Europe's Troubled Region

The countries of the Western Balkans – Albania, Bosnia and Herzegovina, Croatia, Macedonia, Montenegro, Serbia and the province of Kosovo – form a core European region. The region is known for its instability and recent history of wars and civil conflicts, but far less is known about the changes that have taken place in the economic and social welfare systems and the dynamic processes of transition, development and European integration that have been taking place over the last twenty years.

Although economic growth has been firmly established, many problems remain in relation to the labour markets where there is high unemployment, large informal economies and widespread poverty. This book discusses the role of welfare reforms, international aid and European integration in addressing these difficulties. The author argues that the resistance to reforms which were initiated under the communist system in former Yugoslavia led to the break-up of the country but that since then a group of early reforming countries have made fast progress in institutional reform and have been at the forefront of EU integration. He also acknowledges that the main problems have been among a group of late reformers including two international protectorates where aid dependence has held back progress with institutional reforms. This book concludes that the resolution of these problems will unblock the completion of the transition, development and EU integration in the region and open for the way for a more stable and prosperous future.

This book is relevant to all those studying Development Economics, Economics of Transition, International Economics and European Studies and may also be useful to consultants and government officials working in these areas.

William Bartlett is Reader in Social Economics at the School for Policy Studies, University of Bristol.

Routledge studies in development economics

Europe's Troubled Region

Economic development, institutional reform and social welfare in the Western Balkans

William Bartlett

Routledge
Taylor & Francis Group

LONDON AND NEW YORK

First published 2008
by Routledge
2 Park Square, Milton Park, Abingdon, Oxon OX14 4RN

Simultaneously published in the USA and Canada
by Routledge
270 Madison Ave, New York, NY 10016

Routledge is an imprint of the Taylor & Francis Group, an informa business

© 2008 William Bartlett

Typeset in Times by Wearset Ltd, Boldon, Tyne and Wear
Printed and bound in Great Britain by TJI Digital, Padstow, Cornwall

British Library Cataloguing in Publication Data
A catalogue record for this book is available from the British Library

Library of Congress Cataloging in Publication Data
A catalog record for this book has been requested

ISBN10: 0-415-19350-8 (hbk)
ISBN10: 0-203-64489-1 (ebk)

ISBN13: 978-0-415-19350-4 (hbk)
ISBN13: 978-0-203-64489-8 (ebk)

To Djurdja, Esther, Madeleine, Matthew and Thomas

Contents

Figures

Tables

Preface

In the early 1990s, I carried out a research project on the development of small firms in South East Europe funded by the ESRC East-West Research Programme, following which the British Council, the British Academy and the Leverhulme Trust provided crucial support for the research carried out for this book. It would be an understatement to say that the research process has been a more than usually interesting experience as it covered a period of dramatic economic, political and social change in one of Europe's most turbulent yet fascinating regions. Especially memorable were the sight of the long stand-off between the high-spirited but determined student demonstrators and riot police in the centre of Belgrade in the winter of 1996–7 after giving a lecture at the British Council offices in Knez Mihailova street; a visit to Prizren in autumn 1999 to teach a group of clever and enthusiastic pre-university students during a summer school organized by the Soros Foundation; seeing the depth of poverty in rural Albania following a tense journey by car through western Macedonia in the autumn of 2002, and empty and idle wood-processing factories among the forested mountains of North-east Montenegro in 2003. There have been a few practical difficulties in writing this book linked to the changing international position of the countries which have emerged from the former Yugoslavia, especially regarding the names of some countries. The most awkward have been the names of Serbia and Montenegro, which have changed from the 'Federal Republic of Yugoslavia' from 1992 to 2002, to the 'State Union of Serbia and Montenegro' from 2003 to 2006, to their own singular names following independence for Montenegro in 2006. I have used all these names as appropriate to the relevant time period when discussing the countries in the text, hoping that this will not lead to any confusion. I have also used the abbreviations FRY for Federal Republic of Yugoslavia and 'Serbia and Montenegro' for 'State Union of Serbia and Montenegro' for convenience. The name of the Republic of Macedonia has also been problematic since the international agreement to name the country the clumsy 'Former Yugoslav Republic of Macedonia', which I have abbreviated to 'Macedonia' again for convenience, and following the usage that has been adopted by the USA since 2004. I have also used the usual abbreviation 'BiH' for the post-Dayton state of Bosnia and Herzegovina.

The research for this book was carried out through several interrelated research projects funded by the British Academy, the British Council, the European Commission, the Economic and Social Research Council, the European Training Foundation, the Leverhulme Trust, and the UK Know-How Fund in all the countries concerned. The British Council Academic Links and Interchange Scheme (ALIS) provided invaluable support for a collaboration with Vojmir Franičević at the Economics Faculty in Zagreb from 1997 to 1999. The British Council also funded visits to Macedonia and Serbia in the mid 1990s and a Leverhulme Trust Study-Abroad Research Fellowship supported research based at the Institute of Economics in Skopje in 2002 which allowed for a longer and more reflective period of research activity. I have also benefited from participating in conferences and seminars on the region, including a series of conferences on Economic Development in South East Europe at the Inter-University Centre in Dubrovnik from 2002 to 2004 co-organized with Iraj Hashi and Maja Vehovec and the bi-annual Enterprise in Transition conferences organized by the Economics Faculty at the University of Split. I also benefited from my participation as a unit coordinator in a series of Winter Schools organized by the Coimbra Group of European universities held at the University of Split from 2003 to 2005. I am especially grateful to many friends and colleagues in the Western Balkan countries and elsewhere for their support in research and discussions of the issues presented in this book. They include, among others, Biljana Acevska, Mihail Arandarenko, Milford Bateman, Boris Begović, Gojko Bežovan, Ivo Bićanić, Nenad and Snježana Brkić, Božidar Cerović, David Coombes, Drago Čengić, Nevenka Čučković, Marija Donevska, Tim Edmunds, Anastasia Fetsi, Taki Fiti, Vojmir Franičević, Ilir Gedeshi, Iraj Hashi, Gabrielle Hogan-Brun, Milena Jovičić, Michael Kilkommons, Marija Kolin, Miroljub Labus, Ljubomir Madžar, Sanja Maleković, Mustafa Muhamet, Katarina Ott, Jovan Pekovski, Mario Polić, Geoffrey Pridham, Višnja Samardžija, Peter Sanfey, Trajko Slaveski, Vesna Stojanova, Paul Stubbs, Božidar Šišević, Enkeleida Tahiraj, Ilija Todorovski, Milica Uvalić, Verica Hadži Vasileva-Markovska, Maja Vehovec, Mirela Xheneti, Merita Xhumari and Siniša Zrinščak. My thanks also to Djurdja Bartlett for critically reading the manuscript and for moral support through the ups and downs of such a large project. It goes without saying that any errors or misinterpretations are my own responsibility. I am also grateful to the School for Policy Studies at Bristol University for providing a stimulating and supportive intellectual environment in which this book could be completed and to the Institute for Advanced Studies at Bristol University for supporting a series of seminars and conferences on themes related to this book.

Abbreviations

APL	Albanian Party of Labour
APP	Agency for the Promotion of Entrepreneurship (Macedonia)
BAS	Business Advisory Service
BiH	Bosnia and Herzegovina
CARDS	European assistance programme to the Western Balkans
CEDB	Council of Europe Development Bank
CEFTA	Central European Free Trade Area
CEI	Central European Initiative
CHIFs	Cantonal Health Insurance Funds
DfID	Department for International Development
DM	German mark
DOS	Democratic Opposition of Serbia
DPS	Democratic Party of Socialists (of Montenegro)
DS	Democratic Party
DSS	Democratic Party of Serbia
EAR	European Agency for Reconstruction
EBRD	European Bank for Reconstruction and Development
ECHO	EU aid programme
ECU	European Currency Unit
EES	European Employment Strategy
EIB	European Investment Bank
EPL	Employment protection legislation
ESC	Economic and Social Council
EU	European Union
FBiH	Federation of Bosnia and Herzegovina
FDI	Foreign direct investment
FRY	Federal Republic of Yugoslavia
FTA	Free Trade Agreement
GDP	Gross Domestic Product
HAMAG	Croatian Agency for Small Buisness
HBOR	Croatian Bank for Reconstruction and Development
HDZ	Croatian Democratic Union
HGA	Croatian Guarantee Agency

HIF	Health Insurance Fund
HRK	Croatian kuna (unit of currency)
IC	Investment Compact
ICTY	International Criminal Tribunal on the former Yugoslavia
IFC	International Finance Corporation
IFI	International financial institution
ILO	International Labour Organization
IMF	International Monetary Fund
IOM	International Organization for Migration
KLA	Kosovo Liberation Army
KM	Clearing mark
KPST	Kosovo Pensions Savings Trust
KTA	Kosovo Trust Agency
LDK	Democratic League of Kosovo
LFS	Labour force survey
LIP	Local Initiative Project
LSMS	Living Standards Measurement Survey
MVP	Mass voucher privatization
NATO	North Atlantic Treaty Organization
NEPA	National Enterprise Promotion Agency
NGO	Non-Governmental Organization
NSSED	National Strategy for Social and Economic Development
OBNOVA	European assistance programme to the Western Balkans
OECD	Organization for Economic Cooperation and Development
OHR	Office of the High Representative
OMC	Open Method of Coordination
OSCE	Organization for Security and Cooperation in Europe
PHARE	EU assistance programme to Eastern Europe
PHU	Primary Health Unit
PIF	Privatization Investment Fund
PISG	Provisional Institutions of Self Government
PPP	Purchasing power Parity
PRSP	Poverty Reduction Strategy Paper
RS	Republika Srpska
SAA	Stabilization and Association Agreement
SAp	Stabilization and Association process
SDP	Social Democratic Party
SDSM	Social Democratic Alliance of Macedonia
SECI	Southeast Europe Cooperative Initiative
SEECP	South East European Cooperation Process
SIDA	Swedish International Development Agency
SME	Small and Medium-sized Enterprise
SMEA	SME Agency (Albania)
SNP	Socialist People's Party (of Montenegro)
SPA	Serbian Socialist Party

SPO	Serbian Renewal Party
SRS	Serbian Radical Party
SRSG	Special Representative of the Secretary-General (in Kosovo)
SSSH	Croatian trade union association
TAM	Turn-Around Management
TTFSE	Trade and Transport Facilitation for Southeast Europe
TWG	Trade Working Group
UK	United Kingdom
UNDP	United National Development Programme
UNHCR	United Nations High Commissioner for Refugees
UNMIK	United Nations Mission in Kosovo
UNRRA	United Nations Relief and Rehabilitation Administration
USA	United States of America
USAID	United States Agency for International Development
VET	Vocational Education and Training
VMRO-DPMNE	Internal Macedonian Revolutionary Organization – Democratic Party for Macedonian National Unity
WHO	Word Health Organization

1 Introduction

The Western Balkan region includes those countries in South East Europe that have yet to join the European Union (EU). It comprises Albania, Bosnia and Herzegovina (BiH), Croatia, Macedonia, Montenegro, Serbia and its province of Kosovo. Apart from Albania, all emerged from the former Yugoslavia, and all are on the path of European integration at different speeds and with different degrees of enthusiasm.[1] This book is about the complex and inter-connected processes of transition to a market economy, post-conflict reconstruction and development and European integration that all the countries in the region have faced over the last twenty years. It deals with the policy choices that have been taken by the political and economic elites and the associated economic and social reforms that have been carried out, leading to diverse forms of emergent capitalism in each country. The region is an example of the transition process that has marked the all former socialist states of Eastern Europe but has been differentiated by simultaneous processes of war and armed conflict. In the cases of BiH, Croatia and Macedonia, the process of democratization has been mixed with the necessity to create new states out of the ruins of the former Yugoslavia. It is conventional to talk about the 'triple transition' of democratization, state-building and transition to a market economy, which all the former socialist countries had to deal with in one way or another (Elster *et al.* 1998). But the Western Balkan countries stand out, not just in the difficulty of carrying this out in the context of wars and conflicts, but also because in some countries new states had to be built virtually from scratch.

Institutional reform is a central concept in this book. It refers to the process of economic and social change that has been necessary to make the transition from communism to capitalism and to adapt to the wider processes of European integration and change in the global economy. Reforms do not exist in a vacuum. They begin with a particular set of historical and institutional conditions at the outset of the transition process. These initial conditions are an important determinant of the nature and speed of transition. A major focus of the debate on the economics of the transition process has been the relative influence of initial conditions and subsequent policies on the path of transition (Fischer and Gelb 1991; Bartlett and Hoggett 1996; de Melo *et al.* 2001; Falcetti *et al.* 2006). The legacy of the past, which the initial conditions describe, naturally diminishes as time proceeds. Yet especially at the beginning of the transition process, this legacy must have a profound constraining or stimulating effect. The Western Balkan countries are relevant to this debate, since the countries of the former Yugoslavia (Croatia, BiH, Macedonia, Serbia, Montenegro and the almost-country Kosovo) emerged from a very similar set of initial institutional conditions, while at the same time having very different levels of economic development. Their initial institutional conditions comprised a highly decentralized economy based upon a unique system of workers' self-management, while Albania presented a contrast in initial conditions with its extremely centralized communist system. Initial conditions therefore differed along several dimensions. Chapter 2 identifies the main features of these initial conditions in the Western Balkans in some detail by setting out the main features of the communist systems and their evolution up until the end of the 1980s.

At the same time, the reform policies adopted by each country also differed. In this book, I take the view that institutional reforms are the outcome of a policy process which involves a political struggle between pro-reform and anti-reform coalitions which have specific interests in the outcome. In the transition literature, there has been a long debate about the relative influence of 'winners' and 'losers' on the transition process. According to one account, the potential losers from the transition process are likely to resist reform and present the reform process with severe political constraints (Roland 2000). The losers, including workers thrown out of their jobs as a consequence of the privatization and restructuring of state-owned enterprises, may be mobilized into opposition to reform by members of the old elites, including managers of state-owned enterprises and the top echelons of the security establishment who prefer the status quo to radical reform. In order to minimize this opposition to reform, pro-reform leaders should ensure that economic reforms are accompanied by appropriate social reforms and that a social safety net is established to compensate vulnerable groups for their losses (Kramer 1997). Another view holds that it is the winners from reform that are the most dangerous opponents of reform progress (Hellman 1998). The winners are the new elites who gain from the early stages of reform. They include owners of large privatized enterprises, politically well-connected tycoons who gained privatized assets at bargain prices, media barons and directors of public institutions who owe their positions to political connections and political leaders who represent these groups. According to this view, in a partially reformed economy, new elites establish monopoly positions that provide opportunities for rent-seeking, and they strive to prevent further reforms that would undermine their new privileges. Empirical studies of transition countries of Central Europe and the former Soviet Union have addressed the impact of the speed of reform and found that the early reformers which managed to overcome the political constraints to reform had lower inflation and faster recovery from transitional recessions (Aslund *et al.* 1996) and that early success in reform reduces political constraints to reform which in turn encourages further reform efforts (Barlow and Radulescu 2005; Falcetti *et al.* 2006; Kim and Pirttilä 2006).

Chapters 3 and 4 review these reform processes and outline the political context of the macroeconomic stabilization policies that have been adopted in the Western Balkan countries over the last two decades. This analysis identifies a group of early reform countries – Croatia, Macedonia and Albania – which achieved early macroeconomic stabilization and undertook rapid institutional reforms to create capitalist economies. Chapter 3 shows that these countries were assisted in this effort by the fact that their statehood issues were less severe than in other Western Balkan countries and their new post-communist elites were ideologically in favour of reform. Croatia established its statehood after a bitter war with Serbia, Macedonia established its statehood only after a fierce dispute with Greece, while Albania had been independent throughout the communist period. Moreover, international recognition ensured that they were able to obtain assistance from the International Monetary Fund (IMF) and the World Bank to provide the necessary financial resources in the early stages of transition. All three had a difficult time in consolidating their transition processes and met with secondary transition crises involving bank failures and further civil conflicts. Nevertheless, they can be seen as examples of transition countries which adopted early reforms, which in turn enabled them to make faster progress with EU integration than the other Western Balkan states have been able to achieve.

Chapter 4 turns to the case of the late reformers, BiH, Serbia, Montenegro and Kosovo. The analysis shows how conflicts between political coalitions with an interest in stalling or reversing reforms led to the outbreak of severe armed conflicts, which set back economic and social development by many years. Conflict is seen as a strategy by which the anti-reform coalitions were able to mobilize the population against reform. By mobilizing ethnic animosities, the anti-reform coalitions were able to delay reform and for a while maintain their privileges built up under the old system, as well as the additional privileges gained during the subsequent wars and conflicts.

Structural reforms describe the processes of privatization and the entry and growth of new small firms. Reforms to the business environment also attract foreign direct investment and boost domestic investment in the formal economy. Lack of structural reforms can drive entrepreneurial talent into the informal economy and into organized criminal groups (Baumol 1990). These topics are dealt with in Chapter 5 on privatization and foreign investment and Chapter 6 on small- and medium-sized enterprise (SME) policies. A pattern of fast and slow reformers is again identified with greatest early progress with privatization in Croatia, Macedonia and Albania. More recently, Serbia has made rapid progress in improving the business environment and encouraging foreign direct investment and the growth of SMEs, and as a result the international competitiveness of the Serbian economy has improved and her exports have increased. Structural reforms in BiH and Kosovo have been adversely affected by war and conflict, and both have become international protectorates. This has led to rapid changes in the legal systems and the introduction of reform laws, but limited administrative capacity has meant that implementation has often been weak. The World Bank and other donors have been influential in driving forward institutional reforms and encouraging the late reformers to catch up in the transition process but have sometimes fought a losing battle against entrenched anti-reform coalitions.

The economic outcomes of the reform processes are discussed in Chapter 7. Overall, the Western Balkan countries have achieved comparatively high rates of economic growth over the last five years. Albania has been the growth leader and Macedonia the growth laggard, while Kosovo has fallen badly behind. Unfortunately, with the exception of Albania, which began its transition from a very low level, none of the countries has yet regained the level of income and economic activity achieved at the time of the collapse of communism in 1990. Moreover, economic growth has produced little corresponding growth in employment, leading to the phenomenon of 'jobless growth'. This chapter highlights the labour market dysfunctions in the region. Unemployment is worryingly high in many countries, and long-term unemployment and youth unemployment are especially severe. Many people are discouraged from seeking work at all, so participation rates are low and poverty is widespread. There is a large informal economy which has evolved in response to barriers to entry into the formal sector and to high levels of social contributions on wages – the so-called 'tax wedge'. Poorly functioning labour markets and reduced expenditure on education have led to the emergence of significant skill gaps and skill mismatches. World Bank experts have argued that the main problem has been that labour markets have been overprotected, which has reduced job creation and has led to high levels of unemployment and to a large informal economy (Rutkowski and Scarpetta 2005). Experts from the International Labour Organization (ILO) advocate a different set of policies, combining flexible labour markets and employment security, in a model known as 'flexicurity' (Cazes and Nesparova 2007). The EU also has a strong voice in relation to employment policy, since its social policy competence is based largely on labour market measures. It advocates employment protection, social dialogue and measures to combat labour market discrimination. Conflicts between these competing advocacy coalitions have led to paralysis in labour market policy, while public expenditure cuts have undermined attempts to improve active labour market policy measures to assist workers to retrain, improve skills and find jobs.

Chapter 7 also highlights the importance of international trade for the economies of the Western Balkans. These are relatively small economies and their growth is dependent on their ability to export goods and services to European markets and their integration into the global market. The countries face difficult policy choices in this respect. Most have chosen to anchor price stability by fixing their exchange rates, with the notable exception of Serbia which has used currency devaluation as a tool to improve international competitiveness, but at the price of persistent domestic inflationary pressures. While the prospects for economic development look good, and exports and foreign direct investment are beginning to expand, the region still has many social problems to tackle and a long way to go until it is able to catch up to standards considered normal elsewhere in Europe.

These social problems are the subject of Chapter 8 which analyses the process of social sector reform in the region. Transition to the market economy should be supported by an effective system of social protection to compensate the losers from the transition process, but this has not happened in the Western Balkans, and consequently, transition has been slower than it otherwise could have been. Widespread poverty and social insecurity have produced political instability and undermined progress towards the European integration of the region. Weakness in the social safety net has been the outcome of low levels of government expenditure in the poorest countries, especially in Albania, Kosovo and Macedonia. In Croatia, where public expenditure has been higher, the IMF has mandated budget cuts as a tool in the fight against inflation. Public expenditure has been especially low in Albania, undermining attempts to provide effective public services to alleviate poverty. The World Bank has initiated poverty reduction strategies in the poorest countries, based on the idea that the best way to foster investment, stimulate growth and create jobs is by establishing liberal market economies. It has also consistently advised that social protection programmes should be targeted on the poor, but this has been difficult to achieve in countries where the administrative capacity to implement such reforms is insufficient.

Social sector reforms have been directed towards privatization and marketization, and in some countries this has been achieved through partial privatization of the pension system, one of the largest absorbers of public expenditure. Reforms to health systems have been actively discussed, and varying degrees of decentralization, marketization and privatization have been introduced. Housing reforms were carried out at the beginning of the 1990s in many countries, leading to a dearth of public sector housing and growing housing problems. The region still suffers from a large population of refugees which fled their homes during the wars of the 1990s. Donor agencies have been very active in the field of social policy in response to these problems, but they have offered conflicting advice which has led to inconsistencies in the provision of services. Many donors have advocated a welfare mix involving an important role for non-governmental organizations (NGOs) in the provision of social services, but the NGO sector is in its infancy and does not have the capacity to play a leading role.

A distinguishing feature of the transition in the Western Balkans, in comparison with East Central European transition countries, has been the prevalence of wars and armed conflicts which have caused enormous losses in terms of lives, disabilities, refugees and the destruction of property, enterprise assets and social infrastructures. Chapter 9 turns to the international aid effort which was mobilized in response to these crises. Although the inflow of donor grants, concessional loans and technical expertise and advice has been on a large scale, the presence of multiple donors has led to policy confusion. While this has been addressed by the establishment of aid coordination units, the problem has not really been solved. Policy makers in the region are faced with conflicting advice which leads to inefficiencies in implementation and a poor degree of integration of international assistance. Long principal–agent chains have reduced the efficiency of the donor effort, and large inflows of ineffective aid have often substituted for effective reform. The domestic elites in some countries have manipulated donor programmes, and this has led to a growth in corruption which has tended to undermine the effectiveness of local administrations. Large donor presences have also skewed local labour markets, leading to an internal brain drain in which the more skilled workers are drawn away from underpaid local administration to work for higher pay in well-funded donor organizations. Some countries have been affected more than others. Croatia has been more reliant on its own resources and has been less affected by such distortions, while BiH became highly aid-dependent and has faced a difficult process of adjustment as aid money has been wound down. Kosovo is still highly dependent on inflows of international aid which may undermine its ability to function as a possibly independent state in the future. On the other hand, the withdrawal of aid may actually speed up the reform process as anti-reform coalitions are no longer able to benefit from the aid inflow.

As donor aid is gradually being reduced throughout the region, it is being replaced by the increasing influence of the EU as the major external actor. The Western Balkan countries are all included in the process of EU integration discussed in Chapter 10 and have been offered the prospect of EU membership once they meet the extensive set of conditions that have been laid down as hurdles which they must pass before membership negotiations can begin. The early reformers have advanced furthest along the road of EU integration. So far, Croatia and Macedonia have both become candidate members, while Albania has signed a Stabilization and Association Agreement. Montenegro is catching up fast following its declaration of independence from Serbia. Unfortunately, BiH and Serbia still have a long way to go and show signs of unwillingness to make the efforts needed to comply with the necessary conditions. The essential question is how far the anti-reform coalitions benefit from lack of progress with EU integration. Organized crime and informal economy employers probably are not very interested in the implementation of the rule of law that would be required to meet the conditions for EU integration of these countries.

This book explores all these issues and tries to draw connections between the various elements of a complex process. The pace of reform is a critical dimension of economic and social development in the region. Anti-reform coalitions still have the power to block reforms. While the EU is a magnet for policy reform in the region, its policy package might not be suitable for countries at a low level of development. Conformity with the *acquis communautaire* is expensive, and public expenditure will need to be increased in order to implement its provisions, which conflicts with IMF advice to cut budget deficits. Policy advice from external actors is often contradictory, providing a space for anti-reform coalitions to prevent the implementation of effective reforms and so preserve their positions of power and influence. The slower the reforms are, the slower will economic and social development be and the greater the scope for future political instability in the region. This is not an attractive outcome for the EU neighbours or for the populations of the regions themselves. A great deal is at stake in ensuring a smooth completion of the transition process, an effective continuation of economic and social development and a successful process of EU integration which will hopefully eventually see all the countries of the Western Balkans as full members of the EU within the near future.

2 Initial conditions

Yugoslavia and Albania

Both Yugoslavia and Albania emerged from the Second World War with devastated economies. In the early postwar years, the two governments worked together on economic reconstruction and in 1946 agreed on a programme of mutual economic cooperation.[1] Yugoslavia provided financial assistance and food aid to Albania and dispatched advisors to Tirana to assist in Albania's programme of postwar reconstruction. In early 1948, a plan for a federal union between the two countries was put forward by President Tito of Yugoslavia and Koci Xoxe, the Albanian minister of the interior (Crampton 2002). However, this cooperation did not last for long. In 1948, Stalin expelled Yugoslavia from the Cominform, broke off diplomatic relations and withdrew Soviet advisors. Albania, under the leadership of Enver Hohxa, suspended diplomatic relations with Yugoslavia, expelled the Yugoslav advisors and sealed the border. Significant minorities of Albanians within Yugoslavia, and Slav Macedonians within Albania, were to be sources of friction within each country throughout the postwar years.

The subsequent evolution of the communist systems in the two countries could not have been more different. In contrast to the Yugoslav experiment with pro-market reforms and decentralization, the Albanian government persisted with its devotion to the Stalinist system of central planning and state ownership of property. While the Yugoslavs pursued the decentralization of the state and progressively reduced the power of the federal government, in Albania the state became an increasingly dominant influence in all aspects of life. Albania became closed and centralized, while Yugoslavia developed a system of market socialism, open to trade and the out-migration of labour to the West. As a leading member of the Movement of Non-Aligned Nations, Yugoslavia acted as a bridge between the opposing power blocs in the Cold War. In contrast, Albania eventually isolated itself from the outside world and pursued a path of autarchy and self-sufficiency. This chapter explores these divergent experiences and the background to the collapse of the communist systems in the two countries.

Yugoslavia

The Federal People's Republic of Yugoslavia was proclaimed in 1945 as a federation of six republics: Slovenia, Croatia, Bosnia and Herzegovina (BiH),

Serbia, Montenegro and Macedonia; together with the autonomous province of Vojvodina and the autonomous region of Kosovo-Metohija. Politically, it was established as a one-party state. The economy was in a desperate condition. According to the Allied Reparations Commission in Paris, direct war damage to buildings and installations was equivalent to nine times pre-war national income (Hamilton 1968). Two-thirds of agricultural machinery had been destroyed, as had over half the livestock. Two-fifths of the factories had been destroyed, together with over half the land- and sea-transport vehicles and all of the country's large railway bridges. Croatia and BiH were the most devastated areas as they had been the scene of the bitterest fighting. BiH lost 14 per cent of its population during the war (382,000 people), while Croatia lost 8 per cent (295,000) (Matković 1998). Yugoslavia's recovery was assisted by generous amounts of international aid, managed by United Nations Relief and Rehabilitation Administration (UNRRA),[2] including 2.5 million tons of provisions during 1945–6 (Matković 1998). Contributions of railway rolling stock and 15,000 lorries reactivated the railway system and the supply network (Hamilton 1968).

The new communist government set up a Federal Planning Commission which drew up a Five Year Plan along the lines of a traditional Soviet command economy. The commitment to building a classical socialist system continued despite the economic blockade imposed by the USSR in 1948, which led to a complete suspension of imports from the Soviet bloc (Drulović 1978). Nationalization was extended to the entire industrial sector, and peasant farmers were organized into agricultural cooperatives. However, the peasant farmers resisted collectivization, and Yugoslav agriculture was subsequently based mainly upon a system of privately owned peasant smallholdings, the maximum size of which was reduced in 1950 to ten hectares, together with a small number of large state-owned farms concentrated in the flat Danube basin regions of Slavonia and Vojvodina.

The Yugoslav government needed a new approach which would distance its economic system from the Soviet model, and in the early 1950s it replaced centralized economic planning with a more decentralized market-based system. This early institutional reform introduced 'worker self-management' into industrial enterprises, enabling workers' councils to participate in the choice of enterprise managers who were given a free hand to control corporate strategy. State ownership was transformed into 'social ownership' in recognition of the reduced role of the state in the control of enterprises. The adoption of the Marxist concept of the 'withering away of the state' provided an opportunity to resolve the nationalities question through a gradual decentralization of economic power to the republics. The economic system gradually evolved further in the direction of a unique Yugoslav model of market socialism (Madžar 1992).

After its break in relations with the USSR, Yugoslavia benefited from an opening to Western markets, and by the early 1950s most of Yugoslavia's trade was conducted with the West (Dubey 1975). The smallholding peasant farmers were encouraged to enter into marketing cooperatives and agricultural output improved, and industrial output increased by over 10 per cent per annum in the

1950s (Moore 1980). As a result of the introduction of a more flexible economic system, Yugoslavia experienced a long period of rapid economic growth and industrialization which lasted up until the end of the 1970s (Table 2.1).

Further, institutional reforms introduced in 1965, supported by a loan from the International Monetary Fund (IMF), allowed enterprises to keep and reinvest more of their own profits. The effects of the reforms were mixed. Economic growth slowed down from the rapid 7 per cent per annum achieved between 1960 and 1964 to a more modest 4 per cent between 1965 and 1970 (Madžar 1992). Enterprise managers, using their greater freedom, made more rational use of their existing labour force, and employment in the social-ownership sector fell in the two years following the reforms. The agricultural sector, where peasant farms were restricted in size, could not provide sufficient jobs or incomes to the growing rural population and rising industrial wages stimulated massive rural–urban migration. The self-managed enterprises were unable or unwilling to create enough new jobs for the migrant workforce, and unemployment increased steadily in the subsequent years (Bartlett 1979). The existence of open unemployment in former Yugoslavia was a unique phenomenon for a socialist country. Registered unemployment reached 17 per cent by the end of the 1980s, not counting large-scale emigration (Woodward 1995:191). The reforms also affected the distribution of incomes as more prosperous enterprises paid their workers higher wages (Estrin 1983), although the overall level of household income inequality remained low by Western standards (Flakierski 1989).

The constitutional reforms of 1974

The development of self-management had been closely connected to the partial decentralization of political power from the federal state to the republics and two autonomous provinces and pressure mounted for further decentralization.

Table 2.1 Growth of social product per capita in Yugoslavia 1947–90 (% per annum)

	1951–60	1961–70	1971–80	1981–90	1948–90
Bosnia and Herzegovina	3.9	4.0	4.2	−1.2	2.9
Croatia	6.0	5.6	4.9	−1.5	4.0
Kosovo	3.4	4.3	2.6	−3.9	1.6
Macedonia	4.4	6.2	4.3	−2.0	3.3
Montenegro	4.4	7.2	4.8	−2.4	2.9
Serbia	4.6	5.2	5.2	−0.8	3.6
Slovenia	5.8	6.0	5.4	−1.3	4.0
Vojvodina	7.5	5.2	5.4	−0.7	4.0
Yugoslavia	5.2	5.2	4.8	−1.5	3.5

Source: *Razvoj republika prethodne SFR Jugoslavije 1947–90*, Beograd: Savetni Zavod za Statistiku, 1996, 113.

Note
Growth rates calculated at constant 1972 prices.

The party leaders in Croatia demanded that the republic should retain a greater share of the foreign exchange earned by its coastal tourist industry. In the 'Croatian Spring' of 1971, a nationalist movement, led by the Croatian League of Communists, called for greater regional autonomy. The movement was quickly suppressed and the Croatian party leaders were dismissed, but the upsurge of nationalism which was evident in these events induced the Yugoslav League of Communists to counteract what were seen as the adverse effects of pro-market institutional reforms. The solution was found by introducing a system of 'self-management planning' which combined elements of both market and plan in a complicated system of bargaining between the various levels of political and economic power (Madžar 1992). At the same time, nationalist aspirations were accommodated, giving far greater autonomy to Serbia's provinces of Vojvodina and Kosovo. In the latter, Albanian became an official language, and Albanian language newspapers, radio and television stations were established. A new constitution adopted in 1974 enshrined these changes and raised the status of the autonomous provinces to that of federal entities in their own right, with representation in federal institutions, and seats within the federal collective presidency.

The decentralization of power to the republics and the weakening of federal control over the economy were to have fatal consequences for Yugoslavia. Republics borrowed from international capital markets to finance imports of consumer goods and to initiate prestige investment projects. By 1979, the foreign trade deficit had increased to 6.5 per cent of Social Product, and by 1980 the external debt of Yugoslavia had increased to more than $17 billion (Lydall 1989: 44). Policy conflict between the republics was focused on the distribution of foreign exchange earnings. A foreign exchange law introduced in 1977 created republican 'self-managed communities for foreign trade' which were responsible for allocating above-quota foreign exchange among regional importers at a premium above the official exchange rate, effectively bringing about a regionalization of foreign exchange earnings (Bartlett 1987a). The international debt crisis triggered by the second oil price shock of 1979 hit Yugoslavia hard. Increased interest rates and declining export markets created a crisis of debt repayments. But, since federal control over the levers of economic policy had been weakened, the Yugoslav economy was unable to adjust in an appropriate way to external shocks. In 1981, the IMF agreed on a three-year adjustment loan of $2.2 million, conditional on the imposition of tight fiscal and monetary policies, reductions in public expenditure and an increase in interest rates above the rate of inflation. Although these conditionality criteria were not all met, Western governments were disinclined to push the issue too far due to the strategic importance of Yugoslavia as a neutral player in the Cold War. The World Bank also provided substantial loans for enterprise restructuring, with the aim of boosting export growth. Between 1961 and 1982, it lent a total of $2.2 billion for infrastructure investment, often negotiating such loans directly with the republican governments (Dyker 1990).

Throughout the 1980s, the federal authorities strove to bring expenditure on imports into line with export revenues by devaluing the national currency, the dinar. However, the influence of the workers' councils allowed workers to push for wage increases to compensate for devaluation-induced inflation, causing a wage-price spiral. The inflationary spiral was supported by an expansion in the money supply which the central authorities were unable to control. Due to regional decentralization, each republic had its own national bank, and their main debtors – the self-managed enterprises – effectively controlled their local commercial banks. Republican elites were unwilling to restrict the emission of money through the republic banking systems.[3] It was not in their interest to reign in inflationary pressures, since the inflationary impact of money creation in any one republic was dispersed throughout the rest of the federation. Inflation therefore steadily increased through the decade. Even individual companies were able to create virtual money as revealed by the 'Agrokomerc affair' of 1986, in which an agricultural enterprise based in northern Bosnia issued uncovered bills of exchange in order to expand the enterprise and create thousands of jobs in the region (Lydall 1989).[4]

The reforms of 1974 also decentralized the system of social protection which was financed on a republican basis through local 'self-managed interest communities' (Bartlett 1987b). These brought together local governments and local enterprises to finance social services, establish contribution rates and distribute funds to local providers of education, health, pensions and other services.[5] Centres of Social Welfare were established in municipalities to administer social security payments. Although designed to increase local participation, the system was overly complex and bureaucratic. By 1981, there were more than 3,700 self-managing interest communities and over 5,500 laws, regulations and agreements relating to the financing of social services (Lydall 1984). Decentralization led both to spatial inequalities in welfare provision and to rapid growth in social expenditures which were not capped until the late 1980s.

The decentralization of policy making was also reflected in a gradual breakdown of the single Yugoslav market. In a prescient book published in 1982, Kosta Mihailović identified the tendencies towards the development of republican autarchy. He observed that

> with the ongoing independence process of the republics as sovereign states, with decisions about their own development and the high degree of autonomy of the provinces, a single economic system has ceased to exist. Each republic and province has made its own five year development plan, created its own fiscal and monetary policy, as well as its own incomes policy. The crowning achievement of this institutional fragmentation has been the identification of a separate balance of payments position for the republics and provinces. This shows that in Yugoslavia there have emerged eight autonomous economic areas with the republics and provinces as their political and economic centres. The statism of the federation has been transferred to the republics and even in some cases to the counties.
>
> (Mihailović 1982: 276)

Radical decentralization had created a patchwork of separate economic and political entities, which foreshadowed the creation of separate successor states, and initiated a process of economic fragmentation. Commercial transactions within republics became more important than transactions between them. Trade between republics steadily declined, and the single Yugoslav market withered (Goati 1997).

The failures of economic policies in response to the changing international environment brought about what Harold Lydall called 'the Great Reversal' (Lydall 1989). Between 1979 and 1985, real social product per head fell by 10 per cent, real incomes in the social sector fell by 25 per cent and real gross fixed investment fell by 37 per cent. At the same time, employment steadily increased under the stipulation of self-management planning agreements laid down by republican authorities, and declining productivity undermined the international competitiveness of the economy. Further, loans provided by the IMF and the World Bank in the second half of the 1980s were ineffective in an economy in which the reigns of economic power had been devolved to the republics and in which self-managed enterprises faced soft budget constraints.

While fundamental institutional reforms were needed to reverse the decline, an anti-reform coalition including managers of loss-making enterprises who benefited from large subsidies had a strong interest in the continuation of the system. The Yugoslav system of 'worker self-management', like other forms of socialism, relied upon ubiquitous soft budget constraints fuelled by loose monetary emission by the Yugoslav National Bank and its republican counterparts (Uvalić 1992). As Evan Kraft (1995: 470) observed:

> In former Yugoslavia, a key obstacle to stabilization was a coalition in favour of loose monetary policy. This coalition, at the federal level, was spearheaded by the less-developed regions and their representatives in the National Bank of Yugoslavia and the Federal Parliament.

This 'distributional coalition' in favour of loose monetary policy, headed by the political representatives of the loss-making large enterprises, presented a formidable obstacle to the effective implementation of reforms. Such coalitions were present in each republic but were strongest in Serbia where the resistance to the federal reform programme was most entrenched, stalling effective reforms until the end of the 1980s.

The Milošević takeover

Before the federal government could introduce its reform programme, Serbia was swept by a rising tide of nationalism, and in September 1987 the Serbian League of Communists voted for Slobodan Milošević as party leader. The anti-reform coalition in Serbia began to fan the flames of nationalist sentiment and directed its political energy at reversing the gains which the Kosovo Albanians had made since 1974 and which had led to the gradual Albanianization of political institutions in the province. Kosovo was the poorest part of Yugoslavia, with an economy based mainly on agriculture, although industry and mining were developing rapidly (Dogandžić 1987). One of the major grievances of Kosovo Serbs during the 1980s was discrimination in the allocation of jobs in the expanding industrial sector. In fact, there was little evidence of labour market discrimination, and the increased share of Albanians in employment merely reflected a rebalancing of previous labour market inequalities (Bartlett 1990). Nevertheless, Milošević set about consolidating his power by launching the so-called 'anti-bureaucratic revolution' in 1988. The Kosovo Albanian communist leadership was purged and replaced by leaders loyal to Milošević as a prelude to constitutional changes which gave Serbia control of the police and judiciary in the province. In February 1989, the Serbian parliament passed constitutional amendments which gave Serbia direct control over the security forces in the province as well as control of the judiciary, finance and social planning (Vickers 1998: 235).

The federal reform programme

While the Serbian anti-reform coalition was flexing its muscles in Kosovo, the federal government led by Branko Mikulić from Bosnia overcame the objections of the anti-reform faction in the federal parliament and adopted a fundamental and far-reaching reform programme, backed up by a Stand-By Arrangement with the IMF.[6] A new Law on Enterprises introduced in 1988 legalized the formation of joint stock and limited liability companies and other forms of private enterprises.[7] The law stimulated the entry of thousands of new small private businesses over the next two years (see Chapter 6 below). The reforms also liberalized foreign trade by sweeping away the import quotas and special tariffs that had covered most imports. A Foreign Investment Law permitted foreign investment in both private and socially owned enterprises. Foreign investors were offered profits-tax relief, the right to repatriate profits and equal treatment with domestic socially owned enterprises.[8] Mikulić resigned in early 1989 following the wave of street protests against falling living standards in Vojvodina and Montenegro organized by the anti-reform coalition in Serbia, and the reforms were subsequently continued by the next federal prime minister, the Croatian politician Ante Marković. The reforms were subsequently known as the 'Marković reforms'.

A federal privatization law[9] was introduced in 1989 which provided a broad framework within which each republic could adapt the law to its own circumstances. The proceeds from privatization were transferred to republican Development Funds to support local economic development and enterprise restructuring. Privatization agencies were established which were responsible for authorizing the plans of individual enterprises. Social ownership was retained, but the law permitted other forms of private property, while socially owned enterprises could also be nationalized. The legislation permitted enterprises to choose their own form of 'property transformation', but there was an emphasis on the distribution of shares to workers and managers. Shares were offered for sale to workers at a discount of 30 per cent plus an extra 1 per cent for each year of service (Adamovich 1995). The main difficulty was in the valuation of social capital since there was no market for capital assets. The process was open to abuse, and typically auditors would be called in only if the book value appeared to be too high.[10] Once an enterprise was privatized in this way, the workers' council would be suspended and replaced by an 'assembly of owners', eliminating self-management. By March 1991, almost 1,000 enterprises had offered shares to their workers under the provisions of the federal law (Uvalić 1992). Although it was only implemented to a limited extent, the Enterprise Law laid the basis for the subsequent demise of the self-management system and the transition to capitalist market economies in the Yugoslav successor states.

At the beginning of 1990, Marković introduced a radical macroeconomic stabilization programme designed to eliminate inflation. The stabilization programme ended the deficit financing of government expenditure, introduced restrictive fiscal and monetary policies and set up a social protection programme to compensate the losers from the reform (FEC 1990: 14–15). The reform programme also encouraged the development of the small business sector, the break-up of large loss-making enterprises into smaller units and the spin-off of small enterprises from larger parent companies. The dinar currency was made fully convertible at a fixed exchange rate pegged to the German mark. The National Bank ended its practice of issuing selective credits, and base money creation was linked to foreign exchange earnings in the manner of a currency board. Wages were indexed to the pegged exchange rate, which had the effect of freezing wages for six months, and utility prices were also frozen. Inflation was quickly eliminated, and between April and June 1990 producer prices even registered a slight fall. Remarkably, the Marković programme was even more successful than the much-praised Polish stabilization programme introduced at about the same time, achieving a larger decline in inflation at a lower cost in lost output (Coricelli and Rocha 1991).

Failure of the Marković reform programme

However, the federal reform programme ran into the same problem which had defeated earlier less radical attempts to turn the economy around: the independent powers and self-interest of the republics. As part of the overall reform programme, non-communist political parties had been legalized in 1989 and new political parties sprang up with great rapidity in each of the republics. Many had a specifically ethnic or national base and ideology, but there were also greens, human rights parties, regional parties, as well as social democratic, liberals and conservatives. Altogether, 155 political parties were registered in Yugoslavia by October 1990, increasing to 250 by January 1991. In January 1990, the League of Communists collapsed and was replaced by separate republican communist parties with a variety of names. The first multiparty elections were held separately in each of the Yugoslav republics rather than on a national level, reflecting the devolution of power to the republics within the federal Yugoslav system. The first election, held in Croatia in April 1990, was won by a pro-independence opposition party, the Croatian Democratic Union (HDZ), led by Franjo Tudjman.[11] This was followed by elections held in Macedonia and BiH in November. In Macedonia, the nationalist Internal Macedonian Revolutionary Organization – Democratic Party for Macedonian National Unity (VMRO-DPMNE) became the largest party in the republic's Assembly and an interim government of experts was formed by the independent Nikola Kljušev. In BiH, three ethnically based parties won the majority of the seats in the Assembly: the Bosnian-Muslim Party for Democratic Action, the Serbian Democratic Party and the Croatian HDZ. Alija Izetbegović, leader of the Party for Democratic Action, became president of the republic.[12]

In July 1990, the Serbian authorities moved against the national trend towards democratization and suspended the Kosovo Assembly, and in response the Albanian delegates declared Kosovo's secession from Serbia (Vickers 1998: 245). Serbia promptly abolished the autonomous status of both Kosovo and Vojvodina which became mere regions of Serbia and reverted control over police, courts and economic and social policy to the authorities in Belgrade. The Kosovo Albanians protested against the constitutional changes and the imposition of direct rule by Serbia with demonstrations and strikes. In September, the dissolved Kosovo Assembly declared Kosovo to be a republic and adopted the 'Constitution of the Republic of Kosovo' at a secret meeting at the town of Kaçanik (Pula 2004: 806). The Serbian authorities reacted with a severe repression. Many Albanians in leading positions were dismissed, and a process of Serbianization of economic, political and cultural organizations was carried out (Vickers 1998). Schools and universities were no longer permitted to teach in Albanian, and Albanian language newspapers were closed down. In Serbia itself, in contrast to the electoral victories of anti-communist parties elsewhere, elections held in December 1990 returned the renamed communist party to power, partly because the election was boycotted by the Kosovo Albanians, while the renamed communist party also won elections in Montenegro.

The collapse of central political authority opened up a space in which anti-reform sections of the republican elites were able to mobilize the forces of nationalism to prevent or reverse the pro-market changes that were being introduced through the Marković reforms. A reactionary ethnically based political rhetoric was adopted in order to reverse the evident support for genuine market reforms (Gagnon 2004). Despite the apparent nationalist turn in politics, opinion polls conducted in the summer and autumn of 1990 indicated that there was little popular support for the break-up of Yugoslavia.[13] The Marković reform programme had been showing signs of success. New small private businesses had sprung up in all the republics. Shares in socially owned firms had been issued to workers. Inflation had been brought under control. Although unemployment remained high, there was widespread support for the Marković reforms among the population.[14] Nevertheless, the nationalist agenda drew support from the economic conflict between the republics, as each attempted to evade the costs of adjustment implied by the federal stabilization programme. In the absence of a consensus on the reform strategy, the federal government was in a weak position to implement the programme on its own. While the northern republics of Slovenia and Croatia were broadly in favour of market-based reforms, Serbia, now under the control of the nationalist faction under Milošević, was opposed to it. The main problem was the vulnerability of relatively inefficient Serbian industry to the introduction of market forces, which would have exposed its underlying weakness and led inevitably to rising unemployment. Moreover, economic disputes between the republics were already tearing the federation apart. To protect its own industries from competition from more efficient 'imports' from the northern republics, Serbia introduced customs duties on goods from Slovenia and Croatia. Slovenia and Croatia issued new money through the banking system in violation of the federal monetary restrictions imposed by the stabilization programme (Lampe 1966). Serbia soon adopted the same strategy but on a larger scale, drawing 18 billion dinars ($1.5 billion) from the central bank to fund pay rises, pay pensions and subsidize loss-making enterprises in advance of the first multiparty elections. Inflationary pressures in the economy took off again, and inflation reached double-digit figures by the end of 1990. These actions gave the coup de grace to the Marković stabilization programme. The IMF had been supporting the Yugoslav economy on condition that it stuck to the programme, and in response to the Serbian action it suspended its $1 billion Stand-By Arrangement, which in turn led to the suspension of further billions of dollars of Western credits.

In May 1991, as the crisis intensified, Serbia blocked the candidacy of the Croatian political leader Stipe Mesić for the rotating Yugoslav presidency, effectively bringing the Yugoslav federation to an end. Slovenia, Croatia and Macedonia announced their independence soon thereafter in June 1991, heralding the wars of Yugoslav succession which were to last for the following decade, in various manifestations. The Kosovo Assembly declared the independence of Kosovo in October after a referendum received overwhelming popular support. In December, the Bosnian Serbs declared their own 'Serb Republic' in line with the similar pronouncement by the Serbian minority in Croatia. Without support from the largest Serbian political party, BiH declared independence in March 1992.

The Marković reform programme in Yugoslavia in 1988–90 was the first post-communist transition programme to be introduced in Eastern Europe. It threatened the position of those sections of the republican elites who benefited from privileged positions in their own administrations, in the public sector, and as managers of socially owned enterprises. Their interests would have been damaged by the creation of a genuine single market in Yugoslavia, by the full privatization of the socially owned enterprises and by the free entry of new private businesses. As one Macedonian academic explained, the Marković reform programme:

created a real danger for the position of the ethnocentric elites in the republics – which viewed a single Yugoslav market economy as a threat to their own regulatory power within the territories of the republics. In addition, a single market would mean a real cutting down of their privileges, benefits and functions.

(Mircev 1993: 382)

Another analyst made a similar assessment of the

national communist elites in control of each republic and province; these elites naturally refused to implement any economic reform which would have resulted in the loss of their control over the major sources of their patronage in jobs and sinecures

(Pavković 2000: 78)

The threat to established positions was felt especially by the Milošević regime in Serbia which continued to stoke up a crisis situation and pursued a policy designed to break up the federal Yugoslav state and replace it with a state of the Serbian nation.[15] The 'Serbian project' envisioned a new state that would encompass all the 'Serb lands' from BiH and Croatia (Gow 2003). It would divide BiH, which would be shared with what remained of Croatia. Since the transition to a liberal market economy was not acceptable to the anti-reform elite in Belgrade, the only remaining strategy was an alignment with the Serbian nationalist project to create a Greater Serbia which would incorporate 'all Serbs in one state' (Vasić 2005).[16]

The break-up of Yugoslavia accelerated the process of transition from market socialism to a variety of new capitalisms in the successor states. The paths of transition differed in each. Croatia quickly introduced its own privatization laws, while Macedonia concentrated first on macroeconomic stabilization before engaging in full-scale privatization (Uvalić 1997). In Croatia and Macedonia, privatization was effected in large part by sales of shares to 'insider' managers and workers, as envisaged by the Marković reforms. Privatization in Croatia involved the installation of new managers sympathetic to – and in many cases leading members of – the new governing party, the HDZ. In contrast, in Serbia and Montenegro (the new 'Federal Republic of Yugoslavia'), privatization was suspended and much of the industrial sector was effectively nationalized so that the transition to a normal capitalist type of economy was effectively aborted.

The communist regime in Albania

In Albania, the communist-led National Liberation Front formed a new government in 1944 and quickly enacted a legislation to increase state controls and nationalize the entire industrial sector. Although the economy was mainly agricultural, the country was dependent on international food aid provided through the UNRRA and on assistance from Yugoslavia and the USSR. Under an agreement signed in 1945, the USSR provided grain and technical expertise in the oil and mineral extraction industries, in exchange for tobacco, preserved fruits, copper ore and oil (Crampton 2002). The government proceeded to force the peasant farmers into agricultural collectives, and eventually the whole agricultural sector was organized into over 600 collective farms (Prifti 1978). However, collectivized agriculture was never efficient, and the country never achieved the proclaimed goal of self-sufficiency, i.e. the ability to feed the population without imports of food from abroad. Throughout the period up to 1978, Albania ran a balance of payments deficit and was in effect reliant on outside powers for aid in order to support the economy.

The Albanian government broke off relations with the USSR in 1960 after the latter re-established its ties with Yugoslavia. Between 1960 and 1978, Albania depended upon economic aid from China, until that country adopted a more open policy to the West.[17] After breaking relations with its last remaining ally, a new constitution was adopted which prohibited the receipt of loans from other countries and forbade cooperation with foreign or multinational companies. In the 1980s, therefore, Albania was one of the most isolated countries in the world, pursuing a path of economic self-sufficiency and autarchy. During this time, the excesses of Albanian communism reached their peak and the private ownership of both land and farm animals was prohibited. Not surprisingly, international reserves of currency were soon depleted. Equipment became increasingly obsolete and living standards declined. Throughout the 1980s, the economy stagnated and agricultural output, the mainstay of the economy, decreased substantially on a per capita basis (Sjöberg 1991).

It was not until the death of Enver Hoxha in 1985 that a gradual opening to the outside world again became possible, initiated by the new party leader Ramez Alia. Albania began to improve its trade links with Eastern Europe and participated in the Balkan Co-operation Conference held in Belgrade in 1988. In May 1990, the tenth Central Committee Plenum agreed on a programme of cautious economic reforms and the formation of non-communist political parties was legalized. The reforms involved a relaxation of centralized supervision of enterprises which were allowed to retain a part of profits for internal investment and to control the use of up to a fifth of capacity to produce goods for the market independently of the planning targets (Pashko 1991). The reforms also permitted agricultural workers to cultivate small private plots in response to mounting food shortages related to inefficiencies in the state-owned agricultural sector. However, this was insufficient to correct the problem and the country was embroiled in mounting turmoil as food shortages worsened in the summer of 1990, and groups of people began to enter the grounds of Western embassies in Tirana seeking visas to leave the country. At the beginning of 1991, student leaders organized a protest march in Tirana which attracted 100,000 people, and statues of Enver Hohxa were destroyed there and in other towns. In March, crowds of people commandeered boats in Durrës and Vlora and set sail for Italy, where the sight of thousands of desperate and poverty-stricken Albanian refugees became visible to the international media for the first time. Within

Albania, average wages were as low as $20 per month and there was widespread poverty.

Eventually, pushed by a rising tide of protest and civil unrest, multiparty elections were organized in March 1991. Although the Albanian Party of Labour (APL – the communist party) won a majority of seats, the opposition parties had gained two-fifths of the popular vote and considerably more than that in the urban areas. The opposition refused to accept that the elections had been conducted fairly. In May, a general strike in pursuit of a 100 per cent pay increase brought the country to a standstill (inflation was running at 260 per cent per month). Further, mass migrations to Italy were attempted throughout the year. The government resigned on 6 June 1991, and an interim coalition government was formed. At its Tenth Congress held on 10 June 1991, the APL renounced Marxism–Leninism, changed its name to the Socialist Party and announced its adherence to a policy of gradual economic reform adopting the principles of a market economy. In August, thousands of people again tried to leave the country, many of whom were returned by the Italian authorities. In a desperate attempt to turn the tide of refugees, the international community organized an emergency aid package of $150 million, and Italian soldiers were sent to Albania to distribute the aid. The final fall of the communist regime in Albania was heralded by the victory of the opposition Democratic Party led by Sali Berisha in March 1992.

3 The early reformers
Croatia, Macedonia and Albania

Following the collapse of the communist regimes, new elites opposed to the socialist system took power in Croatia, Macedonia and Albania and sought to make progress with radical economic reforms. They drew on experience of reforms elsewhere in Eastern Europe and, in the cases of Croatia and Macedonia, on the experience of the Marković reform policies. They succeeded in implementing reform policies in part because they had a clear idea of their own statehood.[1] Albania's statehood was unchallenged from the communist period, while Croatia was able to draw on a long tradition of autonomy within the prewar kingdom of Yugoslavia. Macedonia was in a more difficult position as it had no recent experience of autonomous statehood to draw on, although it had been a republic of the former federal state. However, all three were relatively weak states with limited resources to finance the adjustments needed for radical reforms. During the early period of stabilization, Croatia was embroiled in war, Macedonia was adversely affected by sanctions and embargoes and Albania was emerging from a long period of international isolation. These factors made their systemic reforms especially difficult and accounted for several setbacks along their different paths to stability and growth. This chapter reviews the macroeconomic stabilization policies in these early reforming countries and charts their progress with democratic consolidation and progress with European integration.

Croatia

Following Croatia's declaration of independence in June 1991, the Yugoslav army (JNA) was determined to impose order within the country which it still regarded as part of Yugoslavia. Army units crossed the border from Serbia into Croatia together with several paramilitary groups. The JNA was met with fierce resistance around the town of Vukovar in eastern Slavonia, which was besieged and subjected to weeks of fierce bombardment, and by the time its garrison surrendered the town was completely destroyed (Tanner 1997). The war in Croatia lasted for six months by which time about one-third of Croatian territory was held by the breakaway Serbian Republic of Krajina. A ceasefire, brokered by the European Union (EU) and the United Nations (UN), came into effect on

1 January 1992, and international recognition of the new state followed soon after. Croatia gained admission to the UN in May, and UN troops were sent to police the border areas within the Serbian enclave. Although the ceasefire temporarily froze the division of the country, most of the breakaway areas were returned to the control of the central government following a large-scale military action in 1995 at which point most of the Serb population fled the Krajina region and became refugees in Bosnia and Serbia. Agreement was reached on the eventual return of eastern Slavonia to Croatia after a further two-year period under UN administration, completing the creation of the new Croatian state.

The war caused massive damage to the economy which the Croatian government estimated at $37 billion (GoC 1999). In 1993, the State Institute for Macroeconomic Studies and Forecasts estimated that 590 towns and villages had suffered war damage, and that 210,000 housing units had been destroyed, equivalent to one-eighth of the entire housing stock of Croatia (Baletić *et al.* 1994). Infrastructure had also been badly affected: thirty-three bridges had been destroyed, the main railway lines from Zagreb to Vinkovci and to Split had been cut and nine major hospitals and many smaller medical centres were destroyed or damaged. The largest single installations destroyed in the war included the Borovo shoe making company in Vukovar, the Ernestinovo electricity generation plant (rebuilt in 2003), the Željezara Sisak steel plant and TLM-Šibenik aluminium plant. In the business sector, it was estimated that 1,142 companies lost assets valued at HRK 14 billion (€2 billion). Further, destruction took place in 1995 when the Croatian government reasserted its control over the Serbian-occupied territories of the Krajina.

Due to increased government expenditure during the war and subsequent reconstruction, the rate of inflation had increased to 634 per cent in 1992 and to almost 1,500 per cent in 1993. After Croatia was admitted to membership of the International Monetary Fund (IMF) in December 1992, it negotiated a Stand-by Arrangement which increased its international credit rating and gave it access to the international capital market. With its international position secure, the government decided to introduce a stabilization programme in October 1993 aimed at eliminating inflation. The programme pegged the exchange rate to the German mark, introduced internal convertibility of the currency, lifted foreign exchange controls and imposed restrictive monetary and fiscal policies. As a result, import prices were stabilized and inflationary expectations eliminated (Anusić *et al.* 1995). The success of the programme enabled the government to introduce a new currency, the kuna, in May 1994, to replace the temporary Croatian dinar in use since independence. Croatia's international creditors agreed to restructure its foreign debt, and by the end of 1994 about $1.4 billion of reserves had been accumulated. The stabilization programme led to a sharp fall in inflation to 2 per cent by 1995, heralding a sustained period of price stability (Figure 3.1).

Between 1995 and 1997, gross domestic product (GDP) per capita increased by an average of 6 per cent per annum. The IMF agreed a $486 million Extended Funding Facility in 1997 which further ensured the international

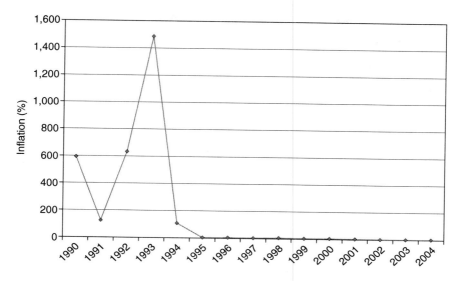

Figure 3.1 Croatia: inflation, 1990–2004 (%) (source: UNECE Economic Survey of Europe, various issues).

credibility of the government's economic policy. Croatia was praised in international circles for its success in achieving non-inflationary growth. However, difficulties were building up beneath the surface. One of the main problems was the deterioration in the balance of payments due to increased imports associated with economic growth, while exports stagnated. Croatia had introduced a liberal foreign trade regime, dismantled import quotas and abolished non-tariff import restrictions, which encouraged imports, while low productivity and high unit labour costs made exports increasingly uncompetitive under the fixed exchange rate that underpinned the stabilization policy. Moreover, the coastal tourism industry had not recovered from the shock of the war. Consequently, by 1997, Croatia's international debt had increased to $6.1 billion or 33 per cent of GDP.

Parliamentary elections held at the end of 1995 to capitalize on the popularity of the ruling party following its success in stabilizing the economy and reuniting the country returned the Croatian Democratic Union (HDZ) to power with 45 per cent of the vote. Its leader, Franjo Tudjman, won presidential elections in June 1997. However, his fierce rhetoric against the International Criminal Tribunal on the former Yugoslavia (ICTY) in the Hague overshadowed the record of actual cooperation and diminished the country's international standing.[2] The authoritarianism of the HDZ, necessary and accepted in wartime, began to look increasingly anachronistic as the economy stabilized and neighbouring Central European countries began to engage with the process of EU integration (Bartlett 2003b).

The economic recovery was interrupted in mid-1998 with the collapse of a number of medium-sized commercial banks. These had built up substantial non-performing debts as a result of bailing out local loss-making companies which were politically well connected and which provided employment to their local populations. The banking crisis was heralded by the collapse of the *Dubrovačka banka* which had made loans to local hotels in southern Dalmatia to keep them afloat, pending the recovery of the tourist industry. Two more bank collapses followed, and the Croatian National Bank stepped in as a lender of last resort supported by the World Bank. The banking crisis led to the re-imposition of a restrictive monetary policy and a tightening of credit conditions bringing the economic recovery to a temporary halt. In 1999, the economy contracted. A new banking law was introduced which gave greater supervisory powers to the Croatian National Bank, and in the following years almost all the commercial banks were sold to foreign investors, mainly Austrian and Italian banks, which came to control most of the banking sector in Croatia.

The consolidation of democracy and the turn to Europe

The death of President Tudjman in December 1999 heralded a fundamental change in Croatian politics. Increasingly unpopular due to its record of corruption and close connections with ruthless tycoon capitalists, the HDZ was unable to fend off the challenge from the opposition parties.[3] A six-party coalition government headed by the Social Democratic Party (SDP) led by Ivica Račan was returned to power in elections held in January 2000, and Stipe Mesić, a veteran Croatian politician who had opposed Tudjman, won the presidential elections in February.[4] The EU welcomed the new government with open arms, and a summit meeting was held in Zagreb in November 2000 to launch the EU's new policy towards the Western Balkans.

The victory of the six-party coalition gave a new start to macroeconomic policy. Economic expansion was assisted by falling interest rates and a rapid growth of credit to both the business sector and households. The government initiated a major road building programme which boosted investment and had multiplier effects throughout the economy. By 2002, the GDP growth peaked at 5.2 per cent, underpinned by a recovery in the tourism industry. However, as in the past, the expansionary policy was brought to an end by the balance-of-payments constraint as imports surged while exports remained uncompetitive. The country's foreign debt rose dramatically. By 2003, the external debt had increased to €19.8 million, equivalent to 78 per cent of GDP, while debt service amounted to 19 per cent of exports.

The coalition government had a troubled relationship with the ICTY. Although proclaiming its willingness to cooperate with the tribunal, in practice it was reluctant to do so, fearing a political backlash from the right-wing opposition. Eventually, its approach backfired as the government lost support from all sides due to its dithering approach to the issue. One of the most prominent inductees, General Ante Gotovina, went into hiding in 2001 and evaded capture for the next four years. When the government agreed to hand over two indicted generals to the ICTY, four cabinet members resigned, eliminating the coalition government's slender majority. In the meantime, the HDZ led by Ivo Sanader began a process of renewal, ridding itself of the most extreme right-wing factions and transforming itself into a party of the moderate centre-right. Gradually, Račan's popularity waned despite presiding over a sustained economic recovery. Living standards had not improved quickly enough to ensure the survival of the government.

In the general election held in November 2003, the HDZ gained the largest number of votes and formed a new government with support from some smaller parties. The country had achieved an orderly transfer of power and seemed set on the road to EU membership, with only the issue of return of refugees and the fulfilment of its obligations to cooperate with the ICTY standing in the way of achieving its ambitions. Croatia applied for EU membership in February 2003, and just over a year later following an exhaustive study of Croatia's readiness for membership, the European Commission issued a positive *Opinion* on the application. In June 2004, the EU confirmed Croatia's status as a candidate country.

In August 2004, the government requested a new Stand-by Arrangement with the IMF for a loan of $141 million over twenty months. The request was approved subject to a number of conditions including a requirement that the fiscal deficit be reduced from 4.5 per cent of GDP in 2004 to 2.9 per cent by 2007, that subsidies to the economy be reduced by 1.2 per cent and that the public sector wage bill be reduced by 1.5 per cent. In addition, the government was required to reduce its expenditure on defence, health care and social programmes and increase expenditure on education and science. The IMF also advised the government to reverse the changes recently made to pension indexation formula and ensure the sale of all remaining state-owned shares in private companies by mid-2005. It was clear that the IMF had come to play a significant role in the determination of economic policy in Croatia.

Croatia has achieved macroeconomic stability with low inflation, a steady exchange rate pegged to the euro and low interest rates. Economic growth has been maintained at relatively high levels averaging almost 5 per cent per annum from 2001 to 2006, and unemployment is on a declining trend. The main problems facing the Croatian economy are low export competitiveness and a slow rate of new business start-up, although this is starting to pick up (Čučković and Bartlett 2007). These problems are linked to the still high level of state ownership of large parts of industry, albeit as minority shareholder in most cases, continued subsidies to large loss-making industries such as shipbuilding and the highest share government expenditure in GDP in the region. Although the government budget deficit has been falling, low international competitiveness has led to a build-up of foreign debt which reached over 80 per cent of GDP in 2005 and required the Croatian National Bank to impose severe restrictions on credit growth. Although the early reforms stabilized the economy and Croatia's model of national, state-led growth has achieved considerable success, it is doubtful whether this approach can be sustained without major improvements in productivity and business competitiveness. Croatia has benefited from a profitable tourist industry, but this has inherent capacity limits and may not be able to support continued growth into the indefinite future.

Macedonia

In Macedonia, an interim government under Nikola Kljušev organized a referendum in September 1991 which, although boycotted by the ethnic Albanian parties, declared Macedonian independence from Yugoslavia. Soon after, the government established an independent National Bank and in April 1992 introduced a new currency, the denar. It adopted an anti-inflation stabilization programme which fixed the new currency to the German mark, introduced restrictive fiscal and monetary policies and imposed a wage freeze and a limited price freeze. Inflation fell from 86 per cent in April to 70 per cent in May and by August had fallen to just 6 per cent. However, owing to the precarious economic climate, this early success in reducing inflation could not be sustained. The major difficulties were the loss of extensive subsidies from former Yugoslavia and the imposition of economic sanctions against the Federal Republic of Yugoslavia (FRY), its main trading partner, together with the imposition of a trade embargo by neighbouring Greece which objected to the name and flag adopted by the new state. The stabilization programme was finally torpedoed when parliament voted for large public sector wage increases and pushed through a vote of no confidence on Prime Minister Kljušev who resigned in July.

In September 1992, a new coalition government was formed led by the young leader of the Social Democratic Alliance of Macedonia (SDSM – formerly the Macedonian League of Communists) Branko Crvenkovski, together with the two main Albanian parties.[5] A second stabilization package was agreed between the government, the trade unions and the powerful Chamber of Commerce which allowed for a more flexible, but still tight, policy towards wages. However, the revised programme again proved insufficient to control inflation, which rose to 20 per cent in December, mainly because the National Bank continued to issue subsidized selective credits to farmers and direct subsidies to loss-making enterprises. The exchange rate was devalued by two-thirds in October 1992 and by a further third in December, and industrial output fell by 15 per cent by the end of the year. One outside observer (Wyzan 1992) judged that while the elimination of selective credits and the creation of a unified exchange rate were needed to stabilize prices, the Macedonian economy was still too weak to achieve success with its stabilization policy in the absence of financial support from the IMF. But without international recognition of the new state, access to IMF resources was blocked.

A significant turning point was reached when Macedonia was admitted to the UN in April 1993, which enabled the country to join the World Bank and the IMF. The government agreed a Stand-by Arrangement with the IMF and additional loans from the World Bank to support the third stabilization programme at the beginning of 1994. This was designed on the lines of orthodox transition policies that had been pursued elsewhere in Eastern Europe involving liberalization, stabilization and privatization. A central aim of the new policy was to achieve macroeconomic stability by targeting monetary policy on the maintenance of a stable exchange rate, pegged to the German mark. Selective credits were abolished, and credit limits were imposed on banks in the form of direct credit ceilings and increased reserve requirements.

When the third stabilization programme began, the Macedonian economy was still suffering from the effects of sanctions against FRY and from the effects of a trade blockade imposed by Greece. Moreover, the stabilization programme involved cuts in government expenditure which were especially hard on public investment in areas such as water resources, energy, transport, environment, health and social services. Tax revenues fell too, as the profits tax rate was cut from 30 per cent to 15 per cent in an effort to stimulate business activity. Unemployment increased as hard budget constraints were imposed on several large loss-making enterprises involved in a special restructuring programme. The stabilization programme initially brought about a decline in output, and GDP fell by 3 per cent between 1993 and 1995.

Although economic conditions had deteriorated, the ruling coalition was returned to power in parliamentary elections in October 1994 with a large majority.[6] The EU belatedly recognized the new state after an accord was reached with Greece in September 1995, under which the government agreed to change the design of its disputed flag and adopt the name 'The former Yugoslav Republic of Macedonia' in international relations, while Greece agreed to lift its trade embargo.[7] The agreement opened the door for assistance from the PHARE aid programme, while an agreement with the Paris Club rescheduled Macedonia's share of the international debt of former Yugoslavia. Price stability was achieved in 1996, and the economy began to grow for the first time since independence (Figure 3.2).

However, the nascent economic recovery was threatened in February 1997 with the collapse of the TAT savings bank in Bitola.[8] The bank had been running a pyramid scheme, and several government officials were accused of involvement in the scandal which led to the dismissal of a deputy prime minister and the foreign minister and the resignation of the governor of the central bank.[9] In the wake of the banking crisis, the Macedonian government agreed a further support programme with the IMF, the World Bank and official bilateral donors under which the IMF agreed to provide an $81 million loan to supplement the reserves of the central bank and to support the balance of payments, while an agreement was reached with the London Club to reschedule the country's commercial debt. Macedonia repaid its arrears to the European Investment Bank in September 1997, paving the way to normalization of its relations with the EU which agreed a €40 million loan to supplement the country's official reserves. Further, large capital inflows began to enter the country from various multilateral and bilateral assistance programmes.

Politically, Macedonia had been seen as a success story of ethnic accommo-

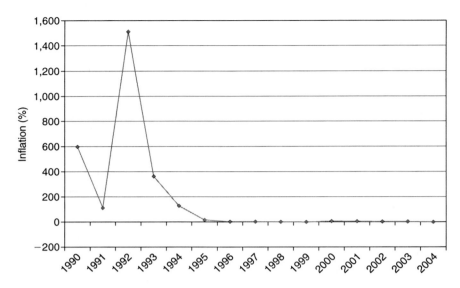

Figure 3.2 Macedonia: inflation, 1990–2004 (%) (source: UNECE Economic Survey of
Europe, various issues).

dation throughout the 1990s. The two ethnic groups, Albanian and Macedonian,
had never formed integrated communities, but they had lived peacefully side by
side, and ethnic Albanian parties had participated in the government. However,
tensions flared in September 1997 when the mayor of Gostivar was sentenced to
thirteen years imprisonment for raising the Albanian flag on public buildings,
while the mayor of Tetovo was sentenced to two and a half years for the same
reason. The Albanian coalition party withdrew from the government, necessitat-
ing new elections in the autumn of 1998. The new coalition government,
although composed of a different combination of parties,[10] continued the tradition of collaboration among the ethnic elites which had held Macedonia together
as a unitary state since its independence. The new government, led by the
nationalist Internal Macedonian Revolutionary Organization – Democratic Party
for Macedonian National Unity (VMRO-DPMNE), emphasized the continuation
of pro-market reforms and job creation as a key element of its political platform.
Relations with the Albanian community also improved with the release of the
mayors of Gostivar and Tetovo, and the EU agreed to construct a new university
in Tetovo that would deliver some courses in the Albanian language. In November 2000, the EU signed a Stabilization and Association Agreement with Macedonia as a first step in its policy of greater engagement in the region following
the Kosovo crisis.

Civil conflict destabilizes the Macedonian economy

However, unexpectedly and dramatically, in 2001 a civil conflict erupted between ethnic Albanian insurgents belonging to an armed group known as the National Liberation Army (NLA) and Macedonian government police forces. The insurgency was brought to an end after several months of fierce fighting due to the timely intervention of the EU in one of the few successful examples of EU peace-making diplomacy in the Balkans. A peace agreement between the two sides was negotiated at the lakeside town of Ohrid on the border with Albania. In commenting on the effects of the conflict, the World Bank (2001: 4–5) noted in August 2001 that:

> The economic impact of the conflict has been growing. The intermittent closing of the main trade routes going north, fighting in some limited areas, and general uncertainty have undermined export performance and business confidence. Industrial production was off by 7.3% in the first five months of the year compared with a year earlier. GDP for the first quarter is estimated to have contracted by 5% compared with the same period in 2000, and growth for the year as a whole is likely to be negative ... economic prospects have been undermined, not only for this year ... but also for subsequent years because of deferred or cancelled investment and a deterioration in investor perceptions that may take years to recover.

The Ohrid Framework Agreement envisaged that the ethnic Albanian minority would gain greater influence over its own affairs and that there would be a significant decentralization of power from the central government to new local authorities which were to be established as part of a fundamental reform of local government. Albanian became an official language in those municipalities where it was the mother tongue of more than one-fifth of the population, and the number of Albanians employed in the public administration and the police was to be increased. Parliamentary elections held in September 2002 were won by a coalition of opposition parties known as *Zaedno za Makedonija* ('Together for Macedonia') led by the SDSM together with the Party for Democratic Integration (DUI), the political party formed by the leader of the former paramilitary Albanian insurgents.[11] Such compromises demonstrated that the Ohrid Agreement had succeeded, at least for the time being, in stabilizing the country and averting another civil conflict on ethnic lines in the Balkans.[12] In April 2003, the IMF approved a Stand-by Arrangement for $29 million to assist the post-conflict stabilization, and the SDSM-led government adopted a new fiscal strategy which called for a 4 per cent reduction in employment in public administration and the 'decompression' of public sector wages to provide greater incentives to motivate public employees. The aim of the policy was to ensure a government budget deficit of just 1 per cent of GDP.

Yet, while macroeconomic policy was focused on reducing government expenditure, the weakness of the state administration was becoming apparent to the international institutions. In 2002, the World Bank published a review of public expenditure and public administration. The report concluded that changes in the structure, processes and capacity of government to implement reforms were needed to underpin the transition to a market economy. Specifically, the report concluded that the processes of budget preparation and execution were disjointed, the government had inadequate information on which to base its proposals and make its decisions, the budgetary process lacked credibility, public administration lacked transparency and there were poor performance incentives in government departments and line agencies (World Bank 2002). While the World Bank was pinpointing the weakness of the state administration and the need to build the state, the IMF called for reductions in public sector employment as an expenditure-reducing measure – policy advice which clashed with the Ohrid Agreement stipulation that more ethnic Albanians should be employed in public administration. A tense political situation arose which pitted the government, supported by the IMF, against the Albanian political parties backed by the Ohrid Agreement provisions, which almost led to the fall of the government towards the end of 2003. That there was a need for reform of public sector employment could hardly be disputed. But, the problem was largely one of poor allocation of available human resources. Public sector jobs, seen as a valuable asset, were handed out by politicians as favours to party members. Not only did it provide a secure income, but also in many cases provided the holder with the ability to gain additional income from bribes. Consequently, some areas of the public sector were heavily overstaffed, while other areas were so short of staff that they were unable to carry out their official functions adequately. Nevertheless, despite all the difficulties, the EU accepted Macedonia as a candidate for EU membership at the end of 2005. Some commentators regarded the application as premature, and the EU implicitly acknowledged the weakness of the application by delaying the opening of accession negotiations.

The VMRO-DPMNE won parliamentary elections in July 2006 and established a new government in coalition with a small ethnic Albanian party. The incoming government inherited a relatively favourable economic situation. Economic growth had reached 4 per cent in 2005, after years of stagnation. Interest rates had fallen on the back of growing international reserves. Inflation was low at 0.5 per cent, the budget deficit was within its 0.6 per cent target and external debt was also low at just 46 per cent of GDP. Despite the resumption of economic growth and stability, and the success of the previous government in achieving EU candidate status, Macedonia faces an uphill struggle in recovering from the long-term effects of the 2001 conflict and increasing its rate of growth to the regional average. Economic growth is narrowly based on a few key sectors, as has the inflow of foreign direct investment which has been concentrated on a few large deals related to privatization in oil refining, telecommunications and banking. A critical weakness is in the field of job creation, where the high cost of starting up new businesses and employing new workers has contributed to extremely high levels of unemployment, while the informal economy accounts for almost 40 per cent of household income (see Chapter 7).

Albania

The new government formed by the Democratic Party in 1992 secured the enthusiastic support of the World Bank and the IMF which agreed a Stand-by Arrangement and helped to introduce radical economic reforms. A shock-therapy stabilization policy was introduced based on restrictive monetary policy. Interest rates were increased to 32 per cent, nearly twice as high as those in neighbouring Greece, to encourage domestic savings (Haderi *et al.* 1999). A tight fiscal policy was imposed to eliminate the budget deficit, and subsidies to state-owned enterprises were reduced to just 2 per cent of GDP. The government's budget deficit fell from 17 per cent to 8 per cent of GDP between 1992 and 1995. Import and export licences were abolished. The exchange rate was allowed to float, and the lek, the national currency, appreciated by 25 per cent. By 1995, inflation had fallen to single digits (Figure 3.3).

However, the consequence of hard budget constraints and tight credit controls was a dramatic reduction in employment in state-owned enterprises which fell from 790,000 in 1992 to 296,000 in 1995, pushing half-a-million people into unemployment or emigration. By 1995, as many as 400,000 people, approximately 13 per cent of the population, were working abroad and the funds they returned home, amounting to 15 per cent of GDP in 1995, played an important role in stabilizing the exchange rate. The austerity measures led to the emergence of open unemployment for the first time in decades, and by the end of 1993 unemployment had increased to 29 per cent of the labour force while real wages had fallen. Social conditions and social services including education, primary health care services, nutrition, maternity and child care, and sanitation,

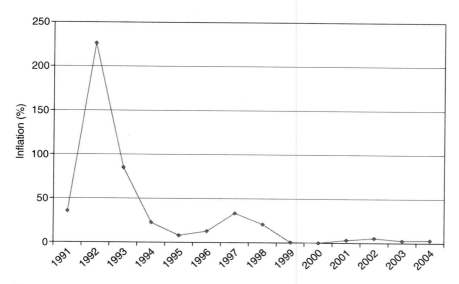

Figure 3.3 Albania: inflation, 1991–2004 (%) (source: UNECE Economic Survey of Europe, various issues).

also deteriorated. Not surprisingly, the 'shock-therapy' reform programme was unpopular among a population which had associated the transition to democracy with an expected improvement in living conditions and quality of life. Support for the Democratic Party melted away, and a referendum on a new constitution held in November 1994 was defeated. Corruption among the high echelons of the government and an increasing tendency towards authoritarian rule further contributed to its declining popularity.

Despite the success of the stabilization policy in controlling inflation, the shock-therapy programme contained a number of fatal flaws. Unlike the countries of former Yugoslavia, there had been no previous experience of a market economy in Albania. The institutional framework which could support the growth of market-based transactions was underdeveloped, and many of the workers thrown out of the collapsing state-owned companies found work in the informal economy or in illegal activities. Albania became a prime route for sanctions-busting trade into FRY. Links with the Italian mafia developed both to smuggle people out of Albania and to smuggle petrol and other banned goods into FRY. More seriously, the banking system was inefficient and unregulated. Most private savings still went into the state banks, but an unregulated private banking sector quickly developed. As the state-owned enterprises posted increasing losses, non-performing loans at the state banks began to accumulate rapidly, and by mid-1995 it was estimated that bad debts amounted to a third of banks' assets. Individuals began to withdraw their savings from the state banks which paid interest of between 17 per cent and 26 per cent depending on the maturity and placed them in the newly established private pyramid savings banks which offered between 85 per cent and 100 per cent (Cani 1997). It was not long before the banking system became highly unstable.

In the parliamentary elections of May 1996, the Socialist Party challenged the Democratic Party and its stabilization policies. Representing the losers from the economic reforms, including pensioners, the unemployed and blue-collar workers, the Socialist Party advocated a larger role for the state in the economy and increased subsidies and social spending. However, the election was won by the Democratic Party amongst allegations of widespread fraud.[13]

In January 1997, the country was plunged into crisis when several pyramid savings banks collapsed. The pyramid schemes had been built upon the incomes from goods smuggled into FRY to evade UN sanctions and on several billion dollars of remittances from Albanian workers employed abroad. As interest was paid out of the funds flowing in from new depositors, the banks were unable to pay existing savers once the growth of new accounts slowed down (Jarvis 1998). Protests against the loss of savings in the pyramid banking scandal soon turned into serious riots, directed by an anti-reform coalition comprising disaffected members of the former regime, including retired army generals and former members of the secret police, the Sigurimi. Organized crime groups also played a role in promoting the popular revolt. In March 1997, the prime minister resigned and President Berisha declared a state of emergency. However, the uprising only worsened, as government buildings were destroyed and factories and shops were looted. Most alarmingly, the military arsenals were plundered and thousands of weapons were seized. Armed gangs took over several towns in the south, and rebel committees demanded Berisha's resignation. In the face of the uprising, the army and police authority disintegrated and a civil war broke out between the government supporters from the north and the rebels with close connections to the Socialist Party in the south. The country slid into anarchy and into a 'social abyss' (Vaughan-Whitehead 1999).

The government was overwhelmed and forced to resign, and an interim government appealed for international assistance. Eventually, the Italian government took the leading role in an international force which entered Albania in April 1997 to restore order. New elections held in July led to a sweeping victory for the Socialist Party. Discredited, President Berisha resigned and a new coalition government led by Fatos Nano came to power which included several members of the previous communist regime, as well as leaders of the recent rebellion in the south. The government moved quickly to restore order. However, the events of 1997 had strengthened the position of organized criminal gangs involved in smuggling drugs, arms and cigarettes and in human trafficking, and in subsequent years this became an important issue in relation to Albania's progress with EU integration. Prospects for the continuation of institutional reforms did not look promising.

The shock-therapy stabilization policy, transferred to a country with an underdeveloped banking system and weak controls over the informal sector, had ended in spectacular failure. The losses in the pyramid scheme crisis amounted to hundreds of millions of dollars. In the months after the collapse, overseas remittances, aid inflows and exports all diminished, the currency depreciated by 40 per cent in the first half of the year and inflation reappeared reaching 42 per cent. The IMF agreed a $12 million post-conflict recovery loan, and international donors pledged to assist in recovery from the economic crisis. Albania was in no position to reject international assistance, and economic policy came under the tutelage of the IMF and the World Bank.

The 1997 stabilization programme

A second IMF-backed stabilization programme was introduced in 1997, which restored macroeconomic stability through a tight monetary policy-based direct control of the minimum deposit rate. The Bank of Albania aimed at a 2–4 per cent target range for inflation, while the exchange rate was allowed to float. Government expenditure was reduced by eliminating subsidies to state-owned enterprises, and the budget deficit consequently fell from 11 per cent of GDP in 1996 to 5.4 per cent of GDP in 1999.

Overseas remittances made a major contribution to stabilizing the economy. By 1998, remittances from family members working overseas, mainly in Greece and Italy, amounted to $452 million. As foreign aid inflows and overseas remittances recovered, the crisis abated and inflation was brought under control. By 1999, the rate of inflation had fallen to 0.4 per cent from previous highs of

32 per cent in 1997 and 21 per cent in 1998. Although direct control over interest rates was phased out in 2000 in favour of more market-based instruments including open-market operations using Treasury bills, monetary policy continued to be restrictive (Muço *et al.* 2004). The high real interest rates associated with the restrictive monetary policy discouraged domestic investment while simultaneously further stimulating overseas remittances, which reached 14 per cent of GDP in 2003. The inflow of foreign exchange led to an appreciation of the exchange rate which undermined the competitiveness of the export sector, and so exports have remained low, at just 10 per cent of GDP.

Albania's international standing rose dramatically following the Kosovo war during which it hosted hundreds of thousands of refugees and cooperated with North Atlantic Treaty Organization (NATO) forces. Consequently, just before the parliamentary election of June 2001, the EU announced the opening of negotiations for a Stabilization and Association Agreement. The Socialist Party, which won the election, had campaigned to bring Albania closer to the EU and had promised to improve infrastructure and repair the roads and the electricity system. The economy continued to perform well under the new government with high growth and low inflation. However, corruption pervaded the political system, and anti-corruption initiatives proved ineffective. Reports revealed that leading politicians and officials had links with organized crime groups and afforded them political and judicial protection (Bogdani and Loughlin 2007). Despite election promises, public infrastructure continued to decay, and public services such as health and education continued to suffer from a lack of funds. Poverty remained widespread, especially in rural areas and mountain regions. Illegal housing construction was rampant especially in and around the major towns and along the main road between Tirana and the main port of Durrës. The privatization plans for the big state-owned companies slowed down under the Socialist government, and EU officials became concerned that the reform programme would stall completely.[14]

The EU viewed Albania's performance in the July 2005 election as a test of democratic progress and a trigger for closer links with the EU. International observers pointed to deficiencies in the conduct of the election, but Olli Rehn, European Commissioner for Enlargement, stated that the elections 'were conducted competitively well overall'. This was a significant evaluation and indicated that negotiations for a Stabilization and Association Agreement would soon be concluded. Following the Democratic Party victory, Sali Berisha once again became prime minister. Domestically, Berisha announced that the priorities of the new government would be the fight against corruption, the creation of a state based upon the rule of law and economic development.[15] In international policy, its priorities were membership of the EU and NATO and dialogue with Serbia. On Kosovo, the new prime minister said that talks on its future status should not be delayed, and that both Kosovars' wishes for self-determination and the rights of the Serbian minority should be respected.

The Albanian economy has performed well since the 1997 crisis, averaging real GDP growth rates of 5.3 per cent between 2001 and 2006. Inflation has been low at around 3 per cent while the exchange rate has been allowed to float, unlike the cases of Croatia and Macedonia. Low inflation has been maintained by restrictive fiscal and monetary policies, although on the downside the share of government expenditure has been exceptionally low at less than 30 per cent of GDP in recent years. Interest rates have been brought down from 11 per cent in 2002 to just over 5 per cent in 2005, supporting growth of investment. While exports have been weak with a deficit of goods and services of 23 per cent in 2005, this has been covered by large flows of remittance incomes and by concessional loans under the IMF's Poverty Reduction and Growth Facility.

A number of factors have been proposed to explain Albania's strong economic growth following the 1997 economic crisis, including the recovery and strengthening of the state institutions, while the imposition of the rule of law has led to the resurgence of overseas remittances and of donor support (Treichel 2002). Improvements in customs administration have led to a reduction in the incidence of smuggling which, while not eliminating the problem, has further boosted government revenue. However, tax evasion has remained a serious problem in Albania, which has the lowest ratio of tax revenue to GDP among all the Western Balkan countries. Thus, despite promising performance in the macroeconomic field, there are many structural weaknesses which threaten the continuation of the country's recovery.

Albania remains a poor country, and although it is moving out of the group of low-income countries, poverty and social insecurity remain prevalent and there is a large informal economy. Albania has pursued a very liberal model of economic growth with a small state apparatus and without a strong regulatory framework to prevent abuses of market freedoms in the form of corruption and criminalization of the economy. In addition, Albania has adopted the path of a labour-export economy, similar to the path followed by Italy, Turkey and Yugoslavia during the 1960s. As Albania moves towards EU integration, it will have to strengthen its state administration and increase the level of public expenditure. So far, however, it has managed to achieve a rapid growth under the guidance of the international financial institutions, primarily the IMF, on the basis of a far more liberal market approach to economic management than has been adopted elsewhere in the Western Balkans.

4   The late reformers

BiH, Serbia, Montenegro and Kosovo

Institutional reforms in Bosnia and Herzegovina (BiH) and in the Federal Republic of Yugoslavia (FRY) were stalled throughout the 1990s.[1] BiH was plunged into war, preventing any reforms from being implemented until after the Dayton peace agreement in 1995. FRY, comprising Serbia including the provinces of Kosovo and Vojvodina, and Montenegro, was held under the sway of the authoritarian Milošević regime, and institutional reforms were effectively stalled until after the overthrow of the regime in 2000. In both cases, the problem of state formation and state-building preoccupied the elites and has only been partially resolved up to the present time. BiH gained a new constitution under the Dayton agreement, but it has required international supervision to monitor and enforce it. FRY became increasingly unstable as two of its component parts, Montenegro and Kosovo, pushed hard for independence. FRY transformed itself into the State Union of Serbia and Montenegro in 2004 under European Union (EU) pressure to maintain a unified state, but in 2006 Montenegro achieved its independence through a referendum. The province of Kosovo had declared independence in October 1991, but this was never recognized by the regime in Belgrade. Following the 1999 war, the province was placed under international supervision by the United Nations (UN). Its final status has not yet been determined, although a form of limited sovereignty seems a likely outcome.

Thus, the resolution of the statehood issue for both BiH and FRY has slowed down both the democratic consolidation and the transition to a market economy throughout the post-communist period. Furthermore, the slow pace of these processes has undermined progress with EU integration. The preoccupation with state-building, and the difficulties which it has encountered, has led to lengthy delays in establishing the formal institutions of the market economy and has opened up space for the emergence of large informal economies on their territories. The delays in resolution of the state-building process, the stalling and reversal of reforms and their delayed implementation have led to quite different outcomes in these states compared to the three early reforming states considered in the previous chapter.

Bosnia and Herzegovina

A referendum on independence held in BiH at the end of February 1992 received overwhelming support from the Muslim and Croatian communities and was followed by international recognition. Soon after, the Bosnian Serb leaders proclaimed the independence of the autonomous 'Serbian Republic of Bosnia', and the Croat leaders declared an autonomous 'Croatian Community of Herceg-Bosna'. Fighting started up in earnest after the declaration of independence, as Serbian forces from within and outside Bosnia moved into action to enforce the independence of their new mini-republic (Donia and Fine 1994; Malcolm 1994). James Gow has argued that 'the core problem was the Serbian state project and the decision to pursue the realization of that project through organized armed violence' (Gow 2003: 31) while in the same vein V.P. Gagnon Jr argued that 'the violence in former Yugoslavia was a strategic policy chosen by elites' (Gagnon 2004: 7). In this view, the intention of the war's instigators was to divide the functioning multicultural Bosnian society and create ethnic constituencies which would support the secession of the new ethnically based mini-states. Beyond the issue of statehood, however, lay economic interests. The war in BiH reflected the interests of the political coalition opposed to economic reforms. The Serbian elite stood to lose from the Marković reform programme, since the socially owned enterprises in both Serbia and BiH received large subsidies from the federal budget that would have been eliminated under the stabilization programme.

The Tudjman regime in Croatia also played a significant role in the crisis, as the annexation of Herzegovina was a strategic goal in the process of building the new Croatian state (Mahmutćehajić 2000: 46). Initially, the Muslim and Croat communities were allied in their common fight against the Serbs, but open hostilities broke out between them following the announcement of the Vance-Owen plan to divide the country in 1993.[2] This conflict within a conflict was resolved through the creation of the Muslim-Croat Federation in March 1994 which eventually became the Federation of BiH (FBiH). However, this was a very different arrangement to the concept of a unified multiethnic state that had been envisaged in the independence referendum of 1992.

Following US intervention, a peace agreement was negotiated at Camp Dayton which was formally signed in Paris in December 1995. A Peace Implementation Council was established to monitor the reconstruction programme, with a steering Board composed of representatives from the G7 states, Russia and the EU. A high representative was appointed by the UN to supervise the peace agreement and the process of reconstruction. The agreement sealed the division of the country, with 51 per cent of the territory held by FBiH and 49 per cent held by the Serb Republic (Republika Srpska – RS). A new constitution was created which established BiH as a federal state, composed of FBiH and RS as two semi-autonomous units or 'entities'. Within the new state, the national government had a parliament, a rotating presidency, a constitutional court and a central bank, but most power was devolved to the two federal units. The central government was responsible only for foreign policy, foreign trade, common and international communications, inter-entity transport, air traffic control, monetary policy, citizenship and immigration. In effect, the entities hold most of the functions of a nation state within their own territories, including their own parliaments, police forces and armies. The new state was built around the concept of ethnic separateness and embodied many of the aims of those who had sought to divide the country on ethnic lines. The three-member presidency of BiH reflected this ethnic division[3].

The Dayton agreement brought to an end over three years of intensive warfare in BiH which had destroyed a large part of the economy, caused over a quarter of a million deaths, injured 3000 people and created two million refugees – more than half the pre-war population. Approximately one-fifth of the housing stock, two-fifths of hospitals, three-quarters of school buildings and half the industrial plant had been destroyed. Industrial output fell to 5 per cent of its pre-war level, electricity and coal production fell to 10 per cent, livestock fell to 30 per cent and per capita income had fallen to just 20 per cent of the pre-war level (World Bank 2004a). The World Bank estimated that $5.1 billion would be required to meet the reconstruction needs of the country and organized a donors' conference to secure pledges of aid for a four-year programme of economic reconstruction.[4]

In the immediate aftermath of the war, the Bosnian Serb leader Radovan Karadžić became president of the RS. He ruled the entity with a ruthless determination to pursue the Serbian agenda of ethnic division. However, in July 1996, Karadžić resigned his post under pressure from both the USA and the Milošević regime. He was replaced by Biljana Plavšić as acting president, who soon turned against his supporters who were blocking the implementation of the Dayton agreement. The power struggle between the moderate faction and the hardliners carried on throughout the summer and autumn. Much was at stake as the section of the Bosnian Serb elite led by Karadžić had established a close relationship with organized criminal groups who were benefiting from stalling the implementation of the Dayton agreement and the reforms that it implied. Together with Momčilo Krajisnik, the Bosnian Serb member of the three-member presidency of BiH, Karadžić had established a number of profitable trading companies which brought in massive revenues from contraband goods (Jeffries 2002: 26). The dominance of the hard-line faction among the Bosnian Serbs alarmed the international community, and at a meeting of the Peace Implementation Council held in Bonn in December 1997, the High Representative was given extraordinary powers to remove obstructive officials and impose measures to ensure the implementation of the peace agreement, including the dismissal of elected representatives who opposed it. These became known as the 'Bonn powers' and led to the domination of Bosnian politics by the High Representative.

BiH joined the International Monetary Fund (IMF) in December 1995 and was the first country to make use of the resources of the Emergency Post-Conflict Fund. The economic strategy agreed between the IMF and the respective governments of BiH, FBiH and RS was based upon the adoption of a fixed exchange rate as a 'nominal anchor' to underpin price stability, the observance of strict fiscal discipline to prevent domestic borrowing by government bodies and reliance on large inflows of concessional financial assistance in the form of grants and loans from abroad. A few months later, in April 1996, BiH joined the World Bank and repaid its share of the former Yugoslav arrears, paradoxically using a new World Bank loan to do so.[5] An exceptional refinancing plan was agreed which involved a new concessional loan with a five-year grace period and a thirty-year repayment schedule. Under the Dayton agreement, the central government budget was financed from the budgets of the two entities, the largest part of which was spent on paying interest on the country's international debt. Agreements to restructure BiH's share of the former Yugoslav debt owed to the Paris and London Clubs of international banks were not reached until December 1997 by which time the total outstanding external debt had reached the equivalent of 90 per cent of gross domestic product (GDP), and payments arrears totalled $2.4 billion.

Macroeconomic stabilization

Parliamentary elections in RS held in November 1997 brought a new coalition government to power led by Milorad Dodik from the small party of Independent Social Democrats. Dodik favoured economic reforms, and a set of new economic laws called the 'Quick Start Package' was adopted to establish trade policy, customs policies and tariffs.[6] A central bank of BiH was established which started its activities in 1997 under a foreign banker who was appointed as governor by the IMF.[7] A new currency, the Convertible Mark (KM), was introduced to replace the Bosnian dinar, pegged to the German mark and later to the euro[8] through a classical currency board, under which the central bank was not permitted to issue new money unless it was backed by foreign currency reserves. The virtue of the currency board was that it ensured a stable exchange rate which underpinned price stability (Figure 4.1), but it also meant that the government could not use the exchange rate as an instrument to adjust the balance-of-payments deficit which remained persistently high. The deficit was partly covered by a Stand-by Arrangement agreed with the IMF in early 1998, by inflows of international aid and by remittances from family members working abroad.

The presidential election held in 1998 in RS was won by the hard-line nationalist Nikola Poplašen and represented a setback to progress in reform. At the first opportunity, High Representative Carlos Westendorp used his draconian powers to dismiss Poplašen from his elected position. At the fifth Donors' Conference in May 1999, Westendorp was able to claim that 'substantial progress' had been made over the previous year and that privatization had begun, BiH was under a single customs administration, taxes and excises had been harmonized between the two entities and illegal fiscal practices had reduced. However, further progress was limited to cosmetic measures, achieved at the expense of huge diplomatic effort, such as the introduction of a common licence plate and a

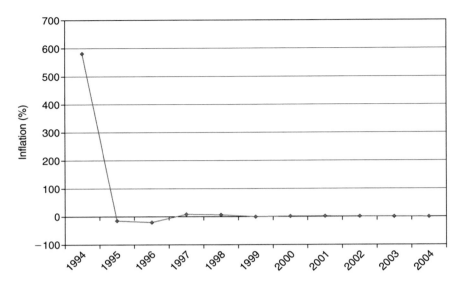

Figure 4.1 Bosnia and Herzegovina: inflation, 1994–2004 (%) (source: UNECE Economic Survey of Europe, various issues).

national flag. The task of creating a single economic space had not been completed – there was neither a unified labour market nor a unified capital market, nor had the problem of smuggling and tax evasion been overcome. Economic activities were under the control of political parties. Public services still needed to be reformed and the problem of corruption and fraud was widespread, and the state lacked a unified border service. Essentially, the entity governments were unwilling to agree on the unification of the state, and politicians in both entities continued to obstruct reform. Between 1999 and the time he left office in 2002, the acting High Representative, Wolfgang Petritsch, had sacked sixty-four local politicians and officials and had imposed 246 laws and other decisions.[9]

In reviewing the 1998 Stand-by Arrangement, the IMF commended the authorities on the maintenance of macroeconomic stability and on the introduction and acceptance of the KM as the unit of currency. It warned, however, that donor funding was about to diminish significantly and that the expenditure plans of the governments were not sustainable. It called for reductions in military expenditure and in budgetary transfers to war invalids and advised the governments that they should prioritize structural reforms, especially the privatization of banks and enterprises, reform the payments and tax systems and reform the labour market (IMF 2000). In their Letter of Intent, the prime ministers of the governments announced that their medium-term macroeconomic strategy was designed to do exactly that. The priorities of the strategy were geared towards fiscal stability, improving the efficiency of the tax system (i.e. reducing tax avoidance in the grey economy) and ensuring fiscal discipline.

Developments after 2000

The democratic turn in other countries of the Western Balkans following the end of the Kosovo war was not reflected in BiH, which remained politically unstable. Paddy Ashdown, former leader of the UK Liberal Democratic Party, took over the position of high representative in June 2002. In an inaugural speech, he declared that his main priorities would be 'justice and jobs – through reform' and added that he would 'step up efforts to fight the war profiteers who have now turned to smuggling weapons, fuel, drugs and even people'.[10] Soon after, a corruption scandal gripped the RS as it was revealed that customs officers had stolen €15 million through false documentation and bribery.[11] Ashdown called for the resignation of the RS finance minister who stepped down, while twenty-seven customs officials were also dismissed.

General elections held in October 2002 demonstrated the continued wide support for the main nationalist parties which won in all three parliaments. Ashdown announced that he was willing to work with the nationalists as long as they were willing to implement reforms, but he soon realized that they were undermining the reform programme and moved to weaken the autonomy of RS. In April 2003, he announced his intention to remove all mention of statehood from the RS constitution and abolish the RS supreme defence council.[12] The latter move was part of a concerted attempt to increase the power of the central government and to create a single economic space within BiH. These efforts bore fruit in November when the House of Representatives adopted a law to unify the country's tax and customs administrations, and a state-level Indirect Tax Authority (ITA) was established in 2005. This enabled a single value-added tax (VAT) system for the whole country to be introduced to replace the sales tax which had been levied at different rates in the two entities.

Despite all the difficulties of a fragmented political system, economic growth has averaged a respectable 5 per cent per annum since 2000. The existence of the currency board, managed by the strong and independent central bank, has ensured price stability. Customs and indirect taxation has been unified at the state level, and a nationwide VAT system was introduced in 2006 which has supported the creation of a single market within the country and should also lead to a reduction in the size of the informal economy. Exports have increased as comprehensive regional free trade agreements have come into effect.

However, the economy still suffers from a number of critical problems. Most notably, structural reforms have been slow, and the economy has been too reliant on outside donor funding. BiH is the least reformed country in the region according to the European Bank for Reconstruction and Development (EBRD) transition indicators, with a private sector share at a relatively low level of just 55 per cent of GDP. Despite economic growth, the current account deficit has hovered around 20 per cent of GDP, unemployment is stuck above 20 per cent of the labour force (nearly 25 per cent in RS), up to half of employment is in informal activities, and it is estimated that more than 30 per cent of the population lives in poverty.

The main difficulty has been that the state-level institutions are too weak and fragmented to carry out the policies needed to complete the transition to a market economy. As donor funding has diminished, pressure on the government budget has increased. The lack of a single budgetary authority has undermined the ability of the government to control expenditure. Separate ministries of finance exist at entity and cantonal levels, and many other non-budgetary bodies such as municipalities and off-budget funds can authorize public expenditure.[13] Furthermore, plans to transfer police and defence functions from the entities to the state-level institutions, to expand municipal investment, to ensure ethnic diversity at all levels of the civil service and to raise public investment have put further pressure on the government budget. BiH remains a fractured economy. Paradoxically, both the central government and the private sector of the economy are weak. Effective power remains with the mini-states in the two entities. The consequence has been that BiH is stuck in the transition stage, and many of the institutional reforms needed to create a functioning market economy still have not been carried through.

The Federal Republic of Yugoslavia (FRY)

Keen to inherit the mantle of the former state and access to its resources and properties, the governments of Serbia and Montenegro created a new state in 1992 known as the 'FRY' whose constitution formally recognized the demise of the Socialist Federal Republic of Yugoslavia (Teokarević 1996). In May, the UN Security Council imposed economic sanctions on FRY on the grounds that it had failed to cut support for the Serbian armed forces in Bosnia.[14] The sanctions prohibited exports from FRY, and all imports except for food and medicines were banned. The sanctions regime was tightened in November, by banning the transit of selected goods through FRY and introducing a blockade of the Montenegrin coast.[15] In April 1993, financial assets held abroad were frozen, and border monitors were put in place to ensure the effectiveness of the sanctions.[16]

Although sanctions were damaging, an inflationary monetary policy, the absence of structural reform and the general mismanagement of the economy were equally responsible for the deteriorating economic situation. In this context, sanctions were a useful cover for the ruling party to deflect popular anger at the worsening economic situation. One of the main negative effects of sanctions was to open opportunities for smugglers to engage in sanctions-busting trade across Serbia's borders, and enormous profits were earned from these activities. Powerful organized crime groups and networks with connections to leading politicians sprang up and began to cooperate with similar groups in neighbouring countries. Structural economic reforms were not on the agenda of the ruling party. According to a leading Croatian economist, 'Serbia showed little interest in transition, especially in marketization and the hard budget constraint involved. It quite clearly attempted to slow it down and tried to avoid implementing the requirements of stabilization policies' (Bićanić 1996: 146).

During 1993, FRY experienced one of the most dramatic hyperinflations in history, brought about not only by the disruptive effect of sanctions, but also by the government policy of printing money to subsidize large socially owned enterprises and to finance its support for the Bosnian Serbs. By the end of 1993, price increases had virtually wiped out the value of individuals' dinar savings, while delays of a few days in paying wages or pensions reduced their value to near zero. Conditions deteriorated in public hospitals where there was a growing lack of medicines, heat and food. Only the highest income groups which could transfer their income into foreign currency could protect themselves from hyper-inflation which, by the end of December, had reached an extraordinary 313,000,000 per cent on a monthly basis (Petrović *et al.* 1999). The average monthly pension had increased to ten billion dinars, but in reality this was worth less than one German mark. The National Bank issued a banknote worth 500 billion dinars (Figure 4.2). The dinar officially collapsed on 6 January 1994 when the German mark briefly became legal tender for the payment of all financial transactions (Lyon 1996). The government became increasingly unpopular as economic conditions deteriorated. Miloševic dissolved the Serbian parliament after breaking with his allies in the ultra-nationalist Serbian Radical Party (SRS), and in elections held in December 1993, the Socialist Party (SPS) lost its overall majority and continued to govern through a coalition with the small New Democracy Party.

Faced with the prospect of almost total economic collapse, the central bank introduced a radical stabilization programme in January 1994, under which the currency was revalued and a fully convertible New Dinar was introduced, pegged at a ratio of 1:1 against the German mark. The government ceased the inflationary financing of its deficit, the central bank introduced a tight monetary policy and new money was printed only in so far as it was backed by foreign

Figure 4.2 The 500-billion dinar bank note, FRY, end of 2003 (source: National Bank of Serbia ©).

Note
The image is of Jovan Jovanović Zmaj, a Serbian doctor and poet.

reserves. The stabilization policy produced immediate effects. Inflation was reduced to single-digit levels in 1994, and GDP and industrial production began to recover.

The ending of sanctions had become a priority for the regime, and in the summer of 1994 the flow of aid to the Bosnian Serbs was stopped, leading to an easing of sanctions in September when international flights to and from Belgrade were permitted, as were cultural and sporting exchanges (Teokarević 1996). The real value of wages and pensions recovered from their disastrously low levels at the beginning of the year, and real GDP increased by about 6 per cent in 1994, although industrial production increased more slowly. However, the stabilization proved to be unsustainable due to lack of support from the international financial institutions, the lack of structural reforms and the lack of commitment of the government to the stabilization policy. Inflation soon reappeared, reaching an annual rate of 72 per cent in 1995 and 90 per cent in 1996 (Figure 4.3).

Political manoeuvres in the post-Dayton period

Trade sanctions were lifted at the end of 1995 following the Dayton agreement, leading to a surge of imports to satisfy pent-up demand which resulted in an enormous current account deficit which reached $1.5 billion in 1997. However, FRY was still subject to an 'outer wall' of sanctions which prohibited businesses and the government from accessing the international capital market or receiving loans from the IMF to cover the ballooning payments deficit (Popović 1997). The government had based its development strategy on the assumption that there

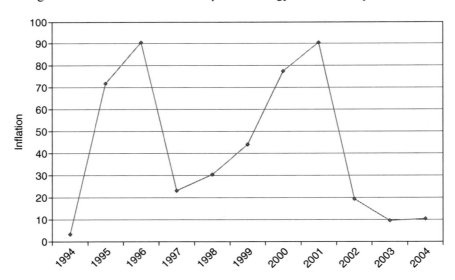

Figure 4.3 Serbia and Montenegro (FRY): inflation, 1994–2004 (%) (source: UNECE Economic Survey of Europe, various issues).

would be a strong inflow of foreign capital to cover the trade deficit, but the outer wall of sanctions made the plan entirely dependent upon privatization revenues raised from the sale of assets to foreign investors.

An opposition coalition, *Zajedno*, had been formed in September 1996 but failed to make a significant breakthrough in the elections to the federal parliament held in the following month. The Dayton agreement had given a temporary boost to the ruling SPS which won the elections in coalition with two other smaller parties. The SPS had presented itself as being committed to reforms and the renewal of the transition process. A new privatization law was prepared, and foreign investors began to arrive in Belgrade in search of business opportunities in one of the few countries of Eastern Europe that had not yet initiated the economic transition. The *Zajedno* coalition consisted of the modernizing, reform-minded Democratic Party (DS) led by Zoran Djindjić and more traditionally nationalist Serbian Renewal Party (SPO) led by Vuk Drašković. The unlikely coalition left many of the supporters of both factions dissatisfied, and the fiercely nationalist SRS secured almost as many votes at the elections (Thomas 1999: 282).

The *Zajedno* coalition made a better showing in local elections also held in November, winning majorities in several towns and cities. These had been first falsified and then vetoed by Milošević in those towns in which the opposition parties had won. A mass protest demonstration of Belgrade university students, supported by the citizens of Belgrade, was held in the centre of the capital. The demonstration was halted in the main street in Belgrade by a line of riot police, and a stand-off developed which lasted several months. The students organized shifts from each of the university faculties to maintain the protest and set up a stage close to police lines from which bands entertained the large crowd of protestors.

In February 1997, Milošević finally accepted the local election results and the demonstrators dispersed. It began to look as though the Milošević regime was on its last legs. However, in June the government sold 49 per cent of the Serbian Telecom company to a consortium of Italian and Greek investors and used the revenue from the sale to increase the salaries of public sector workers in the run-up to parliamentary elections held in September 1997. Regrettably, the opposition coalition split over the summer, and the challenge to the regime dissipated. Although the ruling SPS-led coalition lost its majority in the elections, it remained the largest bloc in the parliament and the Milošević regime hung on to power.[17] The election results represented a shift to the nationalist right as the SRS joined the government coalition, and its leader Vojislav Šešelj became deputy prime minister. The SRS represented the potential losers from institutional reform, the workers in overstaffed large enterprises, pensioners and peasant smallholders (Cohen 2001: 222). Any hopes of further reform were dashed, and the political situation soon began to deteriorate. An upsurge of armed conflict in Kosovo in late 1997, and throughout 1998, was fuelled by the unrest in neighbouring Albania which had released thousands of weapons into the hands of paramilitary groups, including Kosovo Albanian insurgents.

The Kosovo war

The Democratic League of Kosovo (LDK) had led the resistance to Serbian domination under the leadership of Ibrahim Rugova and had established a parallel underground government financed by a 3 per cent 'tax' on the large Albanian diaspora in Western countries (Malcolm 1998). The party won a majority in parliamentary elections to the Kosovo Assembly in May 1992, and Ibrahim Rugova was elected as president of the unofficial government. Under Rugova's leadership, Kosovo Albanians boycotted the FRY parliamentary elections and adopted a policy of non-violent resistance. However, as the repression of the parallel institutions intensified throughout the following years, many Albanians began to turn towards groups advocating more aggressive forms of resistance. An underground paramilitary organization, known as the Kosovo Liberation Army (KLA), was formed and admitted responsibility for the first armed actions in April 1996. The violence intensified over subsequent years and, fuelled by the collapse in law and order in neighbouring Albania in 1997, broke out into open warfare between the KLA and the Serbian paramilitary police in 1998. After almost a year of low-intensity civil war, the Serbian and Albanian sides to the conflict were brought together at a peace conference at Rambouillet in March 1999. The FRY government delegation was presented with an ultimatum to sign the agreement drawn up by the international negotiators or face the use of force by North Atlantic Treaty Organization (NATO). Following the FRY delegation's rejection of the agreement and last-minute negotiations in Belgrade, NATO commenced bombing operations against Serbia on 24 March 1999, which continued with increasing intensity every day for the following three months (Judah 2000).

Once the bombing commenced, the Serbian police and paramilitary forces in Kosovo stepped up their repression of the Kosovar population and began a systemic and brutal programme of attacks and expulsions of ethnic Albanians.[18] Almost immediately, an enormous wave of refugees appeared at the Albanian and Macedonian borders, which quickly grew to unprecedented numbers. It was estimated that 250,000 refugees from Kosovo fled to Macedonia and 442,000 to Albania. Smaller numbers fled to BiH (including 20,000 Muslims from the Sandjak region of Serbia) and to Montenegro. There were also 60,000 refugees from Kosovo within Serbia. Many others became internally displaced within the province, eking out a bleak existence in the hills and forests, while several thousands were killed by paramilitary gangs engaged in a brutal campaign of 'ethnic cleansing'.[19] The total number of refugees registered by the United Nations High Commissioner for Refugees (UNHCR) in neighbouring countries was over three-quarters of a million (around half the population). Many were children, and 85 per cent of the adults were women; most were ethnic Albanians. About 72,000 Kosovar refugees were evacuated from Macedonia mainly to Western countries through the UNHCR/International Organization for Migration (IOM) Humanitarian Evacuation Programme,[20] although relatively few refugees were admitted to the UK which had been one of the main sponsors of the military campaign against FRY (Bartlett 2000). The scale of the humanitarian crisis shocked the world, and the ruthless behaviour of the Serbian forces ensured continued Western public support for the bombing campaign.

In May, the EU had imposed a ban on sale of goods, services, technology and equipment to repair war damage in Serbia, froze funds, prohibited export finance and suspended commercial flights in and out of Belgrade. However, many leading Serbs, and a few Serbian financial institutions, were reported to have already switched their finances offshore to Cyprus.[21] The Milošević regime capitulated once it became clear that the Russian government supported NATO. A peace agreement was reached on 3 June 1999, and Yugoslav forces began pulling out of the province on 11 June. Several days later, NATO forces entered Kosovo and took control of the major towns and cities. Unexpectedly, almost all the refugees returned within a few weeks, and as they did so a reverse wave of up to 250,000 Serbian refugees fled in the opposite direction across the border into Serbia, in a reversal of the ethnic cleansing that had started the war. Under the peace agreement, Kosovo remained formally a constituent part of the territory of FRY, but in practice, as in the case of Bosnia, the province became an international Protectorate under the control of a UN civil administration, United Nations Mission in Kosovo (UNMIK), and NATO forces. The two main factions of the Kosovo Albanian resistance movement (the LDK and the KLA) competed for recognition and political legitimacy as the 'true' provisional government.

The Democratic Revolution in FRY

The Serbian economy had been severely damaged by the NATO bombing campaign in 1999. The destruction of the Zastava car factory in Kragujevac had put 15,000 people out of work, in addition to a further 40,000 people who worked in over 100 subcontractor companies. In Čačak, the Sloboda factory which produced vacuum cleaners for the Russian market as well as ammunitions was destroyed, putting 5,000 people out of work. A further 7,000 people lost their jobs when the 14 Oktobar factory, which made heavy construction equipment and bulldozers, was destroyed in Kruševac. The large factories 21 May, Jugostroj, Rekord and Grmec in Belgrade were destroyed. The DIN cigarette factory, the EI electricity utility and the MIN machine tool factory at Niš were also severely damaged. Numerous small businesses were also destroyed, as well as the Ušće business complex in Belgrade, valued at $50 million. By early May, two oil refineries and most oil depots were reported to be destroyed, and fuel rations of five gallons per month were introduced. Other targets included highways, rail and communications networks and power stations. Output was down by 50 per cent, and over 100,000 people had been put out of work.[22] NATO estimated that damage worth $12 billion was caused in the first eight days of the conflict alone. At the end of the first month of bombing, Vuk Drašković, deputy prime minister at the time, estimated the war damage had reached $40 billion. By that time, thirteen major bridges, twelve railway stations and forty factories had been destroyed.[23] By the end of May, after over two months of bombing, the number of destroyed bridges had risen to fifty, and five airports had also been destroyed. Estimates made after the end of the war varied from the $100 billion by the FRY government to $30 billion estimated by the G17 group of independent Serbian economists. Western estimates of the extent of the destruction wrought by the eleven-week war with NATO were around $60 billion.[24]

In the months following the end of the war, the opposition to the Milošević regime gathered strength, supported by financial and technical assistance from the West. The USA opened an office in Budapest from where assistance to the opposition was directed (Cohen 2001). The student opposition movement *Otpor (Resistance)* protested against the government's attempts to stifle independent activity in the universities and organized demonstrations in several towns and cities. Branded as terrorists, many were arrested and mistreated by the police as the authoritarian regime turned increasingly towards open repression of dissent.[25] One observer noted that, 'as it degenerated, becoming more reliant on violence and intimidation, the regime slid closer to all-out dictatorship' (LeBor 2002). In a show of solidarity, the official opposition parties allied themselves with *Otpor*. Zoran Djindjić and Vuk Drašković pledged unity in the political struggle against the regime and formed a coalition known as the Democratic Opposition of Serbia (DOS), selecting Vojislav Koštunica, leader of the small moderate nationalist Democratic Party of Serbia (DSS), as their presidential candidate. In elections for the FRY presidency in September 2000, Koštunica officially won 49 per cent of the vote, but according to election monitors, the results were rigged by the government. A popular protest movement against the outcome of the election gathered steam, and a mass demonstration of 700,000 protestors took place in Belgrade on 5 October. When a large crowd stormed the Federal parliament building, the Milošević regime collapsed.

Economic stabilization begins in 2000

The regime had bequeathed a harsh legacy to the new coalition government that came to power in FRY at the end of 2000. The economy was in a parlous state with massive hidden unemployment in unproductive state enterprises, widespread poverty and a ruined middle class. A government memorandum to the IMF stated:

> The economic legacy of ten years of regional conflicts, isolation, and economic mismanagement is dismal. Output stands at 50% of its 1989 level; infrastructure is in disrepair; recorded unemployment is about 30% of the work force; 12-month inflation runs at about 120%; average wages are at about DM 140 per month; and the external position is nonviable owing to the crushing burden of debt.
>
> (IMF 2001: 52)

The state was weakened by its association with organized criminal groups and its involvement in the black market and smuggling. *The Economist* magazine summarized the condition of Serbia:

Gangsterism, which has flourished in many ex-communist countries, is exceptionally powerful in Yugoslavia. War-profiteering, sanctions-busting and a corrupt system of import permits have created ideal conditions for well-connected criminals to take over many sectors of the economy. Almost every level of Serbian society is involved with the black market in some way, from wealthy entrepreneurs who have enjoyed the protection of Mr Milosevic junior to petrol-smugglers on the border with Bosnia and small traders selling contraband cigarettes in the flea market. The underworld has exploited Yugoslavia's isolation from the community of law-governed states.

(*The Economist* 12 October 2000)

In December 2000, the DOS went on to win Serbian parliamentary elections, gaining 70 per cent of the seats in the parliament. Djindjić became the new prime minister of Serbia, while Koštunica became the president of FRY. The DS and the DSS were the two largest parties with an equal number of seats, but the DSS had only two ministers in the government, and its requests for greater representation were rejected by Djindjić. The infighting between the coalition partners marred the success that the opposition forces had achieved in the elections. Moreover, the fall of the Milošević regime had not overturned the close nexus between the state and the world of organized crime.

Despite these difficulties, the new pro-reform government moved quickly to introduce a stabilization programme. A comprehensive package of reforms was developed in close consultation with the IMF and the World Bank. The main aims of the policy were to reduce macroeconomic imbalances, restructure the economy, attract additional external assistance and reduce the country's debts. The reform programme involved the liberalization of foreign exchange, trade and prices; radical reform of the public finances; the restructuring of the banking system; and a large-scale privatization of socially owned enterprises.

At the federal level, the stabilization policy aimed to contain the current account deficit at just over 11 per cent of GDP. This, together with the need to clear arrears of debt and to build up international reserves, implied a financing gap of $10.7 billion for 2001, which the government hoped to cover through a combination of debt rescheduling, new concessional loans and transfers from international donors. Under a restrictive fiscal policy, the federal government budget was slashed, salaries in the federal administration and the army were frozen, investment expenditure was cut and military spending was brought under civilian control. Monetary policy was the responsibility of the National Bank of Yugoslavia (NBY), but since the Montenegrin and Kosovo governments had introduced the euro as their official currency, the remit of the NBY ran only as far as the borders of Serbia. The main aim of policy was to reduce inflation, and the main policy instrument was a tight monetary policy. The exchange rate was placed on a managed float, and the NBY permitted the exchange rate to depreciate to ensure external cost competitiveness and to build up external reserves (IMF 2001). In cooperation with the IMF and the World Bank, the government introduced legislation in May 2001 to liberalize foreign trade by abolishing most quantitative restrictions on imports and introducing a new tariff schedule which reduced the average duty rate to 10 per cent.

Fiscal reforms mostly concerned the republic governments. In Serbia, the government proposed a tax reform to simplify and reduce taxes. Public employment was to be reduced by 6 per cent, while social assistance to the most vulnerable families was to increase and be better targeted to the poorest families. The government also planned to change the indexation of pensions from wages to the cost of living. The overall aim was to reduce the Serbian government budget deficit to 3.2 per cent of GDP. In Montenegro, the government budget deficit at 10.5 per cent of GDP in 2000 was a serious problem due to weak tax collection, and expenditure cuts were proposed.

The stabilization policy resulted in a reduction in the rate of inflation from 90 per cent in 2001 to 20 per cent in 2002 (Figure 4.3). The success of the policy increased the credibility of the government and boosted its popular support, enabling it to move politically against the remaining centres of power of the old regime. Western governments insisted that Milošević should be handed to the International Criminal Tribunal on the former Yugoslavia (ICTY) before they would provide aid for economic reconstruction. He was arrested in March 2001 on grounds of financial misdemeanours, damage to Serbia's economy and causing hyperinflation (LeBor 2002) and was extradited in June, a decision opposed by the DSS, but motivated by a threat by international donors to suspend aid to FRY (Cigar 2001). Despite its initial success, the stabilization programme faced difficulties due to political instability within the ruling coalition. Relations between the DS and the DSS deteriorated, and in August the DSS withdrew from the Serbian government. Moreover, the reform efforts were often blocked by the federal parliament where Koštunica and the DSS were supported by the Montenegrin Socialists, the SPS and the SRS. During 2002, the political conflict intensified between the two parties and the two levels of government, bringing the stability of the whole political system into question.

Along with the ambitions of the Djukanović government in Montenegro to secede from the FRY and establish an independent state, the legitimacy of the federal institutions was becoming increasingly problematic. In March 2002, in order to forestall a complete break-up of the federation, the EU brought leaders of the two republics together. The Belgrade Agreement of 14 March 2002, brokered by the EU under the guidance of Javier Solana, the EU's foreign policy supremo, set out the framework for a new constitutional arrangement.[26] From the EU side, the Agreement appeared to have several advantages. It ensured that the two republics would stay together and in doing so effectively blocked the question of change to state borders in other parts of former Yugoslavia, notably BiH and Kosovo. It provided a single point of contact in relations with the EU. In addition, it was expected to diminish the influence of the anti-reform parties in the federal government.

Serbian presidential elections held in September 2002 were indecisive, even after several electoral rounds, due to the low voter turnout. One of the contenders, Miroljub Labus – a founder member of the 'G17' group of dissident economists during the Milošević regime – established his own party known as 'G17 Plus' with a strong focus on reform policies, leading to a worsening of relations within the DOS coalition. Early in 2003, Prime Minister Djindjić threatened the position of the governor of the NBY, pro-reform G17 Plus member Mladjan Dinkić, by suggesting that he would not automatically become governor of the new National Bank of Serbia to be created by the imminent constitutional changes. The announcement positioned Djindjić close to the old anti-reform coalition that had built up around Milošević and in opposition to the reformist group led by Labus to which both Dinkić and the Finance Minister Božidar Djelić belonged.[27] These events demonstrated that the reformists had not yet managed to consolidate effective power within Serbia and that the anti-reform coalition was able to maintain its strong influence on economic policy.

The state union of 'Serbia and Montenegro'

Under the Constitutional Charter adopted in February 2003, the FRY was disbanded and replaced by the 'State Union' of Serbia and Montenegro (known simply as 'Serbia and Montenegro'). The new confederal union retained powers only over joint defence and foreign affairs, while each member state achieved wide autonomy in other areas including economic and social policy. The arrangement was to last for three years until 2006, after which time Montenegro would be able to hold a referendum on independence. Under the new constitution, the province of Kosovo maintained its formal status as an integral part of Serbia. The State Union was run by a six-person Council of Ministers elected by the parliament, whose members were appointed by the two republics. Power was highly devolved to the republics, and the State Union was characterized by a low level of political and economic integration. In effect, the federal state was 'hollowed out' and had little more than an emblematic function to disguise the de facto separation of the two republics as independent states.[28] The new State Union, far from providing a single negotiating partner for the EU, was in fact an empty shell, whose writ had little impact in the two republics that were able to proceed according to their own laws and regulations.

The assassination of Zoran Djindjić

The difficulty of initiating reformist policies in Serbia was highlighted by the assassination of Prime Minister Zoran Djindjić, who was murdered by sniper fire in the courtyard of the Serbian government building in Belgrade on 12 March 2003. The assassination gave a clear message of the fragility of the democratic transition in Serbia since the fall of the Milošević regime. The most likely reason for the assassination was Djindjić's increasingly determined moves against mafia gangs and indicted war criminals, partly brought about by pressure from the USA which threatened to withdraw support if the Serbian government failed to act against these groups. Following the assassination, the government announced a state of emergency and initiated a crackdown on the organized crime gangs in Serbia, arresting as many as 10,000 people of whom almost half were detained for questioning.[29]

The speedy and resolute action represented a setback for the anti-reform coalition which had lingered on from the days of the Milošević regime but did not break it, and nationalist politicians did well in subsequent political contests. In the third round of presidential elections held in November 2003, the ultra-nationalist SRS candidate, Tomislav Nikolić, gained the most votes, although a low turnout invalidated the result. In the general election of December 2003, the SRS made a strong showing, although it was excluded from the minority government led by Koštunica's DSS. Significantly, the reformist DS of the late Zoran Djindjić, now led by Boris Tadić, was also excluded from the government. The continued strength of nationalist sentiment in Serbia, and the need for the government to seek support from the SPS in the parliament, cast doubt on the ability of the government to implement further far-reaching economic reforms.

In July 2003, in a major setback to the reform process in Serbia, Mladjan Dinkić resigned as governor of the Serbian National Bank after accusing the government of seeking to strip the Bank of its independence. Dinkić, who was also deputy leader of the pro-reform G17 Plus party, had earlier stated his disappointment with the police, who had failed to follow up the many criminal charges the Bank had made against companies allegedly involved in money laundering. Following his resignation, Dinkić made further charges of financial irregularities against some members of the DOS government, whom he accused of money laundering. The affair, together with internal conflicts within the ruling coalition, weakened the government, whose popularity began to fall from the high levels which it had enjoyed following the Djindjić assassination earlier in the year. According to a report of the Organization for Security and Cooperation in Europe (OSCE) published in 2005, organized crime continued to be a hindrance to the pursuit of institutional reform '... as well as the country's prospects for European integration. It has penetrated political structures, public administration, the commercial sector, and the criminal justice system. It has created an atmosphere of instability that discourages much-needed foreign investment' (Brunhart and Gajić 2005: 7). Reflecting the drift in support away from the reformist parties, the ultra-right wing political party, the SRS, continued to attract widespread support from disaffected and disadvantaged sections of the population and emerged as the largest party by number of votes in the parliamentary election held in January 2007. However, Kostunica's DSS eventually formed a coalition government with the DS in March, bringing the pro-EU party back into government.

Despite the political turbulence and uncertainties since 2000, the Serbian government has succeeded in implementing some significant institutional and economic policy reforms. Economic growth has been consistently above 5 per cent, having peaked at over 9 per cent in 2003, increasing GDP by nearly two-fifths since 2000. The share of employment in the private sector has also increased as institutional reforms have significantly improved the business climate in Serbia, and foreign investment has been attracted to the country in the wake of a major privatization programme. However, the stabilization policy failed to eliminate inflation which has remained above 10 per cent in most years. Although Serbia is nominally in fourth place in terms of GDP per capita among the Western Balkan countries, when viewed in terms of purchasing power parity which adjusts for price differences among countries, Serbia has a GDP per capita below Albania (see Chapter 8). Unemployment in Serbia is relatively high at around 20 per cent and is increasing as privatization and enterprise restructuring have led to a shake-out of surplus labour. Public expenditure remains a relatively high proportion of GDP at 44 per cent, and many large state-owned and socially owned companies continue to be supported by subsidies. The informal sector remains a significant force despite cuts in direct taxes including corporation tax to a flat 14 per cent, and organized crime remains a worrying element of the economy. The slow development of relations with the EU has been a further negative factor. Since its transition started relatively late, at the turn of the century, it has not yet run its full course and the particular form of capitalism that will eventually emerge is as yet undefined.

Montenegro

In Montenegro, the reformed communist party, the Democratic Party of Socialists (DPS), won the parliamentary election held in November 1996 with a large majority, and in December the reformist Prime Minister Milo Djukanović publicly criticized Milošević, siding with the protest movement that was developing in Serbia. President Momir Bulatović remained loyal to Milošević and left the DPS to establish his own pro-Serbia party, the Socialist People's Party (SNP).[30] Thereafter, politics in Montenegro was deeply divided between the DPS which supported independence for Montenegro and the SNP which supported the continuation of the federal arrangement with Serbia (Bieber 2003).

Until 1997, economic and social policies in Montenegro were essentially subject to the policies decided in Belgrade, but in October that year Djukanović won the presidential elections defeating Milošević's ally Bulatović. The Serbian regime turned against Montenegro and imposed an economic blockade. Trucks were held up at the border for up to five days at a time, and Serbia started importing goods through Thessaloniki rather than the Montenegrin port of Bar (Jeffries 2002). The transfer of federal funds and pension payments to Montenegro was suspended. An FRY government campaign against smuggling focused mainly on the trade through Montenegro and was interpreted as a further action designed to destabilize the Montenegrin government.[31] Bulatović was elected prime minister of the FRY by the federal parliament in May 1998. The Montenegrin parliament voted not to recognize the new FRY government, while the Montenegrin government announced that it would no longer respect federal laws. Opinion in Montenegro began to swing behind the pro-independence parties, and a DPS-led coalition won parliamentary elections held in May.

Thereafter, debate about possible secession became increasingly vocal, and official criticism of the Milošević regime was stepped up. The Montenegrin government began to issue its own import and export licences, and customs revenues
were retained instead of being passed on to the federal authorities in Belgrade.

At the start of the Kosovo war, the situation in Montenegro became
extremely tense. The Yugoslav army attempted to seize control, ordering that
Montenegrin police should be placed under its command, and federal troops
took over the border posts with Croatia. President Djukanović declared that 'the
regime in Belgrade wants to install the Yugoslav army as a dictatorship power in
Montenegro'.[32] For a while, it looked as if an armed conflict between Serbia and
Montenegro might erupt. The airport at Podgorica was closed by the FRY
authorities in December 1999, and a well-armed paramilitary unit was established by the army with the apparent intention of overthrowing the Montenegrin
government. President Djukanović alleged that 'they are devoted to Milošević.
Over 50 per cent of them have criminal records. They are not being retained to
protect the country but to overthrow the government' (Jeffries 2002: 401). The
tension was only defused with the overthrow of the Milošević regime in October
2000.

Parliamentary elections held in Montenegro in April 2001 produced a narrow
victory for the reformist DPS coalition which established a minority government. The EU became even more actively involved in Montenegrin affairs, but
its policy of maintaining the federal arrangement between Serbia and Montenegro was misguided. In the parliamentary election of October 2002, the Democratic List for European Montenegro, led by the DPS, gained a small but clear
majority in the parliament. The pro-independence politicians in Montenegro had
managed to keep their positions in power and settled down to wait for the referendum on independence which was scheduled to be held three years later. The
referendum held in May 2006 secured a narrow majority in favour of independence, and Montenegro declared itself an independent country in June 2006.

Macroeconomic stability had been underpinned by the earlier decision to
adopt the euro as the country's sole legal tender, although this eliminated several
levers of economic control over the economy. Although inflation has been low
since 2000, the rate of economic growth has been less than in Serbia. Unemployment has been over 20 per cent, and poverty is widespread in the de-
industrialized North-East of the country where the main employer, the
wood-processing industry, has collapsed due to the combined effects of sanctions, war and neglect by the central government. Montenegro has moved
quickly to cement its relationship with the EU and signed a Stabilization and
Association Agreement in March 2007 which is likely to give a boost to trade
and investment and speed up institutional reform.

Kosovo

After Kosovo's autonomy was suspended by Serbia in July 1990, many Albanian workers and managers in socially owned enterprises and agricultural kombi-

nats were fired. By 1991, about 150,000 Albanian workers had been dismissed from their jobs, representing 90 per cent of the employed workforce (Pula 2004: 811). The repression of the Albanian institutions in Kosovo spread into the public sector with the dismissal of 6,000 secondary school teachers and 115 school principals, while Albanian students were prevented from entering school premises by the police. In response, the Albanian community set up its own parallel institutions and began a campaign of non-violent resistance against the Serbian repression. During the 1990s, most normal economic activities came to an almost complete standstill. The agricultural kombinats almost entirely collapsed, and the livestock herds were reduced by about two-thirds.

The province was further devastated by the 1999 war. According to one estimate, economic losses caused during the war amounted to some $5 billion (Layne 2000) and included significant damage to the electricity network, key industrial assets and to the agriculture sector where much of the infrastructure of the agricultural kombinats was destroyed (World Bank 2004b).[33] In the aftermath of the war, electricity only functioned intermittently and the sound of generators filled the air of most of Kosovo's towns and villages in the winter of 1999. Many public institutions were looted by the departing Serbs, including the university library in Priština which was left bereft of books and equipment, while the few companies still functioning had been looted of much of their equipment.[34]

The example of the Peja (Peć) brewery demonstrates the difficulties that Kosovo companies had in maintaining production after the war and how a socially owned self-managed enterprise was able to rebuild its production base by drawing on the enthusiasm and hard work of the labour force.

> The Peja (Peć) brewery was established in 1975, and expanded its market to cover Montenegro, South Serbia and Belgrade. After the war, all our company's vehicles were taken to Serbia, and production fell from seventy million to sixty million bottles. In autumn 2003 our company was still under social ownership and workers' self-management and had a twenty-one member workers' council. We employed around five hundred employees, whose wages averaged around €560 per month, rising to €1,000 in the summer and falling to €250–€300 in the winter. We have rebuilt our vehicle fleet to fifty vehicles, and now operate at 60 per cent of capacity, and have an estimated value of €150 million. We think that there would be more opportunities for export if the company were privatized as it would bring new management skills and a new position for both workers and managers.
>
> [Interview with manager, Peja (Peć) Brewery October 2003]

UN Resolution 1244 on the ending of the war with FRY called for 'substantial autonomy and meaningful self-government for Kosovo' within the context of the recognition of the 'territorial integrity of Yugoslavia'. UNMIK was established to provide for the civil administration of the province, headed by the Special Representative of the Secretary-General (SRSG). An international

NATO/Russian peace-keeping force, known as KFOR, was charged with maintaining security and supervising the disarmament of the KLA. While the UN had overall responsibility for implementing the peace agreement, it delegated key functions to other organizations. In particular, the UNHCR took responsibility for humanitarian affairs and the care of refugees, OSCE took charge of supervising democratic institutions and elections, NATO became the lead organization in the field of security and the EU took over the leading role in the reconstruction of the economy. A High Level Steering Group[35] was established to coordinate the activities of all four of these distinct 'pillars' of the new administration. The strategic priority identified by UNMIK was to create an environment conducive to private economic activities, including the resolution of basic property rights, the development and regulation of banking and finance, the clarification of conditions for foreign trade and the creation of procedures for company registration.[36] Other urgent priorities included building a basic civil administration and restoring education and health services. A massive international assistance effort was launched to reconstruct the province and to rebuild the destroyed housing, infrastructure, factories and public institutions. Huge convoys of civilian supplies and military equipment poured into the province along the only functioning road from neighbouring Macedonia. Farmers received donations of equipment and animals, including thousands of high quality cattle to restock the farms.

One of the first actions of the UNMIK administration was to remove all quantitative barriers to trade and introduce a single 10 per cent import tariff which became the main source of government revenue. A Banking and Payments Authority was set up as a central bank, which established the German mark and later the euro as legal tender. A ministry of economy and finance was established to manage the budget and tax system. Real GDP growth was initially rapid owing to post-war recovery and the inflow of aid and grew by over 16 per cent in 2001, but this was not sustained. GDP fell in 2002 and 2003 and, following a small recovery in 2004, fell again the following year. The collapse in growth was largely due to the decline in international aid inflows and the weak export performance, which was not compensated by growth in domestic consumption or investment. The economy came to depend on overseas remittances and on international aid (World Bank 2004b).

Despite all the international assistance, by 2002 agricultural exports were just €3 million compared to imports of €160 million. Owing to its poor initial starting conditions in 1990, the effects of the Serbian repression, discrimination in the labour market against Albanians in the 1990s, the isolation caused by sanctions against FRY and the effects of the NATO bombing campaign, the productivity of the economy has fallen even further behind as equipment has become obsolete, and skills of the labour force have declined. The example of the battery production sector is illustrative of wider problems facing the whole economy.

In the past, batteries were the country's biggest export. There were three battery companies, all linked to the Trepča mining complex, one of which had originally been part of Trepča and was spun off as an independent firm in 1981. Its production line was based on US technology and used inputs of cadmium from the Trepča mines. Its exports were channelled through Yugometal in Belgrade and until 1987 it was one of the Kosovo's largest exporters, sending its batteries to the USSR, the USA and the EU. The company had a large local market within former Yugoslavia and had a stable base in sales to the Yugoslav army. The business environment is now very different and with competition from China the company is no longer internationally competitive. New, more advanced and environmentally friendly lithium-ion technology has overtaken the older toxic cadmium-based batteries. The USA is the leader in this technology and production takes place mainly in China.

(Interview, Euro-Info Correspondence Centre, Priština, September 2004)

A new government for Kosovo was soon established under a Constitutional Framework promulgated in May 2001 that established the Provisional Institutions of Self Government (PISG) consisting of a government, an assembly and a presidency. The Constitutional Framework set out the competences that were to be transferred to the PISG and the powers to be reserved by UNMIK which included full competence over the judiciary and law enforcement. The Constitution required Kosovo to align its legislation and practices with European standards and norms. Kosovo became de facto independent from Serbia, while legally remaining a Serbian province, with its own government, legal system, judiciary, public budget, taxes and customs administration (UNMIK 2002).

In the first elections held in November 2001, the LDK led by Ibrahim Rugova became the largest party in the parliament.[37] Following extended negotiations on its composition, the new government took up office in March 2002, and the parliament voted Ibrahim Rugova as Kosovo's president, while Bajram Rexhepi of the Democratic Party of Kosovo (PDK) became the prime minister. The government consisted of ten ministries assisted by international advisors who played a central role in policy making in the early post-war period but who were gradually withdrawn as the ministries became more capable of organizing their own affairs. The first government programme was endorsed in May 2002 focusing on economic development, institution building and regional and international cooperation. The first law, on the pension system, was passed by PISG in October 2002. The creation of the State Union of Serbia and Montenegro in February 2003 was significant for Kosovo, since under the 1999 post-war peace agreement Kosovo had been negotiated with FRY. The demise of FRY raised the question of the final status of Kosovo and its eventual independence.

Although NATO announced a cut in its garrison in the province from 38,000 to 33,000 soldiers in the spring of 2003, the province remained unstable with over 200,000 Serbian refugees who had left the province at the end of the war unable to return. A major flashpoint was the town of Mitrovica, where the River Ibar marks a boundary between the mainly Albanian south of the province and a northern region populated mainly by Serbs. In November 2003, following an election boycott by Serbian residents, SRSG Michael Steiner introduced direct

UNMIK rule over the northern part of the city. The aim was to promote the gradual integration of the two communities, but critics argued that UNMIK could do little more than provide an institutionalized cover for de facto partition.

Harri Holkeri – a Finnish diplomat – was appointed as the new SRSG in July 2003 at a time of a resurgence of violence in the province. UNMIK revealed that almost 1,000 people had been killed since the end of the war, many as a result of ethnically motivated attacks. In October, leaders from Serbia and Kosovo began talks in Vienna to discuss possible areas of cooperation including electricity supplies, the recognition of Kosovo car license plates and identity documents by Serbia, the return of Serbian refugees to the province and the solution of the fate of 3,700 missing persons.[38] The talks, however, bore little fruit as the Serbs reiterated that Kosovo was an inalienable part of Serbia, while the Kosovars flatly asserted their right to independence on the basis of overwhelming popular support. One of the major aims of the international intervention in the Kosovo crisis and of the NATO bombing campaign had been to halt ethnic discrimination and create a multiethnic society.[39] This aim has failed almost entirely, as Kosovo has become an ethnically divided territory, partitioned between the larger part of the country from which ethnic Serbs have been largely expelled and a smaller region in the north in which Serbs dominate.

Violence flared up again in March 2004, triggered by inaccurate reports that three young Albanian children had been drowned by Serbs. In two days of attacks against Serbian communities across the province, approximately 550 homes were destroyed, numerous churches and monasteries were burned and over 4,000 people, mainly Serbs but also including other minority groups, were left homeless.[40] NATO forces and local police lost control of the situation and were unable to protect the victims, and allegations surfaced that the riots had been planned and organized by sections of the Albanian leadership. The incident demonstrated the fragility and instability of the security situation in the province and the need for urgent actions to bring about a lasting solution based on faster economic development and improved social cohesion.

Kosovo has remained the poorest part of the Western Balkans with GDP per capita of just $790 in 2004 and national income per capita of $1,170, the difference between the two figures reflecting the inflow of remittances. The Albanian population suffered throughout the 1990s from exclusion from the regular economy. Since 1999, the UNMIK administration and the new PSIG government have sought to turn this catastrophic situation around with massive inflows of international assistance. Economic policy has been led by the EU Pillar Economic Policy Office, and new institutions to support a market economy have been built up from scratch under international supervision. Given the alienation of the majority of the population from the pre-existing institutions linked to the Serbian quasi-colonial power, developing an appropriate institutional framework should have been relatively straightforward. Several successes have been achieved in institutional reform under the guidance of the pro-market international administration. A business environment that is favourable to small- and medium-sized enterprises (SMEs) has been established with few barriers to entry of new firms; a new financial sector has been created which consists of registered banks, savings associations, micro-finance institutions and insurance companies; previous labour legislation has been abandoned and the labour market is lightly regulated; and Kosovo has adopted the euro as its legal tender and inflation has been brought under control. Thus, an essentially liberal market economy has been created. However, since 2003 economic growth has stagnated. The mainly agricultural and raw material-based economy produces few exportable goods, and there is a massive imbalance in trade with imports far exceeding exports. The excess of imports is financed by foreign assistance and remittances from Kosovars working abroad. Unemployment is a staggering 50 per cent and reaches 75 per cent among young people. In 2002, over one-third of the population was living below the poverty line of €1.42 per day (World Bank 2005a). With its two million people and rich resource base, Kosovo has a potential to become far more prosperous than it is today. However, in order to achieve this, large inflows of foreign investment will be needed, and this is entirely absent in current atmosphere of uncertainty over question of Kosovo's constitutional status.

5 Privatization and foreign direct investment

In the preceding two chapters, I divided the countries of the region at the macro-economic policy level into two groups: early reformers and late reformers. The former group, Albania, Croatia and Macedonia, conducted macroeconomic stabilization to varying degrees of success in the early 1990s, and by the middle of the decade inflation had been brought under control in each of those countries. The latter group, Bosnia and Herzegovina (BiH), Serbia, including Kosovo, and Montenegro took longer to introduce successful stabilization policies, as these were resisted by coalitions of anti-reform interests, including the potential losers from reforms and the sections of the elites that gained from the continuation of the status quo.

However, the reforms that were carried out at the macroeconomic level were not matched by simultaneous success with structural reforms at the microeconomic level, and each of the early reformers ran into difficulties towards the end of the 1990s due to the incomplete and partial nature of these reforms. Among the late reformers, structural change was almost entirely blocked until 2000, when political changes opened up a space for comprehensive reforms. In this chapter, I examine structural reforms at the level of enterprises by looking at privatization and the inflows of foreign direct investment (FDI), before moving on to the next chapter to examine the entry and growth of new small- and medium-sized enterprises and the institutional reforms required to underpin new entrepreneurial market economies.

The change from social ownership and state ownership to private ownership was intended to trigger enterprise restructuring to improve efficiency, productivity and competitiveness. Whether, and how, it has done so has been a matter of intense debate. A comprehensive survey of the field which summarized the results from more than 100 empirical studies in other transition countries found that privatization typically has led to restructuring and growth (Djankov and Murrell 2002). These authors also examined the argument that productivity is improved more by privatization to outsiders than to insiders who may prefer to maintain employment levels and be less likely to make the required productivity-enhancing changes. They also found that privatization to outsiders has, on average, been associated with more restructuring than has privatization to insiders. The contrary argument has been that insider privatization can have beneficial effects by preserving work teams and improving motivation among the managers and employees with an ownership stake in the company and for the first time have a real interest in their company's business success (Uvalić and Vaughan-Whitehead 1997). Both influences have been relevant in the Western Balkans.

Several hundred companies were privatized in former Yugoslavia under the 1988 'Marković' law which encouraged the sale of shares in socially owned enterprises to their managers and employees. After Yugoslavia collapsed, the successor states introduced their own privatization laws, in Croatia in 1991, in Montenegro in 1992 and in Macedonia in 1993. In Serbia, legislation introduced in 1991 was reversed in 1994 and an effective privatization law was not introduced until 2001 after the overthrow of the Milošević regime, while in BiH privatization was delayed until 1999 and in Kosovo only began in 2003. Albania introduced its privatization legislation relatively early in 1991. The principle difference between these successive waves of privatization was the important role of insider privatization to employees and managers in the Croatian, Macedonian, Montenegrin and Albanian cases, the use of voucher privatization in BiH and the adoption of direct sales through auctions and tenders in the Serbian and Kosovan cases.

Figure 5.1 presents three indicators of transition for the Western Balkan countries in the dimensions of small-scale privatization, large-scale privatization and enterprise restructuring. These indicators have been developed by the European Bank for Reconstruction and Development (EBRD) and have a maximum value of 4.33 indicating a level of reform comparable to that in advanced Western market economies According to these indicators, the privatization

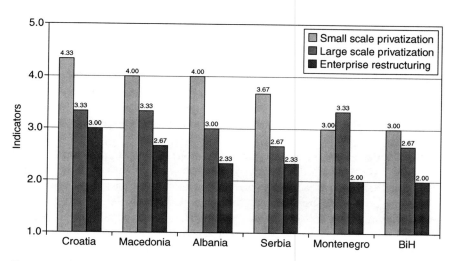

Figure 5.1 EBRD privatization and enterprise restructuring indicators, 2006. (source: European Bank for Reconstruction and Development (EBRD) online database 2006).

process is most advanced in the early reform countries: Croatia, Macedonia and Albania. Croatia has completed small-scale privatization, while Macedonia and Albania are only slightly behind in this dimension. In terms of large-scale privatization, Croatia and Macedonia lead slightly ahead of Albania. Serbia and Montenegro have made some progress in recent years in their privatization reforms, and as a result Serbia has almost caught up with the early reformers in small-scale privatization, while Montenegro has caught up in large-scale privatization. BiH still lags behind the early reformers on both dimensions.

Slowest progress has been made in the dimension of enterprise restructuring, with the most advanced reform country, Croatia, having a score of just 3.0, followed by Macedonia with 2.66 and Albania with 2.33, pointing to significant gaps in this dimension in relation to advanced capitalist countries. Among the late reformers, Serbia has made most progress, having the same level of enterprise restructuring as in Albania but still lagging behind Croatia and Macedonia. Montenegro and BiH have achieved the least enterprise restructuring with scores of just 2.0 each.

Much of the FDI inflow to the Western Balkans has been linked to privatization, especially to large-scale privatization in sectors such as telecommunications, banking and oil refining, while FDI has been less present in new greenfield investments. This has meant that the pattern of inflow has been irregular and lumpy over time, following the vagaries of the privatization process. FDI is conventionally considered to be a benefit to the host economy through the transfer of managerial knowledge, new skills, new technologies and new capital. Economic growth in the Western Balkans has been held back by a lack of finance, and so FDI inflows in the form of privatization of domestic banks by foreign banks, as in Croatia and Albania, have been an important factor in integrating these countries into international capital markets and releasing financial constraints. Early reformers which privatized their banking systems sooner benefited more from this effect than did the late reformers. On the negative side, foreign investors may gain a dominant position in the host country market, manipulate host country governments to gain tax concessions and other advantages, drain resources from a country through transfer pricing and other financial engineering techniques, destroy jobs through out-competing domestic firms and create a wage gap between foreign-owned and domestic companies (Mencinger 2003).

Despite the potential negative effects, the governments of the Western Balkan countries have introduced a variety of measures and policies in order to make their countries more attractive to foreign investors. Laws on foreign investment aiming to give equal treatment to foreign and domestic investors have been introduced in all the Western Balkan countries[1] although administrative barriers are still an important factor in slowing down FDI. In Croatia, for example, foreign investors have found it difficult to complete transactions in the tourism and construction sectors (OECD 2006: 48). Various agencies to promote foreign investment have been established in each country[2] with the most advanced in Serbia and Croatia (OECD 2006: 62). Different types of tax exemptions have been introduced in the Western Balkan states to attract foreign investment,[3] and the region has some of the lowest corporate tax rates in Europe, averaging 16 per cent compared to an average of 25 per cent in the European Union (EU). Corporate tax rates range from 9 per cent in Montenegro and 10 per cent in Serbia and Republika Srpska (RS) to 20 per cent in Albania and Croatia and 30 per cent in Federation of Bosnia and Herzegovina (FBiH) (OECD 2006: 74). Free economic zones have also been established in Croatia and Macedonia. In Croatia, nineteen such zones have been established since 1996, in which businesses are exempt from normal taxes and customs procedures. Most are essentially trading zones, but the Free Zone Varaždin also has a manufacturing capacity. A similar tax-free zone has been established in Macedonia, just outside Skopje, which offers tax and customs exemptions.[4]

FDI inflows to the Western Balkans have increased in recent years, and the upward trend is likely to persist in those countries where institutional reforms are introduced to improve the 'investment climate' and where progress with EU integration continues. Croatia has been the main beneficiary of FDI, having accumulated the highest stock of FDI at $2,750 per capita in 2005. In comparison, Macedonia had accumulated a stock of FDI of less than $1,000 per capita, while Albania, BiH and Serbia and Montenegro had accumulated even lower levels of FDI per capita of just over $500 per capita each (Figure 5.2).

A similar ranking could be seen in terms of inflows of FDI in relation to gross domestic product (GDP). In 2000, Croatia and Macedonia had the highest inflows at 5.9 per cent and 4.9 per cent of GDP, respectively (Figure 5.3). Albania and BiH had inflows of 3.9 per cent and 3.2 per cent each. The inflows of FDI to Federal Republic of Yugoslavia (FRY) were far lower at just 0.2 per

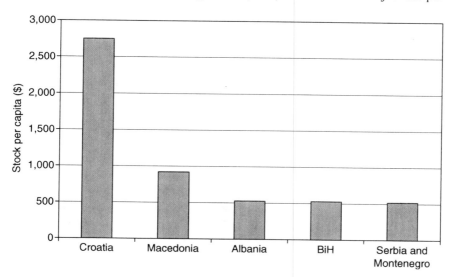

Figure 5.2 Foreign direct investment (FDI) stock per capita, 2005 ($) (source: UNCTAD online database 2007).

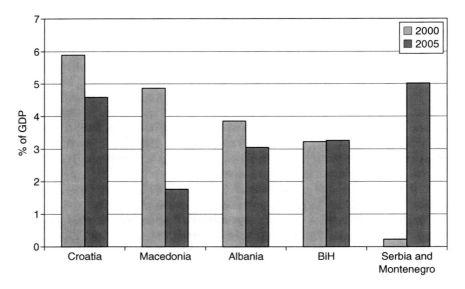

Figure 5.3 Foreign direct investment (FDI) inflows, 2000 and 2005 (% GDP) (source: UNCTAD online database 2007).

cent of GDP, reflecting the long period of isolation under sanctions and the effect of the Kosovo war. However, inflows into FRY began to pick up rapidly in response to the institutional reforms introduced by the new democratic government, and by 2005 the inflows of FDI into what was by then 'Serbia and Montenegro' had reached 5.0 per cent, exceeding the inflows to Croatia. At the same time, inflows into Macedonia had fallen in the aftermath of the 2001 conflict and were still only 1.8 per cent of GDP in 2005. Overall, FDI inflows to the Western Balkans have been close to those of other transition economies reaching 4.1 per cent of GDP on average over the period 1997–2003 compared to 4.9 per cent in the new member states of the EU (European Commission 2004), while econometric studies based on gravity models have shown that there remains much scope for increasing inflows of FDI to the region (Demekas *et al.* 2005).

Early privatization in Croatia, Macedonia and Albania

Privatization had already begun in Croatia and Macedonia under the provisions of the Marković reform programme before they became independent countries. Following independence, the federal laws were replaced by national laws in 1991 and 1993, respectively. In contrast, privatization began from scratch in Albania in 1991. The transformation of the formerly socially owned and state-owned enterprises has been taken furthest in Macedonia and Albania, where practically all enterprises have now been transferred to the private ownership of insider employees and managers or sold to new external owners. Croatia has followed a rather different path of partial privatization with the state retaining significant share ownership in many companies, often on a minority basis.

Croatia

Croatia was the first of the successor states to replace the federal law on privatization with its own privatization law[5] in April 1991. While the federal law had been based on voluntary privatization and the retention of social ownership, the new Croatian law stipulated compulsory privatization and the elimination of social ownership. Socially owned enterprises were to be rapidly transformed into joint-stock or limited liability companies. Management boards were invited to submit their privatization plans to the Privatization Agency by July 1992. Priority in the sale of discounted shares was given to current and retired employees up to a maximum of DM20,000 worth of shares, while total sales were limited to a maximum of 49 per cent of shares in any one company. The general public, including employees, could also buy shares at their full price in instalments over five years, but these remained non-voting until they were fully paid up and could not be sold in a secondary market. Privatization revenues were transferred to the Development Fund which also received two-thirds of any unsold shares, while the remainder of unsold shares was transferred to the Pension Fund and the Disability Insurance Fund. The Development Fund appointed its own managers in enterprises in which it held more than 20 per cent of the shares, while the state-owned banks became significant shareholders in some of the biggest loss-making enterprises. In both ways, the state ended up controlling a substantial number of larger enterprises.[6] The state also took full ownership and control of over 100 important large companies, including major public utilities, and installed new managers who were often members of the ruling party (Bićanić 1993).

At the start of 1993, the Privatization Agency and the Development Fund were merged into a new organization known as the Croatian Privatization Fund (CPF), controlled by a management board consisting of political appointees, politicians and one employee representative. Amendments made to the law allowed small shareholders to trade shares, even if they were not fully paid up, and to receive dividends. A free issue of shares, up to the value of DM20,000, was made to war invalids and families of war victims, and in March 1994 a measure was passed which allowed people to buy shares with frozen foreign currency savings (Škreb 1995).

A ministry of privatization was established in 1995 and, under a new privatization law passed in 1996, 'privatization vouchers' were distributed to war victims. These could be invested in seven privately owned fund-management companies known as Privatization Investment Funds (PIFs) which were established in 1997. Four-fifths of the vouchers issued to the 230,000 beneficiaries were placed with the PIFs, which in turn exchanged them for shares held by the CPF. The new law also envisaged the eventual privatization of the publicly owned utilities, the first of which was Croatian Telecom which sold a 25 per cent stake to Deutsche Telecom in 1999. The privatization programme came under severe criticism from Croatian economists who characterized the new system as one of 'crony capitalism'. One analyst of the privatization process commented that:

> Unfortunately, privatization in Croatia achieved the opposite effect to that which had been expected. Instead of increased efficiency of enterprises, greater market competition, and the growth of employment, the achieved results were diametrically opposed: an increase in unemployment, a reduction of output, falling national wealth and the appearance of criminals in the economy who could be neither controlled nor effectively prevented.
>
> (Petričić 2000: 8)

The Croatian Democratic Union (HDZ) government had created a system in which the largest and most profitable enterprises had been transferred to an elite group of privileged owners with party connections, while the less-profitable non-privatized enterprises were brought under direct state control through the transfer of shares to the Privatization Fund. Many of the new tycoon owners mismanaged the privatized companies, and several stripped the assets of otherwise viable companies to take out short-term profits, paying the employees meagre wages or in some instances no wages at all, or with long delays (Petričić 2000). The new elite that had been created by the HDZ government revealed the negative side of privatization, one which resulted in adverse distributional effects and created social harm rather than improvements to social welfare, having been carried out on the basis of political criteria, clientelism and without effective institutions to ensure public accountability. Public opinion increasingly associated rising unemployment and poor performance of the economy with the privatization methods adopted by the government and with the behaviour of the new tycoon capitalists. As a consequence, the government lost power in parliamentary elections held at the end of 1999.

The new coalition government came into office in 2000 amid high hopes that the worst aspects of the privatization process would be reversed. A law on the revision of privatization was passed in 2001, and a review covering almost 2,000 enterprises was carried out. In 2003, after reviewing 100 cases, the State Office for Revisions pronounced that four-fifths of them had contravened legal norms. A few of the tycoons were jailed for irregularities in the privatization process, but most were soon released and no further action was taken. The government tried to accelerate the privatization of public utilities. An additional 16 per cent stake in Croatia Telecom was sold to Deutsche Telecom in 2001, giving it a majority share holding in the company, and a 25 per cent stake in the INA oil and gas company was sold to the Hungarian company MOL in 2003. However, since then the privatization process has stalled, and it has proved relatively difficult to sell off the remaining shares held by the CPF. A controversial attempt to sell the tourist company, Sunčani Hvar, in 2003 ended in failure when local politicians objected to Croatian tourist assets being sold to a foreign company, in this case from Slovenia. The coalition government lost popular support as the economy continued to falter, and unemployment continued to increase.

The HDZ was returned to power in elections held at the end of 2003 and tried to regain the momentum of privatization. Sales of assets from the portfolio of the CPF accelerated in the early part of 2005, but the government still retained a large stake in the assets of the business sector. Recently, the government has announced its intention to complete the sale of all remaining shares held by the CPF by the end of 2007, with the exception of the shipyards which are to be restructured in consultation with the European Commission and privatized at a later date. The state-owned Croatian Railways are also subject to a restructuring plan which will involve lay-offs of many employees, while state aid to the steel sector will be gradually phased out.

Croatia has been the recipient of the largest share of privatization-related FDI inflows into the Western Balkans, with a total cumulative stock of FDI in 2005 of $12.5 billion. Much FDI has gone into the banking sector, where more than 80 per cent of assets are owned by foreign banks including Italy's Unicredito. Austria, Germany and the USA have been major sources of FDI, while the leading sectors have been the chemicals, metals and food. Greenfield investments have been limited, but some small investments have been made, such as the joint venture between the Italy's Zanussi and a local company in Pakrac which exports electronics components for fridges to Italy.[7]

Macedonia

Privatization took place relatively early in Macedonia where it was largely completed during the 1990s, with the exception of the very largest enterprises and the utility companies. Under the provisions of the Marković law, sixty-seven large- and medium-sized enterprises were privatized before Macedonia became independent, and hundreds of others were partly privatized. A new privatization law[8] was introduced in 1993 under which enterprises that did not meet the deadline for voluntary privatization were subject to compulsory privatization by the Macedonian Privatization Agency. However, few firms opted for voluntary privatization, and the process only really took off in 1995. Enterprises could select from a variety of methods of privatization, including employee and/or management buyout, provided at least 51 per cent of assets were bought; leveraged buyout; commercial sale of the enterprise; issue of shares to outsiders of at least 30 per cent of the shares; debt equity swaps; leasing; or liquidation and sale of assets. Foreign companies were free to participate in the privatization process, without restriction.

In the case of employee buyout, employees were offered discounts of 30 per cent, plus a further 1 per cent for each year of employment in the enterprise. The maximum amount that could be bought by any employee was restricted to DM25,000. Ancillary units such as enterprises' own hotels and restaurants could be bought with a 50 per cent discount. In addition, in every case, 15 per cent of the shares were transferred to the Pension Fund. Remaining unsold shares were transferred to the Privatization Agency, which was to offer these shares to the public after a three-month period. The privatization law was subsequently amended to give greater incentives to outsiders to purchase shares.

Once it began, the privatization programme was carried out rapidly and was largely completed by the end of 1997, by which time over 1,000 enterprises had been fully privatized and only 234 remained in the privatization process. The main methods of privatization were management and employee buyout, with management buyout being the most prevalent in terms of both the employment and the value of equity involved.[9] Managers were required to put up only 10 per cent of the purchase price, with the remainder to be paid in instalments over ten years. Typically, the most profitable, or potentially profitable, enterprises were sold to managers at substantial discounts, often on the basis of low asset valuations. For example, the Prilep Brewery, valued at DM10 million, was sold to its ten-member management team for just DM3.2 million,[10] while Skopje Brewery, one of Macedonia's most profitable companies, was sold to its management team for DM1 million.[11] Weaker and smaller enterprises were often sold to employees at more inflated asset valuations. In several cases, managers subsequently acquired shares from employee shareholders by dubious methods or simply appropriated the voting rights of the employees' shares, consolidating majority holdings to the management group.[12] According to one report:

> The privatization agency's emphasis on management buy-outs reinforces the widespread perception among Macedonians that insiders are being allowed to take over enterprises at preferential prices. The prospect of further job cuts at companies that have been privatized has also fuelled feelings of resentment.
>
> (Kerin Hope, *Financial Times*, 27 July 1995)

In some cases, the new managers created spin-off companies, either wholly or partly owned by the slimmed-down parent firm, to provide new workplaces for redundant workers (Bartlett 1997b). In other cases, contracts with the Privatization Agency stipulated the preservation of jobs in the newly privatized companies, when economic considerations alone would have required dismissals. Although most public utilities have not been sold, the state-owned telecommunications company was privatized in 2001.

By the end of 2001, the privatization process had been completed in 1,678 companies, employing almost 230,000 workers and with assets of DM4.5 billion. Of these, 394 companies with assets of DM155 million were privatized through employee buyouts, while 239 companies with assets worth DM1.4 billion had been privatized by management buyouts. The disparity in the value of the two types of companies indicates that managers had acquired the most valuable part of the privatized enterprises. The emphasis on insider privatization has led to slow restructuring, since many of the newly privatized firms lacked the financial means to invest in new technologies and many privatized companies survived using political connections to avoid paying taxes (European Commission 2005a). In addition, 155 companies with capital assets of DM49 million were sold to foreign owners, and by 2002, according to data of the Privatization Agency, almost €100 million of foreign investment had been invested in privatized companies.

The outcomes of privatization in Macedonia have not been very encouraging. Although privatization has been extensive, relatively little restructuring has taken place, productivity has remained low or even fallen, and there has been little new job creation. A study of 500 privatized enterprises over the period from 1994 to 2000 found that profits were higher in companies with more concentrated ownership, suggesting that dispersed insider ownership was less effective than privatization to a strategic outside investor (Zalduendo 2003). Overall, new small firms had a better economic performance than old established firms, whatever the form of privatization. In addition, the positive role played by strategic investors suggests that the revitalization of the large company sector in Macedonia depends to a large extent upon the ability of those companies to attract foreign investors, who could bring new skills and technology to improve productivity and increase the export potential of the privatized companies.

FDI inflows occurred mainly through privatization and post-privatization transactions on the Macedonian stock exchange rather than through greenfield investment. The largest single transaction of $442 million was the privatization of the telecommunications company in 2001, but FDI diminished following the civil conflict later the same year. In 2002, the inflow had fallen to only $78 million, and it increased only marginally to $95 million in the following year, the lowest in the Western Balkans. Just over half the stock of FDI has gone into the mining and manufacturing industries, while almost two-fifths has gone into the banking sector. By country, the largest inflows have been from Greece, followed by Cyprus, Germany and Austria, while the most important individual investors have been from a diverse group of countries. The telecommunications company Maktel was privatized in 2001 to the Hungarian Matav, itself 60 per cent owned by Deutsche Telecom. In 2003, Westdeutsche Allgemeine Zeitung acquired Macedonia's three largest newspapers, *Dnevnik, Utrinski Vesnik* and *Vest*, for an undisclosed sum believed to be between €1 million and €5 million – a relatively small sum for Germany's second-largest media empire, which owns over 130 newspapers and magazines and dominates the media market in the Western Balkans.

The Greek state-owned oil company Hellenic Petroleum acquired the Okta oil refinery, after it was reduced to virtual bankruptcy by the Greek oil embargo in the years leading up to its sale. The business conditions within which Okta traded were symptomatic of the problems that have beset the Macedonian economy, including dubious privatizations, problems with corruption and uncontrolled smuggling which has threatened to undermine the institutions of a competitive market economy.

The 'new' OKTA started three years ago when the company was bought by Hellenic Petroleum after eight months of negotiations. At that time the company was in a very bad financial position, and the previous manager said publicly that the company only had enough money left to buy the lock with which to close the refinery gates. Hellenic Petroleum formed a joint venture with a construction company, and the joint venture now owns 75 per cent of OKTA. One of the major investments has been the construction of a $110 million pipeline to bring crude oil from Thessaloniki to the refinery here at OKTA. Smuggling is a serious problem for us, and we have had several discussions with the UNMIK authorities on how they can help us to prevent it. The problem is, simply, that the whole system is corrupted, and the customs officers let stuff through the border crossings in return for a bribe. A lorry driver who fills up has lorry at the refinery can save $1,500 per load for a relatively small bribe to an underpaid customs official. The Kosovo guys come here to buy oil, and then smuggle it back across the border. The personnel of UNMIK are changed every six months and cannot control the situation. The sums involved are enormous – a smuggler can fill up ten trucks a day and earn $150,000. Not that he does it every day, but there is a lot of money involved.

(Interview with manager, Okta, October 2002)

Foreign investment in Macedonia has been deterred not only by political uncertainty resulting from the Greek embargo, sanctions against FRY, the Kosovo war of 1999 and the civil conflict of 2001, but also by the high level of corruption in official circles which reached a peak towards the end of the rule of the Internal Macedonian Revolutionary Organization – Democratic Party for Macedonian National Unity (VMRO-DPMNE) government (ICG 2000). Macedonia's acceptance as a candidate for EU membership in 2006 holds out the prospect of an improvement in the enforcement of legal norms and for a change in perceptions of the country by international investors which should lead to an upturn in FDI inflows.

Albania

Agriculture is an important sector of economic activity in Albania accounting for more than 25 per cent of GDP and 58 per cent of employment (INSTAT 2004). Consequently, the privatization of agricultural land which had been entirely under collective and state ownership was high up on the reform agenda following the fall of the communist regime.[13] Under the Land Law of 1991, agricultural land in the cooperatives was distributed to member families and other rural residents on a per capita basis.[14] The privatization of state farms was completed by 1995 with their land, which covered about one-quarter of the agricultural area, being distributed to former specialists and farm workers. The purpose of the radical land reform was to destroy the power of the rural nomenklatura – the former managers and communist leaders in charge of state farms and cooperatives – and to gain political support from the rural population. The actual distribution of the land was carried out by local committees known as the Village Land Distribution Commissions. In areas where land ownership had previously been family-based, rather than owned by large landowners, the commissions allocated land to families according to old boundaries,[15] rather than on a random per capita basis as stipulated in the law (Lemel 1998). Overall, despite some deviations from egalitarian redistribution, the land reform led to an extreme fragmentation of holdings resulting in a post-reform average plot size of just 1 hectare (Vaughan-Whitehead 1999). The radical stabilization programme begun in March 1992 liberalized agricultural prices, and the new private farmers responded by increasing agricultural production. Agricultural output has since grown rapidly, even during the economic crisis years following the collapse of the pyramid banks in 1997.

Following the Privatization Law of August 1991, over 20,000 small retail shops and other small businesses were sold relatively quickly, mostly at discounted prices, to their managers and employees. A National Agency for Privatization was established to oversee the process, but there were many irregularities. In 1993, privatization was extended to small and medium enterprises with fewer than 300 employees. The process was carried out by local privatization committees, and although officially the sales were supposed to be conducted through auctions, in practice most sales were agreed with just a single buyer. Many were sold at below market prices on the basis of political or social connections. The whole procedure was completed by the end of 1994 (Hashi and Xhillari 1999).

An enterprise restructuring agency was established in 1993 to restructure the largest enterprises before their privatization with assistance from the World Bank. The agency was responsible for the thirty-two largest enterprises in Albania, and by 1996, when it was closed, the restructuring programme had reduced the workforce from 50,000 to less than 7,000 (Vaughan-Whitehead 1999). However, only ten of the enterprises were privatized, and the remaining large state-owned enterprises were put into a mass privatization scheme based on the distribution of privatization vouchers to all adults over the age of eighteen. Three PIFs were established in which individuals could place their vouchers which would be invested on their behalf, but they failed to attract many customers and two of them subsequently closed. Most people chose to sell their vouchers on the open market below their face value rather than investing them directly into companies, and the value of the vouchers quickly plummeted. The companies and individual speculators who bought vouchers used them to buy majority shares in some of the more attractive enterprises up for privatization. In many cases, the cash received was invested in pyramid savings schemes which were flourishing at the time and promising vastly inflated rates of return. By 1996, the value of the vouchers had fallen to just 1 per cent of their face value, and the programme was closed amidst admissions of failure by the government (Vaughan-Whitehead 1999).

In early 1997, the government relaunched the privatization of large enterprises, selling them directly through auctions. This represented a policy U-turn following the failure of the mass privatization programme, designed to attract strategic owners to take over the larger companies. In the first two months of 1997, fourteen enterprises were sold in this way (Hashi and Xhillari 1999). However, the privatization process was soon interrupted by civil unrest in March and ceased altogether in June when the Socialist Party returned to power with a large majority. After the pyramid banking debacle, the new government focused its attention on sorting out the chaotic banking sector which was dominated by three large and insolvent state-owned banks (IMF 2005). The Rural Commercial Bank was liquidated in 1998, the National Commercial Bank was sold to foreign investors in 2000 and the important Savings Bank was eventually privatized in early 2004 to the Austrian Raiffeisen Zentralbank (RZB) for $126 million, boosting FDI inflows by a significant amount. The privatization of the large enterprise sector has now been mainly completed, with the exception of the fixed-line telephone company and the oil sector. Apart from the sale of the Savings Bank to RZB, Albania has received only limited inflows of FDI mostly of Italian and Greek origin and mainly concentrated in the capital Tirana and the major port city of Durrës.

Delayed privatization: BiH, Serbia, Montenegro and Kosovo

In BiH, Serbia, Montenegro and Kosovo, the state remained closely involved in the economy throughout the 1990s, and political parties maintained a strong influence in enterprises through the control of appointments to top managerial positions, slowing the growth of the private sector. Privatization has followed different paths in each country. BiH adopted mass voucher privatization (MVP), avoiding the direct sales to insider workers and managers that characterized privatization in Croatia, and Macedonia and Albania. In Serbia, the privatization process ground to a halt after the imposition of United Nations (UN) sanctions in 1992, and previously privatized enterprises were effectively brought back into state ownership. A new privatization programme was only initiated in 2001 based on direct sales through public tenders and auctions. Privatization was also delayed in Montenegro where there was little restructuring of larger enterprises, many of which simply collapsed, especially in the depressed north-east region. Privatization was longest delayed in Kosovo, where the Kosovo Trust Agency (KTA) initiated privatization only in 2003. Most socially owned enterprises were insolvent, and these were liquidated and their assets sold off, leading to large-scale redundancies and increased unemployment.

BiH

Privatization had first taken place in BiH under the Marković programme, and between 1989 and 1991 shares in some 585 socially owned enterprises had been distributed or sold to their workers. However, following the multiparty elections, the newly elected government halted the process in order to conduct a review, and socially owned property was subsequently re-nationalized during the war

(Mulaj 2006). Following the end of the war, the privatization process was eventually revived with a framework Privatization Law at the state level was promulgated by the Office of the High Representative in 1998, and privatization legislation was passed only in 1999. The Bosnian approach, developed under the guidance of US aid agency (USAID), was based upon voucher privatization, the justification for which was to ensure speed, transparency, simplicity and broad citizen participation.[16] Speed was of the essence, since it was thought that large-scale FDI had been held up by the absence of effective privatization.[17] Unlike the privatization process in Croatia and Macedonia, employees were not offered discounts on the purchase of shares in their enterprises.[18]

In FBiH, privatization vouchers were issued to all those over the age of eighteen on 6 December 1997 who had also been citizens of the Republic of BiH on 31 March 1991. All eligible citizens were entitled to 100 points with an additional ten points for every year of employment, while further points could be obtained in exchange for frozen foreign currency savings accounts, unpaid salary claims of soldiers and police, arrears due to pensioners and claims based upon property restitution. Vouchers, with a nominal value of KM19, could be used to buy shares in enterprises, to buy apartments or could be invested in PIFs which, in turn, could invest in enterprises up to a limit of 30 per cent of the subscribed shares. Enterprises could also be sold by public tender to enterprise managers and employees or to foreign investors. Only 65 per cent of the value of shares of an enterprise could be exchanged for vouchers, while the remaining shares had to be paid for with cash to raise capital for the privatized enterprises, a provision that effectively excluded many people with limited cash holdings from the proceedings. In RS, the Privatization Agency issued both coupons and vouchers. Coupons with a monetary value were issued against frozen foreign currency accounts and could be used to buy shares in small enterprises and apartments. Vouchers, without a monetary value, were issued to citizens, veterans and families of soldiers who had died in the war, who were entitled to a basic twenty vouchers, while additional vouchers were allocated in relation to length of employment and military service (Bayliss 2005). Vouchers could only be invested in PIFs, which could use them to acquire up to 55 per cent of shares in a privatized enterprise, while a further 30 per cent of shares could only be acquired with cash. The remaining 10 per cent of issued shares were allocated to the RS Pension Fund and 5 per cent to the Restitution Fund. The government issued a decree that prevented PIFs from appointing more than two members of a company's management board, thus depriving them of effective control and ensuring that the RS government maintained a strong influence within the 'privatized' enterprises (Donais 2002).

In FBiH, many individuals sold their vouchers on the open market to raise much-needed cash, which enabled wealthy individuals to accumulate vouchers at knock-down prices.[19] The director of the Herceg Bosna Privatization Agency, Vinko Banović, admitted that the system was vulnerable to carpetbaggers or *torbari*.[20] In the fractured Bosnian state, this phenomenon inevitably took on an ethnic dimension, with vouchers being accumulated in the hands of 'tycoons' based in the different ethnic communities. The Bosniak Businessmen's Association expressed the fear that Croat-dominated Privatization Funds would be in a position to buy a large proportion of the property put up for sale in the parts of the Federation dominated by Bosniaks. In an expression of ethnic distrust, the Association claimed that 'Croats are organized, they have their goal and they know how to get it ... the goal is the purchase of 70 per cent of the Bosnian economy'. One of the most vociferous critics was Krešimir Zubak, leader of the New Croat Initiative party, who complained about this practice of the Croatian tycoons from Herzegovina. He claimed that the Mostar-based Herzegovina Holding was ready to buy vouchers from ordinary citizens in order to accumulate them for the purchase of enterprises in the Croatian part of Herzegovina. Haris Silajdžić, co-chairman of the Council of Ministers, took a similar position claiming that 'as far as I know, a large number of companies have already been privatized based on the ethnic principle. That's the way of the world: after ethnic cleansing, ethnic privatization comes'.[21]

Advertisements for the sale of vouchers began to appear in the press. The Sarajevo daily *Oslobodjenje* investigated the offers and discovered that the vouchers were being heavily discounted with typical discounts of the order of 90 per cent.[22] The Federation Demobilized Soldiers Alliance requested an amendment to the law so that they would be exempted from the need to make the required 35 per cent cash contribution to participate in the privatization process. Mehmed Fočić, the Alliance spokesman, said:

> we ask that soldiers do not pay 35 per cent in cash for a simple reason: they do not have the funds. We will come to a situation when those who robbed us during the war, war profiteers, will buy certificates from soldiers for 10 to 20 per cent of the true value.[23]

The vouchers were being bought up by the wealthy Herzegovina tycoons and by enterprise managers.[24]

In FBiH, auctions and tenders for the sale of small enterprises were organized in each canton. Bids were evaluated by cantonal branches of the Privatization Agency which established criteria by which the competing bids would be judged. These included the buyer's plans to maintain employment and to invest in improved machinery and equipment. Several of the auctions failed to find any buyers, and the authorities were criticized for beginning the privatization auctions and opening tenders before all the privatization vouchers had been distributed.[25] Many people held back because they preferred to sell their vouchers for cash or exchange them for residential apartments or because they were waiting for the opportunity to place them with PIFs or invest them in larger enterprises which were to be sold in the second phase of privatization or because they simply could not afford to make the required 35 per cent cash contribution, giving ample opportunity to the tycoons to cherry-pick the best enterprises.[26]

The privatization process was also heavily criticized by the Trade Unions.

The Alliance of Independent Bosnian Trade Unions went so far as to ask the High Representative, Carlos Westendorp, to stop 'illegal' privatization and to ensure a new Labour Law would be passed quickly to protect the rights of workers in newly privatized enterprises. The Alliance claimed that Bosniaks and Serbs were being laid off in the enterprises bought out by the 'new Herzegovina tycoons'. The Trade Union leader Sulejman Hrle charged that 'the right to employment is violated there in the most flagrant manner; people were sacked just because they were Bosniaks or Serbs', and they accused Westendorp of 'silence and failure to take action [which] means that he is a direct accomplice to ethnic privatization'.[27]

In FBiH, about 2,000 socially owned and state-owned enterprises worth an estimated $10 billion were included in the privatization process, while in RS, 830 enterprises, comprising 55 per cent of social capital, were offered for sale. In RS, over half the vouchers were invested in PIFs compared to under a quarter in FBiH. About 16 per cent of the voucher holders in FBiH had sold their vouchers on the open market by 2002, and a further 16 per cent had used them to buy apartments, options that were not available in RS. The sale of small enterprises employing less than fifty workers was completed within a few years, and by 2003 more than 1,000 enterprises had been sold in FBiH and more than 500 enterprises had been sold in RS. Ownership patterns differed in each entity. In FBiH, only 20 per cent of the shares in privatized enterprises were owned by PIFs compared to 30 per cent in RS. The state also gained a large stake in the enterprises in RS through the 30 per cent of the shares that had been transferred to state funds. In FBiH, insiders already held about a quarter of the shares in almost 600 enterprises before the privatization programme began, and they ended up with a strong influence in many of the privatized enterprises. In neither RS nor FBiH were there many cases of a dominant outside private shareholder, whether domestic or foreign.

Many of the larger enterprises in the two entities remained unsold, and in reaction to this failure of the policy, the High Representative replaced the head of the FBiH Privatization Agency (Donais 2002). The main aim of the policy turned to the sale of these larger enterprises on a case-by-case approach, and some 440 large enterprises were designated for sale by tender to strategic investors. Of these, a list of 108 strategic enterprises was drawn up in both entities, for which strategic investors were sought with the assistance of the international donors. Within BiH, privatization was criticized on the grounds that it would have an adverse effect on employment and that the new owners would strip the assets of the privatized companies, and perhaps because of these concerns the privatization of larger enterprises proceeded extremely slowly (Bayliss 2005). According to one evaluation study '... the privatization process is bogged down by unresolved problems of ownership, outstanding debts, political and social concerns over possible workforce reductions, and ethnic rivalries over future ownership' (World Bank 2004a: 12).

Overall, while many smaller enterprises have been privatized, larger enterprises have remained in state ownership, especially in RS, and the consequence has been that many of the old industrial enterprises have avoided restructuring. Employment levels have been maintained, but in practice in many enterprises little work is carried out, wages are unpaid and employees work for subsistence in the informal economy (ETF 2006b). Even among those few enterprises that have been privatized, the system of corporate governance is weak, and restructuring has been held back by vested interests and lack of sufficient capital for investment in new technologies. Moreover, BiH has received only limited inflows of FDI, mainly from Austria and neighbouring Croatia, although it has picked up in recent years, more than trebling from $119 million in 2001 to $382 million in 2003. Numerous factors have inhibited foreign investors from making investments in BiH, including political instability, administrative complexity and high levels of corruption.

Serbia

Unlike the other republics of former Yugoslavia, the Serbian privatization law of August 1991 resembled the Marković law in making no attempt to abolish 'social property' (Uvalić 1997). In sectors such as the steel, metal and electronics industries, most enterprises ended up in mixed ownership in which the state had effective control. The state-owned banks held a dominant share of many enterprises which were formally private, and in others the major shareholders were often managers who had bought their shares at heavy discounts. Some enterprises had been nationalized, especially in the public utilities such as electricity, railways, airlines, oil, forestry, water supply, communications, radio and television. In July 1994, the Serbian parliament passed a law on the revision of the privatization, under which the price that insiders had paid for shares was adjusted for inflation. In practice, this involved a drastic increase in their price, and many employees had to surrender their shares as they were unable to afford the extra cost. The Privatization Agency annulled the privatization process in 87 per cent of privatized enterprises which employed 80 per cent of the Serbian labour force, effectively reversing the whole process of privatization that had taken place over the previous five years (Lazić and Sekelj 1997: 1064). According to one account 'the real reason why the ruling elite in Serbia backed the idea of revaluation was ... to keep ... full control over big enterprises and to resume the clientelism of the previous communist period' (Lazić and Sekelj 1997: 1069). The affair demonstrated the intent of the Serbian government to maintain a tight grip on the enterprise sector and its lack of commitment to liberal economic reforms. As Cohen observed:

> one of the main features of the Milošević regime, which allowed it to perpetuate the monolithic political and economic control system of the previous Titoist regime, has been the monopolization of [the] privatization process.... After Yugoslavia disintegrated, the privatization process was further stalled, or fine tuned to favour supporters of the regime.
>
> (Cohen 2001: 131)

Following the signing of the Dayton agreement in 1995, and the ending of UN sanctions, Western companies and investors became interested in buying companies that were offered for privatization and there was a brief upturn in FDI inflows to Serbia and Montenegro. At the federal level, Dragoslav Avramović, governor of the central bank, developed a new privatization programme in 1996 which envisaged the complete abolition of social property.[28] However, the proposal was thrown out by the FRY Parliament in May 1996, and Avramović was forced to resign. Instead, a new federal privatization law was adopted which permitted voluntary privatization by enterprises and effectively preserved social property as the main form of property ownership (Uvalić 1997). The government clearly had no intention of introducing genuine reforms to the systems of enterprise ownership or enterprise governance.

The setback to the federal privatization law appeared to be only as temporary reversal of reforms, however, when a new privatization law was adopted in Serbia in July 1997 following the success of the *Zajedno* opposition in the local elections and the popular desire for change shown by the demonstrations of the winter of 1996–7. In the first round of privatization, free or discounted shares were given or sold at a discount to different categories of beneficiaries. One-half of the money raised went to the Serbian Development Fund, a quarter to the Labour Market Fund and a quarter to the Pension and Invalid Insurance Fund. The basic discount was set at 20 per cent plus 1 per cent per year of service, up to a limit of DM6,000 (Uvalić 2000b). The privatization law covered 4,500 socially owned and state-owned companies and 3,000 companies in mixed ownership. A further seventy-five large companies were put on a special list for privatization under government control. These comprised the large metal producers such as the Sartid steel works and the Glagovac ferrous chrome company. Other prominent companies on the special list included the Trepča lead and zinc mine in Kosovo, the Bor lead and zinc mine, various copper and aluminium smelters and factories in the defence industries. Western companies were keen to become involved in the privatization process, and several foreign investment deals were made under the new law (Bartlett 1999). In September, Messer Greihein GmbH of Germany bought up 60 per cent of Tehnogas, the gas monopoly; the London investment branch of the Banque Nationale de Paris bought 40 per cent of the International Genex Bank in Belgrade; the Swedish TetraPak group bought a Serbian packaging factory for DM24.5 million from the holding company Tipoplastika; Reynolds made a bid to buy the Vranje tobacco company; and a business cooperation agreement was signed between the Ruma Guma tyre company and Germany's Continental Co. The high degree of interest by Western companies in investment in Serbia was further indicated when the Austrian Kreditanstalt Investment Bank opened offices in Belgrade in October 1997. By the end of the year, it was estimated that over 100 German companies had investment stakes in FRY companies. The British investment bank, NatWest Markets, became closely involved in the privatization programme.

However, enterprise managers in Serbia were on the whole uninterested or even hostile to foreign investors who would have threatened their power and influence within the socially owned enterprises, and Serbian policy turned against radical economic reforms after the *Zajedno* opposition movement split in the summer of 1997. The government gave the impression of wanting to postpone privatization as long as possible and enterprise directors, who were free to choose whether to transform their companies through internal distribution of shares or through sale to foreign investors, mostly opted to keep their companies under social or mixed ownership in order to maintain their control and privileges. Foreign investors who had expected to be actively involved in buying profitable enterprises were disappointed, and some foreign embassies declared they would withdraw their trade delegations if there were no further progress. Western investors had been willing to invest large amounts of money in FRY industry, but this investment would only be forthcoming in the event of real structural and institutional reforms which presupposed a genuine democratization. By the end of 1998, the economic situation had deteriorated further, unemployment began to rise and the average monthly wage had sunk to less than $100.[29] The inflow of FDI came to an end and did not pick up again until after the democratic changes and the ousting of Milošević in 2000.

Privatization takes off after the fall of the Milošević regime

After the democratic opposition came to power in Belgrade in 2000, a new, more radical, privatization law was adopted with support of the World Bank, which involved the direct sale of the socially owned and state-owned enterprises. Under the new law, the enterprise sector was divided into two groups. In the first group were the largest enterprises, including eight large state-owned utilities and about 150 socially owned enterprises of strategic importance. These were to be sold off under the direct supervision of the government through public tenders, offering at least 70 per cent of the shares to strategic investors, while half of the remaining shares were to be distributed free of charge to employees and half to the general public. The second group consisted of 4,000 smaller socially owned enterprises which were to be privatized under the supervision of the Privatization Agency. These enterprises were to be sold through either auction or tender, with the aim of attracting a strategic investor, while 30 per cent of the shares were reserved for free distribution to employees as an incentive to support privatization. Enterprises that had not begun privatization within four years were to be taken over by the Privatization Agency.

Between 2001 and 2003, the privatization policy made substantial progress. About 1,000 mostly medium-sized enterprises were sold in auctions, and twenty-five large enterprises were sold by international tenders, and altogether 1,631 enterprises had been privatized by 2005. Although most enterprises were sold through auctions, several large enterprises were sold through tenders, mainly to foreign buyers, raising €1.5 billion between 2002 and 2004, equivalent to 55 per cent of all privatization revenues. The privatization process was most intense during 2003 when 775 enterprises were sold in one year. Mainly, these were the best performing enterprises (Dragutinović-Mitrović 2006). An empirical analysis of the effects of privatization on enterprise performance carried out by a team of researchers at the Economics Faculty in Belgrade found that employment and sales growth after privatization were highest in those companies with some foreign investment, intermediate among companies with local outside ownership and lowest among those which were primarily privatized on the basis of insider ownership (Cerović 2005). Although the sample was small, and the findings are not definitive, they point in the same direction as those from studies of other transition economies discussed in the introduction to this chapter.

As a consequence of the success of the privatization programme, FDI increased steadily to reach $1,360 million in 2003, equivalent to $158 per capita. Slovenian investors became very active in Serbia, and in 2002 the Slovenian supermarket chain Mercator opened a store in the centre of Belgrade. In 2003, the Russian oil company Lukoil paid €210 million for a 75 per cent stake in Serbia's oil and gas company, Beopetrol, in a deal which included an €8 million social programme for employees. In the same year, Philip Morris International bought a tobacco factory in Niš, BAT paid $178 million for the tobacco factory in Vranje, while the Ruma Guma tyre factory was bought by Galaxy Tire. Most subsequent FDI has been in the tourism and the financial sectors. The pace of privatization slowed down in 2004 following the assignation of Serbian Prime Minister Djindjić, and by the end of that year 1,850 socially owned enterprises with 372,000 employees still remained to be privatized, of which seventy were large enterprises employing 140,000 workers (IMF 2004). Recently, the privatization of the banking sector has gathered pace, and by 2005 just over half the banking sector was in foreign ownership (European Commission 2005a).

Montenegro

The Montenegrin privatization law of 1992 differed from that in Serbia by abolishing social property and requiring all socially owned enterprises to become public limited liability companies. Managers and employees received 10 per cent of the value of enterprise assets as free shares and could purchase a further 30 per cent of assets at a discount, while 40 per cent of any unsold social capital was to be transferred to the Development Fund, 30 per cent to the Pension Fund and 10 per cent to the Employment Fund. Almost 300 enterprises were included in the privatization programme, comprising 80 per cent of all socially owned enterprises in Montenegro. Out of the DM4.5 billion which was raised through sales, DM2.6 billion went to the three funds, and most of the shares in the privatized enterprises ended up under majority ownership of the Development Fund.

A new Privatization Law was introduced in Montenegro in 1996 under which state funds were to sell their shares in enterprises to the public or to foreign investors.[30] Altogether, the funds sold majority shares in ninety-six enterprises, a controlling share in eighty-six companies and a managing share in twelve companies. However, by the end of this process, more than two-thirds of enterprise capital still remained in state ownership in the various funds. Prominent among sales to foreign investors was the takeover by the Swiss-based Glencore of the indebted aluminium company Kombinat Aluminijuma Podgorica (KAP), which accounted for more than half of Montenegro's foreign exchange earnings in a controversial sale that occurred under conditions of secrecy and without an open tender. Another major sale was the purchase in 1997 of the Nikšić-based beer and juice company Trebjesa by the Belgian beer producer Interbrew for DM25 million.

A Privatization Council was established in 1998 to oversee the complete privatization of the remaining state-owned shareholdings, and amendments to the Privatization law were introduced in 1999 obliging all remaining state-owned companies to draw up a privatization plan.[31] An MVP process was initiated in 2001, which distributed vouchers free to the public, who then had an opportunity to exchange the vouchers for shares through either directly or PIFs in the 190 companies covered by the programme. However, many of these MVP companies have since closed down or are operating at a significantly reduced level of capacity. Most still have many employees on the books who are hidden unemployed, do not turn up for work, and receive either no or very much reduced salaries and who also have a claim to back pay and to unpaid social security contributions. This legacy deters foreign investors. Even after the completion of the voucher privatization, it is estimated that 45 per cent of industry, including the seventeen largest companies, is still not privatized. Nevertheless, sales of state-owned companies are proceeding, and in October 2002 one of the biggest Montenegrin companies, Jugopetrol Kotor, was sold to a Greek company for €65 million.

Kosovo

When United Nations Mission in Kosovo (UNMIK) took over the administration of Kosovo, the socially owned enterprises in the province were in a parlous state. After a decade of neglect, equipment and technology was obsolete, and enterprises languished, producing little or nothing. Most goods on sale in the shops were imported. Disputes arose concerning the legal ownership and management rights of the socially owned enterprises. The former Albanian managers claimed the right to return to their previous jobs, and except in cases where the Serbian managers had fled the province, disagreements over rights were arbitrated by UNMIK, which frequently imposed joint management committees in the enterprises.

During the early years of UNMIK administration of Kosovo, the issue of property ownership remained unresolved. In order to re-establish production in socially owned companies, many were commercialized by management leasing the assets from the government. One of these was a vegetable-processing company near Prizren with 150 workers, which had been commercialized in 2001 by a partnership of six managers who leased the company from the government and effectively became the new owners.[32] Before commercialization, the farmers that supplied the raw materials were often not paid on time, but the company succeeded in regaining the trust of the farmers, paying for products cash on delivery and providing training and investment to raise the quality of their production. Immediately after commercialization, the company carried out a reconstruction plan and increased production from two tons to twelve tons per day in 2002 and to twenty tons per day by the end of 2003. Finance to renew outdated equipment was supplied by the partners and by commercial loans from an agricultural development bank. The company sourced its inputs from local suppliers, and the increased production it achieved benefited the local economy and increased employment in the Prizren region. Thus, despite criticisms that the leasing system was unattractive to investors because of the short ten-year lease lengths, it is clear that at least in some cases the system worked well and provided a sound base for investment and growth.

There has been relatively little foreign investment in Kosovo due to political uncertainty related to the constitutional status of the province rather than to a lack of viable investment opportunities. One example of a successful foreign investment was that of an Albanian businessman who had returned to Kosovo to set up a fruit juice production business, after working for a number of years in Germany. He had worked in the Western Balkan region as a sales representative of Tetrapak and had taken the initiative to establish his own business in the Prizren region. The example (see box) shows that while foreign investment may bring new skills and technologies, such investments may fail to create strong local linkages, and local multiplier effects may be lower than in the case of domestic leasehold companies.

A Fruit Juice Producer

I leased a disused factory building from the municipality, and began to produce high quality fruit juice, drawing water from nearby mountain springs, having negotiated a deal with both Tetrapak and another company, Combibloc, to supply advanced equipment. The production process is highly mechanized and requires only thirty-seven workers, of which seven are administrative staff. The production-line staff work three shifts a day, five days a week. We import fruit concentrates of grapes, apples, cherries, blueberries and other fruits from Italy, Slovenia, Austria, Germany and Holland. Only 5 per cent of inputs are sourced from within Kosovo, although we could source up to two-thirds of our raw materials locally if we could establish contracts with local farmers at the right price and quality. Each production line can be operated by just three workers and so our productivity is higher than that of our competitors. We can produce a one-litre pack of orange juice for €0.90, while the same imported product costs €2. We export products to the Albanian part of Macedonia, and plan to export to Albania once the free trade agreement between Kosovo and Albania comes into effect. However we can only export to Serbia through informal channels, since formal exports are not possible because of the poor security conditions for Kosovar trucks, and because payments from Serbia are uncertain.

(Interview with owner, Prizren, September 2003)

The privatization process in Kosovo was the last to take place in the Western Balkans. The issue was controversial because the Serbian government had claims to the ownership of the assets. The fact that these ownership claims had not been resolved put many Kosovo enterprises into a limbo, unable to access capital or finance for their restructuring and development. Following the adoption of privatization legislation by the Provisional Institutions of Self-Government (PISG) in June 2002, the previous Serbian privatization legislation was overturned, and the Kosovo Trust Agency (KTA) was established to oversee the privatization of the socially owned enterprises. The KTA announced the first six tenders of enterprises for sale in May 2003, including an electric fuse manufacturer, a limestone quarry, an engineering contractor, two brick makers and an electrical fridge maker.[33] By April 2007, the KTA had carried out twenty-five 'waves' of privatization, 156 enterprises had been privatized and total revenues had reached €166 million. Eight enterprises had been privatized through special spin-offs, in which a new company was established ('NewCo'), and assets from the old company were transferred to it. Shares in the NewCo were owned by the old company before being sold to new owners. In the meantime, creditors of the old company could make claims against it through the Kosovo Supreme Court. Buyers of such special spin-offs have been obliged to implement an investment plan and to maintain an agreed level of employment. One of the companies privatized through special spin-off was the Peja (Peć) brewery, which was sold for €11 million in 2006. The buyer agreed to make new investments in the plant, to maintain the jobs of 600 workers and to purchase 5,000 tons of barley annually from local farmers. By 2005, the total revenues achieved from spin-offs amounted to €48 million, involving investment commitments of €73 million and with a guarantee covering 3,000 jobs, of which one-third were employed in the largest spin-off company Ferronikel.[34]

6 Entrepreneurship and SME policies

Owing to the relatively slow pace of privatization and the weakness of inward investment into most of the Western Balkan countries, the economic development of the region has been highly reliant on the performance and vitality of domestic entrepreneurs who have created new small- and medium-sized enterprises (SMEs). These new entrepreneurial businesses have been the main source of job creation for workers who have lost their jobs in the declining social-ownership and state-ownership sectors. They have introduced a critical element of competition and dynamism into these transforming post-conflict economies, challenging the established monopolies and powerful coalitions which have sought to stall reforms, preserve the status quo and maintain their privileged positions gained during the chaos of the early transition, wars and civil conflicts. In addition, the development of the SME sector has had an important social role in developing a middle class capable of supporting democratic consolidation, and in ensuring a wider dispersion of income among the many thousands of new entrepreneurs and away from the top echelons of the managerial elite in large enterprises.

Between 1990 and 1995, the Western Balkans experienced a rapid entry of new small businesses in the private sector, despite significant obstacles due to lack of finance, adverse government regulation and taxation policies and the market dominance of large enterprises. Entry rates were highest in Albania, Croatia and Macedonia, but slowed down in the late 1990s and early 2000s. The new entrepreneurs faced many obstacles to developing their businesses. One of the principal barriers to growth was the lack of affordable finance through the underdeveloped banking system. Apart from Croatia, lack of confidence in the banks was widespread, and individuals were reluctant to entrust their savings to them. Banks channelled the limited available bank finance mainly to the large-sized enterprise sector, while loans to small enterprises were provided at high interest rates with large collateral requirements. As a result of capital scarcity, relatively few small businesses were able to expand and become competitive and innovative medium-sized enterprises, and the development of the small business sector has been held back. Many entrepreneurs have operated in the informal economy, avoiding the burden of state regulation and taxation. Larger firms have attempted to establish and maintain dominant or monopoly positions, making use of their close connections to the economic and political elites, which themselves rotated between positions of political and economic power. The convergence of these sources of power made it relatively easy for the large-sized enterprise sector to establish and maintain monopoly positions and influence economic policy in ways inimical to the development of the competitive small business sector. Thus, there was relatively little policy impetus for the promotion of the SME sector in the 1990s in most of the Western Balkan states, especially in the late reforming countries.

After the Dayton peace agreement was signed at the end of 1995, an influx of foreign assistance began to ease the financial constraints facing SMEs. The institutional framework for SME development was heavily influenced by international aid donors. They saw the SME sector as a key element in the reconstruction of the Western Balkan economies and began to fund SME development projects in Albania, BiH and Macedonia after 1995, and in FRY after 2000. Microfinance banks were established in several of the Western Balkan states, supported by the EBRD and other international donors. The microfinance concept has become a main form of intervention to mobilize financial resources for small businesses, often with a social motivation to reduce poverty, targeting socially disadvantaged groups including women, refugees and internally displaced persons. The use of microfinance has been an important element of donor-led efforts to stimulate economic development and revitalize localities that were severely affected by the wars and conflicts in the region. Nevertheless, the microfinance institutions were too limited to be a solution to the credit gaps facing small businesses in the Western Balkans. The institutions that were established by outside donors were swamped with requests and applications for credit, and even the international donors could not meet the unsatisfied demand. Although a significant number of new jobs were created, and many people were offered a route out of poverty, high levels of unemployment persisted and the impact on overall macroeconomic performance was limited.

Overall, an extensive private sector has emerged as a result of privatization and the entry of new firms, although to a different extent in each country (Figure 6.1). The greatest transformation has taken pace in Albania where private enterprise was illegal under the former communist regime, but which now has the highest private sector share of GDP at 75 per cent, mainly due to the collapse of the large state-owned enterprises and the privatization of agriculture. In Macedonia, most formerly socially owned enterprises have been privatized, and the private sector now accounts for about 70 per cent of GDP and 55 per cent of employment, while in Croatia, the share of private sector in GDP has stabilized at around 60 per cent due to delays in completing the privatization process. The transformation to a private-ownership economy has been slowest in the late reformers – BiH, Serbia and Montenegro – although the shares of the private sector in GDP and in employment are catching up rapidly, reaching 55 per cent in BiH and Serbia and 65 per cent in Montenegro (EBRD 2005b). Despite progress, these private sector shares in GDP remain below neighbouring Bulgaria (75 per cent) and Hungary (80 per cent).

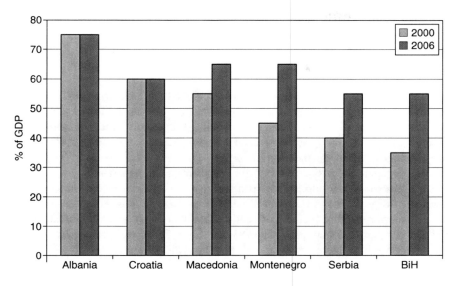

Figure 6.1 Private sector share of GDP, 2000 and 2006 (% GDP) (source: EBRD online data 2007).

Socialist entrepreneurs

The private sector had been an important part of the economy of former Yugoslavia. The agricultural sector was dominated by small private farms alongside a few large state-owned agrokombinats. Outside agriculture, small private enterprises were permitted to operate as sole proprietorships known as craft enterprises, but with limitations on the level of employment – such firms could employ up to a maximum of five workers, a limit that was raised to ten in the late 1980s. Private enterprises operated in all sectors of the economy including the services sector, construction and tourism in addition to small-scale peasant agriculture.

Seasonal activities were exempt from the five-employee rule, and so the private sector flourished on the Adriatic coast supporting a lucrative seasonal tourist industry. By 1967, over two-fifths of the 21,000 registered hotels, pensions and restaurants were under private management (Dirlam and Plummer 1973: 87), and by 1987, there were 23,000 private catering firms throughout Yugoslavia (Allcock 1992: 397). Even regular non-seasonal small businesses often found ways to avoid the regulations on the maximum number of employees and were able to expand their activities. However, the risks of falling foul of the authorities were real enough.

> In 1968 two private craftsmen with ten employees manufactured greasing and cleaning apparatus for automobiles at a rate of 1,500 per month, which they sold at 8,000 new dinars below the price charged by the Auto-moto

Alliance of Yugoslavia. A West German firm (evidently the supplier of the Alliance) offered them 100,000 marks to quit business. The two entrepreneurs were taken to court, their two Mercedes impounded and their giro accounts blocked.

(Dirlam and Plummer 1973: 86)

As the Yugoslav economy became more developed and industrialized, hundreds of thousands of peasants left their villages to find jobs in the towns and cities, and the number of private farmers declined. At the same time, the number of employees in the non-agricultural private sector increased from 120,000 in 1981 to 169,000 in 1988, an increase of 40 per cent over seven years.[1] The private sector engaged about one-third of the workforce in transport and communication, a quarter in catering and tourism and over one-quarter of the workforce in construction and artisan activities (Lydall 1984: 268). It was more developed in the northern republics, including Croatia where there were eighteen private businesses per thousand population in 1983, and lower in southern republics, including Serbia where there were just six per thousand (Bateman 2002: 177). The share of income generated by the private sector was even more substantial since many employees in socially owned enterprises worked on a 'moonlight' basis in the private sector. In addition, hundreds of thousands of emigrant workers were employed as Gastarbeiter in Germany and in other EU countries and sent remittance income back to their families in Yugoslavia, while many of them used the capital they had accumulated abroad to establish private businesses when they returned home. Additional private incomes were also made from renting property to tourists on the Adriatic coast. Taking all these sources of income together, Lydall estimated that in 1979, as much as 40 per cent of personal income was derived from private sector activity in Yugoslavia (Lydall 1984: 269).[2]

The entry of new small firms

In response to the economic crisis of the 1980s, the Yugoslav regime further liberalized the environment for private sector activity through the Enterprise Law of 1988 which permitted the creation of limited liability companies, and abolished the employment limits which had restricted the growth of the craft firms. In response, many new companies were established at the end of the 1980s before the break-up of Yugoslavia. About 26,000 new firms had been registered by June 1990, and by the end of the year this number had increased to over 60,000. In Serbia alone, the number of registered private companies had increased to 55,000 by the end of 1991.[3] Many entered into sectors with low entry barriers such as trade and services. The Yugoslav successor states had inherited relatively liberal laws on the formation and registration of private companies, and after the break-up of Yugoslavia, the numbers of private companies continued to increase rapidly. By 1995, the total number of registered private companies in Croatia had increased to 125,357[4] and in Macedonia to 83,000

(Zarezankova-Potevska 2000: 338),[5] while in Serbia the number of registered private companies increased to 185,256 by the end of 1996.[6] However, in the post-Dayton period up to the present, the respective patterns of entry of new enterprises diverged. By 2003, the number of registered private companies in Croatia had increased by a further 32 per cent to 165,659,[7] whereas in Serbia it had fallen slightly to 182,500.[8]

In communist-ruled Albania, in contrast to former Yugoslavia, private enterprise of any form had been entirely forbidden, but following the collapse of the communist regime, there was an equally explosive growth of new private companies. After the Enterprise Law of 1992 liberalized the registration and start-up of new private firms, the number of registered companies increased rapidly from just over 2,000 in 1991 to almost 20,000 by 1994, and although the rate of entry subsequently slowed down, by 2003, there were 134,000 registered companies. Almost all, however, were very small micro-enterprises concentrated in trade, services and transport, and only 2 per cent employed more than twenty workers.

Despite the growth in the number of new enterprises, many registered companies never began to work, or else failed but were not removed from the register, so that only a proportion of the officially registered companies were actively engaged in economic activity. Data compiled by the Payments Accounting Offices[9] in each of the Yugoslav successor states show that the number of active companies increased eightfold in Croatia between 1990 and 1995 and more than doubled in Macedonia between 1991 and 1995.[10] By 1995, more than nine out of ten active companies were classified as small-sized in each country. By 2005, there were almost 88,000 active SMEs in Croatia[11] and over 44,000 in Macedonia (APP 2006). In Serbia, there were 69,000 active companies in 1995,[12] but there was little subsequent increase and so the number was almost the same a decade later.[13]

Differences have also emerged in the density of SMEs (Figure 6.2). By 1995, Croatia had thirteen companies per thousand inhabitants excluding craft firms, while Macedonia and Serbia had lower densities, at ten and seven respectively. By 2005, the density of SMEs had increased, but it was still noticeably lower than in nearby EU countries, being lowest in Serbia-Montenegro (10) and Albania (11), while the highest densities were in BiH (19), Croatia (21) and Macedonia (22). All, however, were well below the average for the European Union (53), where densities were highest in Greece (72), Italy (78) and Hungary (86).

The distribution of SMEs by sector also shows differences to other comparable countries, with relatively high proportions of SMEs in the trade sector. Data compiled by the EBRD showed that Albania had the highest concentration of SMEs in the trade sector, with 52 per cent in 2001 compared to just 26 per cent in Hungary (Sanfey *et al.* 2004), suggesting that poverty push factors, rather than entrepreneurial pull factors, have been responsible for much of the growth in the number of small firms in Albania. The trade sector was underdeveloped in the communist era, especially in Albania, and the low capital requirement has made entry to the sector an attractive option to provide minimum subsistence. Its prevalence is an indicator of the important role of 'necessity' entrepreneurship compared to 'opportunity' entrepreneurship (Xheneti 2005a). In contrast,

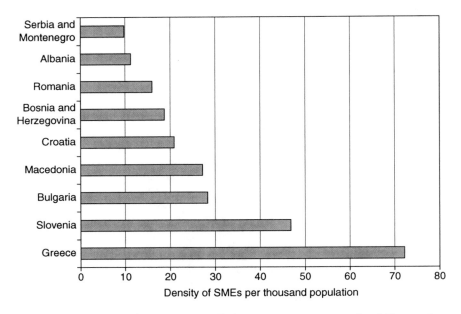

Figure 6.2 Density of SMEs per thousand population (source: International Finance Corporation, July 2006 and SME Observatory of the Republic of Macedonia, report 2004, October 2005).

Croatia had a trade sector share of only 35 per cent, similar to Poland's 36 per cent share. The SME presence in the manufacturing and construction sectors in BiH, Croatia and Serbia and Montenegro was correspondingly higher than in Albania, ranging from 24 per cent to 34 per cent.

Throughout the Western Balkans, most new job creation has been associated with the entry and growth of small-sized enterprises, while employment in large- and medium-sized enterprises has fallen. Between 1990 and 1995, the share of employment in the small-sized enterprise sector in Croatia almost doubled from 15 per cent to 28 per cent, while in Macedonia, it more than doubled from 7 per cent to 18 per cent.[14] By 2005, the share of employment in SMEs in Croatia had increased to 67 per cent, similar to that in Austria (IFC 2006), while the share in Macedonia was 76 per cent, close to the share in Greece and Italy (APP 2006). Albania and Serbia-Montenegro had intermediate positions with shares of about 50 per cent, while BiH had the lowest share, reflecting the prevalence of unrecorded employment in micro- and small-sized enterprises in the informal sector, as well as the slow pace of privatization (IFC 2006). Overall, the SME sector has provided employment for many workers laid off from the large enterprises undergoing restructuring and privatization. However, it has only recently begun to grow fast enough to make a significant contribution to reducing unemployment in Croatia, while in other countries, unemployment remains extremely high, as in Kosovo and Macedonia, or is even increasing, as in Serbia.

The craft sector and self-employment

In addition to the growth of small- and medium-sized companies, many new businesses have been set up by sole proprietors, sometimes referred to as self-employed entrepreneurs. The tradition of the independent sole proprietor has played an important role in the ex-Yugoslav countries, referred to as a 'craft firm' (*obrt*) in Croatia or 'private shop' (*privatna radnja*) in Serbia. Since the break-up of Yugoslavia, the sector has developed rapidly, but is often neglected in studies of SMEs which tend to focus on limited liability companies. However, due to the lower cost of entry and the greater flexibility of sole proprietorships compared to incorporated businesses, the sector has proved to be more dynamic in terms of employment and growth. Even though these firms are typically small enterprises with just a few employees, they have a tradition of skilled work, are important agents for the preservation and development of skills and a source of demand for skilled labour.

Sole proprietorships have increased in numbers in most of the Yugoslav successor states due to the relative simplicity and low cost of the procedure.[15] In Croatia, the number of sole proprietorships, which continued to be known as craft firms, increased from 64,298 in 1991 to 100,500 by 2003 when they accounted for 62 per cent of all enterprises in the economy and 24 per cent of employment.[16] While employment in 'legal entities' (predominantly limited liability companies) hardly changed over the ten-year period from 1995 to 2004, employment in craft firms increased by 50 per cent. In Serbia, the number of sole proprietorships (*privatne radnje*) increased from 166,500 in 1993 (Popović 1995: 47) to 243,000[17] in 2005, providing employment for 522,500 owners and employees[18] at a time when employment elsewhere in the economy was falling.

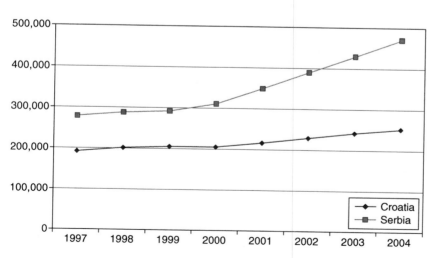

Figure 6.3 Croatia and Serbia – sole proprietors and their employees (source: Statistical Yearbooks of Croatia and Serbia and Montenegro, various years).

In BiH, the number of craft firms exceeds the number of legal entities by a significant margin (43,000 compared to 33,000), and their numbers are growing more rapidly, with the fastest growth between 2004 and 2005 in agriculture, transport and financial services. In Macedonia, in 2004, there were 49,000 active sole proprietors of various types, including craft firms, self-employed persons and 'small traders'.

There has clearly been a large increase in the number of sole proprietors in all the Western Balkan countries, whether setting up as craft firms, 'private shops', self-employed or small traders. There are two main factors driving this growth. The first is poverty, which pushes unemployed or marginalized people into self-employment usually in easy-to-enter sectors such as trade or small retail kiosks with little prospect of capital accumulation and growth. The second factor is the response to new opportunities which pull entrepreneurial individuals, who are capable of adapting to a rapidly changing environment, into dynamic segments of the economy (Bartlett and Hoggett 1996). Research into self-employment in other transition contexts has suggested that self-employed persons with employees are more likely to be dynamic and upwardly mobile entrepreneurs, while self-employed individuals working on their own account are more likely to be struggling to make ends meet (Earle and Sakova 2000; Hanley 2000).

Both types can be observed in the Western Balkans where, due to high unemployment and weak social security systems, many vulnerable people are pushed into self-employment as a means to ensure a living, while there are many other cases of entrepreneurial individuals who have been drawn into self-employment by the new market opportunities opened up by economic liberalization. Table 6.1 shows that Albania has a greater proportion of self-employed people subject to 'push' factors than Croatia and Macedonia, although the similar proportions of 'self-employed with employees' attests to the strong pull factors at work encouraging self-employed persons to expand their businesses and create jobs in each country, albeit to a lesser extent in Albania than in Croatia and Macedonia. However, many dynamic entrepreneurs find their desire for economic advancement through self-employment frustrated by high taxation and administrative burdens, and so avoid the formal registration process for all or part of their activities, preferring to operate in the informal economy which is widespread in the region.

Table 6.1 Self-employed employers and own-account workers (% of all in work)

	Self-employed employers	*Own-account self-employed workers*
Albania (2001)	6.0	48.0
Croatia (2006)	8.0	23.0
Macedonia (2003)	8.0	8.0

Sources: Labour Force Survey, Republic of Macedonia State Statistical Office, April 2003, 50; *Labour Force in the Republic of Croatia First Half-year 2006*, First Release, 9.2.7/1, State Statistical Office of Croatia. People and Work in Albania, INSTAT, 2004 (data refer to 2001).

Entrepreneurship and SME policies 91

Barriers to entry and growth

The relatively low share of the private sector in all the Western Balkan countries except Albania suggests that SMEs face many barriers to entry and growth. In most countries, entry rates slowed down following an initial surge in the early stage of transition, while barriers to formal activity pushed many entrepreneurs into the informal economy. Even in Croatia, the most advanced transition country in the region, entry rates among small limited liability companies have been sluggish in recent years (Čučković and Bartlett 2007). The main causes of slow entry and growth have been a combination of institutional and financial barriers (Bartlett and Bukvič 2002). The 'institutional view' holds that weak security of property rights inhibits the entry of new firms and reduces investment in established firms (de Soto 1989; Johnson *et al.* 2002). The scope of such institutional barriers is wide, and includes property rights, administrative costs, costs of obtaining licences, delays in registering a company, the need to pay bribes to inspectors and so on. Financial constraints present a further important barrier to the entry and growth of small enterprises (Pissarides 1999). The 'finance-first' view holds that in transition countries without a developed capital market, small firms face financial constraints that inhibit growth because they have few resources of their own and are unable to access external finance. Banks may not be willing to lend to new small firms which lack a track record, and small firms often have insufficient collateral to guarantee a loan. Especially problematic have been the political networks that link banks to the state and to larger enterprises and that divert investment finance from profitable SMEs to large loss-making companies supported by political connections. Politically motivated loans and subsidies not only tie up resources in unproductive sectors of the economy, but can also undermine the banking system if it becomes burdened with non-performing debts with little prospect of being repaid.

Barriers to SME entry

According to an assessment of the policy environment facing small business in the region carried out in 2002, 'barriers to business entry ... remain unnecessarily high ... in addition, companies ... face complex and often non-transparent procedures for obtaining and renewing permits and licenses, particularly building and land development permits' OECD (2003b: 11). Since the publication of the report, corrective legislation has reduced many barriers to business entry and improved the investment climate in several countries. Business simplification task forces have been established in Croatia and Macedonia (OECD 2004), while in BiH, a 'Bulldozer Commission' was set up in 2003 to sweep away restrictive legislation, leading to a sharp fall in the number of days needed to register a company. In Serbia and Montenegro, recent reforms have led to major improvements in the ease of starting a business, which propelled the country to the top of a global list of reforming countries in 2004 (World Bank 2006: 2). Albania adopted a detailed action plan aimed at reducing the administrative barriers to investments which focused on easing tax and customs administration and the provision of licences, and which led to a decrease in the average number of days needed to register a business. According to a recent European Commission report, 'company registration time in the Western Balkans is, on average, not altogether worse from what one finds in some Member States and candidate countries' (European Commission 2004: 11).

Surveys carried out by the World Bank have focused on a number of issues which are relevant to the difficulty of starting a business. The most recent survey carried out in 2006 covered 175 countries, including the Western Balkan countries. Although it only covered limited liability companies based in the capital cities, the information provided is useful in gauging progress in reform and in benchmarking the 'ease of doing business' in different countries (Table 6.2).

Typically, a relatively large number of procedures are required to register a company, and the costs of registration are high. By 2006, there were between ten and fifteen procedures needed to register a company, with the lowest number in Croatia and Macedonia and the highest number in Montenegro. The time taken to register a company varies from eighteen days in Serbia, where entrepreneurs can register online, and where a 'silence is consent' rule has been introduced, to as many as fifty-four days in BiH. The cost of starting a business has also been reduced in most countries in recent years, and in 2006 ranged from just 7 per cent of income per capita in Macedonia and Montenegro to 37 per cent in BiH. The minimum capital required to start a business varies substantially from zero in Montenegro to 112 per cent of per capita income in Macedonia. Taking all these factors together, Serbia, Macedonia and Montenegro are placed ahead of the other countries in the World Bank ranking of overall ease of starting a business, while BiH is placed at the lowest rank among the Western Balkan countries. On this dimension, it is clear that Serbia and Montenegro have made great strides in introducing institutional reforms in recent years.

Table 6.2 Ease of starting a business in the Western Balkans in 2006

	Number of procedures	Time taken (days)	Cost (% of income per capita)	Minimum capital needed (% of income per capita)	Overall rank
Serbia	10	18	10	8	60
Macedonia	10	18	7	112	76
Montenegro	15	24	7	0	83
Slovenia	9	60	9	16	98
Croatia	10	45	12	21	100
Albania	11	39	22	37	121
BiH	12	54	37	52	141

Source: World Bank Ease of Doing Business Database.

Barriers to SME growth

When he took up his position as High Representative in BiH in June 2002, Paddy Ashdown stated that job creation was one of his main priorities. In an inaugural speech, he observed that 'the challenge is to stimulate growth in the new private sector and especially among small businesses, which are already becoming the engine that will drive Bosnia's economy. We must sweep away the unnecessary red tape and bureaucracy that makes it so difficult to run an honest business and drives so many into the grey economy.'[19] This emphasis on barriers to the growth of small businesses has been one of the main themes of research into the small business sector in the Balkans.

A survey of 800 SMEs carried out in two of the Western Balkan countries (BiH and Macedonia) with Slovenia as a comparator was carried out within the PHARE-ACE programme in 2000 by the author and colleagues (Bukvič *et al.* 2001). The study found that financial barriers and tax-related barriers were the most serious obstacles to growth (Table 6.3).[20] Institutional barriers including social barriers (lack of trust and the need to bribe officials) and administrative barriers (too much bureaucracy, too many licences required and so on) were also important, but less so than the financial barriers. Employment regulations were perceived as the least important barrier. Lack of support services from the state was a medium-level barrier, suggesting that the state could do more in these countries to improve the provision of business support services, an issue which has subsequently been the subject of several projects organized by international donors and financial institutions.

The results of the survey showed that SMEs in BiH faced the most difficult business environment, reflecting its relatively late transition process and the deleterious effects of the war, while Macedonia faced a less difficult business environment, which was nevertheless worse than in the benchmark case of Slovenia (Bartlett 2003a). Financial barriers, together with high taxation, were the most important barriers facing SMEs in all three countries, and were especially serious in Macedonia. Employment legislation, although it was the least important barrier to growth overall, was a more serious barrier in Slovenia than

Table 6.3 Barriers to growth of SMEs in 2000

	BiH	Macedonia	Slovenia	All
Taxation	66	42	36	49
Finance	48	55	28	45
Social barriers	38	27	22	29
Lack of support services	34	21	18	25
Bureaucratic regulations	31	16	24	23
Employment laws	21	12	22	18

Source: Acevska *et al.* 2002.

Note
Percentage of replies to each question indicating 'very important barrier'.

in the two Western Balkan countries, suggesting that some of the concerns about restrictive employment legislation in the region that have been voiced in the literature may have been overplayed.[21]

The importance of financial constraints to SME growth in the Western Balkans can be explained by a number of factors. First, the banking system is underdeveloped throughout the region with the exception of Croatia, and small enterprises find it hard to obtain loans for expansion. Banks perceive small enterprises to be high credit risks, and typically require two or three times the value of the loan as collateral, so that medium- and large-sized enterprises usually have a better chance of obtaining a loan than do small-sized enterprises. Commercial banks often prefer to lend to larger enterprises, as they considered lending to small enterprises to be too risky, and their capacity to evaluate credit risks is often low (Falcetti *et al.* 2003). Entrepreneurs typically rely on self-financing or borrowing from friends and relatives. When credit is available from banks or other financial institutions, it is often provided on a short-term basis at a relatively high cost. Low-cost, long-term finance is relatively scarce, unless it is provided by subsidized schemes financed by the state or by international donor organizations (Kraft 2002). Credit to small enterprises has more often been provided through foreign donor programmes, frequently through dedicated microfinance schemes. With the exception of Croatia, the banking sector is relatively underdeveloped in the Western Balkans. In Albania, BiH, Macedonia and Serbia and Montenegro, the ratio of private sector credit to GDP was less than 10 per cent in 2001, compared to an average of 43 per cent in the Central European and Baltic states (Falcetti *et al.* 2003). In Croatia, where most banks are foreign-owned, the ratio of private sector credit to GDP was much higher, at 69 per cent, but even there, banks consider small firms to be relatively risky prospects (Kraft 2002).

Taxation was another serious barrier to SME growth at the time of the survey, mainly because business tax rates were still high in the Western Balkans in 2000. Corporate profits tax rates varied from 30 per cent in FBiH to 15 per cent in Macedonia, while VAT and sales tax rates varied from 22 per cent in Croatia to 17 per cent in Montenegro. While these rates were not out of line with tax rates in other European countries, the most burdensome taxes were the social contributions which were as high as 47 per cent of wages in FBiH, although being relatively lower in Croatia, Serbia and Macedonia where they were around 16–18 per cent. Businesses considered taxes to be a barrier to expansion and growth, but their main effect has been to provide an incentive for companies to operate in the informal economy. Even registered companies often declare an unrealistically low wage bill to minimize payment of social contributions or simply avoid paying social contributions altogether. Recently, tax rates have begun to fall, especially in Serbia which has reduced the profits tax rate to just 10 per cent.

Using data from the survey, a regression analysis of employment growth on a set of explanatory variables including the barrier variables revealed that the high cost of credit ($t = 2.2$) and the low quality of equipment ($t = 1.6$) had a significant negative impact on the growth of SMEs in the three countries (see Table 6.4). Despite protestations about high taxes in practice, firms were willing to

Table 6.4 Employment growth and barriers to growth

Dependent variable – (ln) employment growth 1997–9

	Coefficient	*t-statistic*
High cost of credit	−0.293	−2.163**
Too much bureaucracy	−0.131	−0.904
Late payment of bills	0.006	0.045
High profits taxes	0.059	0.042
Low quality of equipment	−0.287	−1.647*
Lack of support from the state	0.140	1.040
(ln) employment	−0.169	−3.543***
(ln) age of firm	−0.354	−4.277***
Owner's university education	−0.457	−3.715***
Macedonia (dummy variable)	0.570	4.167***
BiH (dummy variable)	0.197	1.228
Constant	0.170	0.698
Adjusted R squared = 0.237	$F = 7.904$	Number of. cases = 244

Source: Bartlett 2003.

Notes
'ln' = natural logarithm.
Significance levels: *** 1; per cent, ** 5 per cent; * 10 per cent.

expand despite the high level of profits tax they faced ($t = 0.04$). Equally, administrative burdens in the forms of bureaucratic barriers ($t = 0.9$) had no observable effect on growth nor did late payment of bills ($t = 0.05$). Whether a firm lacked support from the state or not had no effect on growth outcomes ($t = 1.04$), suggesting that the available support services were relatively ineffective and in need of an overhaul.

The regression results revealed two further interesting findings. First, there was a negative relationship between employment growth and the size of enterprises, supporting the view that small firms tend to grow faster than larger firms. Second, the negative coefficient on the level of the owners' education suggests that entrepreneurial success is not linked to the level of educational achievement, an effect that has also been found in studies of enterprise growth in more advanced market economies (Hall 1995: 167). In the present context, this finding suggests that the wrong sort of education has been provided in the past, at least in relation to its usefulness for running a business, and that improved business education may be an important factor in stimulating SME growth. Finally, the significant positive coefficient on the Macedonia dummy variable indicates that given the size of firm, the owner's education and the barriers to growth, SMEs in Macedonia were growing faster than those in BiH and Slovenia, probably reflecting the surge in growth in Macedonia in 2000 in the aftermath of the Kosovo war. Unfortunately, the Macedonian economy took a further blow following the outbreak of civil conflict in the country in 2001, shortly after this research was completed.

These findings have been replicated in other studies of SMEs in the Western Balkans which have found that access to finance has been a major constraint to growth. The EBRD surveyed 1,600 enterprises in all the Western Balkan countries in 1999 and 2002 as part of a larger study of transition economies and found that financial constraints were the main barriers to investment in all the countries apart from Albania, where problems with the judiciary and corruption were even more serious (Falcetti *et al.* 2003). Several studies have emphasized the role of corruption in holding back business growth. Corruption arises in a situation of social disruption and anomie, and the breakdown of moral and legal norms, as has been the case in post-conflict situations in the Western Balkans. The EBRD survey showed that Albanian businesses typically pay 3.3 per cent of their revenues in bribes, while 36 per cent of businesses reported paying bribes frequently. Similarly, the PHARE-ACE survey found a high level of corruption affecting companies in Macedonia. About half of the respondents reported high levels of corruption among state officials and institutions and almost 90 per cent of small businesses had experienced some level of corruption (Acevska *et al.* 2002). In its regional strategy paper for South East Europe, the World Bank argued that corruption was impeding the development of markets in the region (World Bank 2000), a view supported by the findings from its Business Enterprise Performance Survey (BEEPS) which showed that corruption was an important obstacle to SME development. The report observed that 'if SMEs are to be an engine of growth and employment, a frontal attack on corruption is essential' (World Bank 2002: 23).

SME policies

In transition economies, the state has a major role to play in establishing the basic institutional framework in which entrepreneurship can flourish, new firms are encouraged to enter the market and established firms have appropriate incentives to undertake investment and generate employment opportunities (Tyson *et al.* 1994). In addition to macroeconomic stability and secure property rights, governments need to establish an effective institutional support structure for the development of the SME sector (Kolodko 2000). Such structures have been established in most of the Western Balkan states in recent years,[22] and in the rest of this chapter, I set out the differing policies which the Western Balkan countries have adopted in order to support the entry and growth of their SME sectors.

The early reformers

Croatia[23]

Croatia took steps to develop its small business sector after the cessation of hostilities on its territory in the early 1990s. The Croatian Bank for Reconstruction and Development (HBOR) was established in 1992, with half its start-up capital provided by the German government. It provided subsidized loans for small business projects in Croatia's war-affected areas, which were disbursed through the banking system and required no collateral commitment on the part of the entrepreneur, a necessary measure considering the target groups of refugees and internally displaced persons. Four-fifths of the 4,500 loans made by 1998 were for agricultural machinery and equipment. HBOR also provided loan guarantees to SMEs without requiring collateral, and provided training to banks to improve their lending to small businesses. A new Company Law and a Crafts Law were passed in 1993.[24] The Croatian Guarantee Agency (HGA), established in 1994, supported small businesses which had insufficient collateral to obtain bank loans by guaranteeing up to 80 per cent of the value of a loan. Separate programmes were designed for start-ups, business expansion and for entrepreneurs in war-affected areas. The Employment Bureau was also active in supporting small business start-ups by giving financial help to redundant worker and by giving wage subsidies to employers that took on unemployed workers.

A more comprehensive approach to SME development was initiated in 1996 when the Ministry of Economy adopted a 'Programme for Encouraging Small Business' managed by a dedicated Division for SME Development. It established local investment funds which provided subsidized loans to small businesses with support from local authorities (Franičević and Bartlett 2002). Local banks also participated in financing the loan funds. In addition, a network of local consultants was established to provide subsidized consultancy services. The programme prioritized manufacturing businesses, giving equal emphasis to new start-ups and to the growth of established businesses. In 1997, the ministry allocated HRK 32 million (€4 million) to the local funds which were supplemented by HRK 22 million from local administrations and HRK 103 million from commercial banks. The local funds allocated their loans to SMEs on a competitive basis, and by 1998, over 600 loans, guaranteed by the HGA, had been disbursed and 2,600 new jobs had been created. Although the programme succeeded in removing some of the financial barriers facing SMEs, the lengthy bureaucratic procedures led to a slow take-up of the subsidized loans. The programme also assisted the creation of business incubators and business zones, encouraged entrepreneurial activity, assisted the commercialization of innovation and trained professional trainers and advisors. The first small business incubator was established in Pula on the Istrian coast, and by 1998, twelve incubators, twenty-eight small business zones and eight entrepreneurial centres had been established.

The programme operated most effectively where there was a high degree of local involvement. A good example was the town of Čakovec, a market town in the Međimurje region in northern Croatia which had had a tradition of entrepreneurial activity during socialist times and which had retained an entrepreneurial culture throughout the 1990s. In 1997, the county commited HRK 700,000 to the local SME fund, which was multiplied eight times by the participating local bank, the *Međimurska banka*. The county and the town administrations collaborated in setting up a Centre for Entrepreneurship in January 1998 as a non-profit limited liability company. The Centre established the economic and social criteria by which loan applicants would be screened, while a committee representing local business interests and local government selected which applications to pass on to the participating banks for a final decision. In its first year of operation, the scheme attracted 220 applications for subsidized credits, of which thirty-two were successful, a figure which was expected to double the following year.[25]

In Split, the programme was delivered directly by the county administration through its Office for Reconstruction and Development, which adapted the Ministry's model in its own way. The county administration recognized that there was a lack of finance for SMEs, due to illiquid banks, high interest rates and the lack of interest of the banks in financing small businesses. Instead of building up a revolving fund, it provided interest rate subsidies of 50 per cent on loans to SMEs.[26] The scheme was managed through the local *Splitska banka*, and was targeted at manufacturing firms, crafts and business services, including both new start-ups and established small businesses. In 1997, the County contributed 5 per cent of its budget to the loan fund. In the first round of bidding, 836 applications were received, of which nine-tenths were referred to consultants for assistance in preparing a business plan. In the first six months, over forty credits were approved through a number of banks, guaranteed by the HGA.[27] Rather than being selected by a commission, the *Splitska banka* was responsible for selecting projects. In effect, the Split programme backed projects which would have been most likely to obtain loans from the bank in any case, limiting the additional social benefit from the programme. According to one local official:

> Support for SMEs has become a fashion, and is not based on any real analysis. Many 'entrepreneurs' don't have any ideas or resources, but are just trying to capture an economic rent. The banks have their biases in selecting those candidates who are offered the subsidized loans. There is no strategic approach to SME development either at County level or at national level.
> (Interview, Splitsko-Dalmatinska Županija, October 1998)

By October 1998, the programme had received over 3,500 enquiries from potential entrepreneurs, but the disbursement of loans was held back by numerous delays. A key bottleneck was in the preparation of documentation, especially in regard to entitlement over land holdings and property. Typically, it would take a minimum of three months to secure all appropriate documentation, and in practice, it could take much longer. Lack of a secure property rights system was holding back economic development.[28]

In Osijek, the primary city in Eastern Slavonia, the council had carried out a survey of small businesses and found that financial constraints were the main problem facing the estimated 2,000 small businesses in the city. The council established a City Fund for SMEs with an allocation equivalent to 1 per cent of the city's budget, and supported a start-up incubator and a small business zone whose tenants were relieved of local taxes and community contributions.[29] The council also established a Centre for Entrepreneurship in 1997 to provide training and consultancy services for SMEs, and to manage a microcredit programme.[30] The Centre received support from USAID to establish a savings and loan bank called NOA which managed the microcredit fund. Under this arrangement, entrepreneurs clubbed together in small groups and mutually guaranteed their loans from the microcredit fund, which were provided at commercial interest rates. The Centre provided training to support the financial component of the programme, and within a year had 600 clients and had established forty mutual guarantee groups. Its activities had resulted in the creation of 1,200 new jobs, with a loan default rate of just 1.5 per cent.

The Osijek-Baranja county council (*županija*) also viewed small businesses as an essential part of the economic recovery of the region and set up its own SME programme. The county had been devastated during the war in 1991. The last fighting had taken place in 1995, and the region of Eastern Slavonia was only re-integrated into Croatia at the beginning of 1998. Previously, the region had been one of the most prosperous parts of the former Yugoslavia, but its GDP fell by 70 per cent during the war. The large socially owned firms had suffered particularly badly. A local enterprise 'Saponia', a producer of detergent which had originally been established in 1894, had seen much of its infrastructure destroyed.[31] The previously prosperous agrokombinat 'Belje', which covered a large part of the county, had been even more severely damaged and its operations almost completely disrupted. Throughout the county, with unemployment at 25 per cent, only the small business sector, which provided jobs to two-thirds of all employees, was making profits.[32] The county established a small revolving fund in collaboration with the ministry and a local bank to provide loans for equipment for start-up businesses. Applicants were screened by a committee consisting of representatives from the county council, the chamber of economy, the chamber of crafts and a local bank. Unfortunately, the county council was at loggerheads with the Osijek city council as each was controlled by a different political party. County officials complained that although the city had a larger budget, it had done little to support SMEs, having prioritized the repair of civic buildings.[33]

In summary, although the main parameters of the SME programme were set centrally in Zagreb, the local authorities were permitted to vary the design and implementation of the programme at the local level. This discretion was used wisely in Čakovec, but in Split, local discretion at county level resulted in counter-productive rent seeking, while in Osijek, local discretion led to policy conflicts between the different levels of government.

Although the Croatian government carried through its SME development programme largely on the basis of its own resources, it received some limited assistance from international donors. The UNDP supported the establishment of Local Enterprise Development Agencies in war-affected areas in Slavonia and the Krajina; USAID assisted the micro-loan programme in Osijek; the Italian government funded an SME programme in Osijek and the British Know-How Fund provided assistance for SME development. However, despite this international assistance, the SME support programmes in Croatia were essentially home-grown and did not rely on extensive outside financial or technical assistance.

When the SDP-led coalition government came to power in Croatia in 2000, it prioritized SME support by establishing a Ministry for Crafts and Small and Medium Enterprises. The minister in charge was a member of the Croatian Peasants' Party, a traditional promoter of private enterprise in the agriculture sector and a natural leader of Croatia's drive to develop its small business sector. In March 2002, the government passed a Law on Stimulating Development of Small Entrepreneurship, and in June 2002, the HGA was transformed into the Croatian Agency for Small Business (HAMAG). The policy framework continued to be based upon the involvement of local administrations and local banks, and by 2003, twenty-one local business support centres, eleven business incubators and two technology parks had been established. While the main focus of activity has been in the larger towns, there have also been some important initiatives in several smaller towns in the war-affected areas such as Pakrac in Western Slavonia.

The new HDZ government which came to power in early 2004 continued to promote the development of the SME sector as one of its main priorities. The Ministry of Crafts and SMEs was absorbed into a new economic super-ministry, but the policy orientation has remained fundamentally unchanged. A "One Stop Shop" for business registration was established in 2005 which cut registration costs for new enterprises significantly. Major remaining obstacles to small business entry and growth have been the chaotic land registration system and the bureaucratic system of urban land-use planning which has inhibited the acquisition of land and premises for business purposes.

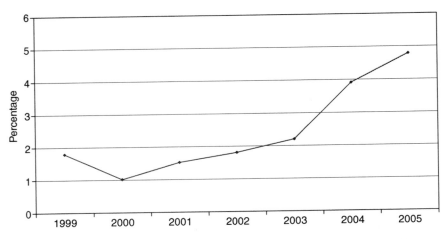

Figure 6.4 Croatia: entry rates of registered businesses (% per annum) (source: *Croatian Statistical Yearbook*, various years).

Despite these shortcomings, the SME sector in Croatia has benefited from a consistent policy approach adopted by successive governments, together with the involvement of local stakeholders. Despite a slowdown during the economic crisis of 1999, the number of registered enterprises has increased steadily since 2000, with the entry rate of new enterprises increasing from 1 per cent in 2000 to 5 per cent in 2005 (Figure 6.4). The strategy of SME development based upon a home-grown policy has begun to achieve its main objective of creating a successful, dynamic and competitive economy based upon a vibrant domestic private sector.

Macedonia

The private sector had developed mainly in the Albanian-populated areas of Western Macedonia in the socialist period, in response to labour market discrimination and the lack of employment opportunities for Albanian workers in the socially owned enterprises.[34] When these began to collapse in the early 1990s, the Albanian-populated areas of the country were less severely affected, and the local economy of Western Macedonia remained relatively vibrant based upon pre-existing trade connections and a flow of remittance income from relatives working abroad. Although the collapse of the large socially owned enterprises through restructuring and privatization led to increasing levels of unemployment among the previously privileged Macedonian sections of the population, the government had no strategy to support the development of the SME sector, and it was left to international agencies to step in to manage SME policy. Macedonia signed a Trade and Cooperation Agreement with the EU in 1996, and the PHARE assistance programme was opened for Macedonia in 1997. One of its first projects was to establish a National Enterprise Promotion Agency (NEPA), which was set up in 1998. The Privatization Agency provided office space for the NEPA, and four Regional Enterprise Support Centres were established to deliver small business services on a decentralized basis. The EU provided a €5 million microcredit line managed through the banking system, which provided loans of up to €30,000 at concessional rates of interest to small enterprises employing up to twenty people, while the regional centres offered advice to applicants and assisted them to apply for loans. One example of the difficulties facing the SME sector was the Company Law of 1996 that required all private firms to transform themselves into 'trade companies' (*trgovska drushtva*) by the end of 1998. When re-registering under the new legal form, business owners had to produce documentation and licenses concerning their current activity. Where this had changed, even only marginally from the original activity, or where business premises were not properly registered according to urban planning regulations, new documentation including at least nine different permits was required. In addition, when registering as limited liability companies, a DM50,000 minimum capital requirement was imposed. The government was strongly influenced by interest groups representing large firms, and policy conflicts paralysed government initiatives in this field. In 1998, for the first time, the government budget included a provision for SME support, but only a token amount was allocated. The measure represented the beginning of a national policy for SME development, but the slow pace of implementation indicated significant resistance by established business interests, especially the interests of the large enterprise sector, and the NEPA programmes failed to work effectively.

In 1996, the UK government supported the setting up of Enterprise Development Agencies in the Western Macedonian towns of Ohrid, Tetovo and Gostivar. The International Finance Corporation (IFC) and the European Bank for Reconstruction and Development (EBRD) provided credit lines to commercial banks for loans to SMEs. The World Bank established four incubators to provide business space, basic equipment and working capital for workers laid off from twenty-five large socially owned and loss-making enterprises undergoing restructuring, supported by a $10 million credit line and subsidized consultancy and training. USAID established the Macedonian Business Resource Centre which provided microcredit and leased capital equipment to SMEs. The German and Swiss governments also provided support for trainers and local consultants to small businesses. Altogether, it is estimated that Macedonia received $100 million from foreign donors for SME development between 1995 and 2000 (OECD 2003a).

Despite the inflow of international assistance, SMEs in Macedonia continued to face many obstacles. In addition to the lack of government support, they faced unfair competition from the informal economy which had grown rapidly during the early 1990s when sanctions had been imposed against FRY, Macedonia's main trading partner, and when Greece had imposed a trade embargo. As noted in one report:

> The informal economy has penetrated deeply into the national economy and its corrosive effects disintegrate the economic environment and inhibit the consistent implementation of legal solutions. It continues to escalate under the pressure of evident discrepancy between the dynamic process of liberalization of foreign trade on the one hand, and the slow process of internal structural, institutional and market reforms on the other.
>
> (Acevska *et al.* 2002: 253)

A further problem has been the adverse influence of the political parties in the development of the small business sector. The same report from 2002 observes: '... the negative influence exercised by the ruling central authorities ... support these illegal operations on a discriminatory principle related to friends from their political party or their relatives, thus stimulating the breakdown of law, nepotism, and corruption' (Acevska *et al.* 2002: 254). In the PHARE-ACE survey of 300 Macedonian SMEs carried out in autumn 2000, more than half the respondents reported that they did not have any trust in the government, the state administration or local government. Small and micro-enterprises had little trust in banks which regarded them as high-risk businesses and were less willing to provide loans to them than to larger enterprises. The survey also highlighted the high level of corruption – almost 90 per cent of the respondents reported that they had experienced at least some level of corruption among state officials.

Macedonian companies have suffered from political interference and pressure from politicians who have sought to use their privileged position for personal advantage. Parties have vied with one another for control of private companies and have sought to gain individual advantage from their political office, to the detriment of economic efficiency and export competitiveness. This is well illustrated by the remarks of the owner of a food-processing company in Skopje:

> The company was established from scratch in 1990 at a time when the creation of new private enterprises was being encouraged within the former Yugoslavia. Then sanctions were imposed against Serbia and Greece imposed a two-year embargo, in 1999 the Kosovo war broke out, and in 2001 there was a war in Macedonia. These disturbances all caused enormous problems for our export activity. Four years ago we began to build a slaughterhouse near the airport and a farm near the Bulgarian border financed with our own money, a loan from the EBRD, venture capital from the SEAF enterprise fund, and with the help of a private investor from Bulgaria. We succeeded in establishing business relations in Greece, Serbia, Bulgaria and Croatia but not in Albania where we were unable to find anyone that we could trust which is important for establishing a long term relationship. The main problems we face are licensing and bureaucracy, and corruption is also a serious problem which has increased unbelievably in recent years. We get no assistance from the government which just puts obstacles in our way. One day a group of politicians came here and said that they wanted to buy the farm. They have their own company which imports 15,000 tons chickens each year without paying any import duties. The politicians were sitting here and offered me only one quarter of the value as a price for the farm! They threatened to make life difficult for me if I did not sell, which is what happened. I'm a businessman, not a politician. If they leave us alone and give us possibilities to work we'll do OK. I don't need any help, I don't need it. If they help me it only makes life more difficult. We could easily employ 2,000 people. We could make fresh meat, make profits and be successful. We are an agricultural country. We won't produce motor cars, but we can easily produce processed food and other agricultural products for sale and for export.
>
> (Interview with owner of a food processing company, Skopje, October 2002)

In the context of widespread corruption and a strong informal economy, international assistance programmes have had relatively little impact. The government SME agency, NEPA, was viewed by its clients as a remote and 'bureaucratic institution, operating under the patronage of government and foreign donors' (OECD 2003a: 17). Its main failing was that it was managed according to political priorities. Despite the criticisms, the agency had presided over a substantial growth in the SME sector, giving Macedonia the highest SME densities in the region. Nevertheless the EU suspended funding to the NEPA and its regional agencies on the grounds that they provided inadequate advice to businesses and failed to provide adequate follow-up services.[35] It was replaced by a new agency known as the Agency for the Promotion of Entrepreneurship (APP) in 2003 which was launched alongside a new government strategy for SME promotion. However, the new agency will be subjected to similar pressures as before, and it is hard to see what benefit will emerge from the change of name.

Despite the hostile environment, the number of SMEs has increased rapidly in Macedonia, which now has the highest density of SMEs in relation to the population among all the Western Balkan countries. In 2004, there were over 44,000 active SMEs and their number was increasing at a rate of 4 per cent per year.

Albania

Following the collapse of communism and the liberalization of the environment for private business in Albania, the number of new small businesses also increased rapidly, mostly in the agricultural and trade sectors. Privatization of agricultural land and the collapse of the large state-owned enterprises led many people to seek work in the agricultural sector. However, the small business sector in Albania has remained relatively weak and fragmented, with most businesses operating at a very small scale of production.

By 2005, there were 45,000 active enterprises employing just over 173,000 workers, the vast majority of which were SMEs (Table 6.5). Almost three-quarters of employees (72 per cent) worked in small enterprises employing fewer than fifty workers, responsible for producing an equivalent share of total turnover. There were only 371 active enterprises which employed more than fifty workers in the whole of Albania. Almost two-thirds of non-agricultural businesses operated in the services sector, mainly in trade.

Several surveys of SMEs performance and barriers to growth have been carried out in Albania. Iraj Hashi carried out a survey of fifty private enterprises

Table 6.5 Size distribution of enterprises in Albania 2005

Employment size group	1–4	5–9	10–19	20–49	50+	Total
Number of enterprises[a]	91.6%	4.3%	1.9%	1.4%	0.8%	45,034
Number of employee[b]	37.9%	7.0%	6.6%	10.5%	38.0%	173,427
Turnover[c]	25.1%	12.0%	11.6%	13.9%	37.4%	n/a

Source: INSTAT, Tirana

Notes
a Per cent of total number of enterprises.
b Per cent of total number of employees.
c Per cent of total turnover of enterprise sector.

employing fewer than 200 employees in early 1997 and found that financial barriers were the most significant obstacles to the growth of small businesses (Hashi 2001). A similar survey of 100 small businesses in Albania in 1999 carried out by the EBRD found that while financial constraints and taxation were among the most serious barriers they faced, the most important barrier was unfair competition from the informal economy (Muent *et al.* 2001). Mirela Xheneti surveyed 110 SMEs in the manufacturing sector through a survey questionnaire carried out in Albania in April–July 2004. The businesses chosen had more than five employees and were located in the districts of Tirana, Durrës, Elbasan, Shkodra, Korça, Gjirokastra and Vlora. The analysis showed that growth was higher in smaller, more recently established firms; in firms run by older more experienced entrepreneurs; and in firms run by entrepreneurs with a recent business qualification and business skills (Xheneti and Bartlett 2006). The analysis also revealed that lack of information was a serious obstacle to growth, reflecting the weaknesses in the institutional support structure in Albania (Xheneti 2005b) and that capital accumulation on its own does not increase the probability of business success, reflecting the weakness of the investment climate.

The SME sector has had relatively little support from the state and has been self-organizing in a largely unregulated environment. By the same token, the sector has been unsupportive of the state, since many businesses operate in the informal economy avoiding payment of taxes, to a greater extent than elsewhere in the Western Balkans. A national SME strategy was adopted by the government in 2001, and the SME Agency (SMEA) was established at the end of 2003. In 2006, the SMEA was merged into *Albinvest*, the state agency for investment promotion.

The late reformers

SMEs in the early reforming countries faced substantial difficulties stemming from the obstacles placed in their way by the lack of access to external finance, and to bureaucratic and other barriers placed in their way by influential lobbies which promoted the interests of the large enterprise sector. The Croatian government had attempted to redress this imbalance by developing special programmes to support and develop SMEs especially in the war-affected areas. The development of supportive SME policies took longer to be established in Albania and Macedonia which relied more on external donor organizations to establish SME support structures. In the late reforming countries, however, the SME sector faced even more serious barriers to their start-up and growth.

Bosnia and Herzegovina

In BiH, the war broke down the pre-existing nexus of economic relations and led to the growth of new, often informal, business structures as survival strategies. In 1992, the government in Sarajevo relied on the smuggling skills of criminal gangs to sustain the city through the early stages of the siege imposed by Bosnian Serb forces, while combatants on all sides traded with each other across the front lines (Andreas 2004). Operators in the informal economy established powerful networks with the political parties that subsequently ruled the divided Bosnian state, while corruption among customs officials supported by political backers has been pervasive. The 'Arizona market' near the autonomous district of Brčko, established initially with the assistance of NATO troops, became a regional centre for the sale of contraband goods. The informal economy was linked to organized criminal groups who engaged in smuggling and human trafficking. This legacy explains why BiH has the highest proportion of informal activities in any of the Western Balkan states, which according to some estimates has reached as much as one-third of GDP.

The involvement of the international donors in post-war reconstruction brought new ideas and new methods to support the small business sector. One of the most innovative and influential new development tools was microfinance which provides small start-up grants or microcredits to individuals without the need to provide collateral. Often, in the case of mutual guarantee systems and credit unions, loans are guaranteed by a group of borrowers who know each other well, and thus are able to screen out unreliable applicants. The first major programme to make use of microcredit was organized by the World Bank in BiH as an instrument of post-conflict reconstruction (Čičić and Šunje 2002). The Local Initiative Project (LIP), which ran from 1996 to 2000, began with an initial capital of $21 million raised from the World Bank and other bilateral donors. By the end of 2000, the project had provided over 50,000 small loans averaging $1,500 which enabled refugees and internally placed persons to begin small micro-businesses. About half of the clients were women and three-quarters were involved in the trade and services sectors. The typical borrower was a small family-owned business which employed up to five people. Repayment rates were high, with less than 1 per cent of loans overdue on repayment. The LIP supported the creation of 34,000 new jobs and sustained 57,000 existing jobs up to the year 2000. It helped to establish seventeen microfinance institutions, of which twelve were local microcredit NGOs and four were international NGOs. The project also led to the creation of a micro-enterprise bank supported by the IFC and the EBRD. A second project, LIP II, was implemented from 2002 to 2005. By the end of 2004, there were forty-six microcredit organizations in BiH, twenty-six of which were based in the Federation and twenty in Republika Srpska. A careful independent statistical study of the impact of the LIP II microcredit programme demonstrated that the loan scheme had had a positive effect on household income, business investment and business registration. The programme had been especially beneficial to returning refugees and displaced persons, the disabled and widowed. In addition to providing productive employment, increasing incomes and reducing the incidence of poverty, it also assisted in bringing these disadvantaged groups into the formal economy. Microfinance was especially useful to refugees who had lost their property and were unable to offer collateral for loans from the commercial banking system.

Despite the success of the microfinance schemes, in 2004, the BiH government recognized that there were still significant barriers to setting up and operating a business, including the length of time taken to register a company, high start-up costs, high tax rates, discretionary inspections and corruption (CoM-BiH 2004: 63). The informal economy was also recognized as a significant hindrance to formal business sector, creating unfair competition. The division of the country has prevented the creation of a single economic space in BiH, and this has created further barriers to the development of a competitive private sector. In this difficult environment, neither of the entity governments has managed to develop a coherent approach to supporting the SME sector. The government admitted that 'generally speaking, one can say that entrepreneurship in BiH is in its infancy' and that 'the banking system presents a particular problem since it considers investing in SMEs high risk' (CoM-BiH 2004). The most recent report on the implementation of the European Charter for Small Enterprises notes that 'only Bosnia and Herzegovina and UNMIK/Kosovo have no fully operational national SME agency ... responsible for implementing SME policies' (OECD 2003b).

Serbia and Montenegro

Policy towards the legitimate small business sector in FRY was underdeveloped throughout the 1990s, and mainly emphasized the continuing role of social ownership and the importance of the large enterprise sector which could be more easily controlled by the ruling party than independent small businesses.[36] The state administration did little to assist the entry or growth of independent small businesses, and numerous administrative obstacles stood in the way of developing SMEs in the formal economy, including onerous reporting requirements and the cost of securing licences for the use of business premises. According to one account published in 1998:

> As soon as one is registered as a private entrepreneur, his telephone, electricity, heating and other utility bills become a couple of times higher. State owned enterprises providing these services have double prices. Much higher prices are charged for services rendered to sole proprietors than to persons who do not run a business. This practice discourages people from engaging in small businesses altogether or else encourages them to operate on the black market instead of the regular one.
>
> (Kovačević 1998)

Imports and exports required extensive paperwork and permits. Customs regulations, high import duties and complicated foreign currency transfers stimulated the development of the informal economy, so many imported goods were smuggled into the country and foreign currency was exchanged on the black market. The Serbian Labour Relations Law required that enterprises were obliged to have at least two persons employed full time for an indefinite period, which effectively discouraged new start-ups. The labour market was heavily regulated and small businesses faced high lay-off costs. At the same time, those businesses which supported the ruling party were privileged and were unhindered by such obstacles. The imposition of sanctions on FRY in 1993 fuelled the growth of corruption.

> Sanctions ... significantly accelerated the impoverishment and criminaliza-
> tion of Serbian society. A parallel economy sprang up, rooted in pre-
> existing Communist era smuggling and black market networks. Previously
> upstanding citizens found themselves engaged in dubious deals with crimi-
> nals and smugglers. Obscure border villages suddenly turned into boom
> towns, made rich on the proceeds of contraband.
>
> (LeBor 2002: 210)

The impact of sanctions spread to neighbouring countries which traded with FRY. Smuggled goods entered FRY from Albania, Bulgaria, Hungary and Macedonia as the incentives for businesses to engage in smuggling became far greater than the incentives to operate legitimate businesses. The government actively promoted smuggling to bypass sanctions, creating a legacy of close con-nections between political parties, state officials and criminal organizations. After the ending of sanctions, the unproductive aspects of the informal economy were acknowledged, and in 1995, the Serbian government introduced a number of measures to regulate it, but these had little effect due to the policy bias against small private businesses. Several programmes were developed to support the small business sector in an attempt to reduce unemployment, but owing to the clientelistic attitudes of politicians and officials, these programmes were often delivered in a partisan and discriminatory way.

The situation improved significantly following the overthrow of the Milošević regime. In 2001, an Agency for the Development of SMEs and Entre-preneurship (ASMEE) was established, together with a network of twelve local business support centres, supplemented by thirty sub-centres. In 2003, the government adopted a new strategy for SME development. Since then, Serbia has moved rapidly in the direction of improving the business environment for SMEs, becoming the World Bank's 'top reformer' in 2004 due to its policy of simplifying the process of business start-up. The process of registering new businesses was moved from the courts to a business registry, online registration was introduced and a 'silence is consent' rule was adopted. As a result, the time taken to start a business was reduced from an average of fifty-one days to fifteen days.

Montenegro

During the 1990s, SME development was the responsibility of the Montenegrin Development Fund, which used the proceeds from privatization to provide sub-sidized credits to private businesses, investing a major part of its income in SMEs. Between 1997 and 2003, the Fund provided loans to the value of €10 million to 640 small enterprises. These were mainly medium-term loans with a grace period of one year, a three-year payback and with a 4 per cent rate of interest. Over 80 per cent of these loans were made to businesses operating in the manufacturing sector, and over 5,500 new jobs were created. However, the funds were distributed highly unevenly to favour businesses located in parts of the country with political or family links to the Fund's directors. While one-fifth were placed with firms in the capital city Podgorica, 26 per cent of the loans were placed with businesses in one town in the North-West part of the country and only 3 per cent of loans found their way to the underdeveloped North-East.[37]

A more successful SME programme was administered by the Montenegrin Employment Bureau which offered subsidized loans to unemployed people to start a business. Applicants could apply for loans of up to €3,000 per employee through any of the four small regional banks which administered the scheme.[38] The loans were offered with a three-year repayment term, a grace period of one year and an annual interest rate of 3 per cent. Regional commissions give a first assessment of the proposed projects, with the final decision being made by the Republic Commission. By 2003, the programme had awarded €17.6 million to 3,782 projects, creating jobs for almost 6,000 people. The contract permitted borrowers to delay payments by up to one year, subject to a very small penalty rate. Although this led to a high rate of default, the Employment Bureau rarely reclaimed the loans.[39]

Microcredit institutions have also been active in supporting the development of small businesses in Montenegro. One such institution, Alter Modus, was established in 1997 by the Danish Refugee Council. Its programme was based on the principle of consecutive loans: clients who succeeded in paying off one loan were entitled to an additional loan with a 50 per cent higher credit limit.[40] Over 60 per cent of the clients were women and most of the loans were for businesses in the trade and services sectors. The loans were made to both registered and unregistered businesses, and in the conditions of underdeveloped capital markets, there was enormous demand for the loans from the organization. Loans were almost always repaid, with a low 2 per cent default level. Another microcredit institution active in Montenegro was AgroInvest, established in 1999 by the Canadian government aid programme, mainly concentrating its lending on agricultural projects. By 2003, AgroInvest had a loan portfolio of €7 million with 3,000 clients, and had created 1,500 jobs throughout the country.[41] It operated a character-based lending scheme, which required village councils to screen applications and to take responsibility for collecting payments from clients. The organization claimed a zero default rate and successfully supported women's businesses that made up 60 per cent of its client base. AgroInvest also established its activities in BiH, Serbia and Albania.

In recent years, Montenegro has made significant progress in further developing the institutional and policy framework for SME support. An agency for SME development (SMEDA) was established in 2000 with support from the European Agency for Reconstruction. SMEDA coordinates a network of local business support centres. However, as elsewhere in the region, the state-run SME programmes have often been distorted by political clientelism and administrative ineffectiveness.

Kosovo

Kosovo has had a long tradition of entrepreneurial activity, and small-scale businesses and agricultural small holdings played an important role in its economy even during the socialist period. During the 1990s, the parallel economy created by the Albanians who had been dismissed from the Serbian-controlled socially owned enterprises was based mainly on small private businesses. This came out into the open after the Kosovo war following the expulsion of the Serbian authorities from the province.

> The rapid return of refugees in June and July of 1999 was immediately followed by a remarkable level of activity in the private sector. New shops, restaurants, and small trading 'companies' began operating literally within days of the arrival of KFOR and the rest of the large international community in Kosovo. Very quickly, these operations became more sophisticated, as goods began to flow into Kosovo and owners responded to a rapidly increasing demand for services. In early September, most major towns had a strong retail and services sector offering a remarkably diverse supply of goods and services. Even during the difficult winter months, this sector continued to expand.
>
> (World Bank 2001: 95)

By 2002, there were 54,400 registered businesses in Kosovo, of which 31,220 were companies and 23,192 were 'individual entrepreneurs' (i.e. self-employed) (SOK 2002). Of the total number of companies, 90 per cent were sole proprietors and only 1.6 per cent were limited liability companies. Amongst the company sector, only 13 per cent employed more than five workers, while among the self-employed, only 5 per cent employed five workers or more. Just over half the businesses operated in the trade sector, while only 10 per cent of companies and 8.5 per cent of the self-employed were active in manufacturing. Kosovo's small enterprises have had to contend with many difficulties, including an unreliable energy supply which leads to frequent power cuts, a large informal economy and difficulties in forging linkages to the European and global markets which would enable small businesses to expand their exports. According to the director of a local organization supporting the development of SMEs:

> Almost all businesses Kosovo are small scale family businesses, but only a few of the larger companies to which the small businesses could previously sell their products are active. The former socially-owned companies are now largely defunct, and one of the main problems facing the Kosovo

economy is that almost all goods are imported. The people of Kosovo are very entrepreneurial which enabled them to survive in the 1990s, but few entrepreneurs think beyond the local market, or are able to compete against the flood of imports.

(Deborah Wahlberg, Kosovo Business Support, Priština, September 2003)

The policy of UNMIK towards the business sector has focused on the privatization of the large socially owned enterprises and has neglected the needs of the small business sector. According to the opinion of a government advisor at the Ministry of Trade and Industry in Priština 2003:

> although there is a dynamic SME sector it has not yet been able to replace the large enterprises which have mainly collapsed. Privatisation has been too long delayed and UNMIK has failed to support the existing businesses which were capable of production.
>
> (Muje Gjonbalaj, Priština, September 2003)

Some international assistance programmes have been active in the field, notably USAID, which has initiated a cluster development programme. The Ministry of Trade and Industry has begun to introduce measures to support the SME sector by adopting a law on SME support in March 2005. The law defined SMEs as companies employing up to fifty workers. It established an SME agency and stipulated that the government should ensure that future legislation should not discriminate against SMEs. It also aimed to reduce bureaucratic barriers and to promote business associations and other civil society organizations in order to develop the support infrastructure necessary to stimulate SME formation and growth.

7   Growth, employment and trade

At the onset of transition, the republics of former Yugoslavia shared a common institutional framework based on decentralized market socialism, which differed fundamentally from Albania's highly centralized version of a socialist planned economy. While managers and workers in former Yugoslavia had experience of markets, Albanian managers and workers had no prior experience of the market economy, and consequently their adjustment to the shock of transition was more difficult. The institutions that supported the transition were also more advanced in the former Yugoslavia than in Albania. Variations in such initial conditions were important determinants of differences in response to the opportunities that were opened up by institutional reform, and therefore in the pace of economic growth.

Although initial conditions have an important influence, successful institutional reforms can overcome the barriers to growth which they impose. Following the break-up of Yugoslavia, the early reformers had pushed ahead with the transition policies that had been initiated under the Marković government, while limited reforms were also introduced in Albania in the final stages of the Communist regime. The reforms were deepened following the collapse of the communist regimes. They involved the creation of an institutional framework to support a market economy; reforms to the legal system, the system of property rights and the ownership of enterprises; and the creation of an economic environment favourable to the development of the private business sector. All these changes provided a stimulus to economic growth, and the early reformers which liberalized their economies sooner, and to a greater degree, than did the later reformers gained an advantage. Together with the variation in initial conditions, variations in the pace and nature of institutional reforms between countries all contributed to differences in the rate of economic growth (Bartlett and Hoggett 1996).

The distinction between initial conditions and reform policy has been observed in all the transition economies, and empirical studies have shown that the effects of some aspects of initial conditions on economic growth can be substantial. One early study found that countries with higher initial macroeconomic imbalances had lower subsequent rates of growth after the onset of transition, whereas initial differences in levels of development did not have any noticeable effect on growth (de Melo *et al.* 2001). The same study also found that, following a negative initial impact, liberalizing reforms have a positive long-run effect on growth and that the effect of reforms is stronger, the more adverse are the initial conditions. Over time, the impact of initial conditions inevitably diminishes and the positive impact of reforms comes to the fore (Falcetti *et al.* 2006). Thus, in Serbia and Montenegro, the anti-reform coalition which initially resisted reforms eventually lost influence as the extent of the losses which the majority had suffered from blocked reforms became apparent, and the pro-reform coalition which came to power after 2000 was able to make rapid progress with reform from that time on. Applying the calculus of winners and losers to the Western Balkans, the early reformers who braved the cost of reform enjoyed a growth premium, with Albania gaining even more than others because of the adverse initial conditions from which it set out.[1] In contrast, the late reform countries, where anti-reform coalitions were able to mobilize blocking majorities from among the potential losers, suffered a growth penalty.

Of course, growth performance cannot be related solely to the issues of initial conditions and the pace of reforms. Investment, the development of new skills, the transfer of new knowledge and an opening to foreign trade and international markets all have an important role to play. This chapter traces the outcomes of all these factors on the growth performance of the Western Balkans, focusing on the overall growth of GDP, industrial production, employment and productivity, taking into account the different phasing of reform in the early and late reforming countries. The last section of the chapter pays special attention to the role of reforms which have liberalized foreign trade and payments, which for small open economies is a further important determinant of their overall growth performance.

Economic growth

Three phases of economic growth can be identified in the Western Balkans since the late 1980s. In the first phase, countries followed their own national transition policies, with each following a set of policies determined by the political decisions of the ruling elites but constrained by the initial economic, political and institutional conditions which they faced. This phase was typically marked by partial reforms and a strong involvement of the state, for example in the banking sector. The second phase, which began after the 1995 Dayton agreement, was marked by the need for post-conflict reconstruction and development and the inflow of massive international assistance. International donors, especially the World Bank sought to guide policy in the direction of a more liberal pro-market model of capitalist development. The third phase, which developed most strongly after 2000, involved a turn towards European integration and a much more focused involvement by the EU which offered a membership perspective to the region, and developed specific pre-accession assistance programmes. Policies became more focused on harmonization of legislation to the EU social market model of capitalist development.

These three phases did not occur simultaneously in each of the countries, and were often overlapping even within an individual country. Early reformers were more successful in the transition phase and in promoting their own national models of capitalist development, although this was not without setbacks and difficulties. Croatia has made a transition towards a set of institutions similar to the Central European corporatist model of capitalism, while Albania and Macedonia have turned towards a more liberal model of capitalism promoted by the IMF and the World Bank. The late reformers, especially BiH and Serbia, have not yet made strong progress into the European integration phase, unlike early reformers who have advanced more rapidly in this third phase, building on their more successful prior transition policies and post-conflict reconstruction programmes.

Transitional recession and recovery

All economies that adopted stabilization policies in the transition from socialism to capitalism experienced initial output falls as individuals and enterprises adjusted to the new institutions and policies (Kornai 1993). In centrally planned economies, the collapse of the planning system brought about a period of disorganization as enterprises searched out new sources of supply in the emerging market (Blanchard 1997). Privatization and enterprise restructuring involved an inevitable fall in output as old inefficient activities were closed down. It also took time for new businesses to enter the market and to provide jobs to workers laid off from the declining or restructuring old enterprises.

The Western Balkan countries were no different in this respect than most other transition economies. In former Yugoslavia, output fell between 1989 and 1991 under the Marković stabilization policies as the economy adjusted to the new policies, even before the break-up of Yugoslavia, the onset of the armed conflicts and the imposition of sanctions on FRY. These factors deepened and prolonged the transitional recessions in the Yugoslav successor states, although they were not the only or even the initiating factors. Rather, it was the response of the elites in the different republics to the reform process, and especially the mobilization of ethnic antagonisms by the anti-reform coalitions, which brought about the conflict in the first place. Therefore, the collapse in GDP and in industrial production should not be seen as the outcome of a spontaneous eruption of ethnic conflict, but as part of a long process of institutional reform, and the responses of the various elite coalitions to reform policies. Between 1989 and 1991, GDP fell by 16 per cent in Macedonia, by 19 per cent in Serbia and Montenegro and by 27 per cent in Croatia – which was also affected by the 1991 war on its territory. Albania, where the communist regime had began to introduce cautious reforms and where bad harvests contributed to the downturn, suffered the most severe transition recession with a fall in GDP of 35 per cent between 1989 and 1991, although output began to recover soon after (Figure 7.1).

The dissolution of Yugoslavia and the outbreak of war in 1991 in Croatia further deepened the economic collapse. The sharpest fall was in FRY where

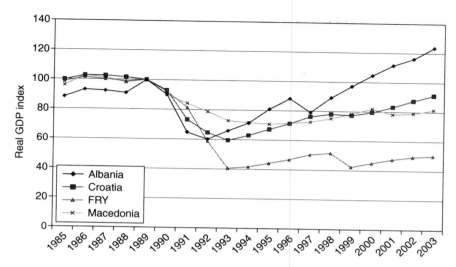

Figure 7.1 Real GDP index, 1985–2003 (1989 = 100) (source: UNECE Economic Survey of Europe 1999(1) and 2005(1)).

GDP dropped by 28 per cent in 1992, and by a further 31 per cent in 1993, reflecting the adverse impact of stalled reforms and hyperinflation which undermined the economy, as well as the effects of UN sanctions (Popović 1997). The transition recessions were relatively short-lived in Albania, Croatia and FRY, with a trough in 1992 in Albania and in 1993 in Croatia and FRY. The Macedonian recession, although relatively shallow, lasted longer and, together with BiH where the recession was deepest due to war, began to recover only in 1995. Overall, the early reformers had relatively shallow transitional recessions, with GDP falling to lows of 60 per cent of the 1989 level in Albania and Croatia at their troughs and 71 per cent in Macedonia. In contrast, the late reformers had much more severe recessions, with GDP in FRY falling to just 41 per cent of the previous level at the trough in 1993.

Economic growth after Dayton, 1995–9

By 1995, the final year of the Bosnian war, economic recovery was established in Albania, Croatia and FRY. Economic growth also began to pick up in BiH which had been devastated by the war, the strength of the recovery reflecting the catastrophically low base to which the country had been reduced. In Macedonia, where the recession had been long but shallow, growth resumed only in 1996.

Despite the growth bounce-backs, the partial nature of the institutional reforms, even in the early reformers, led to setbacks and crises in each country which were manifested in various ways. The first crisis occurred in Albania where the collapse of the pyramid banks caused a sharp fall in GDP in 1997.

Croatia experienced a similar financial crisis in 1998 with the collapse of several medium-sized domestic banks caused by politically connected lending to unprofitable local businesses. Within a few years, almost the entire Croatian banking sector had been taken over by foreign banking groups from Italy and Austria. In FRY, sanctions were partially re-imposed in mid-1998 in the form of bans on new investment and financial transactions, the EU revoked its trade preferences and economic growth came to a halt. The 1999 NATO bombing campaign against infrastructure and industrial facilities led to a sharp fall in real GDP. In Macedonia, the early phase of recovery from the transition recession which had begun in 1996 was disrupted by the civil conflict of 2001.

Economic growth after 2000

Following the end of the Kosovo war, and the democratic changes in Croatia and FRY in 2000, the Western Balkan economies entered a period of more or less sustained recovery. Economic growth was relatively strong compared to performance over the previous decade, averaging 4.3 per cent per annum from 2000 to 2005 (Table 7.1). Albania returned the most spectacular growth, averaging 58 per cent over the same period, although this was based largely on labour export and remittance income rather than on a resurgence of domestic production.

By 2005, GDP growth in region was proceeding at rates above those in the EU including most of the new EU member states from Eastern Europe (Sanfey *et al.* 2004). Serbia and Montenegro recorded a high growth rate of 8.8 per cent in 2004 and 6.0 per cent in 2005. BiH has recorded consistent performance with growth averaging 5.3 per cent, while Croatia experienced a dip in growth in 2004 following monetary tightening in the face of growing external indebtedness. The picture has been different only in Kosovo, which has experienced negative growth due to reduced international assistance and the failure of

Table 7.1 GDP growth rate, 2000–5 (%)

	2000	*2001*	*2002*	*2003*	*2004*	*2005*	*Average 2000–5*
Albania	7.3	7.2	2.9	5.7	5.9	5.5	5.8
BiH	5.5	4.3	5.3	4.4	6.2	5.3	5.2
Croatia	2.9	4.4	5.2	4.3	3.8	4.3	4.2
Macedonia	4.5	−4.5	0.9	2.8	4.1	4.0	2.0
Serbia-Montenegro	5.0	5.5	4.3	2.4	8.8	6.0	5.3
Montenegro	–	–	–	–	–	4.3	–
Kosovo	–	16.1	−2.9	−1.4	3.7	−0.5	3.0
All transition countries	6.0	4.3	3.9	5.7	6.6	5.3	5.3

Sources: Albania, BiH, Serbia and Montenegro: World Bank online database; Croatia, Macedonia, Bulgaria, Romania and Slovenia: European Commission 2006 and European Economy Number 2; Montenegro: IMF; Kosovo: DG-ECFIN 2005 and IMF.

the UNMIK authorities and the PISG government to implement effective reforms of the economy. Projections for 2006 and 2007 indicate a potential for sustained growth throughout the region, with significant improvements in Macedonia.

Despite rapid economic growth since 2000, the countries of the Western Balkans have only just begun to make up the ground lost in the 1990s. By 2003, Albania was the only country which had surpassed the level it achieved in 1989, while none of the Yugoslav successor states had recovered their previous level of real GDP. Taking 1989 as a benchmark year, by 2003, Croatia and Macedonia had made the strongest recovery, reaching 91 per cent and 81 per cent of previous level of GDP respectively, while Serbia-Montenegro had only reached 50 per cent of its previous level of GDP.[2] Overall, the early reformers have recovered more successfully from the various shocks of the 1990s than the late reformers. While there have been differences in extent and timing, the analysis of the overall patterns of economic activity over the last fifteen years bear out the argument that reforms are an important predictor of economic success in post-transition, post-conflict countries. Thus, while the legacy of the past as indicated by initial conditions is important, its impact diminishes over time, and it therefore does not impose fundamental barriers to countries in catching up with their more advanced peers.

Figures 7.2–7.5 show the relationship between reforms and growth for four of the Western Balkan countries for which data is available over the period from 1991 to 2004. The extent of reforms is measured by the EBRD reform index which is a synthetic index of reforms along several dimensions of institutional change.[3] The figures show that among the early reforming countries – Albania,

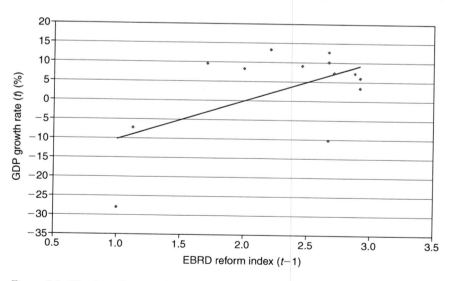

Figure 7.2 Albania: reforms and growth, 1991–2004 (source: UNECE Economic Survey of Europe 2005 and EBRD online data).

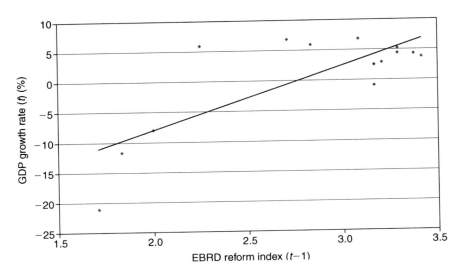

Figure 7.3 Croatia: reforms and growth, 1991–2004 (source: UNECE Economic Survey of Europe 2005 and EBRD online data).

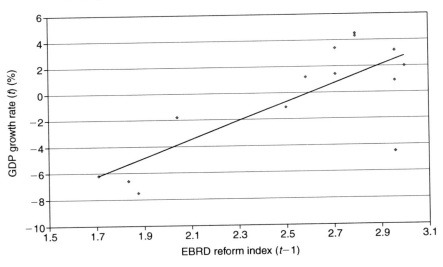

Figure 7.4 Macedonia: reforms and growth, 1991–2004 (source: UNECE Economic Survey of Europe 2005 and EBRD online data).

Croatia and Macedonia – institutional reforms have been positively related to the rate of GDP growth, with a one-year lag. In the late reformers for which data are available, Serbia and Montenegro, there is no observable relation between reforms and growth. This is partly because there were few reform changes in the 1990s, but even taking into account only the period since reforms began in 2000,

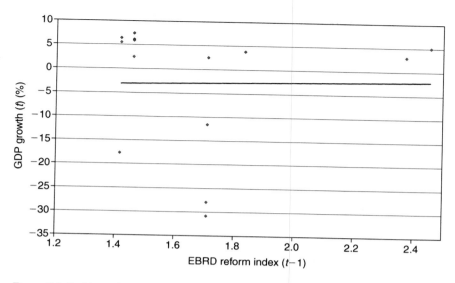

Figure 7.5 Serbia and Montenegro: reforms and growth, 1991–2004 (source: UNECE Economic Survey of Europe 2005 and EBRD online data).

there has been no noticeable impact on growth. Indeed, for the years from 2000 to 2004, the relationship turns out to be negative. This may reflect difficulties in implementation or, alternatively, it may indicate that the lingering impact of adverse initial institutional conditions have imposed a drag on growth despite reforms.

Deindustrializaton

The severity of the economic collapse in the first phase of the transition was further reflected in an intense and rapid process of deindustrialization which took place between 1989 and 1991. The decline in industrial production was initiated by the stabilization programme in former Yugoslavia, and the collapse of the central planning system in Albania, commencing prior to the break-up of Yugoslavia and the subsequent armed conflicts of the early 1990s. Only BiH managed to sustain its industrial production into 1990, but even there, industrial production fell sharply in the following year (Figure 7.6). Deindustrialization was most severe in Albania where industrial production dropped by half between 1989 and 1991. In Macedonia, BiH and FRY, industrial production declined by around a quarter over the two years. In Croatia, industrial production fell by 11 per cent between 1989 and 1990, before the onset of the war on its territory in 1991 which naturally worsened the decline, and by the end of 1991, Croatia's industrial production had fallen by more than any of the other Yugoslav successor states.

In the subsequent years between 1992 and 1995, industrial production

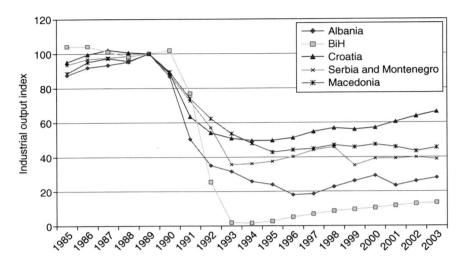

Figure 7.6 Industrial output index, 1985–2003 (1989 = 100) (source: Derived from UNECE Economic Survey of Europe 1999(1) and 2004(2)).

continued to fall by a further third in Albania and Macedonia due to the ongoing process of transition. In FRY where industrial production had fallen to only one-third of its earlier level, the continuing slump was worsened by the imposition of UN sanctions. In BiH, all-out warfare led to a complete collapse of industrial capacity and by 1994, industrial production had practically ceased altogether.

The decline in industrial production reached a trough at different times in each country – in 1993 in FRY, in 1994 in Croatia and BiH, in 1995 in Macedonia and not until 1996 in Albania. The subsequent recoveries were also very different. By 2003, two of the early reformers, Croatia and Macedonia, had recovered most, with industrial production in Croatia at two-thirds of its previous level and on an upwards trajectory, while in Macedonia, industrial production stopped falling but stagnated at around half its previous level. Albanian industrial production never recovered from the shock of transition and stagnated at just over one-quarter of its previous level. In FRY, the incipient recovery after the Dayton agreement and the lifting of sanctions was set back by the NATO bombing campaign of 1999, hovering at around two-fifths of its 1989 level thereafter. In BiH, industrial production has recovered only slightly from the shock of war, and by 2003 was still only 14 per cent of the level achieved in 1989.

In contrast to the pattern of GDP, industrial production change did not divide neatly into the early and late reform typology. Industrial production in Albania suffered a far more damaging transition shock than in FRY, even though the latter was subjected to damaging sanctions and military attack. Albanian policy makers never managed to introduce effective structural policies that were capable of rebuilding the industrial capacity that had been lost in the 1990s by the decline of the old state-owned industries, and the disruption following the collapse of the pyramid savings banks. The legacy of the past and the role of initial institutional conditions had a particularly strong impact on the industrial sector in Albania, since under central planning the development of industry had been far more irrational than in market-socialist Yugoslavia. A prime example was the large steel mill that had been built in Elbasan in the 1980s with Chinese assistance, but which was unable to continue production after the fall of communism due to its poorly conceived location far inland away from any major port. Policies, embodied in the pace of reform, were unable to overturn this historical inheritance.

Employment and productivity

The sharp declines in GDP and industrial production were matched by equivalent but shallower reductions in employment. In former Yugoslavia, a gradual decline in employment levels began in 1988 under the Marković reform programme. By 1991, when Yugoslavia broke up, employment levels had fallen by 10 per cent or more in BiH, Croatia and Macedonia, compared to the 1989 level, while the decline in employment was slower in Serbia and Montenegro which resisted the Marković reform programme (Figure 7.7). In the Yugoslav successor states, the output fall of the 1990s had only a muted impact on the labour market, as jobs were preserved through subsidies and strong employment protection legislation. Reductions in employment were initially achieved by encouraging early retirement and by the natural attrition of the workforce. In some

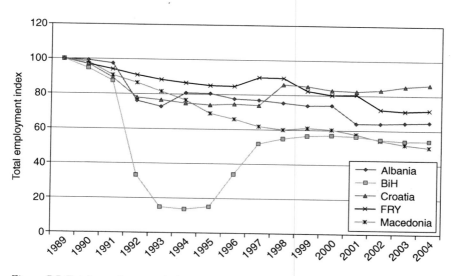

Figure 7.7 Total employment index, 1989–2004 (1989=100) (source: Derived from UNECE Economic Survey of Europe, various years).

cases, managers and skilled workers left the collapsing state firms to set up their own businesses. This was a common escape route in the early 1990s when many thousands of new small firms were established, but the economic downturn affected them too, and only a minority survived more than a few years as going concerns.

The picture was different in Albania where there was a sharp drop in employment after the collapse of the communist regime. Although there was no previous experience on unemployment under communism in Albania, workers had less employment protection than in the former Yugoslavia. When subsidies to state-owned enterprises were slashed in 1991, the impact on employment was immediate, and thousands of mainly unskilled workers were thrown out of their jobs. When central planning collapsed, unemployment shot up to 27 per cent in the space of a couple of years.

In FRY, lay-offs in socially owned industries were prohibited following the imposition of sanctions in 1992, leading to the growth of surplus labour and hidden unemployment within socially owned enterprises. Many workers were put on 'paid vacation' as there was no work to be carried out in their factories. Employment nevertheless continued to decline gradually apart from a brief upturn from 1996 to 1998, before falling sharply between 1998 and 1999 due the adverse impact of the Kosovo war on industrial production. A further shake-out in employment took place in 2001–2 as a result of the restructuring and privatization programme implemented by the new pro-reform coalition government.

In BiH, there was a sudden collapse of employment in 1992 due to the war and to forced migrations, and by 1994, employment had fallen to just one-fifth of its previous level before partially recovering in the two years following the end of the war. Employment levels in Macedonia had also fallen to relatively low levels by the end of the 1990s. Since then, employment increased only in Croatia where new job creation has taken place, although by 2004, employment was still only 86 per cent of its 1989 level.

The weak relationship between employment growth and GDP growth in several of the Western Balkan countries is demonstrated by a regression analysis performed on panel data for the period 1990–2004. The results for the country slope coefficients reveal a positive relationship between output and employment growth in Albania, Croatia and Macedonia, in which a one percentage point increase in GDP growth is associated with an approximately 0.4 percentage point increase in employment growth (Table 7.2). In Macedonia, the negative intercept indicates that a substantial increase in GDP growth is needed to trigger growth in employment,[4] reflecting the role of the informal economy in absorbing fluctuations in economic activity and the collapse of the large enterprises in the formal economy. In the case of Serbia and Montenegro (taken as the baseline), there is no relationship between output growth and employment growth, reflecting the delayed transition to a market economy. The Milošević regime had preserved unproductive jobs in the socially owned enterprises on a large scale, and employment levels only began to fall following the institutional reforms introduced by the new government which came to power at the end of 2000.

Table 7.2 The relationship between GDP growth and employment growth

Dependent variable (employment growth)	Coefficients	t-statistic	Significance level
Constant	−0.486	−0.448	0.656
GDP growth $(t-1)$	−0.111	−0.853	0.398
Country intercepts			
Albania	−1.735	−1.222	0.227
Croatia	−0.908	−0.669	0.506
Macedonia	−3.465	−2.449	0.018**
Country slopes			
Albania	0.406	3.261	0.002***
Croatia	0.371	2.503	0.016**
Macedonia	0.437	1.928	0.060*
$[\text{GDP growth } (t-1)]^2$	−0.009	−1.700	0.095*
Adjusted R^2	0.373		
Durbin-Watson	1.914		

Source: UNECE database.

Note
Statistical significance: *** 1%; ** 5%; * 10%.

Despite substantial employment protection, the level of employment in the industrial sector gradually fell in all the countries as deindustrialization took hold. In Croatia and Macedonia, industrial employment fell by more than industrial production, reflecting the greater restructuring of the economy during early transition. In contrast, in FRY, the government attempted to buy social peace by maintaining employment levels in old industries, minimizing the amount of economic restructuring that took place.

Industrial productivity fell following the early stabilization programmes as employers avoided laying off workers, even though output was falling sharply. The fall in productivity was relatively shallow in Croatia and Macedonia, reaching its lowest point between 1993 and 1994 before recovering (Figure 7.8). In Croatia, productivity surpassed its previous level in 2001. FRY experienced deep falls in productivity, and although productivity began to recover in 1993, by 2002, it was still less than two-thirds of the level achieved in 1990. Productivity did not turn around in Albania until after the introduction of the 1997 stabilization programme, and has been the slowest to recover. Overall, the productivity pattern tells a compelling story. Productivity growth has been strongest in the early reformers of former Yugoslavia and slowest in the late reformers. Albania is an exception, as the initial institutional conditions were so different and have clearly had a long-lasting impact.

The informal labour market

The informal economy, which comprises both private unregistered firms and undeclared work in registered firms, is widespread in the Western Balkans since

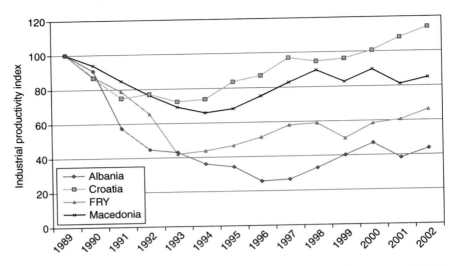

Figure 7.8 Industrial productivity index, 1989–2002 (1989=100) (source: UNECE Economic Survey of Europe, various years, own calculation).

many employers avoid paying social insurance contributions. In contrast to the strong employment protection for workers in the formal economy, the informal economy is characterized by a high degree of flexibility. However, it imposes a number of externalities and social costs on the formal economy: it places a burden of unfair competition upon formal firms, reducing their profitability and their demand for labour; it deprives the government of tax revenue which could be used for social expenditures; and it imposes costs on workers who are deprived of social protection, health and safety protection and access to government training programmes. There are several causes of the phenomenon. The lack of job creation in the formal sector has pushed unemployed people into informal activity to make a subsistence income, while employers have embraced informality to avoid restrictive regulations. Lack of trust in formal institutions also plays an important role in pushing both employers and workers into the informal economy. The PHARE-ACE survey[5] found that entrepreneurs in BiH are more likely to base their business dealings on the 'strong ties' of interpersonal trust in known business partners in the informal economy, than the 'weak ties' of institutional trust in anonymous business partners in the formal economy (Rus and Iglič 2005).

Informal economic activity is notoriously difficult to measure, although statistical offices make estimates of it in compiling official measures of GDP. Various independent studies have come to different conclusions about the extent of informal economic activity in the Western Balkan countries. The most straightforward method has been to estimate the share of undeclared household income using estimates of taxes that would be due given observed consumption, compared to taxes actually paid on declared income (Christie and Holzner 2004). Calculating this for data from 2001, Edward Christie and Mario Holzner found that Albania has the highest share of informal economic activity with 52 per cent of household income being undeclared and that Kosovo and Macedonia also have a high share at 45 per cent and 39 per cent respectively. These levels of informal activity are significantly higher than in RS with 26 per cent and Montenegro at 27 per cent, while FBiH, Serbia and Croatia have the lowest levels at 18–19 per cent. If these estimates are accurate, they suggest that the extent of informal activity has a strong geographical and cultural component, being higher in the south of the region than in the north, and also associated with the level of economic development, and hence initial institutional conditions, rather than with subsequent policy developments. However, estimates of the extent of the informal economy vary widely. The OECD has carried out a careful study of the informal economy in Albania and concluded that it accounts for about 26 per cent of GDP, excluding agriculture (OECD 2004). For Croatia, Katarina Ott estimated that the informal economy had been substantially reduced since the early 1990s when it accounted for over 30 per cent of GDP and had fallen to about 7 per cent of GDP by 2000 (Ott 2002).

Labour Inspectorates operate in all countries of the Western Balkans to combat the informal economy by monitoring the effective implementation of the labour and employment laws, inspecting health and safety arrangements at work and identifying unregistered labour and avoidance of social contributions. However, the Labour Inspectorates are underfunded and underequipped, and the inspectors themselves are underpaid, leaving them vulnerable to bribes from informal economy employers. In RS in 2002, the Labour Inspectorate introduced an amnesty for employers, under which they would be obliged to pay just one-fifth of the owed contributions if they regularized their employees' status. In that year, the inflow of social contributions to the pension fund increased by almost a third, but since it was a temporary measure, the progress has not been sustained. The inspectorate failed to close down any of the non-conforming companies because of delays and costs associated with court procedures.[6]

Falling participation rates

Participation rates have fallen as workers laid off from old socially owned and state-owned enterprises have dropped out of the labour market. Many of the unemployed, especially women and older people, simply left the labour force, while early retirement was also used to reduce employment levels of over-staffed enterprises. All this led to falling participation rates, which in 2004 ranged from 68 per cent in Serbia to 46 per cent in Kosovo, compared to over 70 per cent in the EU-15. The relatively high participation rate in Serbia is due to the delayed transition process, and can be expected to fall as institutional reforms lead to enterprise restructuring, while the participation rate for young people, at just 36 per cent, is much below the national average, reflecting the very low level of new job creation (World Bank 2004c). Participation rates are also low in Macedonia, but vary by ethnicity and gender, with the participation rate for Albanian women at just 11 per cent in 2000, compared to 51 per cent for Macedonian women (ETF 2005a).

Albania also has a relatively high participation rate, at 66 per cent, partly due to massive out-migration of active workers in search of work abroad. About 1 million Albanians have emigrated since the early 1990s in search of work (ETF 2006a), mainly to Greece and Italy, and their remittances have made a substantial contribution to the economy. Moreover, many migrant workers return home and bring newly acquired skills with them, and in many cases establish new small businesses. In contrast to Albania's experience of out-migration, Serbia has experienced a substantial inflow of labour, including mainly ethnic Serb refugees who have left, or been expelled from, BiH, Croatia and Kosovo. It is estimated that there are around half a million refugees and internally displaced persons in Serbia who are specially disadvantaged on the labour market.

Unemployment

The Yugoslav successor states inherited labour markets with already high levels of unemployment. Labour force adjustment has continued to be a difficult aspect of the transition process, since the successor states inherited a set of employment laws which protected incumbent workers and led to low rates of labour force turnover. Workers who lost their jobs through restructuring or privatization found it hard to find a new job in the formal sector. Unemployment has also had a pronounced regional dimension with some localities experiencing intense economic decline. There are many unemployment black spots, for example, in South Serbia, North-East Montenegro and Eastern Slavonia.[7] In contrast, there was previously no official unemployment in Albania's centrally planned economy where unemployment was not recognized, and the transition was marked by a sudden increase in unemployment due to weak job protection in the formal sector following the collapse of central planning.

Registered unemployment in the Yugoslav successor states remained high throughout the 1990s. However, data on registered unemployment over-estimate its true level, since many people who work in the informal economy, or who have left the labour force, have a strong incentive to register as unemployed in order to qualify for health insurance payments. In Croatia, registered unemployment peaked at 23 per cent in 2001 before falling to 19 per cent by 2003, while in FRY, registered unemployment hovered around 25 per cent in the 1990s and increased to 28 per cent in 2003. Registered unemployment reached extremely high levels in BiH and Kosovo, at 44 per cent and 50 per cent respectively by 2003. In Albania, incentives to register went in the opposite direction, since unemployment benefit payments were extremely low and eligibility requirements were tight. After peaking at 27 per cent in 1992, a combination of economic growth and mass emigration soon reduced the level of unemployment to an average of 16 per cent between 1995 and 2003.

A better measure of the real level of unemployment can be gleaned from the

Labour Force Surveys (LFS) which have been carried out in a number of countries according to standard criteria developed by the International Labour Organisation (ILO). In Croatia, according to the LFS, the unemployment rate in 2005 was just over 12 per cent, more than four percentage points below the registered rate, having fallen for several years as economic growth had begun to create jobs (Table 7.3). In Serbia and Montenegro, the LFS unemployment rate remained steady at around 13 per cent in the 1990s and began to increase in 2001 as post-Milošević institutional reforms led to lay-offs associated with enterprise restructuring. In Serbia, the unemployment rate increased from 12 per cent in 2001 to 21 per cent in 2006.[8] The unemployment rate is highest in Kosovo, at a disastrously high level of nearly 41 per cent, followed closely by Macedonia where it is 37 per cent. In BiH, the unemployment rate was 22 per cent in 2004 according to the Household Panel Survey (24 per cent in RS and 21 per cent in FBiH). In Albania, registered unemployment, at 14 per cent, corresponds more closely to the LFS measure since there is no incentive to register to obtain health insurance.

Unemployment in most countries adversely affects the younger sections of the population due to the low level of job openings and the relatively strong protection of insider employees. Youth unemployment among the 15–24 age group is extremely high in the Yugoslav successor states, ranging from 69 per cent in Kosovo in 2002 (La Cava et al. 2005) and 66 per cent in Macedonia in 2003 (ETF 2005a). Youth unemployment rate is also high in Montenegro at 51 per cent (ETF 2005b), in BiH at 42 per cent in 2004 (ETF 2006b) and in Serbia at 34 per cent in 2002 (La Cava et al. 2005). Youth unemployment is lower at 16 per cent in Albania (ETF 2006a), probably due to out-migration.

An alarming feature of the labour market in the Western Balkans has been the high proportion of long-term unemployed, which has led to the deterioration and obsolescence of the skills base of sections of the labour force. The share of the unemployed who had been out of work for more than one year in 2002 reached 85 per cent in Macedonia (World Bank 2003c), 72 per cent in Serbia and 85 per cent in Montenegro (World Bank 2005b). Studies of labour market flows in the region have found very low rates of exit from unemployment to formal sector

Table 7.3 Unemployment rates, 1996–2005 (%)

	1996	1997	1998	1999	2000	2001	2002	2003	2004	2005
Albania	12.4	14.9	17.8	18.4	16.8	16.4	15.8	15.2	14.4	14.2
Croatia	10.0	9.9	11.4	13.5	16.1	15.8	14.8	14.3	13.8	12.3
Macedonia	31.9	36.0	34.5	32.4	32.2	30.5	31.9	36.7	37.2	37.3
Serbia and Montenegro	13.2	13.8	13.7	13.7	12.6	12.8	13.8	15.2	–	–
Serbia	–	–	–	–	12.1	12.2	13.3	14.6	18.5	20.8
Montenegro	21.9	23.5	25.7	27.3	27.8	24.8	–	–	–	30.5
Kosovo	–	–	–	–	–	57.1	55.0	49.7	39.7	41.4

Sources: Labour Force Survey data for Croatia, Serbia and Montenegro, Serbia and Macedonia; for Kosovo, based on LSMS survey data, Labour Market Statistics 2005, Statistical Office of Kosovo, Prishtina; household survey data for Montenegro (1996–207701) from Montenegro Economic Trends, 12, ISSP Podgorica; official registered unemployment data for Albania, INSTAT, Tirana.

employment. In Croatia, job-to-job flows within the formal sector, and flows out of the labour force into inactivity, dominate the labour market, while flows out of unemployment into formal employment are sluggish (Crnković-Pozaić 2005). The loss of skills due to long-term unemployment presents a challenge to policy makers seeking to reintegrate the unemployed into the labour market.

Labour market policies

Policies to deal with high unemployment have mainly focused on passive measures to provide income support to unemployed people, while active measures to get people back into work have only recently been introduced in some countries. Budgetary restrictions have however meant that the duration, coverage and level of unemployment benefits are generally low. Despite long formal maximum periods, the average duration of unemployment benefit in the Western Balkans is below the EU average. Apart from Croatia, unemployment benefit replacement rates are also below the EU average, and the coverage rate (the share of unemployed receiving benefits) is low and falling[9] due to increasing proportions of long-term unemployed (Micevska 2004). In Albania, for example, the coverage of unemployment benefit was just 8 per cent in 2003. Moreover, passive policies, including both unemployment compensation and social assistance, have become less generous over time (Arandareko 2004). In Serbia, although unemployment benefits account for 85 per cent of the expenditure of the Employment Service, it only covers 81,000 unemployed people, so that despite significant expenditure in relation to available resources, the benefits do not meet demand for assistance. Under such circumstances, the unemployment benefit system can hardly be thought to provide disincentives to job search by the unemployed.

In Albania, open unemployment was not permitted under the communist system, although there was disguised unemployment in state enterprises. With the rapid adoption of the market economy, many workers were laid off from restructured and privatized enterprises, and unemployment rapidly increased. An Unemployment Benefit and Social Assistance Act was passed in January 1992, and unemployment insurance was introduced in 1993 covering all employees in the public and private sectors (Xhumari 2004). However, the flat-rate unemployment benefit hardly provides for a minimum living standard. Owing to budgetary limitations, benefits were not indexed between 1993 and 2003, although they have since been increased annually in line with the price index. At the start, benefits were equal to the minimum state pension, but by 2003, the benefit was just 3,960 lek per month (€32) compared to the minimum state pension of 6,728 lek per month (€55).

The World Bank has been influential in promoting the view that employment protection legislation (EPL) is a prime source of labour market rigidities in the Western Balkans, and has campaigned for institutional reforms that would reduce the role of government in collective bargaining, strengthen the voice of employers, decentralize bargaining to firm level, increase flexibility in minimum wage setting, reduce minimum wages, liberalize the use of temporary employment contracts and improve enforcement of EPL by reinforcing labour inspectorates (Rutkowski and Scarpetta 2005). An earlier influential World Bank study argued that strong EPL had reduced the flexibility of the labour market in Croatia and contributed to high levels of unemployment (Rutkowski 2003).

In response to this policy advice, EPL has been weakened over the last decade in several countries. The advice was taken up in Croatia, where amendments to the Employment Law were adopted in 2003 to increase the flexibility of the labour market and reduce employment protection. The main changes included a relaxation on the use of fixed-term contracts that has made part-time work and temporary work possible; a reduction in the pre-conditions for valid dismissals; a shortening of the notice period for dismissal from six to three months; a reduction in the amount of severance pay; a relaxation in the definition of mass lay-offs; and an increase in the retirement age. These institutional reforms have significantly liberalized the labour market (Šošić 2005). Serbia and Montenegro had already passed new labour laws in 2001. The measures introduced new labour standards including the freedom of association and participation in collective bargaining while also reducing employment protection. Employers were able to more easily terminate employment, hiring procedures were simplified and rights to paid leave and maternity benefits were restricted. In 2003, a new Employment Law in Serbia liberalized employers' ability to make redundancies and significantly reduced job security. It reduced entitlement to unemployment benefit and cut the replacement rate to 60 per cent of the average wage in the final three months of employment, falling to 50 per cent after three months' unemployment (Arandarenko 2003: 39).

More recently, the EU integration process has brought new policy initiatives and support for labour market reforms in the region, in line with the European Employment Strategy (EES). Since the publication of the Kok report (Kok 2003), the EU has promoted employment growth to the top of its economic policy agenda. Within the revised EES, the European Commission has set out Employment Guidelines on the basis of which member states are required to produce national action plans for employment. The guidelines lay a heavy stress on full employment, the quality of jobs, social and territorial cohesion, inclusive labour markets, employment security, social dialogue and training. Although the Western Balkans states are not involved directly in this process, they are nevertheless being drawn into it as part of their gradual alignment with EU policies. In 2004, the European Commission formulated a set of 'European Partnership' documents, spelling out policy priorities for EU integration, which prioritized the development of employment strategies, and in response, Croatia, Macedonia and Serbia developed national action plans in accordance with the Employment Guidelines. National Action Plans for Employment have been adopted by Macedonia for 2004–5, by Croatia for 2005–8 and by both Macedonia and Serbia for 2006–8. These national action plans embody the EU priorities for more regulated labour markets and to a significant extent work against the liberalizing labour market policies recommended by the World Bank.

International economic performance

An important aim of labour market reforms has been to improve the international competitiveness of export industries, which until recently had been unable to make much progress on the international markets. The Western Balkan economies are all relatively small by European standards, and so exports represent an important driver of growth. The population of the region, at 24 million, is 5 per cent of the EU population, while GDP at €50 billion is equivalent to just 0.4 per cent of that in the EU. International trade and openness to the wider European and global economy is therefore an essential element for their economic development.

An important policy choice facing the newly independent countries in the 1990s was the nature of the exchange rate regime. Countries which fixed their exchange rates to an anchor currency such as the German mark and later the euro, as did Croatia and Macedonia, were more successful at reducing inflation than countries which allowed their currencies to float as did Albania and FRY.[10] Some countries went further and fixed their exchange rates irrevocably. The Dayton Agreement established the German mark as BiH's official currency, and in 1998, a new currency called the Convertible Mark (KM) was introduced and a currency board was established. The German mark became the official currency in Kosovo in 1999 and in Montenegro in 2000. Both countries switched to the euro in 2002. Some commentators have argued that all the countries of the region should adopt the euro as their official currency in order to insulate their economies from exchange rate risk and to 'influence the political economy' inside the countries and give a boost to growth (Gros and Steinherr 2004: 315). However, growth has, in practice, been more dependent on effective institutional reforms rather than the technical fix which euroization implies. The adoption of a currency board in BiH has stabilized the exchange rate and prices but has not led to a significant improvement in growth performance due to the absence of reforms. Montenegro adopted the euro for political purposes, to emphasize its economic detachment from Serbia, while the currency boards in BiH and the adoption of the euro in Kosovo were linked to the unstable post-conflict situations in which they found themselves at the time.

All the countries of the Western Balkans, with the exception of FRY, achieved exchange rate stability by the mid-1990s (Figure 7.9). The Milošević regime in FRY allowed the dinar to depreciate in an attempt to improve international competitiveness through export price reductions, but this policy proved counter-productive, only stimulating inflation instead of the intended lowering of export prices, and exchange rate stability was only achieved after the new government came to power in FRY in 2000. In those countries which pursued effective stabilization policies, the stable exchange rates that were required to eliminate inflation imposed constraints on the use of monetary policy to stimulate domestic demand. Some countries attempted to use expansionary fiscal policies to stimulate domestic demand, but where this was tried, as in Croatia, it soon led into rising domestic and international debts, and increasing balance of

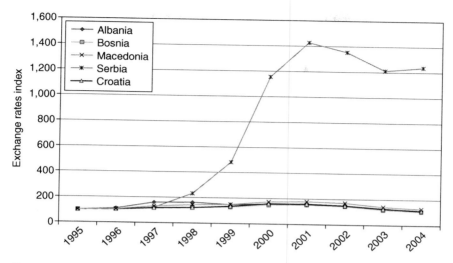

Figure 7.9 Exchange rates index, 1995–2004 (1995 = 100) (source: UNECE Economic Survey of Europe, various years).

payments deficits imposed a constraint on growth. With little leeway to stimulate domestic demand under stabilization policies, increases in growth came to depend on export performance, and hence on improved international competitiveness. This in turn could only be achieved in the wake of institutional reforms which would enable the entry of new firms and improvements in productivity and innovation in all sectors of the economy.

Export performance

In the 1970s and 1980s, former Yugoslavia had been the most open socialist economy in Eastern Europe and Yugoslav enterprises traded extensively with the West, while Albania had been almost completely closed to international trade. Following the break-up of Yugoslavia, the successor states lost ground in traditional export markets, while the wars and conflicts disrupted export capacities. Throughout the 1990s, all the Western Balkan countries had a dismal export performance (Table 7.4). Total exports fell sharply between 1990 and 1995 and only increased by a modest amount by 2000. BiH experienced a near total collapse of trade in the early 1990s due to the effects of war, while sanctions against FRY inevitably caused a steep decline in trade with the outside world. Between 1990 and 2000, the early reformers managed a small increase in the absolute value of their merchandise exports, while exports from the late reformers, BiH and FRY, decreased substantially, falling to less than half the level they had recorded in 1990.

The situation has improved noticeably since 2000, as exports from all the countries have increased sharply, with total exports from the region increasing

Table 7.4 Total merchandise exports, 1990, 1995, 2000 and 2005 ($ million)

Year	Albania	BiH	Croatia	Macedonia	FRY	Total
1990	231	1,850	4,020	1,113	4,651	11,865
1995	202	24	4,633	1,204	1,531	7,594
2000	255	832	4,567	1,321	2,084	9,059
2005	671	2,072	8,992	2,040	6,601	20,376

Sources: UNECE, Economic Survey of Europe 2005 and EBRD online database 2007.

by 72 per cent. Between 2000 and 2006, exports from Albania, BiH and Serbia and Montenegro more than doubled, exports from Croatia increased by 60 per cent and exports from Macedonia increased by 30 per cent.[11] The increases in exports largely reflected the opening of the EU markets due to the autonomous trade preferences that the EU granted to the Western Balkan countries in 2000. By 2006, exports per capita from Croatia had reached $2,026 and from Macedonia were $1,020, but they were far lower at $832 in Montenegro, $620 in Serbia, $545 in BiH and only $210 in Albania. Serbian exports are relatively uncompetitive on foreign markets, being in eighty-seventh place among the 125 countries surveyed by the World Economic Forum in 2007. Kosovo was in an even more precarious situation with total exports in 2003 of just €37 million, against imports of €971 million, financed by aid inflows and overseas remittances. Kosovo's main exports of processed agricultural goods are limited by the low capacity of the processing industry, while other important exports including electric equipment, leather products and clothes are insufficiently competitive to capture a large market share abroad.

Although small economies usually have a relatively high ratio of exports of goods and services to GDP, the export shares in the Western Balkans are still relatively low. The highest export shares are in the EU candidate countries, Croatia and Macedonia, which have export ratios of above 40 per cent of GDP, reflecting their better relationship to the EU markets (Figure 7.10). Albania, BiH and Serbia and Montenegro all had export ratios below 30 per cent of GDP, although Albania's ratio doubled since 1997 and Serbia's increased by a quarter. The worst performance was in BiH, whose share of exports in GDP actually fell.

Owing to their relatively poor export performance in relation to the growth of imports, the Western Balkan states all suffer from persistent current account deficits, despite surpluses on invisibles arising from tourism and migrants remittances (Table 7.5). BiH has by far the largest current account deficit, which has

Table 7.5 Current account deficits (% GDP)

	Croatia	Macedonia	Albania	BiH	FRY
Average 1996–9	−7.7	−6.0	−8.8	−25.6	−6.2
Average 2000–5	−5.3	−5.7	−7.5	−19.3	−8.5

Source: EBRD Transition Report 2005.

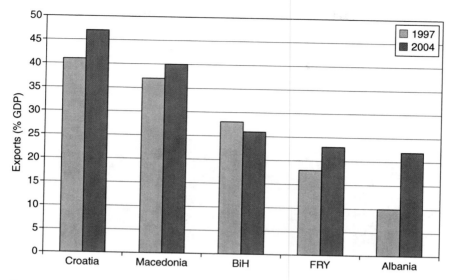

Figure 7.10 Exports of goods and services, 1997 and 2004 (% GDP) (source: World Bank online database 2007).

been covered by donor financial assistance. Its currency board arrangement has prevented exchange rate adjustment, and so the burden of adjustment has to fall on wages and employment, a difficulty which also faces Kosovo and Montenegro which have adopted the euro as their official currencies. In order to reduce their external deficits, all the countries have cut government budget deficits in an attempt to restrain domestic demand and reduce the growth of imports.

Nevertheless, persistent current account deficits have led to extremely high levels of external indebtedness in several of the Western Balkan countries (Figure 7.11). Croatia has the highest levels of external debt to GDP, a high debt-service ratio and low international reserves, and so is especially vulnerable to external shocks (Vlahinić-Dizdarević *et al.* 2006). Serbia also has high levels of external indebtedness, although this is on a downwards trend, while the other countries have more moderate levels of international debt in relation to GDP. Croatia's relatively high level of international debt is due to its heavy borrowing from abroad to finance both private consumption and public expenditure. Private borrowing was made possible by the integration of the Croatian banking system into international capital markets as the domestic banks were gradually sold to foreign banks after the banking crisis of 1998, and after 2000, much of the private borrowing financed the import of consumer goods such as motor cars. The large increase in public borrowing during the period of the SDP government financed a major road-building programme.

Measures to boost exports through improving international competitiveness have been high up on the policy agenda throughout the region, but this has not always been easy to achieve. The policy actions required to increase

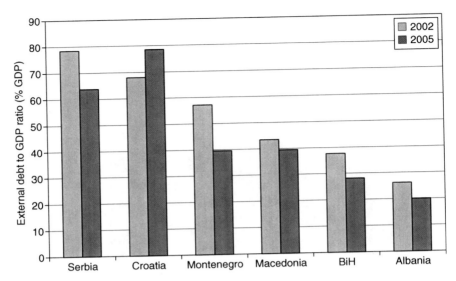

Figure 7.11 External debt to GDP ratio, 2002 and 2005 (% GDP) (source: EBRD online data 2007).

competitiveness involve structural reforms such as improving conditions for the entry of new firms, improving the supply response of existing firms through privatization and increased foreign direct investment, increasing labour productivity through improved education and training, and ensuring unit labour costs are in line with competitors in export markets. Such structural reforms are inherently more difficult to carry out than macroeconomic stabilization policies, since they are often resisted by interest groups which would prefer to maintain the status quo.

Trade with the EU

The EU granted Autonomous Trade Preferences to the Western Balkan countries in 2000, which provided for the unilateral dismantling of import tariffs and duties for almost all their exports. The EU tariff ceilings on industrial products originating from Albania, BiH and Croatia were removed in June 2000, while Serbia and Montenegro were included in the measure after the fall of the Milošević regime.[12] The Western Balkan countries, therefore, have broadly free access to EU markets, and more than 84 per cent of the total trade of the region now goes to the EU, of which Croatia is responsible for about half. Croatia and Macedonia, as signatories of Stabilisation and Association Agreements with the EU, are also eligible for diagonal cumulation of rules of origin with one another, which enables them to count inputs imported from each other as originating in their own countries. This increases the scope for their processed agricultural goods to enter the EU market free of import duties.

Since 2000, exports from the Western Balkans to the EU-25 have increased faster than the region's exports to the rest of the world. The EU is therefore a magnet for the region's exports and the major supplier of its imports, and economic growth within the EU will be a major force driving export expansion of all the Western Balkan states for the foreseeable future. Textiles are the main export commodity, accounting for 18 per cent of total exports from the region, while base metals and machinery and electrical equipment are also important export products. Exports from Albania are heavily concentrated in textiles and footwear. Macedonia's exports are almost exclusively concentrated in two sectors: textiles, and machinery and electrical equipment. Other countries have a more diversified mix of exports, but with notable concentrations in BiH in base metals, textiles, footwear and wood products; in Croatia in machinery and electrical equipment and textiles; and in Serbia-Montenegro in base metals, vegetable products and textiles.

There are considerable variations in the skill-mix of exports among countries. The largest part of exports from the Western Balkans to the EU-25 consists of low-skill or medium-skill goods, which accounted for four-fifths of total exports to the EU in 2003. Albania and Macedonia export predominantly goods with a low-skill content which account for three-quarters of Albania's exports to the EU-25 and half of Macedonia's exports. Low-skill goods account for two-fifths of exports from BiH. Serbia and Montenegro export the highest share of medium-skill goods which account for about half of their exports. No other Western Balkan country is close to Croatia in the proportion of exports classed as high-skill goods and which is responsible for three-quarters of all high-skilled goods exports from the region (Bartlett forthcoming).

Trade within the Western Balkan region

Trade within the Western Balkan region itself has been limited, and there is scope for its further expansion of trade between countries. The break-up of Yugoslavia severed many pre-existing trade and transport links between the successor states, while there had been little trade between Albania and former Yugoslavia for many years during the communist period. However, the reduction in official trade was also accompanied by an enormous growth in unofficial trade flows of smuggled goods.[13] Trade flows were seldom cut entirely, even over the front lines in the conflict zones. The creation of new state borders, UN sanctions against FRY and the arms embargo provided opportunities for smugglers to make huge profits. The new entrepreneurs in the grey economy soon became entrenched in the Western Balkans states most affected by sanctions, and the practice of smuggling persisted well after the end of the conflict, branching out into drugs, cigarettes, counterfeit goods and human trafficking, as well as more mundane commodities such as clothes and textiles. The practice of undervaluing goods at the border in collusion with customs officials who could expect a corresponding pay-off provided fertile ground for the spread of corruption amongst public officials, made more attractive by the low level of wages and salaries in the public sector.

Soon after the end of the Kosovo conflict, a strong advocacy coalition comprising representatives of the World Bank, the WTO and the EU promoted the virtues of a free trade area, pointing to the fact that trade in the region was below its potential and that trade liberalization could provide a boost to economic growth. A Trade Working Group (TWG) was established to coordinate the creation of a network of bilateral Free Trade Agreements (FTAs) envisioned in a Memorandum of Understanding signed in 2001, which covered non-tariff barriers, rules of origin and liberalization of services. The Memorandum stipulated that over 90 per cent of the products covered under the FTAs should have 0 per cent tariff rates. This caught the imagination and support of those business interests which were keen to re-establish the trading relationships which had been broken by years of war and conflict. There was therefore a certain degree of self-interest which could be mobilized behind the strategy. By the end of 2004, the Stability Pact countries had signed thirty-two bilateral Free Trade Agreements with one another, establishing a *de facto* free trade area in the whole of South-East Europe, covering a market with fifty-five million consumers. At the same time, Albania, Croatia and Macedonia joined the WTO, which required them to lower their external tariffs to the rest of the world as well.

Although regional trade liberalization succeeded in increasing trade flows within the South-East Europe region, the system of multiple bilateral agreements was haphazard and confusing. In June 2005, the Western Balkans' foreign ministers agreed to establish a single Free Trade Agreement for the region. However, the Croatian government, seeing Croatia as part of Central Europe, objected to the South-East European framework, and so negotiations eventually began under the umbrella of the Stability Pact to open the Central European Free Trade Agreement (CEFTA) to the Western Balkan countries. This proposal was energetically pursued by the TWG and at the end of 2006, the Western Balkan states joined CEFTA, replacing the network of thirty-two bilateral free trade agreements with a single free trade agreement for the whole region. The agreement, including Bulgaria and Romania, was signed in Bucharest on 19 December 2006. However, twelve days later, on 31 December, these latter two countries renounced their CEFTA membership, since they were about to join the EU on 1 January 2007. Therefore, paradoxically, 'CEFTA' has become an association solely of the Western Balkan states, with the sole outside addition of Moldova.

The impact of the free trade agreements

The proponents of a free trade area pointed to the fact that trade in the region was below its potential and argued that trade liberalization would provide a boost to economic growth (Uvalić 2000a: 68). In its regional strategy paper published at the launch of the Stability Pact, the World Bank argued that '... intra-regional trade can expand and be a stimulus for growth ... progress in intra-regional integration is needed both for its direct economic benefits and the contribution it makes to the wider political integration of these countries'

(World Bank 2000: 64). The creation of a free trade area was furthermore expected to lead to a much-needed increase in FDI which would boost productivity and export competitiveness. For trade optimists, therefore, there was a strong case for a revival of trade within the region. On the other hand, trade pessimists argued that even current shares of intra-regional trade were already too high, and should be expected to fall further as the share of exports going to the EU expands and that

> [p]olicy attempts specifically designed to engineer recovery of this trade are bound to fail, as there is not much, if anything, to be recovered. Intra-SEE-5 trade will not become ... a lever of economic growth of countries of the region any time soon.
>
> (Kaminski and de la Rocha 2003: 47)

Before the introduction of the free trade agreements, almost half the measured trade flows in the region took place between Croatia and BiH, reflecting the close political and economic ties between Croatia and the Herzegovina region, while trade between Serbia and Macedonia accounted for a further quarter. There seemed to be plenty of scope for increasing trade between the other partner countries. The free trade agreements were introduced over a period of several years, and most were signed by early 2004. In line with the expectations of the trade optimists, the agreements had a substantial impact on the growth of trade within the region. However, some countries benefited more than others, suggesting that free trade may cause divergent growth trends within the region. A comparison of data on trade flows between 2004 and 2005 (shown in Table 7.6) identifies some of the winners and losers from the policy of trade liberalization.

Following trade liberalization, Croatia's exports to Serbia-Montenegro increased by 35 per cent, while exports to BiH and Macedonia increased at a slower rate.[14] Equivalently, Serbian exports to Croatia increased by 34 per cent, exports to BiH also increased substantially, but exports to Macedonia increased only by a small amount.[15] Considering overall trade patterns, between 2004 and

Table 7.6 Croatian and Serbian exports to neighbouring countries, 2004–5 (€m)

	2004	2005	Increase (%)
Croatian exports to			
Bosnia-Herzegovina	927	1,014	9.4
Macedonia	59	66	10.4
Serbia and Montenegro	235	318	35.0
Serbian exports to			
Bosnia and Herzegovina	504	604	19.8
Macedonia	207	211	2.2
Croatia	120	160	33.9

Sources: State Statistical Office, Zagreb, First Release; Republic of Serbia Statistical Office, Communication ST16, No. 026, 31 January 2006.

2005, trade between Croatia and Serbia increased to a far greater extent than did Macedonia's trade with either country. Therefore, although the FTAs led to an overall increase in trade in the region, the benefits of this trade growth have been unequally spread since Albania, BiH and Macedonia have gained far less than Croatia and Serbia from trade liberalization. The competitive pressure on the Bosnian economy from increased imports was reflected in public protests by Bosnian farmers against imported processed food products from Croatia.

Non-tariff barriers and trade facilitation

However, free trade agreements on their own are unlikely to stimulate a significant further growth of trade in the region in the absence of measures to remove non-tariff barriers. Such measures, sometimes referred to as 'deep integration', would involve the harmonization of legislation, quality standards and other measures which facilitate trade including infrastructure development, action against the grey economy, developing the financial framework for trade, and liberalizing the visa regime to permit free movement of labour. Furthermore, the use of tariff quotas for agricultural goods and foodstuffs in the free trade agreements encouraged rent-seeking by importers and corruption in the allocation of quotas. Complex regulations concerning the rules of origin of imported products raised transaction costs, increased bureaucracy, and reduced transparency in the customs administrations. Deficiencies in transport networks and border-crossing infrastructure increased costs for exporters and placed them at a competitive disadvantage. The road from Skopje to Tirana, for example, was barely passable in 2002, although it was being upgraded with international assistance. Inadequate road and rail networks and delays at border crossings were also an obstacle to increasing exports to the EU market.

Trade facilitation policies have been adopted with international assistance to overcome some of these difficulties. They have involved measures such as training customs officers, improving infrastructure at the borders and improving customs procedures. The most important policy initiative of this type has been the Trade and Transport Facilitation for Southeast Europe programme (TTFSE) developed in 1998 by the World Bank. The programme aimed to strengthen mutual cooperation in trade and to reduce smuggling and corruption at border crossings. TTFSE achieved a significant reduction in waiting times at border crossings. However, the programme suffered from a lack of cooperation between some of the border agencies, and proved unable to successfully reduce smuggling and corruption within the customs administrations.

To gain a deeper insight into the problems facing exporters in the region, I interviewed commercial managers of several exporting companies in Macedonia in autumn 2002.[16] This revealed that Macedonian producers faced major difficulties in expanding their exports to neighbouring countries. Bribery by customs officers, higher-level officials and politicians imposed high transaction costs on Macedonian companies. The use of tariff quotas, which permitted a limited amount of imports with reduced or zero tariff rates, proved to be a recipe for the institutionalization of corruption. The introduction of bilateral free trade agreements did little to solve the problem, since many agricultural goods were covered by tariff quotas. Furthermore, Macedonian exporters faced additional difficulties due to political interference and corruption. These difficulties were well illustrated by the case of one confectionary producer, Kraškomerc of Skopje, which experienced unfair practices in the distribution of import licences under the 1997 free trade agreement with Croatia.

> Kraš was founded in 1911 in Zagreb, and the Skopje branch was established in 1955. Today, Kraškomerc in Skopje is a separate company although it is 100 per cent owned by the parent company in Zagreb, which was privatized in 1992. Kraš is an exporter to the EU market, and 30 per cent of its exports go there. There is a significant amount of international trade within the Kraš Group. For example, Kraškomerc Skopje obtains its final products from Zagreb, while it exports cherries for filling sweets to the Zagreb parent company. It also purchases hazelnuts and other raw materials from Turkey and other neighbouring countries. Macedonia has a trade agreement with Croatia which is regulated by quotas. Previously we had to pay 50 per cent duty for imports from Croatia. Now within the quota, we can import at a tariff of just 1 per cent. However, these quotas are now the main obstacle for a company like ours. Before the war we imported 3,000 tons of products, but now there is an import quota for only 1,200 tons. The critical question is who gets what proportion of the quota? The quotas are handed out to companies by the relevant committee of the Ministry of Economy. It is a political and not an economic decision which provides opportunities for corruption. Some of the companies which are granted part of the quota are not even in the confectionery business. They sell their quota on to Kraškomerc for a profit which greatly increases the costs of importing the goods.
>
> (Interview with manager, Kraškomerc, Skopje, October 2002)

A further difficulty facing exporters was the uncertainty over the reliability of payments for goods supplied to other countries. Most companies reported that they had to pay for international transactions either in cash or on a barter basis because the banking system was unable to handle cross-border payments and there were no export credit guarantee facilities. One company based in Tetovo which exported products to Albania, Kosovo, Bulgaria and Greece commented that 'our main problem is getting paid for our invoices. If we had a bank to guarantee payments it would be much easier for us'. This issue is related to the degree of trust in business partners. Where trust is low, business risks and transaction costs are correspondingly high. Trust takes time to be established, and does not necessarily follow ethnic lines. An Albanian businessman based in Tetovo observed:

> For the moment we do not envisage exporting our products to Albania. We have tried to do business there but it was not a success as we could not find

companies that we could trust. Trust is missing between the companies there, and there is a high risk that we would not get paid. So we have had to start with more stable markets such as Croatia.

(Interview with SME owner, Tetovo, November 2002)

The creation of trust-based business relationships, backed up by bank guarantees, could do much to encourage the growth of trade in the Balkan region. Business contacts facilitated by organizations such as business associations and chambers of commerce have an important role to play in this process, and the Export Credit Guarantee Fund established by the EBRD through local banks in a number of countries has been an important initiative.

Overall, Macedonian companies have been disadvantaged in their competition on the regional market compared to companies in more developed countries such as Croatia. Macedonian companies are less competitive than Croatian companies, as they are relatively less capitalized and employ a lower amount of qualified labour. Given this competitive disadvantage, adverse location effects under which new industries locate in the places where industries already agglomerate may overwhelm the potential comparative advantage gains from regional trade liberalization (Krugman 1993; Schiff and Winters 2003). A likely outcome of trade liberalization is a further deindustrialization in Macedonia and an increasing divergence in economic growth, incomes and living standards in the region.

8   Social policies and welfare reforms

The transition in the Western Balkans involved major structural readjustments which led to a significant rise in long-term unemployment, an increase in informal economic activities, a drop in labour market participation and an increase in poverty. Social protection systems were focused mainly on passive measures to shelter individuals from poverty, and until recently relatively little has been done to actively assist unemployed people to find work. The privatization of socially owned and state-owned enterprises led to the loss of many of the social benefits which they had provided, while privatization was also extended into the social sector through the sale of social housing stock and the privatization of parts of the health services and pension systems.

The development of social protection systems has also played an important role in the context of post-conflict reconstruction. The wars and civil conflicts in Croatia, Bosnia and Herzegovina (BiH), Albania, Kosovo and Macedonia destroyed numerous schools, hospitals, welfare centres and significant parts of the housing stock. They displaced hundreds of thousands of people many of whom became refugees in other countries in the region. All this has increased problems of physical and mental health, disrupted educational programmes and led to a 'brain drain' of many talented young people. The enormous reconstruction effort in the region, and the inflow of technical advisors in almost all policy fields, has resulted in the importation of new ideas about the delivery of welfare services, including ideas about the welfare mix, the role of non-governmental organizations (NGOs) and the reform of pension, health care and education systems.

Welfare reform is also significant in the context of European integration. The social dimension of the European Union (EU), elaborated in the social acquis, focuses on labour market policies, including social dialogue, gender equality, discrimination and portability of pension and social security entitlements. Accession states must comply with these laws and regulations before they are able to enter the EU. Alongside this 'hard law' element of social policy, there is also a 'soft law' element which has emerged in recent years through the bottom-up 'open method of coordination' (OMC) which extends EU competence into social policy fields such as health, education, housing and social security. The OMC was developed in order to implement the EU's Lisbon Agenda on competitiveness and social cohesion and which has brought social policy as a whole within the focus of EU policy concern.[1] Therefore, the development of EU-compatible social policies is fast becoming a necessary part of the preparation for the integration of the Western Balkan countries into the EU.

Poverty and inequality

The Western Balkans region includes some of the poorest countries in Europe. According to World Bank data, Albania had a gross national income per capita in 2006 of just $2,960, similar to Albania ($2,980) and Macedonia ($3,080), while per capita income in Serbia was only slightly higher at $3,910. In contrast, average per capita income in Croatia, at $9,330, was more than three times the level achieved in Albania, and higher than in some of the new EU member states, although still significantly lower than the EU average.

A similar picture emerges from a comparison of the gross domestic product (GDP) per capita which, apart from Croatia, is consistently below that of most of the EU's newest member states, including Romania. Croatia's GDP per capita is at about the same level as that in Slovakia, while for comparison, GDP per capita in Slovenia is twice as much as in Croatia and six times greater than in BiH. Taking into account price relativities, purchasing power parity (PPP) measures of GDP per capita reveal that Albania and Serbia are the least prosperous of the Balkan countries and that Macedonia and BiH are well below the standards achieved in Bulgaria and Romania.

Poverty

Although poverty increased dramatically during the transition period and following the various wars and conflicts in the region, relatively little was known about the characteristics of the poor until fairly recently. Following the

Table 8.1 GDP per capita, 2005 ($)

	GDP per capita	GDP per capita at PPP
BiH	2,384	6,035
Albania	2,673	5,405
Macedonia	2,810	7,748
Serbia	2,880	5,348
Bulgaria	3,459	9,223
Romania	4,539	8,785
Croatia	8,675	12,325
Slovakia	8,775	16,041
Slovenia	16,986	21,808

Source: IMF online database 2007.

Note
PPP is Purchasing Power Parity.

end of the Kosovo war, the World Bank began to carry out household surveys within the framework of its programme of Poverty Reduction Strategy Papers (PRSPs), which showed the extent of poverty in the region. Measured at a minimum poverty line of $2.15 per day, over one-fifth of the population in Albania lived in absolute poverty in 2002, as did 9 per cent in Serbia and Montenegro, 6 per cent in BiH and 4 per cent in Macedonia (World Bank 2005c). Taking a more realistic poverty line of $4.30 to measure vulnerability to poverty, and which is more consistent with national poverty lines, as many as 70 per cent of the Albanian population were vulnerable to poverty, 42 per cent in Serbia and Montenegro, 35 per cent in BiH and 24 per cent in Macedonia (Figure 8.1).

The poverty situation is also serious in Kosovo where a household survey carried out in 2002 showed widespread poverty, with over one-third of the population living below a poverty line of €1.42 per day (World Bank 2005a), while about 15 per cent of the population is living in extreme poverty with insufficient income to cover basic food needs. The incidence of poverty is greatest among families where the head of the household is unemployed and among children and the elderly. Poverty in Kosovo is reflected in poor housing quality and poor amenities. Only one-third of dwellings have a piped water supply compared to four-fifths in Serbia, only one-third have a bathroom and less than one-tenth have central heating.

In Albania, poverty is most severe in the rural areas where about 30 per cent of the population is poor, according to the Living Standards Measurement

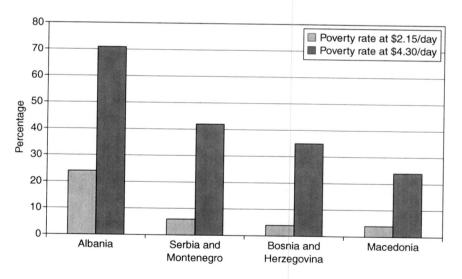

Figure 8.1 Poverty rates, 2002–4 (absolute poverty) (source: Derived from World Bank 2005c).

Note
Albania, Serbia and Montenegro 2002; Macedonia 2003; BiH 2004.

Survey (LSMS) carried out in 2002 (World Bank 2003b). In the northern mountain areas, over two-fifths of the population lives in absolute poverty, while the rural areas have been left out of the modernization of infrastructure and services which has primarily taken place in urban areas. This neglect has stimulated migration to the cities, where shanty towns and illegal housing have grown up especially in the environs of Tirana. Many dwellings in these deprived urban areas lack basic services such as water, electricity and waste disposal. In response to widespread poverty and lack of job opportunities, about one-fifth of the population has left the country and lives abroad.

In Serbia, poverty has been measured by an LSMS carried out in 2002, which showed that 800,000 people are living in poverty and about 1.6 million are at risk of falling below the poverty line (GoS 2004). The poverty risk of refugees and displaced persons is far greater than that of the general population, while poverty has also become a rural phenomenon, as incomes in the rural areas have not kept pace with urban wages. The most vulnerable sections of the population are the unemployed who face a poverty risk 60 per cent greater than average and pensioners who face a poverty risk 40 per cent above the average. Households with children and people with low educational levels were also at greater than average risk of poverty.

In Montenegro, a United National Development Programme (UNDP) survey, carried out in 2000, reported that at least one-fifth of the population lives in poverty (UNDP 2003). The most vulnerable are members of large families, the elderly living alone, the unemployed and those without a pension. Poverty is related to unemployment and gender in a situation when more than two-fifth of the labour force is unemployed, while women are more at risk of poverty than men.[2] The north-east part of the country is affected to an even greater extent, due to deindustrialization and the collapse of the traditional wood-processing and paper-making industries, following the withdrawal of subsidies from Belgrade at the end of the 1990s. Some 40,000 refugees and internally displaced persons (IDPs) put additional pressure on the already scarce social funds.

In BiH, a household survey (LSMS) carried out in 2001 revealed that one-quarter of the population in Republika Srpska (RS), and one-sixth of the population in Federation of Bosnia and Herzegovina (FBiH), lives in absolute poverty, while fewer live in poverty in the more developed Croat-populated areas. In BiH as a whole, about half the population lives below or close to poverty (World Bank 2003d). The social groups most at risk of poverty include children under five, displaced persons and returnees and people with low education levels. Despite the low unemployment benefits, almost two-thirds of the poor lives in families with at least one person in employment, owing to low wages (CoM-BiH 2004: 26). Elderly people are mostly protected from poverty by pensions which are indexed to wages and are just enough to raise the elderly above the poverty line.

In Macedonia, poverty is measured by household budget surveys carried out by the State Statistics Bureau. According to these data, about one-fifth of all households lived below the poverty line in the period from 1997 to 2000 (GoM

2002). The level of education and a rural location are two of the most significant indicators of poverty risk, while old age does not present any greater risk of poverty than among younger age groups. The Roma and Albanian populations have a higher than average poverty risk. Overall, three main groups of poor households can be identified: the traditionally poor comprising rural households with low education; newly impoverished households, including urban households who have lost out from the transition process; and the chronic poor, including the elderly disabled, institutionalized individuals and rural households without a permanent source of income.

Poverty indicators in Croatia are calculated from the Household Budget Survey on the basis of total net income of households. They show that absolute poverty is relatively rare and affects only specific disadvantaged groups in the population, including mainly the long-term unemployed and people living in war-affected areas, many of whom have not benefited from recent economic growth. In Croatia, poverty is measured in relative rather than absolute terms. In 2003, the overall relative poverty rate was 17 per cent, while the relative poverty rate among the unemployed was 32 per cent.[3] Women were more likely to be in poverty than men. Among pensioners, the poverty rate was 21 per cent, while one-person pensioner households had a relative poverty rate of 42 per cent, explaining the political sensitivity of the pension issue and the electoral success of the Pensioners Party. The importance of social transfers and pensions in sustaining a large section of the population above the poverty threshold is indicated by the fact that the relative poverty rate measured before such transfers was 42 per cent compared to just 17 per cent for the after-transfer relative poverty rate.

Inequality

Inequality already existed within the market socialist system that had been developed under the Titoist regime in former Yugoslavia, both between and within republics, since enterprises that were more capital intensive, or had a stronger market position, could pay higher wages for the same work than other less-productive, more labour-intensive enterprises. However, the overall level of inequality in Yugoslavia was relatively low by Western standards (Flakierski 1989: 81).

The shift to a market economy had profound implications for the distribution of income and wealth. Property transformation changed access to assets, while the liberalization of entry for new firms opened up opportunities for new forms of income. Privatization increased income inequality whenever the new owners were able to capture a stream of property income that was previously unavailable, enabling them to transfer wealth from their companies to their own accounts by asset-stripping, running down companies and depriving employees of incomes and jobs. These socially adverse consequences of privatization have occurred mainly in cases in which privatization has led to the monopolization of the market and where the institutions of public accountability have been weakened by civil conflict and a failure of democratic consolidation, circumstances which occurred in all the Western Balkan countries to differing degrees.

Inequality increased in former Yugoslavia soon after the transition started in the late 1980s. The Gini measure of inequality reached 0.36 in Croatia by 1990, significantly higher than levels recorded in the 1970s, although it has since decreased, while inequality has remained at a relatively high level in Macedonia. In Albania, the Gini coefficient was 0.19 in 1987–90, but pro-market reforms widened inequality so that by the late 1990s inequality had increased to levels approaching that in Croatia. Greater inequality has therefore followed early pro-market reforms in Albania, Croatia and Macedonia (Figure 8.2). Inequality is lower in the late reformers, BiH and Federal Republic of Yugoslavia (FRY), where the potential losers from reform were protected by redistributive policies which maintained low-productivity jobs in socially owned enterprises through state subsidies.

Expenditure on social welfare

Throughout the Western Balkans, attempts to boost economic activity through expansionary fiscal policies have provoked deficits on the balance of international payments leading to inflationary pressures. Consequently, the International Monetary Fund (IMF) has advised countries to reduce their budget deficits, which in practice has meant cutting public expenditure or improving tax

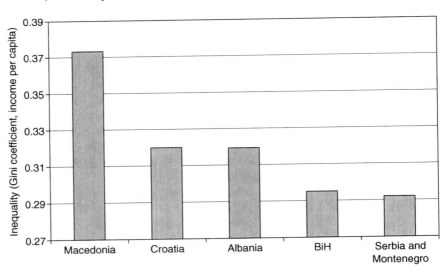

Figure 8.2 Inequality, 2002–4 (Gini coefficient, income per capita) (sources: World Bank 2005c and Croatian Statistical Office).

Note
Serbia and Albania 2002; Albania 2003; BiH and Croatia 2004.

collection. Some countries have been more successful at increasing tax revenues than others. In 2000, Croatia had the highest tax-to-GDP ratio at 38 per cent, while Albania had the lowest at just 16 per cent. The low tax collection rate in Albania has meant that government expenditure has also been low, and a very narrow range of public services has been provided, while Croatia has maintained a relatively high share of public expenditure in GDP.

In 2000, public expenditure in both Croatia and BiH was almost 57 per cent of GDP, but since then both countries have conformed to IMF and World Bank advice to reduce their expenditure, which by 2004 had fallen to around 50 per cent of GDP in each country (Figure 8.3). In Serbia and Montenegro, the share of public expenditure has been at an intermediate level but since 2000 has increased to over 40 per cent of GDP. The lowest spenders are Albania and Macedonia. While the latter has increased its public expenditure share since 2000, Albania has continued to cut its already low share to below 30 per cent of GDP. With the exception of Albania, the Western Balkan countries are converging to the EU average, which was 47 per cent of GDP in 2005.

Total public expenditure on the social sector as a proportion of GDP is relatively low, only matching the EU-25 average in Croatia (Table 8.2). The same is true of social protection expenditure, which covers all social transfers including pensions and expenditure on health care. Croatia, FBiH and Serbia and Montenegro have the highest proportions of social protection expenditure, while it is comparatively low in Albania, Kosovo and Macedonia. Spending on health care is high in all countries, with the exceptions of Albania and Kosovo which spend less on health care than the EU-25 average. Education spending follows a

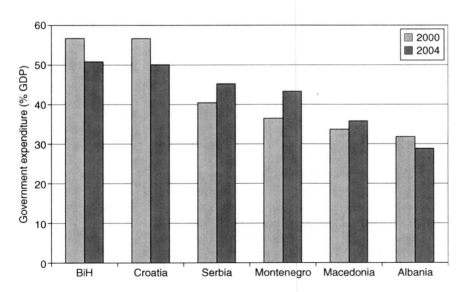

Figure 8.3 Government expenditure, 2002–4 (% GDP) (source: EBRD online database 2007).

Table 8.2 Social expenditure in 2003 (% GDP)

	Social security	Health	Total social protection	Education	Total social expenditure
Albania	6.7	2.1	8.8	2.9	11.7
BiH[a]	15.3	6.1	21.4	5.6	27.0
FBiH	16.9	6.6	23.5	6.4	29.9
RS	13.5	5.9	19.4	4.3	23.7
Croatia	19.3	7.2	26.5	4.2	30.7
Kosovo	5.8	4.5	10.3	6.1	16.4
Macedonia[b]	6.8	5.8	12.6	3.5	16.1
Montenegro	15.7	7.3	23.0	5.9	28.9
Serbia	15.3	5.6	20.9	3.5	24.4
EU countries[c]	22.0	5.0	27.0	4.9	31.9

Source: ILO 2005: 19.

Notes
a World Bank 2005d: 20.
b Health and education from UNDP 2005 [data for 2002], social protection from Bulletin, May/June 2005, Ministry of Finance, Skopje.
c Petrášová 2006 and Eurostat 2007.

different pattern, with Albania, RS, Croatia, Macedonia and Serbia all spending below the EU average. Overall, the countries are divided into a group of high spenders, which includes BiH, Croatia, Montenegro and Serbia, and a group of relatively low spenders including Albania, Kosovo and Macedonia. In the latter group, the low public expenditure on health and education is offset to some extent by relatively high levels of private expenditure, either through informal payments to medical personnel in the public health sector or through private providers in the education sector.

These data suggest that the Western Balkan countries have been converging on rather different models of capitalism. Recent research has identified several varieties, or 'models', of capitalism in developed Organization for Economic Cooperation and Development (OECD) countries (Esping-Andersen 1990; Amable 2003). The 'Anglo-Saxon model' has relatively low levels of employment protection. Its US variant of neo-liberalism also has a relatively low level of social protection, while the UK variant combines low employment protection with relatively strong social protection, sometimes referred to as the Beveridge model. In contrast, the 'Central European corporatist model' of capitalism combines strong employment protection and strong social protection. A further group of countries, characterized as the 'Mediterranean model' of capitalism, combines high employment protection with low social protection.

This 'varieties of capitalism' approach can be applied to the Balkan economies (Bartlett 2006). Viewed from this perspective, Albania has adopted the neo-liberal market model of capitalism, with a strong reliance on the market combining low social protection and low levels of employment protection. A similar approach has been adopted in Kosovo under the governance of the United

Nations Mission in Kosovo (UNMIK) authorities. Croatia, BiH, Montenegro and Serbia have followed the more traditional Central European corporatist models of capitalism, with relatively high shares of public expenditure combined with relatively high levels of employment protection. Recent reforms to employment protection legislation may be weakening this dimension of the model, but the picture is unclear since the adoption of EU compatible employment action plans will tie these countries into the corporatist model of 'social Europe'. Macedonia is a rather different case on account of low social protection combined with high levels of employment protection, placing it closer to the 'Mediterranean' model of capitalism. However, other dimensions should be taken into account including the size of the informal sector which is relatively large in Macedonia. This reduces effective employment protection and makes its economy more similar to the neo-liberal variety of capitalism developed in Albania and Kosovo.

Social assistance in transition

In the former Yugoslavia, the system of social welfare consisted of a mix of contributory and non-contributory cash benefits and a range of benefits in kind, most available on a universal basis, with some provided by enterprises to their workers (Pošarac 1993). The main contributory benefit, based on social insurance principles, was the pension related to a person's contribution record. Workers' health contributions covered family members, while unemployed persons' health insurance contributions were paid by the Employment Bureau, so that almost all the population was covered by social insurance for health care. Owners and employees in the crafts sector and in private agriculture had inferior benefit entitlements, while uninsured people were entitled to a reduced package of health care entitlements. Non-contributory cash benefits included child benefit, family benefit, maternity benefit, disablement benefit, war veterans' benefit and housing benefit. Education was provided on a universal basis. Workers had extensive employment rights, and strong job protection meant that dismissal from employment was rare, so that few people were eligible for unemployment benefit. Subsidized low-cost housing, subsidized holidays and subsidized transport were provided by socially owned enterprises to their full-time employees. Utilities such as heating and running water were provided to households at subsidized prices.

At the beginning of the 1990s, the cost of providing such an extensive social welfare system had become increasingly unsustainable. New legislation was introduced to reform the system which transferred funding from local self-management communities of interest to centralized republican funds for family welfare, while owing to the growing awareness of poverty, entitlement to social assistance was extended to any family whose income fell below a minimum subsistence level (Arandarenko 2003: 27). Following the break-up of Yugoslavia, each of the successor states inherited their republic-based welfare systems.

Albania under communism had a classic centralized approach to social welfare based upon full employment. After the collapse of the communist system, social welfare reforms were introduced in line with the transition to a market economy (Xhumari 2003). A social assistance programme known as *Ndihme Ekonomika* (*Income Support*) was introduced in 1992 for urban families with no independent source of income, rural families with small plots of land and disabled people under the age of twenty-one. The scheme provided means-tested monthly benefit to the one-fifth of the population who met the criteria and was administered by a new institution known as the State Social Services. Funds were distributed by communal administrations according to a needs formula. This decentralized system relied on a subjective assessment of needs and directed about half the available resources to the poorest one-fifth of the population (Alderman 2002). More recently, the policy of the State Social Services has evolved to combine the social assistance scheme with active employment policies, backed up by a World Bank project to develop community-based social services.

Social security systems are relatively weak in most of the Western Balkans due to pressure on governments to cut budget deficits and restrict public expenditure. The average monthly social security payments for eligible recipients in 2004 averaged just €53 in Croatia, €27 for urban families and €17 for rural families in Albania, €17.50 in Serbia, €16–€19 in Montenegro and just €15 per month in FBiH. Despite widespread poverty, eligibility criteria are restrictive. In 2004, only 16 per cent of the population in Albania was in receipt of social security benefits, 15 per cent in Kosovo, 11 per cent in Serbia and 3 per cent in Croatia. In BiH, about one-fifth of the population is entitled to social security benefits, although in practice the poorer municipalities are unable to provide any benefits to the poor, and about half of the most severely disabled is not adequately protected (CoM-BiH 2004: 33). Most of the resources to finance social security have been provided by international donors, and declining donations have reduced social security for the most vulnerable groups of citizens.

In countries badly affected by conflict, the social welfare of war veterans, war victims and their families has been a contentious issue. In Croatia, war veterans and their families are entitled to more favourable levels of social security benefits than other citizens, and political support from veterans' groups played an important role in the electoral victory of the Croatian Democratic Union (HDZ) in 2003. In BiH, relatively high social benefits are made to war veterans and their families. In RS, a specialized department of the Ministry of Veterans' Affairs provides veterans with better social services than those available to other groups, and attempts to reduce their privileges have led to vociferous public protests. A reform of veterans' invalidity insurance benefits was carried out in BiH in 2004 under the terms of a World Bank loan. Certificates of wounds and deaths were reviewed, and means-tested disability and survivors' benefits were reduced. However, the reform met with strong protests from veterans' associations, which argued that they were entitled to compensation for loss of income during and after the war.

Pension reforms

Pensions are the largest item of social protection expenditure throughout the region owing to the increase in early retirement that accompanied privatization and enterprise restructuring. The ratio of employees to pensioners, the dependency ratio, has fallen sharply in recent years placing severe financial pressure on the pension systems (Figure 8.4). The dependency ratio is especially low in RS where there are more pensioners than there are active pension scheme contributors. Even in Croatia, there are only 1.4 active contributing employees for each pensioner, having fallen from three employees for each pensioner in 1990. Only Albania and Kosovo have demographically youthful populations, although due to the low employment rates, the funding of pensions is problematic in those countries too.

The countries of the former Yugoslavia inherited an income-related pay-as-you-go system which covered workers in socially owned enterprises and agricultural cooperatives, and self-employed craft and professional workers, but which excluded private farmers. Pensions were indexed to wages, and as the number of pensioners increased and dependency ratios worsened in the successor states contribution rates were increased in an attempt to cover rising pension deficits. In Croatia, the government tried to solve the problem in 1993 by breaking the index link to wages, without, however, amending the law to make the decision legal. This became politically contentious when, in 2004, the newly elected Pensioner Party MPs demanded the return of the 'lost' pensions from the government. The controversy was resolved only when the government agreed to establish a special fund to cover the outstanding debts, financed by HRK4.8

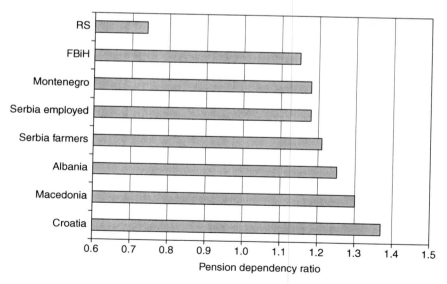

Figure 8.4 Pension dependency ratios, 2004 (source: ILO 2005).

billion (€700 million) of shares from companies owned by the Croatian Privatization Fund.

In Albania, a pay-as-you-go pension system based on social insurance principles was introduced in 1993 to replace the previous universal state-funded system. It covered employees, self-employed people and university students, with a voluntary scheme for other groups. Pensions consist of a basic pension and an earnings-related component of 1 per cent for each year in employment. The basic pension is set at the minimum living standard, while the maximum pension is equal to twice the basic pension.

Pensions are low in relation to subsistence needs, with minimum pensions around 20 per cent of average gross wages in each country, although average replacement rates in relation to gross wages are significantly higher in Serbia and Montenegro than in Albania, Croatia and Macedonia (Table 8.3). Pensioners are therefore protected from poverty more effectively in Serbia and Montenegro than elsewhere, especially in relation to Macedonia where the average pension is below the official poverty line. Although pensions in BiH are apparently relatively generous, in practice in RS pensions are often not fully paid, and typically pensioners receive only half of their entitlements. Contribution rates are universally high, being everywhere above 20 per cent of gross wages which has led to widespread avoidance by businesses, and stimulated the growth of the informal economy. Pension expenditures account for a relatively high share of GDP in Montenegro, Croatia and Serbia, where deficits in the state pension funds have put pressure on government budgets. In response to difficulties in financing the growing cost of pension expenditures, several countries in the region have introduced pension system reforms, which have, however, varied widely in their scope.

The introduction of privatized pension schemes: Croatia, Macedonia and Kosovo

The Croatian pension reform law of 1998, supported by a $27 million World Bank loan, envisaged a three-pillar pension model. The first pillar is the pre-existing compulsory pay-as-you-go system within which the retirement age was extended, to which employees contribute 15 per cent of their gross wages. The second compulsory privately managed pillar, introduced in 2002, is based upon individual contributions amounting to a further 5 per cent of gross wages. The third pillar comprises additional voluntary contributions. Four private pension funds have been established, between which contributors can choose to allocate their pension contributions.

The Macedonian pension reform law passed in 2002, supported by a $9.8 million World Bank loan, envisaged a three-pillar pension system similar to the Croatian system.[4] The reform to the first pillar has involved a gradual increase in the retirement age, a decrease in the replacement rate, a change in the pension indexation method, the ending of early retirement and a change of the pension formula. Introduced in 2006, the privately managed and fully funded second pillar is compulsory for new entrants to the labour market who are required to

Table 8.3 Pension benefits and expenditures, 2004

	Average monthly pensions (€)	Replacement rate (%)[a]	Replacement rate of new pensions (%)[b]	Minimum pension replacement rate (%)[c]	Pension/poverty line[d]	Pension contribution rates (%)[e]	Share of pension expenditure in GDP (%)
Albania	50	33.0	33.0	–	132	29.9	5.0
BiH	100	–	–	–	–	24.0	–
Croatia	–	34.0	26.0	20.0	122	20.0	14.0
Macedonia	–	42.0	–	24.0	56	21.2	9.0
Montenegro	90	51.0	52.0	17.0	–	24.0	17.0
Serbia	–	61.0	70.0	20.0	193	24.0	12.0
Kosovo	40	–	–	–	–	20.6	–

Source: ILO (2005).

Notes

a Average replacement rate to gross wages.
b Average replacement rate of newly awarded pensions to gross wages.
c Replacement rate of guaranteed minimum to average gross wages.
d Average pension to official poverty line.
e Pension contribution rates in relation to gross wages.

pay 7 per cent of their salary to one of two new private pension funds. The contribution rate to the first pillar is reduced to 14 per cent but will provide only a modest pension with an estimated replacement rate of 30 per cent. It will be supplemented by the pension derived from the investments in the second-pillar private pension funds, but by design the returns to these investments are not guaranteed and depend upon the performance of the funds. Given the underdeveloped state of the Macedonian capital market, this is a high-risk strategy since there are few financial institutions in the country that could manage a large investment fund, and even fewer high yielding opportunities in which the accumulated contributions could be invested. An independent assessment carried out on behalf of the World Bank has raised concerns about the introduction of the privately managed second-pillar pension scheme in Macedonia, on the grounds that the projections for future pensions made in designing the scheme were overly optimistic (Fornero and Ferraresi 2007).

These concerns would appear to be even more serious in the case of Kosovo. The first law which the new Kosovo Parliament passed in 2002 created a new pension system based on the three-pillar pension model. The publicly managed non-contributory first pillar provides a flat rate pension of €40 to all citizens aged over sixty-five, financed out of the government budget.[5] The second pillar is a privately managed defined-contribution system in which contributions are saved in individual accounts and fully funded through a 5 per cent contribution by employees on their gross wages.[6] The new pension system was introduced in August 2002 for public sector employees of government and workers in socially owned enterprises and was extended to all workers in 2003. The third pillar consists of six small occupational schemes.

The private, second-pillar pension fund is administered by the Kosovo Pensions Savings Trust (KPST) which was established with assistance from the US Agency for International Development (USAID). Remarkably, the KPST placed the entire scheme consisting of members' individual savings accounts outside Kosovo, in mutual investment funds managed by ABN-AMRO and Legal & General. By February 2007, the total amount invested had reached €213 million and was increasing at €3 million per month. The argument in favour of investing the funds abroad was that the level of risk would be lower than if they were invested inside Kosovo. However, there could be some serious negative consequences of this strategy. First, the funds are leaving the country and are not available for investment within Kosovo which could underpin improved productivity and competitiveness. Second, there can be no guarantee that the eventual pensions derived from an overseas private fund would be greater than could have been provided by the state on a pay-as-you-go basis, drawing on the economic growth that the reinvestment of the funds in the Kosovo economy might have generated. Third, the capital outflow involved will significantly worsen the Kosovo balance of payments, leading to increased foreign debt and higher future taxes, which have to be set against the eventual pension payments. These issues were glossed over by the USAID advisors who designed the system and who held a strong aversion to state-funded pensions.[7]

Reforms to state pensions: BiH, Montenegro and Serbia

In BiH, the traditional pay-as-you-go pensions are the responsibility of the entity governments, and reforms have focused on the harmonization of the two separate systems.[8] Many disabled pensioners in BiH receive enhanced pension and invalidity insurance benefits, but the system for assessing disability is not consistent across the entities and cantons and is open to abuse, for example through informal payments to doctors to register healthy individuals as disabled.[9] In FBiH, the fragmented pension system was only consolidated at the federal level in 2001, with the creation of a unified Federation Pension and Invalidity Fund.[10] The RS pension system also faces difficulties since many companies avoid paying pension contributions on behalf of their employees. In an attempt to resolve the situation, the Office of the High Representative (OHR) passed a regulation that pensions should be calculated in accordance with the capacity of the pension funds, rather than by established entitlements. This has had the unintended consequence that since the RS pension fund only needs to distribute as much as it collects, it has had little incentive to enforce payment from recalcitrant employers and has therefore failed to enforce the collection of debts through the courts. Moreover, the government has not pressured the fund to enforce the rules, arguing that employers cannot afford to make the required payments. Due to the consequent deficit, pensions are often paid at a reduced rate, while the pension fund has come under criticism for its inefficient practices including the construction of luxurious offices and the padding of employees' remuneration.

The Serbian government decided against introducing a private pension reform and has concentrated instead on the reform of the compulsory pay-as-you-go system. The Serbian pension system is split among three different funds, for employees, farmers and the self-employed, of which only the fund for the self-employed is solvent. In 2004, the state pension fund for employees had a deficit equivalent to 5 per cent of GDP, mainly because less than three-fifths of the labour force was making regular pension contributions. The farmers' fund has also relied on transfers from the government budget. Reforms to the state pension system were introduced through the Pension Law adopted in 2004. The law increased the retirement age from sixty to sixty-three for men and from fifty-five to fifty-eight for women; changed the indexation base from wage inflation alone to an average of wage and price inflation; and fixed the minimum pension at 20 per cent of the average wage. In Montenegro, a new pension law envisaged the introduction of a three-pillar pension system, although its introduction has been delayed due to the weakness of the pension system administration. The strengthening of its administrative capacity has been supported by a $5 million World Bank credit designed to build the capacity of the pension fund administration.

Overall, liberal pro-market pension reforms have been introduced in Croatia, Macedonia and Kosovo, while state pension funds have been subject to relatively minor reforms in BiH, Serbia and Montenegro to deal with pension fund deficits. The diversity of pension systems has created problems of coordination between the different schemes in cases where individuals live and work in different countries. For example, Kosovars who are working in Albania or Macedonia and have a residence in Kosovo can benefit from both countries' pension schemes, by drawing both a basic pension in Kosovo which is unrelated to the individual's work record and a contributory pension in either Albania or Macedonia.[11] Others are worse off, such as the 90,000 Kosovars who are entitled to a pension on the basis of their prior employment history of working in Serbia but who do not receive their entitlement because of the breakdown in relations between Priština and Belgrade. In order to begin to rectify some of these problems, the Council of Europe has initiated a programme to promote social security coordination in the Western Balkans and has established a regional office in Skopje in 2005 to manage this programme.

Housing

One of the most significant changes in the social sector that took place in the Western Balkans in the early stages of transition was the privatization of the public sector housing stock. In most of the Yugoslav republics, tenants were given the right to buy socially owned housing at discounted prices. In Croatia, almost three-quarters of the stock was sold under the Law on the Sale of Apartments, with protection for tenants who could not afford to buy their own apartments. In Macedonia in the early 1990s, almost all the social housing stock was privatized at hefty discounts under the Law on the Sale of Socially Owned Housing. In Albania 98 per cent of the housing stock was privatized following the 1993 Law on Privatization, although many high-rise apartment blocks had been poorly built and were in need of repair or replacement (CEDB 2004), and many apartments continued to deteriorate after privatization (UNECE 2002). In Serbia, a Housing Relations Law was passed in 1990, and by the end of 1992, about one-fifth of the stock had been sold. According to one analyst, the properties were sold mainly to 'elite members who bought the largest and most desirable housing' (Petrović 2001: 222). A Residence Law was passed in 1992 which restricted the sales of social housing to current tenants who were offered further discounts, and by the end of 1993, 93 per cent of social housing had been privatized. Housing privatization in Serbia had two political purposes. The first was to ensure a transfer of property to the elite, and the second was to provide a means to build support for the Socialist Party.

By 2001, there was hardly any social housing left anywhere in the Western Balkan region apart from BiH, and almost all property was in private ownership (Table 8.4). Since the private rented sector was underdeveloped, migrant workers from rural areas were pushed into overcrowded accommodation and illegally constructed housing with inadequate public utilities. Moreover, the housing stock had been depleted by the wars of Yugoslav succession. One-eighth of the housing stock was destroyed in Croatia, one-fifth in BiH and one-half in Kosovo,[12] and less but still significant destruction took place in Macedonia in 2001. Many homes have been reconstructed with both domestic

Table 8.4 Tenure structures (% of national housing stock)

	Year	Public rented housing	Private rented housing	Owner occupied housing	Other forms of ownership
Albania	2001	0.0	4.0	93.6	4.2
BiH	2001	9.0	1.3	78.3	12.5
Croatia	2001	2.8	10.8	83.0	–
Macedonia	2002	0.6	8.9	90.4	–
Serbia	2002	2.1	2.0	95.9	0.0
Kosovo	2002	1.4	–	95.1	6.5

Source: Tsenkova 2005.

resources and international assistance, although significant rebuilding gaps still remain in some regions.

Lack of clear property ownership records has increased transaction costs in the housing market, and the problem of illegal construction has worsened due to the lack of an effective system of land registration.[13] In Albania, widespread illegal housing construction has taken place in the areas surrounding Tirana and alongside the road to Durrës, and many of these housing units are not connected to water supplies, electricity or sewerage. Although unregulated urban development together with a breakdown of previous control over the land market and urban planning and building processes has taken its most extreme form in Albania (Tosić 2005: 73), the phenomenon of illegal construction has also affected some of the Yugoslav successor states. In Macedonia, as many as one-quarter of the population lives in settlements without building permits. Illegal and unregistered housing construction has also been a serious problem in Serbia and Montenegro. By 1996, the number of illegally built dwellings in Belgrade was approaching the number of legally built ones, and a law on Planning and Construction was passed in 2003 to legalize such housing units retrospectively (GoS 2004). Some of the worst housing conditions could be found in Roma settlements in Albania, Serbia and Montenegro, where up to half of Roma households live in shacks rather than in properly constructed housing.

Refugees

The population structure in the Western Balkan countries has changed radically as a result of the movement of refugees and IDPs, while many of the most educated simply emigrated. Under the Dayton peace agreement, the Croatian Serbs from Krajina and Western Slavonia were guaranteed the right to return home. Up to 200,000 had fled Croatia following the recapture of Krajina in 1995 by which time up to 600,000 refugees from BiH and other parts of former Yugoslavia were living in poor conditions in various parts of Serbia. Most refugees stayed with relatives or other families, while about 100,000 lived in collective refugee centres. One-third of the refugees settled in Belgrade, many others went to Vojvodina or central Serbia and some settled in Kosovo (Pošarac 1997).

The Croatian authorities passed a series of laws and regulations on the return of refugees. A Programme for the Return and Accommodation of Displaced Persons was adopted which encouraged refugees from FRY and RS to return to Croatia. The government argued it was doing all it could to facilitate refugee return, but critics claimed that in practice the government was implementing the law in such a way as to discourage refugees from returning. The main impediments to return arose from the difficulties that returnees faced in regularizing their status, in accessing welfare benefits, in repossessing property and in unequal access to reconstruction assistance.[14] A large numbers of refugees chose not to return while the HDZ government was in power in the 1990s. The EU interpreted this as evidence that the Croatian government was hindering the return of Serbian refugees and consequently would not allow Croatia to participate in the PHARE assistance programme.

In BiH, many of the more than two million people who had been forcibly displaced from their homes returned in the years immediately following the end of the war. A significant but diminishing number continued to return thereafter, but by mid-2003 about half a million had still not returned.[15] About 400,000 have decided to settle in the country to which they fled, mostly in Serbia, while the rest who wish to return to BiH, but have been unable to do so, live in unsuitable accommodation or in collective centres where living conditions are inadequate. Refugees and IDPs outside the collective centres have also suffered acute housing problems, especially in Serbia. Many of these people are among the most vulnerable, and the lack of affordable social housing, along with the lack of employment opportunities, has been a significant barrier to their effective social inclusion.

Health

The publicly provided health care system provided good quality services in former Yugoslavia, but the break-up of the country and the associated wars and conflicts have led to a decline in the level and quality of health service provision, especially in BiH, Serbia, Montenegro and Kosovo, and to some extent in Macedonia. About one-third of health centres and hospitals were destroyed in Croatia and BiH during the wars of the early 1990s, while in Albania many health centres and hospitals were looted in the 1997 uprising (WHO 2006). The quality of health care provision has been maintained in Croatia but only at a high and rising cost. Life expectancy has increased between 1990 and 2002 by 2.5 years in Croatia, while in FRY life expectancy increased by only 1.1 years and in Macedonia by just one year. Despite the difficult circumstances, life expectancy in Albania has increased over the same period by 4.0 years in Albania but from a lower base than elsewhere.

Infant mortality rates were lowest in Croatia at 6.0 per thousand in 2004, but more than double that, at 13.0 per thousand, in Macedonia, Serbia and Montenegro. In Albania, infant mortality rates have fallen from 41.5 per thousand live births in 1990 to 16.0 in 2004. Under-5 mortality rates have fallen in all the

Western Balkan countries since 1990, being initially highest in Albania (Figure 8.5). In Macedonia, however, the rate of under-5 mortality increased between 2000 and 2005, reflecting the impact of the civil conflict in 2001.

Health care finance

In the Yugoslav successor states, health care services are financed through compulsory health insurance contributions paid in proportion to wages and salaries and collected by national health insurance funds (HIFs), the successors of the former Republican HIFs. Eligibility to receive health care at all levels is linked to an individual's health insurance contribution record, while co-insurance is provided to family members. Health insurance contributions are paid by Employment Bureaus on behalf of the registered unemployed, which creates a strong incentive among those not actively seeking work to register as unemployed. Pensioners' contributions are paid by the pension funds.

Health expenditures are highest in Croatia, where cost escalation is a significant problem, and the Ministry of Health has introduced a set of restrictive measures to cap health expenditures made by the HIF. In Macedonia, where the HIF has lacked sufficient resources due to the non-payment of insurance contributions by many companies, policy has focused on cost containment.[16] Government expenditure on health services is lowest in Albania but is supplemented by almost equivalent private expenditures paid directly, but informally, to health workers. Patients are typically required to make side payments to doctors and other health workers to access public health care.

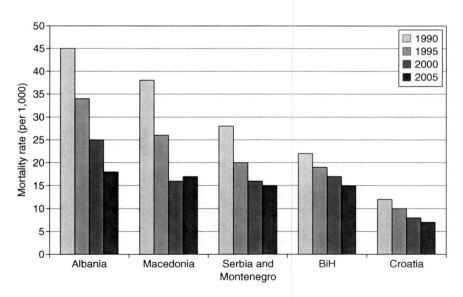

Figure 8.5 Under-five mortality rate, 1990, 1995, 2000 and 2005 (per 1,000) (source: World Bank online database 2007).

In BiH, the provision of health services collapsed during the war, and the health sector came to depend on donor assistance (Deets 2006). Following the Dayton agreement, ten separate HIFs were set up in RS and in the separate cantons of FBiH. These Cantonal Health Insurance Funds (CHIFs) were relatively small and incapable of pooling risk. The fragmentation of administration and finance froze the pre-war distribution of health facilities, and there has been little incentive to reallocate resources between cantons to achieve a more efficient pattern of provision, especially in the hospital sector. The absence of arrangements for cross-financing of health care between cantons has led to significant spatial inequality in health care provision. Moreover, one-third of the population of FBiH and one-sixth of the population of RS are not covered by health insurance due to the large informal economy and to the failure of many employers even in the formal sector to regularly pay health contributions. In addition, farmers and self-employed people who make contributions on a voluntary basis also often fail to pay their health contributions.[17] Although free emergency treatment is offered to non-contributors, there is a charge for the provision of elective non-emergency care, and the system is expensive and inefficient owing to duplication of facilities between cantons. In Serbia, public expenditure on health care decreased under the Milošević regime, leading to deterioration in the quality of public provision, and there has been a corresponding shift to private services by those who can afford it. Private health services now account for almost one-third of health expenditure.

Health care reform

Health care reforms accompanied other pro-market reforms in the early reform countries. They began in Croatia in 1993, with the aim of reducing costs and improving efficiency. The reforms gave a greater role to primary health care and the development of family medicine, shifting resources out of secondary care. Specialist services in polyclinics were replaced by generalist family health care teams in which family doctors act as gatekeepers to secondary care. Partial privatization was introduced by allowing primary care physicians and dentists to lease their premises from the state, and by 1999 about a quarter of primary care practices were supplying services on a private basis.

In Macedonia, similar reforms carried out in 1991 legalized the private provision of health services by primary care practitioners, and a system of capitation payments was introduced for family doctors in 1996 (Nordyke and Peabody 2002). In 2004, amendments to the Law on Health Care provided for the privatization of pharmacies and dental services through a leasing system. The World Bank loaned $10 million to finance the reform of health sector management with a focus on reforms in the provision of day care and primary care services and improvements to revenue collection. The HIF began to negotiate fixed-price contracts with hospitals in an attempt to reduce cost overruns. The Ohrid Agreement has mandated the decentralization of the health care responsibilities to the municipal level, and representatives of municipalities have begun to participate in the boards of primary health care centres (Gjorgjev *et al.* 2006).

In Albania, a compulsory health insurance scheme was introduced in 1995 which covered primary health care services, polyclinics and some basic medicines. Secondary and tertiary health care remained publicly financed and managed, with treatment notionally free at the point of delivery, although in practice patients often make an out-of-pocket payment to access treatment. A new Basic Health Care Law was adopted in 2004, which transferred competences and financial responsibility for health care services to the regional level, gave more autonomy to hospitals and extended the scope of the social insurance system. Central government remained responsible for capital expenditure, while the primary care sector was to be further developed and family doctors were to adopt the role of gatekeepers to filter access to secondary and tertiary services.[18]

Amongst the late reforming countries, health care reforms did not begin until after 2000. In BiH, the pre-war system of health centres (*Dom zdravlja*) which provide specialized services and local primary care outposts (*ambulanta*) staffed by family doctors has remained intact (WHO 2006) while health care reforms have brought about a significant change in their functions with an emphasis on promoting family medicine and quasi-market competition. *Ambulanta* have become primary health units (PHUs) with a community board to oversee their activities. Family doctors working within PHUs are funded on a weighted capitation basis, with additional bonus payments for meeting set targets for specific treatments such as child immunization. Patients are allowed to choose their PHU, introducing an element of competition into the public provision of primary health care services. The *Dom zdravlja* and the secondary and tertiary care hospitals are, however, unaffected by the reforms and will continue to be funded by the HIFs and CHIFs.

In Serbia, health care reforms have not yet been carried out. Low salaries of medical workers have resulted in low motivation and poor quality services. Health policy has focused on innovations in public health, such as information campaigns to reduce the incidence of smoking which is a major cause of ill health. The deteriorating quality of public services has led to the growth of an unregulated private health care sector. This has taken on significant proportions, and it has been estimated that almost one-third of health services are provided by unregulated private practitioners.[19]

In Kosovo, the first priority after the end of the war was to restart and repair the damaged and deteriorated hospitals. In 2000, UNMIK established a Department of Health as a precursor to the new Ministry of Health which was established a year later. The World Health Organization (WHO) provided technical assistance to develop a health policy, which was drawn up by local experts in 2001. The objective of the health policy was to transform the health centres into family-based, preventative primary care organizations in the municipalities in place of the specialist, curative polyclinics. With international assistance, 300 family doctors were trained by 2004, and 800 nurses were trained in family medicine, while a further 600 doctors were trained in health specialisms. A health insurance system was established in 2005. Despite progress in rebuilding the public health system, a significant private health care sector has also emerged in Kosovo.[20]

Education

Education is a key factor in restoring social cohesion in ethnically divided post-conflict societies where it can either promote or block reconciliation depending on the policies adopted and the way in which they are implemented. In transition societies, education is a fundamental element in promoting and facilitating change in society. For example, the reform of vocational education and training (VET) is essential for the wider aim of labour market reform, labour reallocation and structural adjustment. Without the people trained in new skills appropriate to the emerging market economy, the wider hopes for economic reform and economic revitalization and recovery are likely to flounder. Moreover, education is an essential element in sustaining the growth process in the globalized world economy and in developing the competitiveness of open market economies. Finally, education has been identified a key factor in reducing the risk of poverty.

Years of conflict and instability have resulted in significant deterioration in the extent and quality of education provision throughout the region. Several countries have introduced overarching strategies of education reform and established an institutional structure to implement education policies. In VET, reform projects have been directed essentially at the secondary school system and have rarely addressed the pressing problem of retraining the unemployed and redundant workers that have been left stranded by deindustrialization and the loss of career expectations that has affected thousands of adult workers. Projects in the field of adult education and in lifelong learning to enhance the adaptability and employability of the workforce are only just beginning to be introduced, for example through EU CARDS programmes in Croatia and Montenegro.

Problems of implementation of reform policies abound. In Croatia, even though the education system is better funded than in other countries, problems remain in relation to damaged school buildings in the war-affected areas. However, the most pressing problem in Croatia is the low pay of teachers which has led to demoralization among teaching staff. In Albania, inadequate public provision in overcrowded schools has motivated parents to supplement public provision with private resources through additional informal contributions and by buying additional tuition from the private sector. Data on illiteracy rates show the concentration of problems in Albania. There are also problems of corruption within the education system, related partly to low pay and demoralization. In Macedonia, access to schooling is affected by corruption and political pressure in the appointment of school directors.

The provision of education is particularly problematic in BiH where ethnic discrimination hinders equal access to the education system. There are different curricula for the three ethnic groups, and children are often taught in different classrooms in the same school. In FBiH although education expenditure is relatively high, the multiplication of administration at the various levels of government and the duplication of facilities within some cantons have led to an inefficient use of resources. Equipment is out of date and obsolete, there is a shortage of teachers in some fields of education and there is a lack of appropriate infrastructure for adult education (CoM-BiH 2004: 179). The financial resources that are available are spent almost entirely on teachers' salaries and little is left for the maintenance of buildings, leading to a gradual deterioration of the physical infrastructure. In Serbia and Montenegro, the school system has suffered from a chronic lack of investment over the years, and in Montenegro only 1.3 per cent of the education budget is available for capital expenditure and maintenance. In Kosovo, the education system has had to be rebuilt both physically and academically in the aftermath of a decade of exclusion of the Albanian minority from the school system and following the destructive impact of war. In addition, a high rate of illiteracy among girls reflects the phenomenon of early school dropout especially in traditional rural villages, which represents a challenge to policy makers concerned with issues of gender equality and social inclusion.

EU integration has brought significant new policy initiatives and international support for the reform and renewal of the education and training systems, and the CARDS programme has assisted the reform of VET systems. EU involvement has stimulated governments to pay greater attention to education and training in order to catch up to EU norms, practices and targets, for example in higher education through adherence to the Bologna process of education reforms, although adult education and vocational training has been relatively neglected. There is also a problem of access to education in rural areas in Kosovo, Montenegro and Serbia for children from poor and vulnerable families of refugees and IDPs and for female pupils after the fifth grade in some rural and mountainous communities.

Roma

The large Roma minority in the Western Balkans suffers from widespread discrimination on the labour market, as well as in education and in other areas of social life. A regional programme for the whole of south-east Europe to assist the social inclusion of Roma populations, the 'Decade of Roma Inclusion' was launched in June 2003. Gathering support from eight European governments, and many international organizations, it represents the first international effort to change the lives of Roma in Europe. As a framework for governments to work towards Roma integration, the initiative will monitor progress in ending the severe discrimination and devastating poverty faced by Roma communities. Croatia, Macedonia, Serbia and Montenegro are among the founding sponsors, which will span 2005–15. Their backing signals a sea change in Roma policy and in the political will necessary for reform. To accelerate social inclusion and improve the economic status of Roma in these countries, each country has set a limited number of measurable national goals for improvements in priority areas. Full Roma participation is envisaged in the planned course of action. The initiative is guided by an International Steering Committee, made up of representatives of governments, Roma from each country and international organizations, which established four priority areas – education, employment, health and housing. The Steering Committee also determined three cross-cutting themes: income poverty, discrimination and gender. Each participating country's action plan identifies goals and indicators in these areas.

Social welfare reforms and the welfare mix

In the post-Dayton period, the international institutions and international donors became more active in the Western Balkans. One of the main new ideas that the international organizations introduced was the idea of the 'welfare mix', based upon the opening up of the provision of social services to private and non-profit providers including NGOs. The aim was to add extra capacity to welfare provision in the face of declining public resources. It also embodied the belief of the officials working in donor organizations that public provision is less efficient than private or non-profit provision. The welfare mix approach also encompassed the idea of decentralization of services to the local level. Laws on social welfare reform were introduced in Macedonia in 1997 and in RS in 2003. These envisaged a shift to a welfare mix involving greater participation of civil society, including NGOs, in the provision of social services, in partnership with municipal authorities and the private sector. A similar law in Serbia based on the welfare mix approach began the deinstitutionalization of care homes and decentralized funding and competencies to municipalities. A Social Innovation Fund (SIF) was established to mobilize innovative NGOs in the provision of social services. In Croatia, a team of experts funded by the World Bank studied social welfare reform and recommended similar changes, although implementation of the proposals was stalled following the election of the new HDZ government at the end of 2003.

In Albania, the decentralization of social services has been promoted by international donors, and pilot projects testing the viability of decentralized provision were implemented in Tirana, Durrës, Shkodra and Vlora. In September 2004, a new draft Law on Social Assistance and Welfare, prepared with support from the World Bank, was discussed in the Albanian parliament. It aimed to develop community-based social services involving NGOs and other civil society organizations in the provision of social services. In Kosovo, a Law on Social Welfare was introduced to improve the legal framework established by UNMIK after the war. FBiH was the only exception, as its welfare reforms envisaged centralization of the dispersed cantonal organizations that had been established under the Dayton agreement and which had led to significant spatial inequalities in the provision of social welfare services and social assistance payments.

These new laws introduced by international donors and aid agencies were based on a large dose of optimism. In seeking to promote a welfare mix based upon a plurality of providers including the state, the private sector and non-profit

NGOs, they attempted to introduce ideas that are still only in an experimental stage in some of the advanced market economies in the West. The policies have been largely ineffective due to the weakness of the NGO sector. The NGO sector had received donor funding in the 1990s, but this was mainly to promote 'political' NGOs, and the promotion of genuine social sector NGOs capable of providing social services has been relatively neglected.

European integration and the social acquis

With the prospect of future EU membership in view, the countries of the Western Balkans are, at varying speeds, putting in place the necessary institutional infrastructure required for EU entry. As noted above, in the field of social policy, this essentially reflects the EU's 'social acquis', the parts of the *acquis communautaire* that relate to social issues. Since social policy competence of the EU is essentially structured around the creation of labour mobility and equal treatment of labour in the single market, the social acquis is primarily focused on labour issues such as social dialogue, gender equality, equal opportunities and health and safety at work and has recently been further extended into related fields such as youth policy and disability policy (Geyer 2000).

Social dialogue

Institutions of social dialogue were established in the early reforming countries during the 1990s: in Croatia in 1993, in Macedonia in 1996 and in Albania in 1997. In line with their generally delayed reforms, these institutions were not established until 2001 in Serbia, Montenegro and Kosovo. In Croatia, the Economic and Social Council (ESC) was initially founded in 1993 and revised in 1996 (Djurić 2002). However, due to disagreement on its representativeness, and to the authoritarian tendencies of the government of the time, the work of the Council was effectively blocked until 1999 when a law was passed determining the criteria on which the representative nature of the trade union associations was determined.[21] The ESC operates at national level and through eighteen regional branches. It is a tripartite consultative body on which each of the social partners has six seats. Each has the power of veto over labour laws presented to the government. The social partners are also involved in the tripartite boards of the pension fund, the National Council for Occupational Health and Safety, the Employment Bureau and other institutions. Croatia can be considered to be the furthest advanced in the practice of social dialogue, although weaknesses still exist. The high point of the influence of the trade unions on government policy came immediately after the election of a new government in 2000 which overturned the previous authoritarian regime. After the election, the new government signed a partnership for development with the trade unions and employers' organizations which defined seventeen common goals. The document covered various issues including the basis for social policy and social priorities, an agreement on wage policy, the method of implementing restructuring and privatization of the economy and the programme for making an analysis of the European Social Charter. The agreement broke down in 2002 when amendments to the Labour Law were introduced by the government that were unacceptable to the Croatian trade union association (SSSH). Following the defeat of the Social Democratic Party (SDP)-led government in 2003, the HDZ government and the social partners developed an agreement 'Through Social Partnership to the European Union' as a basis for the development of social dialogue. A priority of policy in this field has been to develop the institutions of arbitration and conciliation in the field of labour relations.

In Albania, the National Council of Labour is the main tripartite body with twenty-seven members (ten each from the social partners and seven from the government). Although it is supposed to work closely with the Ministry of Labour and Social Affairs on issues of social policy and labour policy, in practice it rarely meets. The social partners also participate in the tripartite boards of the Social Insurance Institute, the Health Care Insurance Institute, the National Employment Service (the Training Enterprise and the Employment Fund) and the State Labour Inspectorate. The practice of social dialogue is weak in Albania, and the institutions of social dialogue are largely ineffective.

In BiH, there is no ESC at state level because the trade unions are divided on ethnic lines. The BiH Council of Employers has recently been recognized by the government, but there is no counterpart Trade Union Council (TUC). Instead, the two ESCs operate at entity level. The RS ESC was established in 1997, and the FBiH ESC was established in 2002. The RS ESC is not provided with any resources by the government which has little interest in the process of social dialogue. The social partners on the ESC include the RS Employers Association which was formed in 2000 and the RS TUC, an association of trades unions which covers 97 per cent of the workforce and has offices in all municipalities. The RS TUC was established in 1992 and later reformed in 1998. Its membership encompasses 97 per cent of all employees in the entity and claims to be independent of the political authorities, professional interests and ethnic and religious groups. In 1997, it signed a general collective agreement, subsequently amended, with contracts for each of the fourteen branches of the economy it represents. The situation was explained by a trade union leader in Banja Luka:

> Of the 230,000 workers in RS, about 55,000 work in the private sector. They are paid irregularly because their companies suffer from huge losses, while public sector workers and civil servants are paid on a regular basis. In the textile and leather industry the situation facing workers is catastrophic. On paper, 20,000 people are employed in the industry, but in practice only 6,000 are actually working and 14,000 are placed on a 'waiting list', where they are idle but not formally discharged because the employers cannot afford to make the required redundancy payments. Under the new bankruptcy law, these workers are to be dismissed without compensation, but the law is not being implemented because of the government's fear of a popular backlash. On the other hand companies such as the Post Office, the Tele-

coms, and power plant companies all pay high and regular salaries and are over-staffed with employees. Their directors are politically appointed, and they are not interested in dismissing surplus workers. The trade unions in these companies are fighting against privatization because they are unwilling to lose jobs in those industries. In this, the trade unions act as hidden spokesmen for the government which is also against privatization, but does not say so because of fear of sanctions from the international community. Although the RS TUC says all this quite openly in the Economic and Social Council it feels that its opinion is ignored. The RS Trades Union Council estimated that as many as 70,000 workers would be dismissed if the bankruptcy law is put into full effect.

(Interview with Trade Union leader, Banja Luka September 2004)

Overall, despite the creation of an institutional framework for social dialogue in the Western Balkans, practice trails behind aspirations. As regards the differences of degree between the various countries, a recent International Labour Organization (ILO) report has indicated, on the basis of a survey research, that Albania and Croatia have acquired significant experience in tripartite social dialogue. In other countries, the experience of social dialogue is more recent and remains fragile, and the central institutions of social dialogue lack the human, financial and administrative resources to operate effectively.

Gender equality

Gender equality laws were passed in BiH and Croatia in 2003 and in Albania and Kosovo in 2004, while in Macedonia the Labour Relations Law of 2005 contains prohibitions on discrimination. National Action Plans for Gender Equality have been adopted in Macedonia in 2000 and in Kosovo in 2004, while a National Policy for Gender Equality was adopted in Croatia in 2003, and a National Action Plan has been prepared in RS. In order to implement the provisions of the laws and the associated action plans, government offices for gender equality were established in RS and FBiH in 2001 and in Croatia and Kosovo in 2004, while a gender equality agency has been established in BiH at the state level, and a council for gender equality has been established in Serbia. Administrative capacity among these offices has been variable. In 2004, the RS Gender Centre had a staff of six and many associates, whereas the Croatian government's Office for Gender Equality had a staff of just four.[22] In Croatia, the office of an Ombudsman for Gender Equality has been created to monitor the implementation of the gender equality law, but as a self-funding organization it had insufficient administrative capacity.[23] In Albania, a committee for equal opportunities has been the main organization promoting gender equality.

Parliamentary committees for gender equality have been established in Albania, Croatia, RS and Serbia. In RS, gender commissions have been established at the municipality level, and focal points have been established within the ministries to monitor the implementation of the gender equality laws.

In Kosovo, institutional structures have been created within ministries with a similar role. In 2004, Croatia had not yet established gender equality units within the line ministries, while in Macedonia the Ministry of Labour and Social Affairs had established a unit for gender equality, and in Albania the government was in the process of establishing a network of focal points within ministries.[24] Least progress has been made in addressing gender equality issues in Serbia and Montenegro, where there are no specific laws on gender equality, mainly because of a lack of political will. Although new laws had been introduced in 2004 to combat family violence and organized trafficking, the laws on labour relations provided little support for women to appeal against discrimination in the labour market.[25]

Thus, institutional and legal structures for the improvement of women's position have been put in place in several of the countries in the Western Balkans. The issues that they have been actively concerned with have included the representation of women in the political process and the improvement of the position of women in the labour market, in business and in social positions in civil society. Women's business associations have been active in several countries, aiming to improve the representation of women within the small business community. In Kosovo, for example a network of women's businesses was established in 2003, with plans to create seven regional centres to support women setting up small businesses.[26] The NGO sector has also been involved in the promotion of gender equality issues, for example through the Alliance for Gender Equality in Albania and in the fight against trafficking and domestic violence. Trafficking in women is a serious problem in the Western Balkans (UNICEF 2002). Countries with a large presence of international military forces, including BiH and Kosovo, are destination countries for trafficked women, while other countries including Serbia, Montenegro and Macedonia are mainly transit countries (Malarek 2004). The Organization for Security and Cooperation in Europe (OSCE) and the International Organization for Migration have been involved in tackling this problem in conjunction with local NGOs and governments.

9   International aid and regional cooperation

Speaking to the Economic Club of Chicago in April 1999, Tony Blair announced 'We need a new Marshall Plan for Kosovo, Montenegro, Macedonia, Albania and Serbia too, if it turns to democracy.'[1] Although the ambitions for a new Marshall Plan were not realized, the Western Balkan countries have been host to an enormous inflow of humanitarian and developmental aid over the last decade and a half. International assistance peaked in 2002 and has been declining since then, mainly because aid from bilateral donors has fallen sharply. Aid was not always effective due to the difficulty of donor coordination and the reactions of the recipient countries to the aid programmes. Established in 2000, the Stability Pact attempted to address the problem of donor coordination. In doing so, it acted as a policy broker between various advocacy coalitions composed of donor organizations which promoted distinct approaches to transition, development and post-conflict reconstruction. The reactions of the recipient countries to the aid programmes proved to be more difficult to manage, and various conditions were laid down by donors to ensure the implementation of their programmes. As a consequence, the influence of the domestic elites over key elements of institutional reform diminished in those countries that became more dependent on aid. Among the late reformers, aid inflows sometimes substituted for effective reforms, while the early reformers developed a greater capacity to design their own reform programmes and had less need of international assistance.

Aid effectiveness, reforms and policy transfer

A major issue is whether aid has been effective in increasing growth in the Western Balkan countries. Several empirical studies have questioned the impact of international aid on economic growth and found that aid is often used to support increased consumption rather than being channelled into productive investment (Boone 1996). Aid to the post-socialist Balkan countries was argued to be more effective where there has been a domestic political consensus amongst pro-reform coalitions on the distribution of gains from growth (Bartlett 1997a). However, a study of twenty-six transition countries including all the Western Balkan countries except BiH over the period 1990–8 found little evidence that aid flows had any impact on growth in the region (Kekić 2001). Even where aid has been effective because pro-reform governments pursue supportive policies, there is often a point beyond which aid loses its effectiveness due to the limited 'absorptive capacity' of recipient countries and the ineffective use of aid by weak public administrations (Dalgaard and Hansen 2001). Nevertheless, aid can often be effective in post-conflict societies where government revenues have collapsed, and infrastructure has been destroyed in the aftermath of war (Collier and Hoeffler 2004).

Aid effectiveness may be adversely affected by long chains of principals and agents, in which donors and recipients have different interests (Gibson *et al.* 2005). In such a chain, an aid agency typically has two principals: a donor government and a recipient government. If the aims of the donor and the recipient government are aligned, and both are agreed on the set of reforms to be supported by the aid programme, then the existence of two principals should be manageable. On the other hand, if the recipient government is controlled by an anti-reform coalition, the effectiveness of the aid agency may be compromised unless the donor is able to set conditions on the use of aid. Such conditionality may effectively circumscribe any negative influence of an anti-reform coalition over the aid programme but may also undermine the legitimacy of the programme and diminish the collaborative commitment to implementation. The institutional arrangements within which aid is organized are thus extremely important in determining the link between aid and growth, and the principal–agent relationship is a likely culprit in explaining the weak association that has been observed between aid and economic growth on numerous occasions. There are many examples of the ineffectiveness of such aid chains and donor–recipient relationships in the Western Balkan countries.[2]

Problems can also arise when there are many donors acting as principals, each with conflicting objectives which send confusing messages to recipient government policy makers, especially if each donor imposes a different set of conditions. Attempts by recipients to meet inconsistent conditions laid down by multiple donors can undermine the coherence of development policies and lead to administrative inefficiency. The issue of donor coordination has been raised on many occasions in the Western Balkan countries in relation to the problems of conflicting objectives and overlap between donor aid programmes, and aid coordination units have been set up in several recipient countries.

Each donor organization has brought its own vision of the appropriate set of policies that are needed to revitalize war-damaged transitional economies. Bilateral donors have often favoured institutional reforms that have been inspired by the institutional framework adopted in their own country. Amongst multilateral donors, the World Bank, the International Labour Organization (ILO) and the European Union (EU) each have their own view of what a capitalist economy in the Western Balkans should look like and have therefore championed a variety of strategies and policies with varying aims, whether promoting transition, post-conflict development or EU accession (Deacon *et al.* 1997). Such 'policy transfer' by international aid agencies and non-governmental organizations (NGOs) raises many issues of effectiveness and appropriateness, including whether policy transfer is voluntary or coercive, whether it leads to policy convergence or divergence and what are the determinants of success or failure (Dolowitz and Marsh 2000). Policy transfer may fail where the transferred policies are uninformed by an understanding of the local context, which is more likely where policy design is too heavily influenced by donor organizations. Policy transfer may also fail if the transfer process is incomplete or inappropriate, which is likely to occur where donor agencies disagree about the policies to be transferred. Examples of failed policy transfer are common in international aid programmes, and the Western Balkan countries have not been immune from this problem.

The donor agencies

Most official international finance, including both concessional and non-concessional loans, originates from the international financial institutions (IFIs) including the World Bank and the European development banks. The EU is the largest provider of grant aid through its pre-accession funds which aim to prepare Western Balkan countries for eventual EU membership. The EU has also provided humanitarian assistance through its external aid office ECHO. Bilateral donors have also been active, including many from EU countries, while both financial and in-kind assistance have been provided by numerous NGOs including organizations connected to various faith groups, for example the Catholic 'Caritas' aid organization.

The largest part, about one-third, of the flows of international financial assistance to the Western Balkans has been provided for infrastructure projects, a sixth has been provided for private sector development and a further sixth for institution building in government administrations. Relatively small proportions have been devoted to agricultural development and social sector support. Grant aid declined by almost a half between 2001 and 2005, mainly due to a sharp fall from bilateral donors which was only partly offset by an increase in grant aid from the EU (Figure 9.1). Loans of all types provided by the IFIs stayed about the same so that, overall, the total financial flows fell from €3.6 billion in 2001 to €2.8 billion in 2005.

This decline in overall flows of international financial assistance implies a need for increased inflows of private finance either in the form of remittances, foreign direct investment, or borrowing on international capital markets, unless the countries' own earnings from exports of goods and services can be substantially increased.

In practice, international assistance may have some unintended consequences and spill-over effects in the local economies. In Macedonia, Kosovo and BiH, the donor community presence became especially prominent in the capital cities, Skopje, Priština and Sarajevo. Its presence and ability to pay high salaries led to distortions of the local labour market and generated an 'internal brain drain' away from government offices, ministries and public organizations. International aid workers have put pressure on housing markets and pushed up the price of rents in the centre of major cities (Barakat and Kapisazovic 2003).

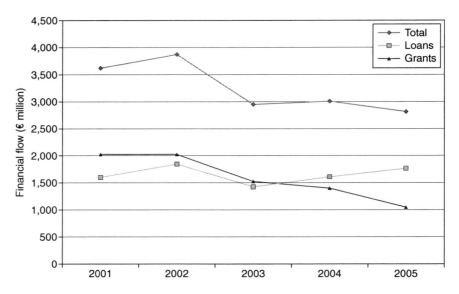

Figure 9.1 Financial flows to the Western Balkans, 2001–5 (€ million) (source: Derived from 'Financial Flows to South East Europe', European Commission/World Bank Office of South East Europe 2005).

The World Bank

The World Bank has a resident representative in each of the Western Balkan countries, directing local offices with relatively large staffs of analysts and sector specialists. These have been involved in analysis of a wide range of policy areas covering both economic and social development issues. Country assistance strategies (CASs) have been developed for each country, for example the CAS for Bosnia and Herzegovina (BiH) for the period 2005–7 was adopted in September 2004 and was the result of a long period of negotiation and consultation with local stakeholders. In recent years, the Bank has led the preparation of Poverty Reduction Strategy Papers (PRSPs) which have been developed in Albania, BiH, Serbia and Montenegro, written by the governments of the recipient countries. A PRSP sets out macroeconomic, structural and social policies and programmes to reduce poverty and identifies the external financing needs and sources of financing.[3] The first PRSP in the region was the Albanian National Strategy for Social and Economic Development (NSSED) launched in 2001, followed by PRSP policy documents for Serbia and Montenegro (2003) and for BiH (2004). The PRSPs adopted the UN Millennium Development Goals, which prescribe targets for poor countries aimed at cutting poverty in half by 2015 and set out aims around which donor support can be mobilized and coordinated. They involve recipient governments in a complex process of project cycle management built around stakeholder participation. Croatia and

Macedonia are not part of the PRSP process since they are more closely under the guidance of the EU with which they have signed Stabilization and Association Agreements. A draft PRSP was developed for Macedonia, but the final version was abandoned when Macedonia 'graduated' from the category of low-income country with access to concessional loans and adopted the EU accession process as its main policy objective. Even so, the World Bank has adopted a CAS for both countries to guide its assistance programmes.

Despite its apparently participatory approach, the World Bank also adopts coercive practices when its CAS is questioned. For example, in the case of BiH, the World Bank Country Director warned the entity prime ministers in 2005 that they were in danger of losing $108 million World Bank funding due to the slow implementation of reforms. According to a press release, three projects were at risk and their suspension

> would not only jeopardize implementation of the ongoing reforms but it would [also] affect the level of future World Bank investments in the country . . . and would certainly have further negative effects on the attitude of some other investors and development partners.[4]

The conditionality applied by the World Bank and the IMF is an example of 'development governance' in action, especially in those countries where a PRSP process has been used to define a set of development priorities.

The European Development Banks

The European Investment Bank (EIB) was established by the Treaty of Rome in 1958 to finance European infrastructure projects.[5] It made a series of loans to the former Yugoslavia starting in 1977 for the power transmission network, the trans-Yugoslav highway and railway system.[6] Between 1991 and 1997, the EIB's only activity in the region comprised loans to Albania for road-building, port infrastructure and power transmission projects. Lending to the Yugoslav successor, states re-commenced in 1998 with a loan to Macedonia for road-building. In 1999, the EIB established a Balkan Task Force to assess infrastructure needs in South-East Europe which identified thirty-five Quick-Start projects leading to a large programme of infrastructure investment. In June 2001, Federal Republic of Yugoslavia (FRY) agreed to repay its €225 million debt to the Bank, financed through a loan from the Swiss government, opening up its access to EIB finance.[7] Since the resumption of its operations in 1995 up to the end of 2004, the EIB had lent a total of €2.1 billion to the Western Balkan countries. Four-fifths of the total has gone to Croatia, Serbia and Montenegro primarily for investment in transport infrastructure to improve connections with the EU. Loans have also been made to Croatia for environmental protection, to Serbia and Montenegro for small and medium-sized enterprise (SME) development and to Albania for the construction of a power plant in Vlore (EIB 2004). EIB activity in the region has mainly been focused on basic infrastructure, energy and transport but has also included support for local municipalities, environmental protection, health and human capital and the private sector.

The second major European development bank, the European Bank for Reconstruction and Development (EBRD), was created in 1991 to finance restructuring and development in the transition countries of Eastern Europe and the CIS,[8] through a number of financing instruments including loans, equity participation and guarantees. According to its Articles of Agreement, the EBRD can only lend to countries that apply 'the principles of multiparty democracy, pluralism and market economics'. This conditionality is more relaxed than that applied to EU assistance programmes such as PHARE and CARDS, and it has therefore been able to engage with Western Balkan states at times when they have been excluded from EU programmes. The EBRD invested over €2.9 billion in the Western Balkans from the start of its operations in 1991 up to the end of 2004, mainly supporting projects for the privatization and restructuring of financial institutions and for the development of local and regional infrastructure (EBRD 2005a). Almost half of EBRD loans have been made to Croatia, where €1.3 billion had been lent by 2004. In 2006, the bank launched a €10 million Western Balkans Fund and had a pipeline $800 million of projects under consideration for the region. Overall, the EBRD has made almost 11 per cent of its total loans to Western Balkan countries.

The EBRD provides project-specific financing on a commercial basis in support of restructuring, privatization and SME development, usually channelled through local commercial banks,[9] and has been instrumental in establishing a number of specialized microfinance institutions which have provided loans to more than 3,000 small businesses. It manages two programmes financed by other international donor organizations: the Business Advisory Service (BAS) and the Turn-around Management (TAM) programme. BAS helps microsized enterprises and SMEs to improve their competitiveness through advice from local consultants. TAM provides outside management expertise to larger companies to assist their restructuring and the development of new management skills. The EBRD has also established a Trade Facilitation Programme which provides finance for exporters through local banks.

The third main European public finance institution active in the region, but on a much smaller scale, is the Council of Europe Development Bank (CEDB) whose members and principal shareholders are thirty-eight European states.[10] It provides long-term loans for social projects, including support facilities for refugees and displaced persons, for social housing, for job creation through SME development and for environmental and educational projects, while a Selective Trust Account provides subsidized interest loans to projects with a high social content. For example, in 2004, it provided €18 million to Croatia to co-finance the reconstruction of school buildings for the benefit of refugees and displaced persons, while an €8 million project was approved for BiH for the rehabilitation of 1,100 dwellings damaged during the war.[11] Between 2000 and 2004, the CEDB approved projects in the Western Balkans to a value of €212 million and disbursed loans to a value of €122 million. The main beneficiary was Croatia which received 85 per cent of the total amount disbursed to support the process of refugee return.

Overall, the European Development Banks have funded infrastructure projects, SME development and a wide variety of social projects. The assistance has been in the form of concessional loans which have demonstrated the commercial viability of projects and drawn in additional private finance to countries that were previously perceived as too risky for private investment. However, the commercial basis of the funding decisions has meant that the allocation of the available resources has been skewed to the more developed and stable economies. Thus, Croatia has received by far the greatest share of funding from the development banks among the countries in the Western Balkans, while Serbia and Montenegro have also received significant amounts since 2001. The other Western Balkan countries have received proportionately little funding from these sources.

The European Agency for Reconstruction

Immediately after the end of the Kosovo war, the EU established a Task Force for the reconstruction of Kosovo (EC TAFKO) which operated from July 1999 to implement an emergency programme. In February 2000, it was replaced by the European Agency for Reconstruction (EAR), which as a decentralized agency of the EU was directly accountable to the EU Council of Ministers and the European Parliament. The main aim was to ensure that the EU aid programmes were delivered more effectively and more speedily, by having an independent agency on the ground which would eliminate some of the bureaucracy which had slowed down the implementation of EU aid in BiH. The Agency was responsible for the entire project cycle including identifying, designing, contracting, managing, implementing, paying, monitoring and evaluating projects. The EAR headquarters were established in Thessaloniki in Greece and a local operational centre was set up in Priština. Following the democratic turn in Serbia, the EAR extended its operations to Serbia and set up an office in Belgrade in 2000. A further office was established in Podgorica in Montenegro in 2001. Following the civil conflict in Macedonia in 2001, a fourth office was opened in Skopje in March 2002. In each of these countries, the EAR took over responsibility for the delivery of EU aid programmes from the local EU delegations. By 2005, the EAR had committed funds amounting to €2.6 billion in aid projects to Kosovo, Serbia and Montenegro and to Macedonia (EAR 2006). Initially, the main focus had been on emergency reconstruction, rebuilding destroyed buildings and facilities. For example, €41 million was spent on rebuilding the Sloboda Bridge in Novi Sad which had been destroyed by NATO bombing. Other emergency reconstruction activities included repair and improvement of power and water supply infrastructure, transport, sewerage and agriculture. Following on from that, the focus moved to economic development, including support for SME development through training and loans to small businesses, promoting trade with the EU, establishing banks and privatizing and restructuring socially owned enterprises. Attention was also paid to strengthening social structures, interpreted as support for civil society development, through training and loans for NGOs. As the European integration agenda has gathered pace in recent years, the focus of attention has again shifted to supporting pre-accession activities, and especially towards building the capacity of the public administration, decentralizing government to local level and improving the justice system in order to strengthen the rule of law (EAR 2003).

The United Nations agencies

The United National Development Programme (UNDP) has offices based in each country in the Western Balkans supported by its regional headquarters in Bratislava. Since 1998, the UNDP has delivered more than $226 million of assistance programmes to the region for post-conflict income generation and microcredit programmes, support for the return of refugees and internally displaced persons, capacity building through public administration reform programmes to foster effective governance, development of strategic approaches to the Millennium Development Goals, youth programmes and support to SMEs. It has been especially active in building up civil society through capacity building in the NGO sector and more recently has moved towards a focus on local economic development.

The Office of the UN High Commissioner for Refugees (UNHCR) has been responsible for providing aid to the hundreds of thousands of refugees which were created by the wars of the 1990s. While almost two million people have returned to their homes, a further 420,000 people remain displaced, including 110,000 refugees in BiH, 119,000 in Croatia and 190,000 in Serbia and Montenegro. While many of the refugees from the wars in Croatia, BiH and Macedonia have returned home, very few of those expelled from Kosovo in 1999 have done so. The resolution of the final status of Kosovo could trigger a further wave of refugees from among the 160,000 ethnic minority population in the province. The civilian staffs of the UNHCR have carried out dangerous work in conflicts throughout the region, bringing essential relief to refugees and displaced persons. The direct relationship between the donor and the recipient in the case of refugee relief has curtailed the length of the aid chain and increased the effectiveness of the aid that has been provided.

Bilateral donors

In most of the Western Balkan states, there are a large number of smaller donor organizations and agencies which compete against each other for the attention of the government. These include the national aid agencies of the main donor countries, as well as various sorts of NGOs, many of which operate on a global scale, and others which have been established specifically to act in the Western Balkan region. Among the bilateral donors, the most prominent has been the USA which has provided about two-fifths of all grant aid from the bilaterals. Other large donors included Germany, Italy, Netherlands, Sweden and Switzerland. Greece became a significant donor more recently, while aid from Germany, Italy and the Netherlands has fallen back (Table 9.1). Bilateral agencies tend to focus on development projects at local level, if for no other reason than that their smaller capacity limits the scope of their operations. Major bilateral donors include USAID (USA), DfID (UK), GTZ (Germany), SIDA (Sweden) and others.[12] USAID is one of the largest bilateral agencies with a strong focus on local economic development and the development of the capacity of municipal administrations.

Many international NGOs, such as Caritas and World Vision, have been active in delivering assistance funded by direct donations or working in cooperation with the major multilateral or bilateral agencies. The increase in international aid has stimulated a rapid growth in local NGOs, which are a relatively new phenomenon in the region. NGOs have been most heavily engaged at local level, with an emphasis on short-term emergency relief and small-scale operations. While having a significant impact in some instances, their capacity to carry out sustainable developmental interventions has been rather low. In recent years, the most effective NGO activity has been in the provision of microfinance, which provides small-scale financial resources to individual entrepreneurs, often women, in an effort to kick-start business activity in deprived rural or urban areas, where more conventional sources of finance are scarce.

Table 9.1 Financial assistance to South East Europe by country (€ million)

	2001			2005		
	Grants	*Loans*	*Total*	*Grants*	*Loans*	*Total*
Canada	42	0	42	15	0	15
France	53	0	53	0	0	0
Germany	252	0	252	35	23	58
Greece	0	0	0	155	0	155
Italy	115	0	115	0	0	0
Luxembourg	0	0	0	9	0	9
Netherlands	182	0	182	55	0	55
Portugal	11	0	11	8	24	32
Spain	9	0	9	12	1	14
Sweden	86	0	86	82	0	82
Switzerland	124	0	124	81	0	81
UK	57	0	57	33	0	33
USA	752	0	752	310	0	310

Source: 'Financial Flows to South East Europe', European Commission/World Bank Office of South East Europe 2005

Note
This list is not exclusive.

The Stability Pact and donor coordination

The Kosovo war inspired an urgent search for appropriate policies to underpin economic and social development, and the international alliance which had forced the Milošević regime to leave Kosovo agreed to the creation of a 'Stability Pact' for South-East Europe in Cologne in June 1999.[13] The Stability Pact was to oversee the international effort to establish political stability in the region and therefore promoted the principle of 'regional cooperation' as a basis for security, democracy and economic development.[14] The intended beneficiaries were Albania, BiH, Bulgaria, Croatia, Macedonia and Romania. The prospect of eventual membership of the Pact was held out to FRY on condition of effective democratization, while Montenegro was given special consideration in recognition of the reformist policies of the Djukanović government. FRY eventually joined the Stability Pact after the overthrow of the Milošević regime.[15] Despite its political rhetoric, the practical role of the Stability Pact was to ensure coordination between the various donor organizations.

The Stability Pact was led by a Special Coordinator[16] appointed by the EU with an office and secretariat in Brussels. Its main activities were divided into working tables, on (i) democratization and human rights, (ii) economic reconstruction, development and cooperation and (iii) security issues. Working Table II on economic reconstruction evolved to encompass a wide variety of policy areas with numerous task forces covering issues such as regional infrastructure, the energy market, trade liberalization, private sector development, enterprise development, employment generation, foreign investment, the environment, housing and urban management and social cohesion. A division of labour was established between the lead agencies responsible for different policy areas. For example, the Organisation for Security and Cooperation in Europe (OSCE) was to oversee and monitor the development of democratic practices in the region; the Council of Europe contributed through its experience with the development of conventions in the social field, human rights, justice and education; the UNHCR took a lead role in the protection and return of refugees; the Paris-based Organization for Economic Cooperation and Development (OECD) contributed to policy development for economic reconstruction and private sector development; while the IFIs contributed financial resources and policy advice. The USA, Russia and NATO were identified with specific policy fields related to economic development and security. Although the governments of the region were identified as the main beneficiaries, they had no specific role in policy design. The establishment of the Stability Pact underlined the fact that key elements of economic, political and security governance of the region had slipped out of the hands of the domestic elites and that outside powers were now closely involved in the governance of the affairs of the region.

A High Level Steering Group, composed of representatives from the EU, the World Bank and other international financial institutions, organized the first Regional Funding Conference in March 2000 in Brussels to gather pledges of support for economic reconstruction from donor organizations.[17] The World

Bank presented a Regional Strategy Paper (World Bank 2000), the EIB presented a framework for the development of infrastructure and the EBRD presented a regional framework for the development of the private sector. The liberalization and facilitation of trade, both between the countries of the region and with the EU, was emphasized as a key objective that would eventually lead to a reduction in reliance on outside aid. The importance of infrastructure development and a vibrant private sector were emphasized at the conference, but 'numerous speakers' also underlined the need to overcome the 'underlying causes of tension' by addressing the issues of internally displaced persons, minorities, social cohesion and unemployment, building democratic institutions and strengthening the rule of law in the region.[18] All the main institutions and organizations set out their plans for the future assistance to the region to promote economic reconstruction and development. Donor organizations pledged €2.4 billion to finance a €1.8 billion Quick-Start package of projects and to contribute to a set of further projects for economic reconstruction and development.

Thus, many different national and international actors were involved in assisting the development of policy in many different fields under the umbrella of the Stability Pact, working through numerous transnational policy networks and advocacy coalitions. Policy conflicts between these advocacy coalitions were mediated by the Stability Pact acting as a 'policy broker'.[19] From this perspective, the main object of its activities has been managing the policy conflict and debate among transnational advocacy coalitions comprising various combinations of international organizations and IFIs. Expectations that the Stability Pact would bring about a rapid increase in donor funds and a regeneration of economic activity were disappointed. The Stability Pact did not evolve into a new Marshall Plan for the region, and relatively few projects of a regional nature were funded. Instead it focused on supporting actions geared towards developing regional cooperation, donor coordination and policy development. Indeed, it could almost be said that the practice of regional cooperation had more to do with cooperation between the major donor organizations than with cooperation between the recipient countries.

Advocacy coalitions: the Investment Compact

Several organizations have been active within the Stability Pact to promote private sector development at a regional level. One of the most active has been the 'Investment Compact' (IC) established by the OECD whose main objective has been to boost private sector investment in the region. Among its various activities, the IC has actively followed reforms relevant to the development of the private sector through annual 'Monitoring Instruments', which provide a checklist of progress in general pro-market reforms in each country, and through annual 'Enterprise Policy and Performance Assessments' which focused on policy reform in the SME sector.[20] The IC has applied the rational policy cycle methodology used by the OECD in other contexts involving target setting, implementation, monitoring and evaluation. It has emphasized private sector involvement in the policy process. Foreign Investors Councils have been established in each Western Balkan country to lobby governments on economic policy and legislation. A Business Forum has been established to enable businesses to lobby at the highest policy levels to promote opportunities for investment.[21]

In recent years, the IC has promoted a greater involvement of the countries of the region in the policy process through encouraging regional 'ownership'. It has ensured that the South-East Europe Investment Forum has been chaired by countries of the region, by Romania in 2003/4 and by Albania since 2005. It has established a Regional Network of Foreign Investor Councils with a Secretariat in Serbia since 2004. Since 2005, the policy cycle methodology has emphasized target setting based on an 'Investment Reform Index' and has introduced horizontal policy evaluation through the mechanism of 'peer review' along the lines of OECD practice in other contexts (Dostal 2004; Schafer 2006).

Advocacy coalitions: the initiative for social cohesion

In contrast to the IC emphasis on private sector development, a number of regional projects and programmes have been developed in different fields of social policy. The most prominent of these has been the Social Cohesion Initiative, established in collaboration with the Council of Europe. Under the umbrella of the Stability Pact, the Social Cohesion Initiative has promoted regional networks in the fields of social security and pensions, health and housing. Various policy networks have been established in these four areas of activity on a regional level. The Council of Europe has sponsored a 'Social Security Coordination Network' in cooperation with the ILO which has trained civil servants in techniques of social security coordination. The CARDS programme has funded a 'Social Institution Support Programme' focusing on cross-border social security including the coordination of social security policies and the mutual recognition of acquired pension rights. A regional Centre for Coordination of Social Policy Issues has been established in Skopje. In the health sector, the Council of Europe and the WHO have sponsored the 'South-Eastern Europe Health Network' which brought health ministers together in 2001 to sign the 'Dubrovnik Pledge' on cooperation in the field of health policy. A 'Housing Network' has been supported by the CEDB.

Separately from the Stability Pact, a 'South-East Europe Educational Cooperation Network' was established as an information network coordinated from a regional hub in Ljubljana. The ILO has supported the South-East European Employers' Federation to exchange information between employers' organizations in the region. Its priority areas have included discussion of the establishment of labour courts, freedom of association and collective bargaining, criteria for the representation employers associations in social dialogue, arbitration at national level and services to members on labour law issues.

Transnational advocacy coalitions

Several advocacy coalitions have been sponsored by a 'patron' country outside the region aiming to promote trade relations on a regional basis and to foster the interests of their own investors. The most prominent are the Central European Initiative (CEI) and the Southeast European Cooperative Initiative (SECI). The CEI was an essentially Italian grouping founded by Austria, Italy, Hungary and former Yugoslavia. Its membership increased to ten in 1994, to sixteen in 1996 and to seventeen in 2000 with the accession of FRY. The CEI cooperates through a number of forums involving senior officials from CEI member states. Its aims are to stimulate political, technical, economic, scientific and cultural cooperation. Annual Summit Economic Forums provide an opportunity for businesses, officials from central and local governments of the region and from international financial institutions and organizations to meet one another and present their projects and proposals.[22]

SECI, a US initiative launched in December 1996, is a coordinating organization with an Agenda Committee consisting of high-ranking officials from the participating states. It identifies projects of a regional nature relating to the economy and the environment focusing on cross-border projects in the areas of trade and transport infrastructure development, security, energy and private sector development. It has set up the so-called 'PRO' committees in several countries of the region to help improve procedures at customs posts and has also created a network of Business Support Offices in countries outside the region to provide information and assistance to foreign companies wishing to trade and invest within it.

Outcomes: infrastructure and trade

Regional infrastructure networks such as roads, railways, energy networks, telecommunications and water supply are classic examples of the need for regional cooperation to deal with the externalities that arise from cross-border impact of these major systems. Significant economies of scale can be achieved by planning infrastructure investments at a regional level (World Bank 2000). Compatible technical standards need to be agreed for infrastructure investments that span borders. For example, new border-crossing infrastructures were needed following the break-up of Yugoslavia. Lack of maintenance has reduced the quality of roads and railways throughout the region. The NATO bombing campaign against FRY alone caused an estimated €1 billion of damage to infrastructure and blocked the Danube, a major pan-European transport route. Despite the enormous need for the repair of damaged infrastructure, the Western Balkan countries have had limited budgetary capacity and have had to rely largely on aid and foreign borrowing to meet the challenges involved. The Stability Pact established an Infrastructure Steering Group in 2001 led by the EIB to coordinate activity in this policy area. The largest investments have been in the transport sector, since major international highways link together not just the countries of the Western Balkans but wider afield to other European countries, while major pan-European transport corridors pass through the region.[23]

The development and repair of energy systems has been another priority. The energy grids in the Western Balkans had deteriorated badly as a consequence of a decade of war, conflict and underinvestment. Frequent power cuts had become a part of daily life, and a regional energy network was badly needed to overcome the critical energy shortages in countries such as Albania and Kosovo where power cuts are an everyday occurrence. In order to create an environment attractive to private investment in energy infrastructure, the Stability Pact promoted the creation of a regional energy market, in collaboration with the EBRD and other international financial institutions. The aim was to create a regionally integrated energy market for electricity and natural gas networks and to integrate the market into the wider EU market for energy. An 'Energy Community' was established which included the EU, the Western Balkan states, Bulgaria, Romania and Turkey, the members of which were obliged to create electricity regulators and transmission system operators and to open the market for non-domestic consumers (Petrović 2007). A similar arrangement was developed for the provision of gas supplied throughout the region on the basis of the Athens Memorandum of 2003. This obliged the signatories to implement relevant EU Directives on gas, electricity, environmental impact assessment and the reduction of sulphur content of fuels and large combustion plants. A Treaty on the South-East European Energy Community, designed to create unified markets for electricity and gas supplies in the region, was signed in Athens in October 2005 and came into force in July 2006.

The recipient countries

Despite these successes in regional cooperation and donor coordination, the provision of international aid has had some unintended consequences. Recipients have often behaved in ways which they would not have considered in the absence of aid and have diverted some of the additional financial resources into consumption expenditures rather than investment. Aid has often enabled regimes to delay reforms that would have otherwise been carried out and has given regimes in late reform countries perverse incentives to delay reconstruction efforts and postpone anti-poverty programmes expecting that further aid would be available in the future. Under such circumstances, it is not difficult to see how late reformers became dependent on aid. In contrast, early reformers were less aid-dependent and followed more closely their own paths of institutional reform.

All the Western Balkan countries received official development assistance from the donor countries and organizations. While BiH received the largest amount of assistance in the second half of the 1990s, assistance to Serbia and Montenegro including Kosovo grew to a substantially greater amount after the end of the Kosovo war in 1999. Total official development assistance peaked in 2002 at $3.2 billion and has since been on a declining trend, although remaining far higher than before the Kosovo war (Figure 9.2). Throughout this period,

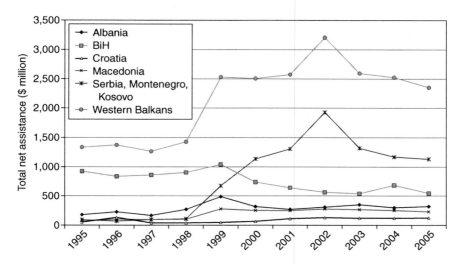

Figure 9.2 Total net official development assistance, 1995–2005 ($ million) (source: OECD online database).

Note
Net official development assistance (ODA) includes official grants and concessional loans with a grant element of at least 25 per cent, for the promotion of economic development or welfare, includig technical cooeration and excluding loans for military purposes. Data are in current prices.

Croatia received the smallest amount of official development assistance, reflecting its position as a more developed country.

The share of aid in national income has declined since 2003 in each country, due to both the reduction in total aid and the economic recovery which has raised incomes (Table 9.2). Between 2003 and 2005, the share of international aid in national income fell in Albania by over one-quarter and in BiH by more than one-fifth. Official international aid as a share of national income has continued to be highest BiH and lowest in Croatia.

Table 9.2 Total net ODA as a share of gross national income, 2003–5 (%)

	2003	*2004*	*2005*
Albania	6.0	3.9	3.7
BiH	7.4	7.8	5.7
Croatia	0.4	0.4	0.3
Macedonia	5.8	4.7	4.0
Serbia and Montenegro (including Kosovo)	6.4	4.9	4.3

Source: OECD Recipient Aid Charts.

Note
ODA includes official grants and concessional loans with a grant element of at least 25 per cent, for the promotion of economic development or welfare, including technical cooperation and excluding loans for military purposes.

The balance of international assistance between concessional loans and grant aid has shifted towards the former. In per capita terms, total grant aid was highest in the years immediately after the end of conflict and fell off quite quickly thereafter. Flows of grant aid to Kosovo were extraordinarily high between 1999 and 2001, when they reached €250 per capita but have fallen back sharply each year since then. A similar effect occurred after the Macedonia conflict, with per capita grant aid peaking in 2002. Grant aid per capita has been noticeably lower in Croatia and Albania than in other countries in the region.

The recipient countries: early reformers

Croatia, Macedonia and Albania adopted their institutional reforms in the 1990s with relatively little international assistance from aid donors, although the involvement of the IMF was important in providing support for macroeconomic stabilization. The interests of the domestic pro-reform coalitions took precedence in the design of the reforms, and they were therefore able to design reforms in their own way. Many of the reforms turned out to be incomplete, such as the partial privatization in Croatia, and domestic elites were able to capture the reform process for their own benefit, at least for a while. After the increased involvement of the EU from 2000 on, the elites in all these countries adopted EU accession as a primary strategic goal. The EU became more and more involved in their reform process and in the case of Macedonia succeeded with a successful intervention to defuse the civil conflict in 2001. Croatia and Macedonia and later Albania negotiated association agreements which required them to carry out reforms to align their institutions with the EU. Pre-accession assistance became a key driver of reform policies in these countries.

Croatia

In 1991, the new Croatian state began the process of postwar reconstruction on its own terms and with relatively little international assistance. The Croatian Bank for Reconstruction and Development issued bonds on the international market which financed a small business start-up programme and provided concessional loans to entrepreneurs and refugees in war-affected areas and underdeveloped islands (see Chapter 6). Croatia did receive some limited international assistance during the 1990s, in the form of loans from the IFIs. In June 1994, the World Bank approved a $128 million Emergency Reconstruction Loan for the repair of damaged housing, schools and health centres, and between 1994 and 1999, it financed fourteen projects through concessional loans which totalled $762 million in areas such as transport and mine clearance. The International Finance Corporation lent $57 million to specific enterprises, and the EBRD lent ECU 230 million for four credit lines to banks and to specific projects including a brewery, air navigation systems, roads, electricity networks and the tourist sector.[24] However, Croatia was excluded from the main EU assistance programmes until the change of government in 2000 led to an improvement in relations with the EU, and most of the reconstruction effort was carried out in the absence of substantial international aid. Croatia's relatively higher level of income compared to other Western Balkan countries also mitigated against large aid inflows. To compensate for the absence of aid, Croatia borrowed heavily on international capital markets at commercial rates of interest and built up a large international debt.

Macedonia

Macedonia also received little international support in the early stage of its transition, partly because it was excluded from EU assistance by a Greek veto, connected to the dispute over the name of the country and its flag. Once this issue was resolved, Macedonia began to receive assistance from the EU PHARE programme in 1996. Further international assistance was stimulated by the outbreak of the Kosovo war in 1999 and after the resolution of the civil war within the country in 2001. At the outbreak of the Kosovo crisis, an emergency donor meeting raised $252 million for humanitarian financial assistance to cover immediate needs and further support was promised to cover the economy's estimated finance gap of $400 million. The IMF supported macroeconomic stability with a $32.6 million stand-by credit, while the World Bank provided a $50 million Emergency Recovery Credit to finance imports and support the government budget[25] and a $1 million Post-Conflict Fund to finance support to refugees. With Macedonia's acceptance as an EU candidate country, the focus of economic and social reform turned towards adopting the acquis communautaire and away from the World Bank agenda for liberal reforms. Financial assistance for pre-accession reform has increased, and future EU assistance will be provided through the Instrument for Pre-accession Assistance (IPA) focusing on institution building, cross-border co-operation, regional development, human resource development and rural development, with planned funding of €210 million over the three-year period 2007–9.

Albania

International aid inflows to Albania have been relatively low, both in terms of grant aid per capita and as a proportion of gross national income. IMF assistance was important in supporting the macroeconomic stabilization policies in the 1990s and beyond. The EU has had the largest donor programme, while other international donors such as UNDP and USAID have also been active. However, aid coordination has been problematic, and '[e]ach important donor has developed its individual approach, which brings with it the vision, practices, and procedures of each organization, creating in many cases confusion in the Albanian administration and government's programmes' (Ruli 2003: 158). In response to this problem of donor fragmentation, lack of coordination and duplication of activities, the four lead multilaterals formed a Donor Technical Secretariat in 2004 headed by the European Commission to manage the coordination process.

Quarterly donor–government roundtables, chaired by the deputy prime minister, have addressed strategic issues of coordination, monitored aid effectiveness and provided a forum for dialogue between donors and the government. However, the main source of assistance to the Albanian economy has been 'private aid' in the form of workers' remittances sent back to their families by mainly young people who have left the country to work abroad. Albania has benefited from large inflows of remittances which, at $889 million in 2003, far exceeded the inflow of international aid which amounted to $349 million (Mansoor and Quillin 2006). By 2005, remittances had increased to almost $1 billion, equivalent to 14 per cent of GDP and to 64 per cent of the trade deficit.[26] Remittances have played a crucial role in sustaining consumption levels and supporting investment in small businesses, often in the informal economy.

The recipient countries: late reformers

The late reformers, BiH, Montenegro, and Serbia and Kosovo, have relied much more on the inflow of international assistance, and donor organizations have had a far greater influence over the design of reform policies. Some of these countries, BiH and Kosovo in particular, have become aid-dependent. In such cases, perverse incentives can arise in which the more aid that is provided the weaker is the reform effort, and the stronger become the anti-reform sections of the governing elite. Aid dependency is difficult to break but can entrench delayed reform. BiH which has had the highest share of international aid in national income is a classic case of this syndrome, while it can also be observed to a lesser degree in other countries.

Bosnia and Herzegovina

The competing and often contradictory policy advice of the international donor agencies became most visible in the case of postwar BiH which received massive inflow of international assistance from a wide variety of organizations (Deacon and Stubbs 1998). By the time the Dayton peace negotiations began the major international donors had already identified a support package for priority reconstruction which was used to encourage a reluctant Bosnian leadership to endorse the peace agreement.[27] A donors' conference attended by representatives from fifty countries and twenty-seven international organizations subsequently pledged reconstruction assistance of $5.1 billion, an amount that was committed and disbursed between 1996 and 1999 (World Bank 2004a). Since BiH was not a member of the World Bank, a Trust Fund was set up to finance sixteen emergency reconstruction projects (Kreimer *et al.* 2000: 33).[28] Donor conferences held annually between 1996 and 1998 raised a total of $3 billion to finance reconstruction projects. However, as time passed and local political actors failed to introduce the expected reforms required to build a modern capitalist economy in BiH, donors began to question the effectiveness of the aid flows. Carlos Westendorp, the high representative, pleaded with the donor representatives at the fifth Donors' Conference in 1999 for a continuation of financial assistance, in order to support the moderates in the RS 'who should be given the chance to carry out their policies in favour of the people'.[29] As Westendorp pointed out at the conference, 'all reforms lack money. Without your support, I just cannot carry out on your behalf the reforms that you have tasked me with' and, in a candid admission of the dominant role of the international institutions over the internal affairs of BiH, that 'the pace of reform is in your hands. You control it.'[30] The admission that reforms depended on the inflow of international assistance underlined the lack of commitment of the entity governments to the implementation of the reform process.

More than 200 foreign organizations took part in Bosnia's reconstruction, aimed at repairing the estimated \$20 billion of damage caused during the war.[31] As time went by, the coordination of the efforts of the many different donor organizations became a critical issue undermining aid effectiveness. The main donors participated in eleven 'sector task forces' to coordinate aid delivery, each chaired by the donor with most expertise in the relevant area and under the overall guidance of an Economic Task Force whose members were the World Bank, the IMF and the EU. However, according to a World Bank evaluation report, '... success in carrying out fully coordinated programs on the ground has been limited. ... Despite best efforts, donors continue to work independently with respect to project selection, priority setting, and procurement methods. This remains problematic' (Kreimer *et al.* 2000: 85–6).

Different donors had different aims and objectives, and this led to contradictions in policy design and implementation. The OHR strove to have projects finished as quickly as possible to meet the peace implementation timetable, while the World Bank had a longer time frame and was driven less by immediate political concerns. While the World Bank was willing to formulate policies at entity level and deal with the entity governments as counterparts, EU assistance programmes were implemented only in collaboration with the weak central- and state-level authorities because EU assistance programmes were constitutionally prohibited from contracting directly with the entity authorities.

Unofficial assessments voiced concern that a large part of the inflow of donor financial assistance found its way to organized criminal groups or was misappropriated by corrupt officials. The OHR established an Anti-Fraud Office to assist in the identification of cases of official corruption. Although an IMF report from 1998 declared that 'neither international nor domestic investigators have found evidence of systematic corruption in the management of donor funds',[32] a report published in the *New York Times* alleged the Anti-Fraud Office had found that as much as \$1 billion had disappeared or been stolen from international aid projects.[33] In Tuzla, it was alleged that \$500 million was 'missing' from the city budget and that schools had been repainted four times in one year using donor funds. In another case, donor funds deposited in a local bank were allegedly lent to fictional businesses or given as personal loans to friends of the bank's owners. More recently, a report produced on behalf of the Swiss aid agency SIDA identified numerous examples of aid being diverted from its intended use. Since nationalist politicians controlled the local business environment, they were able to ensure that lucrative reconstruction contracts were won by politically connected companies. Companies which won reconstruction contracts would pay a percentage to the local political leadership. NGOs that received funding to deliver a donor project would be required by local leaders to provide 'balancing projects' for the benefit of the local officials or politicians, such as assisting a local business or building a local road (Devine and Mathiesen 2005).

The aid programme in BiH was a prime example of the difficulties that donor agencies faced in monitoring the delivery of aid in an environment of asymmetric information. Aid programmes are often distorted by the differing objectives of the donor and recipient. To counteract this defect, the inclusion of the recipient in the design of a project can create a closer alignment of donors' and recipients' objectives, and by giving a greater sense of 'ownership', create better incentives for recipients to ensure that donor funds are not misdirected into private hands. To implement this philosophy, the World Bank turned to a more participative approach in providing its assistance programme through its Poverty Reduction Strategy in collaboration with the governments of the state, the entities, cantonal governments and civil society. A Coordination Board for Economic Development and European Integration composed of prime ministers and representatives of the international community was established to manage the process. The PRSP involved the work of forty-nine experts over two years with numerous public consultations with interested parties and stakeholders. In the opinion of the experts involved in the process, the exercise was a success because its action plans represented a realistic compromise between competing views of different policy makers, and it was based upon the government's own Medium Term Expenditure Programme. However, the Republika Srpska Employers' Association, although formally supporting the PRSP, was unhappy with many of the details of the document. It claimed that the World Bank had pushed the Council of Ministers to produce it, that the consultation process was purely formal and that the strategic plans were not the product of a real consensus.[34]

Serbia

Aid to Serbia increased rapidly after the overthrow of the Milošević regime as soon as the country resumed its membership of the international financial institutions. The World Bank re-engaged, offering concessional loans and approving five projects financed by grants from a $30 million Trust Fund for emergency reconstruction, while direct budgetary support of $540 million was linked to the implementation of reforms under the new government's Economic Reconstruction and Transition Programme. Among the key objectives were restoring macroeconomic stability and fostering economic growth, improving the well-being of the most vulnerable, reducing the social costs of privatization, restructuring enterprises, targeting the social safety net and improving the use of resources in health and education.

The Serbia Poverty Reduction Strategy, a joint effort of the World Bank, the

IMF, the UNDP and the Serbian government, recognized the multidimensional nature of poverty and stressed social inclusion and equal opportunities. The UNDP launched a large project for employment generation and conflict prevention in Southern Serbia focusing on the development of the administrative capacity of local government. USAID was the largest bilateral donor in Serbia, and the USA actively used its aid programme to influence the Serbian government into compliance with the ICTY. In 2004, Serbia lost $20 million of a planned $100 million aid budget owing to its refusal to hand over indicted war criminals to the international tribunal, and a further $7 million was withheld in 2006.

The EU has also been active in Serbia through the EAR. Serbia has been one of the main beneficiaries of the CARDS programme and received a cumulative €1.1 billion up to 2005. Priorities have been in the fields of public administration, health, energy, infrastructure, enterprise, rural development, civil society and media, regional development and the environment. Improvements to the health care system were an immediate priority as this had been worn down under the Milošević regime and suffered from obsolete equipment and facilities and a lack of basic medicines for patients. By 2003, €67 million had been spent on supporting the renovation of health care in Serbia. The largest amounts of assistance were, however, disbursed for energy and other public utility projects, for economic development including enterprise and the rural economy and for infrastructure and transport. Repairs to the energy sector were urgently needed. According to the EAR, '[d]ecades of poor management, a lack of funding, the impact of sanctions and the effect of NATO bombing in 1999 [had] left the Serbian energy sector crippled and in a state of almost terminal decline' (EAR 2003: 11). By 2003, the aid programme had provided 144,000 tonnes of emergency fuel oil for schools, hospitals and municipalities, heating oil for sixty municipal heating systems, electricity imports, rehabilitation of four thermal power plants and other projects. In the field of enterprise, the EAR provided over €10 million in credits for SMEs which had created 2,000 new jobs and detailed restructuring studies for thirteen enterprises and assistance with their privatization. In the infrastructure sector, the programme had provided 225 repair programmes in 160 municipalities, repairs in over 600 schools and repairs of other local infrastructure. However, the agency faced a more difficult task in moving beyond the basic aim of reconstruction to projects dealing with institutional reform and capacity building in the public administration, as the enthusiasm for reforms which had been prominent when the democratic government had come to power in 2000 had all but vanished after the assassination of Zoran Djindjić in 2003. Although the government adopted a public administration reform strategy and action plan in November 2004, there has been little progress with its implementation. According to the Serbian economist Dušan Vujović (2004: 3):

> The real challenge to the continuation of the process of reforms rests on the gainers from the first stage of transitions. ... They use their financial and political power to block further progress of reforms in order to preserve

their advantages, increase their wealth and prevent the introduction of the second generation of incentive and disciplinary measures, especially those which increase the quality of governance in the private and public sectors.

Montenegro

The World Bank has become a major donor in Montenegro and in 2004 approved an $18 million structural adjustment loan to support key institutional reforms designed to promote growth and fiscal consolidation. The EU aid programme to Montenegro focused largely on the improvement of public administration and reform of the judiciary, while the European Agency for Reconstruction (EAR) funded projects on the reform of vocational training, the rehabilitation schools and TAM for enterprise restructuring especially in the wood-processing sector. The European Investment Bank financed several major infrastructure projects including the rehabilitation of the Port of Bar, the repair and reconstruction of the main north-south highway and the rehabilitation of the railway system. In the tourism sector, EBRD funded projects to develop the coastal region and an environmental project to reduce pollution in Kotor Bay, an important coastal tourist attraction. Several NGOs, including AgroInvest and Alter Modus and Opportunity Bank, have been active in providing microfinance schemes. These have had some success in releasing financial constraints on small businesses in rural areas and in the underdeveloped north-east of the country but have not been able to kick-start regional growth or make significant inroads into the high unemployment which has resulted from deindustrialization in the region. Several bilateral assistance programmes have also been active in the north-east region from where many people have emigrated to EU countries claiming asylum. A major objective of the bilateral programmes has been to create jobs which could support refugees returning from the EU. Mainly these have failed to achieve their aims since they have relied on large-scale projects that have been insufficiently integrated into the local economy (Bartlett 2006).

As in other Western Balkan countries, numerous donor organizations have provided economic assistance in Montenegro, but many of these were adversely affected by the weakness of the federal level of government of Serbia and Montenegro. EU programmes were especially affected. According to one evaluation study, '[d]ysfunctional state structures are clearly slowing down the process of EU approximation in both republics'.[35] The dissolution of the federation following the independence referendum in Montenegro in 2006 has created greater clarity in relationship between donors and recipients.

Kosovo

After the end of the Kosovo war, the World Bank and the European Commission developed a Reconstruction and Recovery Programme for physical and institutional rebuilding.[36] Initially, the World Bank could not provide financial support for reconstruction since Kosovo was formally part of FRY which was not yet a

World Bank member, and financial support for the programme was mainly provided by other donors.[37] Moreover, as part of FRY, Kosovo was initially formally under the sanctions regime which caused legal problems for aid agencies in the procurement of services from local companies. The Reconstruction Programme financed supplies for the repair of housing, the rehabilitation of basic infrastructure, mine clearance and the restoration of customs services. Its activities began immediately after the end of the war in August 1999 with a 'Village Employment and Rehabilitation Programme' designed to provide employment for 10,000 unskilled workers in the repair and reconstruction of damaged villages. The programme created temporary jobs for the rural labour force and paid wages directly to the workers involved, while tools and equipment were sourced locally to boost the local economies.[38]

The first Donors' Conference for Kosovo was held in July 1999 and was attended by high-level officials from more than 100 donor countries and international organizations along with representatives of the international organizations. The United Nations Mission in Kosovo (UNMIK) requested funding of $45 million to cover the province's budget deficit; the UN agencies requested $200 million for immediate basic needs, while the EU identified a need for €300 million for immediate reconstruction. In all, the conference gathered pledges of almost $2 billion. Subsequent evaluations have observed that the levels of per capita assistance provided to Kosovo in the aftermath of the war were far higher than in other contemporary international disaster situations. In 2001, the inflow of international assistance amounted to €250 per capita (see

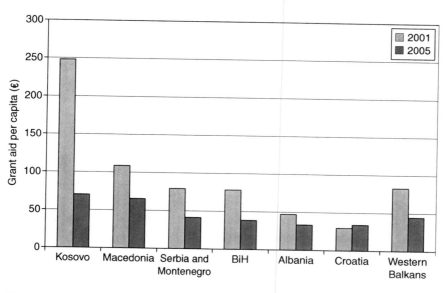

Figure 9.3 Grant aid per capita, 2001 and 2005 (€) (source: European Commission and World Bank Office for South East Europe 'Financial flows to South East Europe 2001–2005', 9 June 2005).

Figure 9.3), contributing significantly to the minimum subsistence standard. Although the aid inflow quickly fell to €70 per capita by 2005, the amounts involved were still large. According to an evaluation by the Danish aid agency Danida:

> By any conventional humanitarian standards, the international response to the Kosovo crisis was disproportionate. The mortality, morbidity and malnutrition rates[34] recorded at the time offer little justification for the scale and intensity of the actual international response. For example, Oxfam reported that infant mortality rates were 10 times higher in several African crises in 1999. Yet, the international donor community spent over 100 times the amount per capita upon the victims of the Kosovo crisis than, for example, upon those in the Democratic Republic of the Congo where, during the same period, it has been estimated that over 3 million people died.[39]
>
> (T&B Consult 2004)

A large part of the resources were used to pay the salaries of the international community presence in the country. Indeed, it is no exaggeration to say that the international presence in Priština in the early 2000s far exceeded the presence and influence of the Serbian authorities in the city in the 1980s.[40] It is tempting to remark that if the international community presence in the country were to depart tomorrow, and simply hand out the equivalent cost as a social dividend to the Kosovo population on a per capita basis, the population would be immediately better off than it is today.

Nevertheless, the reconstruction programme provided major benefits to the province by repairing roads, schools and health centres. Economic growth reached 16 per cent in 2001, which, however, turned negative in 2002 as aid inflows gradually decreased from their initial high levels (World Bank 2005a). Total EU assistance channelled through the EAR amounted to €1.1 billion by 2005, the same amount as had been provided to Serbia with its five times greater population. The largest amount was in 2000 when €432 million was disbursed. By 2005, the annual aid inflow had fallen to €77 million. As in Serbia, following initial emergency reconstruction, the emphasis has shifted to institution building and promoting the rule of law. Energy and housing has received the largest assistance of €351 million and €129 million, respectively, by 2003 (EAR 2003), which provided a boost to growth, but when the reconstruction programme was completed, the economy regressed.

Although much has been spent, the aid programme has been relatively ineffective in promoting the development of the SME sector and has instead focused on privatizing the large socially owned enterprises. This sequencing of reforms was probably a mistake, since the socially owned enterprises could have been revitalized first on the basis of leasing or through working more closely with the workers' councils which were rebuilding their enterprises from scratch as in the case of the Peja brewery (see Chapter 5). The economy faces a difficult time as international assistance is progressively withdrawn and will depend upon the entrepreneurial activity of the SME sector to achieve improved export growth in the future, especially if the province achieves independence.

Regional cooperation and local 'ownership'

In addition to responding to the needs of individual countries, the largest donor organizations and institutions have been keen to view the interests of the region on a collective basis. The expression of this concern for a wider perspective has been the prioritization of regional cooperation policies and projects among the Western Balkan countries (often incorporating the other South-East European neighbours, Bulgaria, Romania and Moldova). The Stability Pact has been a main promoter of the idea of regional cooperation. Initially, this seemed rather far-fetched in the light of the preceding decade of conflict. While some sections of the domestic elites were in favour of greater cooperation with neighbouring countries, in most cases this took a nationalistic flavour, for example in the desire for special relationships between Serbia and the Republika Srpska and between Croatia and the Herzegovina. Moreover, the main objective of most countries, especially Croatia, Macedonia and Albania, was greater cooperation with the EU, rather than among themselves. Croatian policy makers in particular have been very suspicious of any pressure to cooperate more closely with other Western Balkan countries, and some have viewed the emphasis on regional cooperation as a back-door method of restoring the former Yugoslavia. The Stability Pact and the EU therefore had great difficulty in promoting the policy of regional cooperation, which from their perspective appeared to be a natural expression of the desire to restore peace and stability to the region.

In addition, the desire of the international donors to promote regional cooperation has in practice often run counter to other policy prescriptions that emphasize competition between private sector organizations and the strengthening of the competitive capacity of individual countries. Countries compete against one another to attract foreign investment, while private companies compete for market share and lobby their governments to introduce measures which favour them in relation to their competitors in neighbouring countries. In practice therefore, injunctions for regional cooperation often fail because they are unable to harmonize competing economic interests. Examples are not hard to find. The inequalizing effects of free trade agreements were discussed in Chapter 7, and significant gaps are also opening up in the flow of FDI between the more advanced and less advanced countries in the region, so much so that the regional share of FDI going to Albania, BiH and Macedonia fell from 14 per cent of total regional FDI in 2002 to just 9 per cent in 2006.[41]

Despite the unpromising environment, the office of the Stability Pact persevered in promoting the idea of regional cooperation. It organized meetings of civil servants from the Western Balkan countries to address a wide range of policy areas, to find some common ground and exchange policy ideas and 'best practice' examples among themselves. This approach succeeded in creating a policy community whose participants have benefited from greater mutual understanding, from exchange of experience and best practice and from involvement in international meetings, even if at times these have appeared to be little more than talking shops. Over time, these regional policy networks became firmly established and laid the ground for the transformation of the Stability Pact into a more locally owned Regional Cooperation Council (RCC).

The South-East Europe Cooperation Process and the RCC

The Stability Pact has coordinated the development of many new policy initiatives funded by international donors. In this, it has played not just the role of a policy broker but even more ambitiously as what might be called a 'policy incubator'. However, the countries of the region had far less say in the development of regional policies or in setting the agenda on key issues such as trade policy and employment policy. In practice, regional cooperation has been more about coordination between donors and international organizations than about cooperation between countries of the region.

One exception to this dominance of outside organizations on the regional policy process has been the South-East Europe Cooperation Process (SEECP) launched on the initiative of Bulgaria in 1996 to promote confidence building, good neighbourly relations and stability in the region (Hyde 2004). Although being the only genuinely indigenous advocacy coalition, it initially had relatively little influence (Lopandić 2001). Its member states are Albania, BiH, Bulgaria, Greece, Macedonia, Romania, Serbia and Montenegro and Turkey, while Croatia has participated in meetings as an observer. The basic goals of SEECP have been consolidation of security and political stability; intensification of economic relations; and cooperation on democracy, justice and actions against illegal activities. SEECP has also aimed to assist its members to meet EU integration conditionality by demonstrating good neighbourly relations. An Informal Consultative Committee has been established as an advisory body to coordinate the activities of the SEECP, with the EU and the Stability Pact. Over time, the SEECP has developed its capacity to take on the role of a regional council which could manage a locally owned process of regional cooperation.

In May 2005, the Stability Pact began to consider ways in which the regional cooperation process could be handed over to local ownership of the governments of the region. A Senior Review Group was established to consider the issue and delivered its report in March 2006. According to the review, '...regional cooperation has improved significantly ... [but] many of these processes are still largely driven from the outside ...'.[42] The review led to the development of plans to ensure greater involvement and 'ownership' by the countries of the region of the regional cooperation agenda. It called for the SEECP to be strongly involved in the future framework for regional cooperation, for the streamlining of Stability Pact initiatives, for the closer alignment of regional cooperation with the EU integration process and for continued financial support from donors and international financial institutions. The special coordinator responded to the review by asserting that the 'priority in the upcoming years must be on ensuring long-term sustainability of the regional cooperation processes . . . by enhancing regional ownership'.[43] In pursuit of this ambition, the Stability Pact is to be transformed into a RCC under 'local ownership' by early 2008. The RCC will focus on six priority areas including Economic and Social Development, Infrastructure, Justice and Home Affairs, Security Cooperation and Building Human Capital (i.e. education and training) to replace the twenty-five initiatives and task forces that had been established under the aegis of the Stability Pact.[44] In addition to a continuing emphasis on regional cooperation, the main aim of the RCC will be to support the European integration of its member countries. The creation of the RCC represents the culmination of the activities of the Stability Pact and the transition of SEECP from a 'voice of the region' into a significant 'regional actor' with the ability to align the principles of regional cooperation to the EU integration process.[45]

10 European integration

Over the last decade, the relationship between the EU and the Western Balkans has developed in a new direction with the opening of the prospect of EU membership to all the countries of the region. The EU has taken a leading role in providing financial assistance to promote democratization and economic development and to support pre-accession adjustment. The ensuing process of European integration has been a major influence in shaping the path of institutional reform and economic development. The early reformers, Albania, Croatia and Macedonia, have embraced the opportunity for integration and taken decisive steps to introduce reforms and institutional adaptations in accordance with the requirements of the accession process, while the late reformers, BiH and Serbia, have had a more ambivalent approach and have been more hesitant in engaging with the complex and costly reforms required by the accession process. Montenegro, however, has made rapid strides towards EU integration since independence in 2006. Countries have therefore differed in the extent of their progress with EU accession, partly from their own choosing and partly from the decisions of the EU to speed up or slow down the pace of the integration process depending on each country's compliance with a set of conditionality criteria.

The EU's engagement with the region has been both political and economic. On the political side, the EU has been involved through its external foreign policy, seeking to broker peace agreements rather unsuccessfully during the early 1990s, but with greater success in relation to the conflict in Macedonia in 2001. On the economic side, EU policy has focused mainly on trade relations and control of emigration. More recently, policy has moved with increased emphasis to the accession process. Following the fifth enlargement in which the EU took in ten new members, followed soon after by Bulgaria and Romania, responsibility for relations with the Western Balkans has been transferred from the EU's foreign policy wing, DG External Relations, to the accession wing, DG Enlargement, thus signalling a firm commitment to the eventual inclusion of the region into the EU.

EU conditionality after Dayton: the 'regional approach'

The EU had long experience of contractual relations with the former Yugoslavia.[1] After the break-up of the country in 1991, the EU suspended its Cooperation Agreement but, with the exception of FRY, maintained autonomous trade preferences for the successor states, enabling some industrial goods to enter EU markets with reduced customs duties (World Bank 2000: 60). Although it introduced sanctions against FRY in May 1992, it continued to provide humanitarian assistance through its ECHO programme, and the EU Delegation in Belgrade continued to operate quietly as a virtual embassy of the EU. Albania had no links with the EU before the collapse of the communist regime, but quickly negotiated a formal Trade and Cooperation Agreement which was signed in 1992, putting the country ahead of the Yugoslav successor states in the extent of its relationship with the EU for several years.

The first EU assistance programme for the countries of Eastern Europe, PHARE, provided analytical and advisory support to the transition process.[2] It was extended to Yugoslavia in 1990 but soon suspended when the country broke up, while Albania was included in PHARE in 1991. In March 1995, the EU agreed to extend PHARE to Croatia, and to open negotiations for a Trade and Cooperation Agreement, but the plans were shelved following Croatia's offensive against the self-proclaimed Krajina Serb Republic in August 1995. The EU provided humanitarian assistance throughout the conflict period, channelling €2.1 billion of assistance to the Western Balkans through ECHO between 1991 and 1999. Smaller amounts were provided through a variety of assistance programmes supporting the creation of democratic institutions, the return of refugees, the independent media, human rights and demining.

After the end of the Bosnian war, the EU set out a new policy towards the Balkans, called the 'Regional Approach',[3] to support the Dayton Peace Agreement through region-wide projects funded through the €400 million OBNOVA (Reconstruction) assistance programme which was initiated in 1996 for BiH, Croatia, FRY and Macedonia.[4] Additionally, both BiH and Macedonia were admitted to PHARE in 1996, by which time it had been reoriented towards the EU pre-accession strategy.[5] The Luxembourg Summit of April 1997 further defined the Regional Approach, setting out a policy framework for trade preferences, financial assistance and economic cooperation.[6] Conditions for the renewal of trade preferences included respect for the principles of democracy and human rights and a willingness to develop economic relations with neighbouring countries. Conditions for receiving financial assistance through the PHARE programme were more stringent, requiring in addition compliance with obligations under the peace agreements including support for the return of displaced persons and refugees, cooperation with the ICTY and a commitment to pursue economic reforms. Specific conditions were imposed on FRY which was required to initiate a dialogue on the status of Kosovo, while assistance was provided to BiH for refugee return and building inter-entity links without any conditions at all.

A more complex process was imposed for negotiating cooperation or association agreements, with a lower level of compliance required to begin negotiations than to conclude them. Only the conditions for the start of negotiations were set out in detail. They comprised a set of ten general conditions, and a number of others specific to BiH, Croatia and FRY. In addition to the general stipulations on democracy, respect for human rights and return of refugees, a specific economic condition was established: 'implementation of first steps of economic reform – privatization programme, abolition of certain price controls.'[7] The elements which would indicate the successful implementation of market reforms included:

• Macroeconomic institutions and policies necessary to ensure a stable economic environment
• Comprehensive liberalization of prices, trade and current payments
• Setting up a transparent and stable legal and regulatory framework
• Demonopolization and privatization of state-owned or socially owned enterprises
• Establishment of a competitive and prudently managed banking sector.

This list was extensive in its scope and embodied a clear vision of the required institutional reforms. Countries which met the conditions would be eligible for autonomous trade preferences, receipt of financial assistance and the development of contractual relations with the EU. However, a major flaw in the Regional Approach was that despite the stick of conditionality, it did not have any very powerful carrots to incentivize compliance, such as a promise of future potential EU membership, or even a promise of an Association Agreement, a lure which had been successfully used to propel institutional reform elsewhere in Eastern Europe (Bartlett and Samardžija 2000).

In practice, the Regional Approach split the Western Balkans into two subgroups. In the first group were Albania and Macedonia which negotiated Cooperation Agreements with the EU. In the other were the parties to the Dayton Agreement – BiH, Croatia and FRY – which failed to fulfil the conditions needed to develop closer contractual links with the EU. Further distinctions were made within the latter group of countries with Croatia and BiH both benefiting from autonomous trade preferences and being eligible for assistance from the OBNOVA assistance programme, while BiH gained access to the PHARE programme along with Albania and Macedonia, which was denied to both Croatia[8] and FRY. In addition, FRY was subjected to an 'outer wall of sanctions' which prevented it from accessing official capital flows from the IFIs. The largest beneficiary of PHARE during this period was Albania which received assistance of €0.6 billion between 1991 and 1999. Overall, funding for PHARE and OBNOVA amounted to €1.8 billion between 1991 and 1999.

In April 1998, the EU began to support the anti-Milošević government in Montenegro with short-term assistance for institutional reform, while its relations with FRY again deteriorated in 1999 and the EU imposed an oil embargo, an arms embargo, a flight ban on FRY-registered airlines, a visa ban on those responsible for the repression of the independent media, a supply ban on equipment which could be used for terrorism or police repression, a moratorium on export credit, a freeze on Serbia/FRY Government funds held abroad and a prohibition on new foreign investment in the country.[9] Relations collapsed entirely with the NATO bombardment of Serbia which began in March 1999 over the issue of Kosovo.

Total EU assistance to the Western Balkans between 1991 and 1999 amounted to €4.5 billion. In per capita terms, the greatest amount of assistance was provided to BiH in the immediate post-Dayton years. In 1996, EU assistance to BiH was equivalent to €111 per head. This declined in subsequent years, although remained much larger than to other countries in the region. Following the conclusion of the Kosovo war in 1999, EU assistance to Kosovo and FRY increased to levels which exceeded the per capita equivalent amounts allocated to BiH (Figure 10.1).

After the Kosovo war: the stabilization and association process

The failure to find a diplomatic solution to the Kosovo crisis demonstrated that the Regional Approach had been an insufficient basis to promote stability in the region,[10] and at the outset of the Kosovo war, other international actors took the lead to develop a long-term strategy. At the end of April 1999, a high-level meeting of the governments and international agencies was convened in Washington by the World Bank and the IMF to coordinate international aid in response to the Kosovo crisis. It was attended by representatives of thirty-three

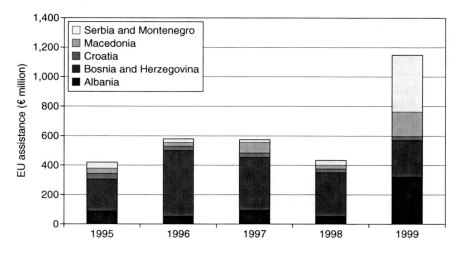

Figure 10.1 EU assistance to the Western Balkans 1995–9 (€ million) (source: European Commission, DG External Relations).

countries, including the six neighbouring countries of FRY most affected by the war and seven international organizations. The organizers estimated that the costs of stabilizing the region would be between $2 billion and $10 billion. The meeting endorsed the idea that aid should be provided within a comprehensive regional framework, a call that was echoed by the G8 meeting in St Petersburg at the beginning of May 1999 which proposed a comprehensive approach to economic development and stabilization.[11]

Following on from these proposals, the EU announced that it would take a leading role in the Stability Pact, its main contribution being the adoption of a new policy approach to the Western Balkans called the Stabilization and Association process (SAp). This represented a major policy U-turn, as it opened up the prospect for EU membership for all the countries of the region. A formal declaration issued at the June 2000 Feira European Council stated that all the Western Balkan countries 'are potential candidates for EU membership.'[12] The SAp was officially launched at an EU–Balkan Summit held in Zagreb in November 2000 to support the domestic reform processes with aid, trade preferences, dialogue and technical advice. It envisaged 'privileged political and economic relations' between the Western Balkan countries and the EU. In signing the Zagreb Declaration, the countries undertook to pursue policies of regional cooperation in a number of areas in order to underpin regional security.[13] The European Commission set out a comprehensive regional strategy for the Western Balkans and prepared a set of Country and Regional Strategy Papers to guide the allocation of financial assistance (EC 2002).

A centrepiece of the SAp was the introduction of the Stabilization and Association Agreement (SAA) as a precursor to EU accession, modelled on the earlier association agreements with the East-Central European and Baltic states. The SAAs provided for asymmetric trade liberalization with the EU, economic and financial assistance, political dialogue, approximation with EU legislation and cooperation in other policy areas. They required signatories to implement EU-compatible competition policies, rules on limiting state aid and subsidies to the business sector, rules on protecting intellectual property and rules of establishment, bringing these in line with EU practice. They set out a framework for political dialogue, provided a basis for cooperation in the field of legal and home affairs, and provided for the gradual adoption of the *acquis communautaire* (the legislative framework of the EU Single Market), a massive task considering the tens of thousands of pages of legislation involved, covering issues ranging from competition laws and the regulation of state aid to industry to more detailed legal norms concerning standards and the classification of goods.[14] They also required signatories to engage actively in a process of regional cooperation with one another.[15] The SAAs also created of a number of new institutional forums to enable ministers, civil servants and politicians to engage in dialogue with their EU counterparts including a Stabilisation and Association Council, a Stabilisation and Association Committee and an Association Parliamentary Committee. This method of exerting influence over the reform programmes in each country has been referred to as a system of 'enlargement governance' (Dimitrova 2002).

The conditions for both beginning and concluding negotiations for an SAA remained the same as those set out under the Regional Approach for negotiating contractual relations with the EU. The conditions to *begin* SAA negotiations included the establishment of the rule of law; establishing democratic institutions and compliance with human/minority rights; free and fair elections and full implementation of results; absence of discriminatory treatment; implementation of the first steps of economic reform; proven readiness for good neighbourly relations; and Dayton compliance (ICTY cooperation, refugee return) for BiH, Croatia and FRY. The conditions to *conclude* SAA negotiations included substantial progress in achievement of the conditions for opening negotiations; substantial results in the field of political and economic reforms; and proven cooperation and good neighbourly relations. Regular annual Stabilisation and Association Reports on the Western Balkans as a whole and on each country individually were published as instruments to monitor compliance with the conditions and to highlight policy areas on which countries seeking to make progress with the accession process should focus attention.[16] This was far from being a scientific process since the conditions were rather general and open to subjective interpretations. The mechanism, therefore, gave the Commission some scope to adjust its annual assessments to conform to prevailing political preferences over the speed of enlargement within the EU.

At the same time, a number of policy areas were to be developed without conditions. These included trade relations with the EU, financial assistance programmes, assistance for democratization, civil society, education and institution building, cooperation in justice and home affairs especially relating to asylum and immigration within the EU and the development of political dialogue. All this opened a path for the rapid implementation of EU policy initiatives in the region and thus marked the SAp as a far more flexible approach to EU intervention than the Regional Approach had been. This greater flexibility has been borne out in practice as each of the Western Balkan states has proceeded along paths of EU integration at varying speeds under the SAp, with Croatia and Macedonia at the forefront and BiH and Serbia lagging behind (Table 10.1).

Macedonia, considered by the European Commission after its cooperation with NATO during the Kosovo war to be a leading factor of stability in the region, was the first country to benefit from the new arrangements. Negotiations were opened in April 2000, and an SAA was signed soon after in April 2001. Croatia's SAA negotiations were opened next, leading to an agreement in October 2001. Interim Agreements with both countries covering the trade protocols entered into force immediately. These involved asymmetric trade liberalization with the EU which removed customs duties and quantitative restrictions on imports from the two countries. The SAAs came into force with Macedonia in 2004 and with Croatia in 2005 after ratification of the agreements by the EU member states. Negotiations for an SAA with Albania were launched in January 2003 and were concluded in June 2006, the lengthy negotiations owing to difficulties in Albania's ability to meet the necessary conditions. The European Commission conducted a Feasibility Study for an SAA with BiH in November

Table 10.1 Stabilization and association agreements

	Status	*Date*
Macedonia	SAA negotiations opened	April 2000
	SAA in force	April 2004
	Candidate status achieved	December 2005
Croatia	SAA negotiations opened	Autumn 2000
	SAA in force	February 2005
	Candidate status achieved	
	Accession negotiations opened	October 2005
Albania	SAA negotiations opened	January 2003
	Negotiations for SAA concluded	June 2006
Bosnia and Herzegovina	Feasibility Study for SAA approved	November 2003
	SAA negotiations opened	November 2006
Serbia and Montenegro	Feasibility Study for SAA approved	April 2005
	SAA negotiations opened	October 2005
	SAA negotiations suspended	May 2006
Montenegro	Negotiations for SAA concluded	March 2007

2003 which set out sixteen conditions for opening negotiations. Although fifteen of these were met, the issue of police reform proved to be a sticking point, and BiH has not yet signed an SAA as a result. Serbia and Montenegro began SAA negotiations in October 2005 but these were soon suspended following Serbia's unwillingness to fully cooperate with the International Criminal Tribunal on former Yugoslavia in The Hague.

The Thessaloniki agenda

The EU Summit held in Thessaloniki in June 2003 reaffirmed that all the Western Balkan states were potential EU members. It proposed European Integration Partnerships[17] to identify short- and medium-term reforms for each country and to guide assistance under the CARDS programme.[18] At the summit, the European Commission also called for the extension of 'Twinning' projects which would involve the secondment of civil servants from EU member states to work as advisers in ministries and other government agencies in the Western Balkan countries.[19] It pointed to the importance of trade as a driver of economic development and proposed the creation of a free trade area in the region. It also emphasized the importance of SMEs as a 'source of jobs, innovation and wealth' and proposed that the Western Balkans should adopt the European Charter for Small Enterprises. The Commission also emphasized the importance of the further development of regional cooperation in the creation of a regional energy market.

The adoption of the European Charter for Small Enterprises throughout the region was an important milestone, highlighting the issue of small business growth as a key source of competitiveness, and galvanized government policy initiatives in support of SMEs. The Charter set out a package of policy measures to promote the development of small businesses, and promoted policy coordination between countries. The Charter set out ten key areas to which signatories were required to harmonize their support for small businesses. Country reports were prepared to monitor the implementation of SME policy against a set of targets, some common and some specific to each country. The second regional report, published in January 2005, set out fifty-six policy targets. The policy process was modelled on the Open Method of Coordination adopted in the EU for various sectoral policy areas. In this and other ways, the Western Balkan countries have begun to Europeanize their policy environment well before the formal process of EU integration has been completed.

European partnerships

In accordance with the Thessaloniki agenda, the European Commission issued European Partnerships for each country in 2004, setting out specific short-term and medium-term priorities for EU-compatible reforms. The EU encouraged countries to respond by preparing a plan for implementing the identified priorities.[20] The countries themselves had no role in the design of the Partnerships but were expected to passively accept them and implement their aims. As an example,[21] the key short-term priorities set out for Serbia included:

- Reform of public administration
- Reform of the judiciary
- Ensuring effective democratic control over the military
- Full cooperation with the ICTY
- Intensifying dialogue with Priština
- Respecting human rights and rights of minorities
- Fight against organized crime and corruption

The accession process moved slowly forwards in the following years, leading to candidate status for Croatia and Macedonia, and towards SAAs for Albania and Montenegro. In November 2004, the European Council approved the signing of Framework Agreements to open up a number of Community Programmes in the social and education fields for participation by the Western Balkan countries, including programmes such as Combating Social Exclusion (2002–6), Youth (2000–6) and Gender Equality (2001–6).[22] At the June 2005 EU summit in Brussels, the European Council adopted a declaration on Kosovo, reiterating the EU engagement that the future of 'the Western Balkans, including Kosovo' was in the European Union.

EU assistance after the Kosovo war

The Kosovo war provided an opportunity for a rethink on the provision of EU assistance to the Western Balkans, and the European Commission decided on a large pre-accession assistance programme. In addition, the promises made to rebuild Kosovo and FRY after the end of the NATO bombing campaign inspired a continued injection of funds into the region over the period 2002–6 through the €4.65 billion CARDS assistance programme, which was firmly tied to the SAp pre-accession agenda.[23] Despite the rhetoric, the total amount of grant aid steadily diminished from 2000 onwards, especially to Kosovo and BiH, with a relatively increasing amount provided to Serbia and Montenegro (Figure 10.2).

The strategic framework for the assistance was set out in a set of Strategy Papers and in a Multi-Annual Indicative Programme (MIP), which were prepared both for the region as a whole and for the individual countries. The EU had promoted the idea of regional cooperation both as a means to ensure political stability and as an instrument of economic development, and a willingness to engage in regional cooperation was established early on as one of the key conditions for negotiating an SAA. The CARDS assistance programme allocated 10 per cent of its funds to regional projects (i.e. projects with a regional scope) managed directly from Brussels. However, the countries themselves did not always agree with this perspective, a position which is understandable since they had just emerged from a decade of conflict and ongoing political fragmentation. Therefore, the commissioning officials in Brussels had great difficulty finding any projects that would fit within the regional cooperation framework, and much of the available funds went unspent.

Reactions to enlargement governance

The Western Balkan countries have reacted in differing ways to the EU policy of greater engagement with the region. The SAp has required countries to gradu-

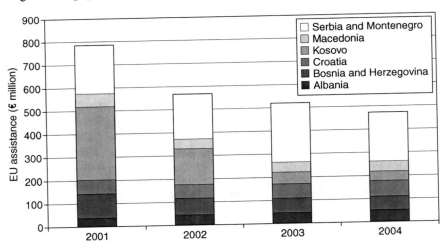

Figure 10.2 EU assistance to the Western Balkans 2001–4 (€ million) (sources: 'Financial Statistics' EuropeAid Co-operation Office website and European Commission and World Bank Office for South East Europe Report on Activities 2003).

ally adopt a set of EU-compatible reforms including the harmonization of laws to the *acquis communautaire*, the creation of new EU-compatible institutions such as Competition Agencies and Equal Opportunity Agencies and the reform that requires existing institutions and domestic political practices to meet EU standards. Within each country, pro-Europe coalitions have derived support from the potential gainers from eventual accession, including reform-minded elites which welcome the opportunity to make further progress with democratization and the introduction of competitive market rules. At the same time, anti-European coalitions have gained support from the potential and actual losers from the reforms required by the accession process. These include workers threatened with unemployment as a result of further privatization and restructuring; entrepreneurs active in the informal sector and organized crime threatened by reforms in the judiciary; managers of privatized monopolies whose positions would be endangered by competition laws; and managers of partially state-owned firms who would lose subsidies from the implementation of tight EU regulations limiting the provision of state aid to the private sector. In order to win political support for accession, the EU has a number of strategic and tactical instruments available to compensate potential losers, through its assistance programmes, through negotiating cooperation and association agreements to open up the EU market and through the prospect of lucrative jobs to top members of the elite in Brussels. All these instruments can be deployed to overcome resistance to the integration process. In deciding whether to proceed through any stage of the accession process, ruling elites have had to weigh up the benefits of accession against the costs of adopting new rules and implementing reforms. If the costs of accession are greater than the benefits for the key decision-making elite, then a country may turn away from the EU integration process (Schimmelfennig and Sedelmeier 2004). Although the benefits of EU accession appear to be large for most of the Western Balkan countries, a strategy of non-accession might be chosen by anti-reform coalitions who would lose from adopting EU rules. As Milada Anna Vachudova has noted:

> In order for the Balkan states to become stable, democratic, and prosperous, the region's moderate elites must hold power and revitalize the economy. All the while, these elites must fend off extremist forces by convincing voters that difficult reforms of the economy and the state will lead to greater prosperity and to membership of the EU. For its part, the EU must help convince them by providing intermediate rewards that demonstrate the merits of EU integration.
>
> (Vachudova 2003: 160)

By imposing conditions on progress with the accession process, the EU has been able to manipulate the costs of non-compliance so as to steer countries in the desired direction.[24] Conditionality has been applied to all the stages that the Western Balkan countries must pass through in their process of EU integration. By exercising it, the EU has been able to exert pressure on governments which have resisted the required reforms, preventing them from passing to a subsequent stage of the accession process. Examples include the delay to the start of Croatia's EU membership negotiations imposed in 2005 in reaction to the failure to arrest the fugitive General Ante Gotovina who had been indicted by the ICTY, and the suspension of Serbia's negotiations for an SAA in 2006 in reaction to its failure to arrest the fugitive General Ratko Mladić, another ICTY indictee. The leverage that the EU has been able to exert to ensure that desired policies are adopted has therefore been substantial. Conditionality is a fairly blunt instrument, but by breaking the accession process down into ever more discrete stages, the EU has been able to sharpen its control over the process by tightening or loosening the terms of conditionality. Progress with EU integration, therefore, has depended not only on whether a country has met the technical conditions of entry, but also on the EU's willingness to permit the entry of new members.

The speed of accession has also depended on the willingness of the potential applicants themselves to actively engage with the process of enlargement governance and to undertake the reforms needed to meet the entry conditions. These reforms are costly. Not only do they require a large and competent bureaucracy, but they also distribute costs unevenly between different interest groups, generating both political support and opposition to the accession process. In making the strategic decision about participation in the process, governments have had to weigh up the costs and benefits of EU accession and of the required reforms. Where the governing elites have been unwilling to carry out required reforms, the pace of integration has been slower than in countries that have had a more positive approach to the process.

The applicant states: Croatia and Macedonia

The cases of Croatia and Macedonia which have travelled furthest along the path of European integration demonstrate the effectiveness of enlargement governance in the Western Balkans. The governments of both countries have perceived the accession-related reforms to be in line with their own reform agendas and have embraced the opportunity to implement them. National programmes for the adoption of the *acquis communautaire* have been drawn up which have involved whole-scale transfer of EU legislation to the applicant states. This large administrative effort and commitment to a sustained process of reform requires a determination by the ruling elites to carry it through to a successful completion. Cross-party consensus, at least among the main parties, is a necessary condition to achieve the accession goal. Both Croatia and Macedonia have achieved cross-party unanimity on the benefits of EU membership, and the pace of accession has therefore been more rapid than in other Western Balkan countries where such consensus has been noticeably absent. The differences in reaction of the Western Balkan countries to the process of enlargement governance therefore demonstrate, more clearly than in previous enlargements, the nature of the strategic game being played out between the EU and the accession states.

Croatia

Croatia submitted its application for EU membership in February 2003. The EU responded with a 4,560-item questionnaire which the government returned in November 2003 just prior to parliamentary elections. The European Commission issued a positive *Opinion* on Croatia's membership application in April 2004 in which it recognized that Croatia met the Copenhagen criteria for EU membership, with a functioning democracy, stable institutions guaranteeing the rule of law and a working market economy. It observed that the ICTY chief prosecutor, Carla del Ponte, had confirmed Croatia's full cooperation with the Tribunal. The *Opinion* was less certain about whether Croatia could withstand competition within the single market, one of the economic criteria for membership. To meet these criteria, Croatia would have to pursue further economic reforms including further enterprise restructuring and privatization, especially the modernization of the shipbuilding and agriculture sectors. It also pointed to the need for further reforms in the fiscal and social security systems; for improved public administration; for greater efforts to facilitate the return of Serb refugees from Serbia and BiH; for substantial improvements in the judicial system; and for stronger efforts to fight corruption. Despite these weaknesses, the Commission recommended the opening of membership negotiations, and in June 2004, the European Council granted Croatia the status of an official candidate for EU membership. Negotiations were due to begin in March 2005 but were briefly postponed because of a negative statement from Carla del Ponte, the ICTY chief prosecutor, to the effect that Croatia was no longer cooperating sufficiently in the pursuit of the fugitive general Gotovina. The delay caused considerable political damage to the government, but Croatia eventually began its negotiations for EU entry in October 2005 following a further statement by Carla del Ponte that the country was fully cooperating with the ICTY due to the expected imminent arrest of General Gotovina. The decision was important in maintaining the momentum for European integration, not just for Croatia but for the region as a whole.

The success of Croatia's application for EU membership reflected the cross-party political support for accession. Under the nationalist Tudjman regime in the 1990s, the ruling elite in Croatia had been unenthusiastic about the prospect of EU membership. However, after the defeat of the HDZ in the election in 2000, its new leader Ivo Sanader had set about converting it into a pro-European centre-right party committed to EU membership, notably ejecting a right-wing faction led by Ivić Pašalić in 2002. The HDZ began to claim in its electoral propaganda that it would succeed in achieving EU candidate status even faster than the SDP-led coalition government which had long held a pro-Europe stance. Agreeing on the importance of EU membership, the parties put aside their ideological differences ensuring cross-party unity, and several measures were carried out to comply with EU conditions. In late 2002, a law on minorities was passed by the Croatian parliament which reserved between five and eight seats in the parliament for the country's ten officially recognized minority groups, among whom the Serb population was still the largest, comprising 4.5 per cent of the population.[25] The law also established a Council for Minorities and provided for the education of children in their own minority languages. The new law was approved by the Organisation for Security and Cooperation in Europe (OSCE), and Croatia thus fulfilled one of the key criteria set down under the SAA.

Opposition to EU membership came from the far right-wing of Croatian politics, representing primarily the nationalist factions and war veterans who were most commited to Croatia's sovereign independence, and from managers of state-owned enterprises who were wary of increased competition and of further privatization. Entrepreneurs operating in the informal economy also opposed the more regulated law-based society promised by EU membership. This right-wing section of opinion was represented in the polls by the Croatian Party of Rights (HSP), which by early 2005 had become the third largest in the country. The HSP had gained 12 per cent of the vote in local elections, boosted by the controversy over the government's attempts to arrest General Gotovina. Although the leader of the party, Ante Djapić, became the mayor of Osijek, the economic strength of the anti-European groups was relatively insignificant compared to the political influence of the large formal private sector of the economy which stood to gain from accession to the EU and its large single market. Despite the consensus among political elites in Croatia in favour of EU membership, there was surprisingly little popular enthusiasm for the policy. At the end of 2006, the Eurobarometer opinion poll reported that only 42 per cent of Croatians thought that they would benefit from EU membership, while 49 per cent expected that the employment situation would deteriorate upon accession to the EU.[26] Despite this pessimism about the benefits of EU membership, 68 per cent of Croatians support their country's bid for EU membership, although it had fallen from 74 per cent in the previous year.

Macedonia

For several years after achieving independence, Macedonia received little support from the international community to assist its economic recovery. In the early 1990s, the development of Macedonia's relations with the EU were blocked by Greece which disputed the country's flag and its right to call itself the 'Republic of Macedonia'. EU assistance to Macedonia was limited to humanitarian aid. Eventually, reeling from the effects of the Greek embargo, Macedonia changed its flag and altered its constitution in 1995 and agreed to be called 'The Former Yugoslav Republic of Macedonia'. EU recognition followed the resolution of the dispute with Greece and the PHARE assistance programme was opened for Macedonia in 1996. A Cooperation Agreement came into force in January 1998 which provided preferential terms for certain categories of Macedonian exports to the EU.

In Macedonia, as in Croatia, the main right-wing nationalist party VMRO-DPMNE reinvented itself as a moderate centre-right Christian-Democratic party. It had held power from 1998 to 2002 before losing elections to a coalition led by the reformed former communist party, the SDSM. After its electoral defeat,

VMRO-DPMNE purged its nationalist and anti-European wing led by former prime minister Ljubco Georgievski, which established the breakaway VMRO-People's Party. Echoing the evolution of the HDZ in Croatia, the main body of the VMRO-DPMNE led by Nikola Gruevski evolved in a firmly pro-European direction, and a political consensus for the EU accession process was established.

Macedonia submitted its membership application to the EU in March 2004[27] and received the standard Questionnaire from the European Commission on the country's economic, legal and administrative system. The Questionnaire was delivered by Romano Prodi, the European Commission president, during his visit to Skopje in October 2004. He advised the government of the need to implement 'reforms in the judiciary and ... police, fight corruption, and pursue economic reforms reducing the bureaucratic burden and guaranteeing a level playing field for business so as to attract foreign investment.'[28] A 14,000-page document containing Macedonia's answers to the EU Questionnaire was presented in Brussels in February 2005. In delivering its *Opinion* on the membership application in November, the Commission pronounced that Macedonia was 'well on its way' to satisfying the political criteria for EU membership, being a functioning democracy with stable institutions which 'generally' guarantee the rule of law and respect for fundamental rights. However, the *Opinion* also stated that it needed to make additional efforts to improve the electoral process, to implement reforms in the judiciary and the police and to strengthen the fight against corruption. On the economic criteria, it had taken 'important steps' towards establishing a functioning market economy, but would not be able to cope with competitive pressure within the Union even in the medium term. Further institutional reforms needed to be carried out in a wide range of policy areas such as land and property registration, improving the business and investment climate, decreasing the size of the informal economy and improving the functioning of labour and financial markets. On the ability to assume the obligations of membership, the *Opinion* considered that Macedonia lagged behind in the areas of technical norms and standards, protection of intellectual property rights, competition policy, financial control, and environmental policy.

Although there is cross-party support for EU accession, the institutional and administrative capacity of the Macedonian government is much lower than is needed to implement the required reforms and transpose the *acquis communautaire* into Macedonian law. In June 2002, Dragan Tilev, former head of the Macedonian government Sector for European Integration, observed that:

> Croatia learnt from the Macedonian experience in negotiations over the SAA. But, the political commitment and understanding is much higher in Croatia than in Macedonia. About 140 people work in the Slovenian Office and about 150 in the Croatian ministry for EU Integration. But only 23 people work in the Macedonian sector for EU Integration ... Support from abroad is very much needed, but there also has to be an investment from our own budget.

> (Interview, Sector for EU Integration, Skopje, June 2002)

This institutional weakness has been rectified to some extent since then, but the administrative capacity of the state to deal with the very demanding process of membership negotiations still presents an enormous challenge to the country. Despite becoming a formal candidate, the opening of negotiations was held back by the EU, pending further progress in meeting the Copenhagen political criteria and in the effective implementation of Macedonia's SAA.

The potential applicants

Other governments in the region have been less willing to introduce the reforms required by the EU accession process. The adoption of EU rules designed to create a 'functioning market economy' requires the elimination of the soft-budget constraints to politically well-connected firms which would lose out from implementation of such rules. The reforms implied by rule transfer during the accession process have therefore been resisted by anti-reform coalitions which have benefited from delayed and stalled transitions and from the perpetuation of partial reforms.

Unlike Croatia and Macedonia, the political parties in BiH have not developed a pro-Europe consensus. In the RS, there appears to be little interest in pushing forward the EU membership agenda, as the key proposals for the unification of the two entities' police forces, the last of the sixteen conditions laid down in the EU Feasibility Study for a Bosnian SAA, were rejected by the RS parliament.[29] Police reform was the final barrier to the start of negotiations for an SAA between the central government and the EU. In a statement issued in September 2005, the High Representative declared:

> Just over a week has passed since the RS Government ... blocked police restructuring, and in so doing, dashed this country's hopes. ... The European Union has been very clear that it wants BiH, and the rest of this region, to join the Union. ... But if you want to join the club, you have to meet the standards it sets. Police restructuring is one of the last requirements it has set for BiH. ... No police restructuring means no negotiations on an SAA, and no progress towards Europe – it means isolation. It's as simple as that.
>
> (Press release, OHR Sarajevo 22 September 2005)

The reasons for the opposition to police reform are linked to the unwillingness of the RS elite to impose the rule of law in the entity. In addition, opposition to EU membership is widely held among the population in both entities in BiH, which according to recent opinion polls does not regard EU membership as a priority (Massari 2005).

In Serbia, the anti-reform faction has dominated the strategic decision making of the government. In September 2005, the ICTY chief prosecutor Carla del Ponte announced that Serbia had established cooperation with The Hague tribunal through its handover of sixteen fugitives wanted since October 2004. In reaction, the EU agreed to launch preparatory talks on an SAA, putting Serbia on the path to eventual EU membership. However, political parties are divided about the benefits of EU membership. The Serbian Radical Party (SRS), supported by losers from the economic transition, the unemployed and the many ethnic Serb refugees from the other republics of former Yugoslavia (Cohen 2001), has been opposed to EU membership in principle. The anti-European orientation of the right-wing and nationalist sections of Serbian politics also draws support from the old elite associated with organized criminal groups that had developed during the Milošević period. In 2006, the government failed to meet a deadline to hand over the remaining fugitives from the ICTY, in particular General Ratko Mladić who was charged with responsibility for the Srebrenica massacre in Bosnia. As a result, the SAA negotiations were suspended, signalling the continuing influence of the anti-reform coalition in Serbia. The rapid privatization and other pro-market reforms that have been implemented in recent years have undermined to some extent the power of the old elite composed of the managers of socially owned enterprise, the bureaucracy and military institutions that supported the previous authoritarian regime. The new pro-European liberal elite that supports the reformist parties such as the Democratic Party (DS), and the G17-Plus, struggled to form a coalition government with the nationalist DSS after the February 2007 elections. The difficulty they faced in doing so, including an inter-regnum in which the deputy leader of the anti-European SRS, Tomislav Nikolić, became the speaker of the Parliament, demonstrated the weakness of this pro-reform coalition in Serbian politics.

In Albania, there is a broad political consensus on the importance of European integration and on eventual EU membership. The goal of EU accession is broadly supported by the population, and opinion polls show the highest level of support for EU membership among all the Western Balkan countries (Bogdani and Loughlin 2007: 190). However, the support for the EU accession process by the governing parties is often pitched at a rhetorical level, while the really substantial intention to implement pro-Europe reforms has been absent. Thus, although Albania began its negotiations for an SAA in 2003, these were not concluded until 2006 due to numerous delays in fulfilling the conditionality requirements laid down by the EU. In the opinion of Mirela Bogdani and John Loughlin, '[o]ne of the main reasons for this gap between rhetoric and reality is the fact that the political class is under pressure from the structures of organized crime that are interested in keeping Albania out of European Union control' (Bogdani and Loughlin 2007: 147).

In 2007, the issue of the final status of Kosovo was brought to the fore, with the report of the UN negotiator Marti Ahtisaari. His report recommended *de facto* independence for Kosovo with all the trappings of statehood. The proviso was that the Kosovo government should provide firm guarantees of respect for minority rights. There was also to be a substantial devolution of power to local municipalities, several of which would have an ethnic Serb majority. Although the proposals were rejected by the Serbian parliament, the EU supported them strongly and appeared willing to do a deal to restart the SAA negotiations in return for Serbian support for the Ahtisaari proposal. Carla del Ponte complained bitterly that she and the ICTY were being sidelined. The EU appeared to be compromising its principle of conditionality for the sake of progress in the Kosovo status talks.

EU financial assistance: the IPA programme and beyond

The CARDS programme, together with other EU assistance programmes to the Western Balkans ended in 2006 and was replaced by a single Instrument for Pre-Accession (IPA) covering the period 2007–13. Support will differ between the countries with candidate status and others which are defined as potential candidates.[30] Potential candidate countries will receive support along the lines of the CARDS programme for actions and projects in the fields of institution building and democratization, economic and social development, regional and cross-border cooperation and some alignment with the *acquis communautaire*. Candidate countries will, in addition, receive assistance for meeting the Copenhagen and other accession-related criteria for EU membership and for improving their administrative and judicial capacity. Additionally, candidate countries will receive help in preparing systems for the management of EU Structural Funds, Cohesion Funds and Regional Development Funds, for which they will qualify after accession and for regional, rural and human resources development.

The planned assistance to be provided under the IPA programme is projected to increase steadily in the coming years (Figure 10.3). This will involve some gradual increases for the candidate countries, Croatia and Macedonia, as well as

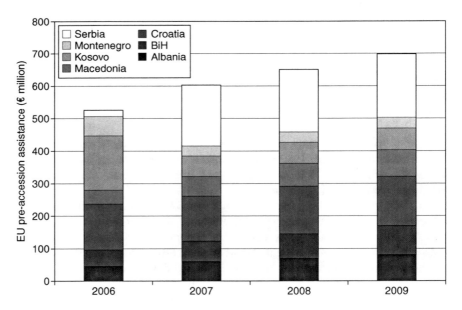

Figure 10.3 EU pre-accession assistance 2006–9 (€ million) (source: European Commission, Brussels).

for Albania and BiH. Serbia is projected to be one of the largest beneficiaries, reflecting its population size. Assistance for Kosovo is projected to return to more normal levels, although in relation to its needs, it will experience a significant reduction of EU support compared to recent years. However, whether or not these plans come to fruition depends largely upon the outcome of the Kosovo status negotiations and the continuation of Serbia's willingness to pursue reform policies that would eventually lead to an opening of EU membership negotiations.

Some perspectives on EU integration process

The Western Balkans face a far more difficult EU accession process than did the new member states from Central Europe and the Baltics, as they have a greater 'reform gap' to traverse with fewer resources. Moreover, there are a number of contradictions between the reforms required under the accession process and the reforms which have been required and implemented in the twin processes of transition and post-conflict reconstruction in which the Western Balkan countries have been engaged for the last decade. The democratizing and competitive market-building aspects of the enlargement process should not be overstated. In comparison to the clear pro-market model of development promoted by the World Bank and the OECD and other international institutions, the EU influence is ambiguous. First, in relation to the creation of a competitive market economy, the process of alignment to the EU *acquis* involves the creation of a set of regulatory institutions and agencies which tend to undercut the competitive market and impose a large new layer of bureaucracy creating a 'technocratic regulatory state' (Schimmelfennig and Sedelmeier 2004: 676). Second, in relation to the consolidation of democracy, the enlargement process sidelines and undermines the democratic process through the one-sided imposition of EU rules. Thus, while integration speeds up reforms driven by EU conditionality and negotiations, the quality of democracy may be harmed by pressure from the EU and the marginalization of political debate (Raik 2004). Third, there is a contradiction between the fiscal restraint demanded by the Maastricht criteria and the need to increase public expenditure on harmonization with the *acquis communautaire*. This fiscal tightening by reducing social expenditure can be especially harmful to the level and quality of social services, health and education (Barr 2005).

At the same time, it should not be overlooked that the willingness of the EU to accept the Western Balkan countries is not a foregone conclusion and that the enlargement fatigue which set in following the recent 'fifth' enlargement may not be easily overcome, requiring, as it does, some profound changes in the working arrangements and Treaties which currently define the possibilities for an expansion of the EU as a political organization and a governance system. However, the ongoing accession process has a sufficient momentum of its own to ensure that, at least for the next few years, the existing commitment to enlargement will guide the actions of the officials and politicians involved in the process, in both the Western Balkan countries and the EU.

11 Conclusion

Looking at the map of Europe, it is apparent the Western Balkan countries are geographically a core region of the continent. Surrounded on all sides by EU member states, it is paradoxical that the region remains outside the Union and that it is in many ways politically far away from it. This is all the more surprising considering that the former Yugoslavia was the most liberal and economically advanced of the Eastern European communist countries in the 1980s, only to turn into the most conflict-ridden part of Europe. The problems began with the Milošević ascendancy in 1987 and the ensuing imposition of direct rule over Kosovo. While all other issues including the independence of Croatia and Macedonia, the Dayton Agreement over Bosnia and Herzegovina (BiH) and the independence of Montenegro came and went, Kosovo still had a problematic relationship with Serbia twenty years later. While Albania, Croatia, Macedonia and Montenegro were set on a path to EU membership, the resolution of the Kosovo final status issue and the issue of police reform in BiH stood in the way of closer ties between Serbia, BiH, Kosovo and the EU.

In Chapters 3 and 4, I contrasted the early reform countries – Albania, Croatia and Macedonia – with the late reformers – BiH, Serbia, Montenegro and Kosovo – on the basis of their progress with macroeconomic stabilization and transition to a private-ownership economy. Regardless of their different initial conditions, the early reformers gained a growth premium, reflected in the positive relationship between reforms and growth. The distinction between early and late reformers was to some extent resolved once the late reformers began to adopt institutional reforms, following the Dayton Agreement in BiH, and the democratic turn in FRY (Serbia and Montenegro), as both countries introduced stabilization policies and institutional reforms involving privatization and improvements to the investment climate. However, in relation to progress with EU accession the distinction has remained valid, as the early reformers are well on the way to EU membership, while the late reformers have been held back by strong anti-European interest groups which prevented their compliance with EU conditionality.

Why have the countries of the region experienced such divergent paths of transition, development and EU integration? Yugoslavia was the first country in Eastern Europe to introduce institutional reforms in line with the transition paradigm that would later sweep the former socialist economies of Eastern Europe. The Marković reform programme, begun in 1988, was popular, involving the distribution of shares to workers in their own enterprises, the entry of thousands of new small firms and the elimination of inflation. It was assessed as more successful than the widely praised Polish stabilization and transition programme, having stabilized prices at a lower cost in output foregone. However, the Marković programme was ultimately unsuccessful because factions within the republic elites resisted the reforms which threatened their positions of power and privilege. This political economy of the transition process had disastrous consequences for the federal state, as the republic elites turned to the mobilization of nationalist sentiments to counter the reforms. If this worst outcome could have been avoided, then it is likely that Yugoslavia would have been a front runner for EU membership, possibly some time in the 1990s. In that case, Albania's transition might also have been easier, with a secure and prosperous Yugoslavia on its doorstep. However, this potential outcome was forestalled by the wars and conflicts which tore the country apart.

The wars of Yugoslav succession led to the independence of Croatia and Macedonia in 1991. Together with Albania, their independence solved their statehood problems and they were able to turn towards early reforms, their stabilization programmes backed by financial assistance from the IMF. All three achieved price stability in the first half of the 1990s. By 2006, the European Bank for Reconstruction and Development (EBRD) indicators of transition in the field of privatization were well ahead in Albania, Croatia and Macedonia, although enterprise restructuring remained problematic in Albania. Matters were very different among the late reformers. BiH eventually realized its sovereignty in 1995, but only as a fractured state under international supervision. Since then BiH has had difficulty in introducing effective reforms, in part because the large international assistance effort replaced the need for them. In Kosovo, which achieved de facto independence in 1999, also as an international protectorate, reforms were imposed from above by the international administration. In Federal Republic of Yugoslavia (FRY), effective reforms were blocked by the Milošević regime, which benefited from that strategy despite runaway inflation and the collapsing economy which it ruled over, having mobilized support from the potential losers from reform by maintaining jobs for surplus workers in loss-making enterprises. The imposition of sanctions also played into the hands of the regime, as it was able to control the smuggling routes and gain enormous rents from the monopoly position this provided over illegal imports.

Yet, all was not well with the early reformers either, as the institutional reforms that had been introduced in all three countries were only partial. The political economy of reforms suggests that such partial reforms can become stuck as early winners seek to prevent further progress and consolidate their advantages. In this case too, it was the winners that stalled the completion of the reforms by preserving monopoly positions and benefiting from weaknesses in the unreformed judiciary and from the collapse in the rule of law, exploiting workers in privatized companies whose wages or social contributions often went unpaid and asset stripping the companies for their personal gain. Such rampant tycoon capitalism was most prevalent in Croatia in the 1990s. In Albania, most large companies simply collapsed as the central planning system came to an end, and many of their workers lost their jobs through either restructuring or privatization. Many of them either emigrated or turned to organized crime, as smuggling goods to break the sanctions imposed on FRY became a profitable trade. Towards the end of the 1990s, all the early reformers experienced crises to do with their unreformed banking systems. The most serious crisis was in Albania following the collapse of the pyramid banks, when large-scale social unrest brought down the government. In Croatia, bank collapses led to the takeover of Croatia's banking system by foreign bank groups from Italy and Austria. In Macedonia, the banking crisis which erupted with the collapse of the TAT savings bank in Bitola happened on a lesser scale but further indicated the difficulties of partial reforms.

Following the banking crises, Albania and Macedonia sought international assistance from the International Monetary Fund (IMF) and the World Bank. Both pushed through their reforms at a more urgent pace, and to a greater degree than did Croatia, and by the end of the decade, both had essentially privatized their economies, whether through the sale of the socially owned and state-owned companies or through the entry of new small firms. Macedonia had a higher density of small- and medium-sized enterprises (SMEs) than any of the other countries, while Albania had a large self-employment sector into which many workers had been pushed to ensure a subsistence income, as well as a large informal economy. In consequence, by 2005, Albania and Macedonia had the highest private sector shares in gross domestic product (GDP) in the region, while also having weak labour market outcomes, with high unemployment in Macedonia and high out-migration from Albania. Overall, Albania and Macedonia adopted a liberal variety of capitalism, in which social protection expenditure was low, and the share of the private sector in the economy was high. In 2007, Albania went even further by introducing a 10 per cent flat tax, giving it the lowest corporate taxes in the Western Balkans. Yet, as the late reformers were catching up between 2000 and 2005, Croatia made little further progress and its private sector reforms were firmly stalled. With its high levels of social and employment protection, Croatia resembled the Central European corporatist variety of capitalism on which the image of 'Social Europe', embodied in the social acquis, has been modelled.

The Kosovo war marked a turning point among the late reformers. In FRY, it led to the downfall of the Milošević regime and the initiation of transition reforms with the assistance of the international financial institutions (IFIs). Montenegro, within the 'State Union of Serbia and Montenegro', achieved de facto independence which was sealed by the 2006 referendum. Both countries initiated radical institutional reforms, involving privatization and the easing of the conditions for new firm entry. By 2004, Serbia had surpassed the other countries in the region in reforming the business environment. Yet, reforms stalled after the assassination of the Prime Minister Zoran Djindjić in 2003, since when there has been ongoing uncertainty about the direction that the transition in Serbia would take.

BiH and Kosovo have proved to be the most difficult cases of transition in the region. Both are international protectorates, and both have unresolved statehood problems, which have blocked the domestic political impetus for reforms. While BiH has recorded rapid economic growth in recent years, partly in recovery from the devastation of the war, the Kosovo economy has regressed with negative rates of economic growth in recent years. Both economies became internationally uncompetitive with significant trade deficits as privatized industries with little foreign direct investment (FDI) failed to achieve sufficient restructuring. Both have depended upon large inflows of international aid and assistance. While the large size of the international aid inflows has been justified in each case by the need to respond to the devastations of war, the countries have become subject to the syndrome of 'aid-dependency' with international aid becoming a substitute for reform. Although some reforms have been pushed through by the international administrators, the domestic anti-reform coalitions have been able to resist their effective implementation. This has been especially problematic in BiH where institutional reforms have lagged far behind those in the other Western Balkan countries. Thus, in relation to other countries in the region, BiH occupies the last place in the World Bank's ease of doing business indicators, has the lowest private sector share in GDP and is lowest on the EBRD ranking of transition indicators with respect to privatization and enterprise restructuring.

The experience of BiH and Kosovo highlights the role of international institutions in the processes of institutional reform in the Western Balkans. With the failure of the national transition programmes in all the countries, international actors including IFIs and aid agencies have become deeply involved in supporting economic growth, postwar reconstruction and development, and the EU accession process. The extent of this involvement has been unprecedented in comparison with the transition countries in other parts of Eastern Europe. These international actors have mainly been from the public sector, including IFIs, non-governmental organizations (NGOs) and the European Union (EU). Significant problems of aid effectiveness and donor coordination emerged as this process unfolded. The Croatian case has been an exception, since there has been a much higher involvement of international actors from the private sector in the form of FDI, especially in specific sectors such as banking and finance, telecommunications, and the oil and gas industry. Croatia has also relied much less on international aid than other countries in the region and has carried out its postwar reconstruction mainly through its own efforts while also borrowing on the international capital markets which early membership of the IMF and World Bank facilitated. Croatia has also received more assistance from the IFIs including the European development banks than the other countries.

The World Bank has been a predominant influence on policy design, and together with the IMF, and the OECD through the Investment Compact, has promoted a neo-liberal and pro-market approach to transition, post-conflict reconstruction and development. In the low-income countries in the region, Albania, BiH, Serbia and Montenegro, the World Bank has promoted its Poverty Reduction Strategy Paper (PRSP) approach, based upon a set of pro-market institutional reforms to create jobs and stimulate economic growth. Croatia and Macedonia were bypassed by the PRSP policy package and instead turned towards the EU social model following their nomination as candidates for EU membership. This involved the adoption of the acquis communautaire which had a far less liberal tone to its policies in regard to labour market issues, laying greater stress on equality of access, non-discrimination and employment protection. While this fitted in well with the Croatian policy orientation towards the Central European corporatist model of capitalism, it represented something of a U-turn for Macedonia which had hitherto directed its policy effort towards a more liberal model. This is no doubt one of the reasons why, despite its acceptance as a candidate, the EU hesitated with opening membership negotiations.

The World Bank has also been influential in social policy, complementing the relative lack of activity by the EU in this policy area. Although this is changing with the extension of EU competence into social policy more widely, its traditional focus on labour market issues had previously left a vacuum which the World Bank was able to fill. This is particularly noticeable in the field of pensions, with Croatia taking the lead in pension reform and the introduction of three pillar models based upon partial privatization of the pension system, followed by Macedonia and Kosovo. Pro-market reforms have also been introduced in the health systems in Croatia and Macedonia, while health has been privatized by default in Albania owing to the low level of public provision. Housing was privatized in all countries early on in the transition process leading to a severe lack of social housing and the growth of illegal settlements and substandard urban environments in the poorer countries. The education systems have been run down by budget cuts and remain unreformed, which together with the growth of long-term unemployment and the large informal economies has reduced the skills base and undermined international competitiveness in all the countries of the region.

The involvement of the international aid agencies, including bilateral aid agencies and NGOs, highlights the importance of economic development, as an issue overlapping with the economic transition that was unfolding at the same time. Whereas transition essentially involves a transfer of resources from the social- or state-ownership sector to the private sector through reallocation and restructuring, development involves additionally a set of policies to overcome a lack of capital resources. This was relevant to the Western Balkans because wars and conflicts had destroyed large parts of the infrastructure and because the undeveloped banking system did not efficiently recycle individual savings into productive investments. The other developmental aspect was the institutional deficit in the field of property rights, which are known to hold back growth in developing countries and which were weakened in the Western Balkans by blocked and stalled reforms. Additional institutional deficits have included the weak rule of law, the growth of organized crime, the spread of corruption and the poor quality of the judiciary. The themes of financial constraints and institutional weaknesses sparked a fierce debate over the priority of these two issues for policy purposes, with the EBRD emphasizing financial constraints and the World Bank emphasizing more the issue of institutional gaps and the investment climate.

Since 2000, the EU has become a major actor in the region, and its Stabilization and Association process for the first time promised eventual membership to all the Western Balkan states once the required conditions were met including full cooperation with the International Criminal Tribunal on the former Yugoslavia (ICTY), refugee return and a commitment to regional cooperation. The CARDS programme was introduced to support pre-accession projects, followed by the IPA programme with increased funding from 2007 on. The process of EU integration raised further reform challenges for the countries concerned since EU integration and membership requires the introduction of a whole new set of EU-compatible reforms and the adoption of the acquis communautaire, a massive task of legislation and implementation involving large-scale rule transfer from a more advanced environment, together with all the attendant costs of doing so. Moreover, the EU rules ran counter to some of the policy prescriptions of the World Bank, IMF and Organization for Economic Cooperation and Development (OECD) neoliberal agenda. Croatia has clearly chosen the EU social model, but adjustment to the new set of rules has been more difficult for Albania and Macedonia. The response of the domestic elites to the EU accession agenda has depended on the outcome of struggles between pro-EU and anti-EU coalitions in each country. While political consensus has been reached in the early reformers on the strategic importance of EU membership, significant opposition to the implementation of the rules remains, especially in Albania where sections of the elite which benefit from the weak rule of law have not supported a quick accession. In BiH and Serbia, there has been significant opposition to the accession process, and a successful outcome of the EU integration is uncertain.

EU integration also raised the question of regional cooperation. This culminated in the accession of the Western Balkan countries to the rather inappropriately named Central European Free Trade Area (CEFTA) and to the creation of a new Regional Cooperation Council which will become operational in 2008. The Stability Pact has also created numerous regional cooperation task forces and networks in various policy areas, from investment promotion to housing policy. In this respect, the Stability Pact has acted as a classic policy broker. The involvement of the international institutions in these networks has demonstrated that the concept of regional cooperation has been as much about donor coordination as it has been about cooperation between the countries of the region themselves, which have often been involved more on a declarative basis to meet EU conditionality criteria than out of any real commitment to the principle. Indeed, this has often run counter to other policy advice to countries, to increase international competitiveness and to outdo one another on a series of league tables related to reform progress and economic performance.

Overall, what are the prospects for the region? The stability which EU membership would bring to the region would open the door for foreign investment, knowledge transfer, expanded tourism, competitive economies and a reversal of the steady brain drain of the most talented young people and would lead to faster economic growth and a more prosperous future. Thus, EU membership is the most favourable outlook, but it is not inevitable, nor is it a panacea. The EU has enlargement fatigue, and in the late reforming countries there are powerful interest coalitions set against it. Even supposing these groups are overcome, and the EU accepts all the Western Balkan states as members some time in the next decade, difficult reforms will still need to be carried out. Administrative capacity will need to be developed, and the rule of law imposed. It would be better that these issues were dealt with and solved before membership is achieved rather than afterwards. Yet, delay in achieving membership is also a dangerous option, as this would give a boost to the anti-reform coalitions which oppose entry and strengthen the hand of organized crime in the region threatening to create a black spot of instability in Europe for years to come.

Notes

1 Introduction

1 Slovenia, the sixth former Yugoslav republic, joined the EU in 2004.

2 Initial conditions: Yugoslavia and Albania

1 In July 1946, the two countries signed a Treaty of Friendship, Cooperation and Mutual Aid (Jelavich 1983: 331).

2 UNRRA was created at a forty-four-nation conference at the White House in November 1943. Its mission was to provide economic assistance to European countries after the Second World War and to repatriate and assist refugees who came under Allied control. UNRRA provided health and welfare assistance, vocational training and entertainment to refugees. In 1948, its tasks were taken over by the International Refugee Organization.

3 Harold Lydall (1989: 157) reported that:

> [a]ccording to the Vice-Governor of the National Bank ... the governors from the different republics and provinces prevent the formulation of effective regulations to put a stop to illegal, or 'grey', increases in the money supply, which has been a persistent problem in Yugoslavia ... the National Bank ... gives the impression of being feeble and ineffective. It shows no evidence of resisting the demands either of the federal government or on the national banks (and hence the governments) of the republics and provinces. From the point of view of policy, it might just as well not exist.

4 The director in question was Fikret Abdić who later established Bihać as an autonomous area in northern Bosnia during the Bosnian war, trading with all sides and maintaining a neutral position between the warring factions.

5 In practice, the rates of contributions were established by the republican governments, and participation in decision making by representatives of enterprises and other stakeholders was limited.

6 Mikulić had been former president of the Bosnian communist party before taking up his position as federal president. His hold on power was undermined by the Agrokomerc scandal of 1987.

7 The Enterprises Law, Službeni list SFRJ No. 77/88, 40/89.

8 The Foreign Investment Law, Službeni list SFRJ No. 77/88. According to Article 8 of the Law, '[e]nterprises with foreign investments shall have the same status, rights and responsibilities on the single Yugoslav market as socially-owned enterprises'.

9 The Social Capital Circulation and Management Law, Službeni list SFRJ No. 84/89. Article 1 of the law stated that '[s]ocial capital may be sold wholly or in part, to domestic or foreign legal entities and natural persons'. According to Article 2, '[t]he

decision to sell social capital shall be made by the workers' council, unless otherwise provided by the Enterprise's by-laws'. The law was amended in August 1990 when its name was changed to the Law on Social Capital (Uvalić 1997: 268).

10 Interview with Professor Ljubomir Madžar (1990).

11 Elections also took place in Slovenia in April 1990 and returned the opposition DEMOS coalition with a majority in two of the three chambers of the Slovenian parliament.

12 Fikret Abdić, a popular but eccentric Bosnian businessman, had won more votes than Izetbegović but stood down in favour of the latter.

13 Opinion polls conducted throughout Yugoslavia recorded 61 per cent disagreeing with the statement that every (Yugoslav) nation should have a national state of its own (Mueller 2000).

14 Marković was popular with the Serbian public, and in an opinion poll carried out in May 1990 he received a higher approval rating than Milošević.

15 'The reforms that Marković was championing were exactly the kind of changes that were most threatening to the conservatives who had taken control of Serbia at the end of 1987 . . .' (Gagnon 2004: 91).

16 According to the Serbian journalist Miloš Vasić, an important turning point was the failure of the counter-revolutionary coup by the hardliners in Moscow against the Yeltsin government. This dispelled all hope among the Serbian elite in Belgrade for a restoration of the communist system.

17 One of the legacies of this period is the enormous, defunct, steel mill at Elbasan which was built with Chinese assistance. It was ambitiously but unsuccessfully intended to transform the Albanian economy.

3 The early reformers: Croatia, Macedonia and Albania

1 The central importance of statehood is recognized in the literature on the transition to democracy. As Juan Linz and Alfred Stepan have observed '[w]ithout a state, there can be no citizenship; without citizenship there can be no democracy' (Linz and Stepan 1996: 28). Statehood is equally relevant to the economic aspects of transition and the ability of the state to implement effective institutional reforms.

2 For example, the EU refused to admit Croatia to the PHARE programme.

3 Tapes and documents discovered in the presidential quarters that had been made by Tudjman revealed the extent of some of the dealings of the HDZ in corrupt and illegal financial activities.

4 Stipe Mesić had been Croatia's representative on the presidency of the former Yugoslavia. He later joined the HDZ but resigned over Tudjman's policy to support the Croatian autonomy movement in Herzegovina and set up his own party – the Croatian People's Party – together with Vesna Pusić and Radovan Čačić.

5 These were the Party for Democratic Prosperity and the People's Democratic Party. The small Reformed Forces Party also joined the government.

6 The size of the majority was largely due to the fact that the two main opposition parties, the VMRO-DPMNE and the moderate Democratic Party both boycotted the second round of the election, claiming electoral fraud (Szajkowski 2000: 256).

7 The dispute centred over Macedonia's use of the Star of Vergina on its flag, which Greece claimed as its own symbol.

8 The Macedonian financial crisis preceded by several months the financial crisis in East Asia which began in July 1997.

9 The owner of TAT was arrested and charged with forging documents, tax evasion and abuse of office. Investigations revealed that DM40 million of deposits had disappeared from the bank.

10 The government was formed by the nationalist VMRO-DPMNE (Internal Macedonian Revolutionary Organization – Democratic Party for Macedonian National Unity),

the small Democratic Alternative and the Democratic Party of Albanians (DPA) led by Arben Xhaferi.

11 The coalition also included the Liberal Democrats together with a number of smaller ethnically based parties of Bosniaks, Roma, Turks, Serbs and Vlachs.

12 However, some minor incidents revealed the underlying tensions. The Ohrid Agreement had promised a radical decentralization of government functions. Despite the agreement, ethnic and political tensions persisted, and there were a number of violent incidents, some instigated by a group known as the Albanian National Army (ANA) which was also active in Kosovo and Southern Serbia. In January 2003, members of the Lions interior ministry militia unit staged a blockade of the Blace border crossing with Kosovo after it was announced that the unit was to be disbanded and absorbed into the regular Macedonian police, alongside ex-members of Albanian paramilitary formations. In another incident in June 2003, the police station in the village of Aracinovo was stormed and taken over by angry Albanian residents, and a dozen police were taken hostage for a few hours.

13 Election observers declared that 32 out of 790 clauses of the election law had been broken (Crampton 2002: 304).

14 'Power struggle', *The Economist*, 28 August 2003.

15 'Albania's new leader sets out his goals', RFE/RL report 9(25), 9 September 2005.

4 The late reformers: BiH, Serbia, Montenegro, and Kosovo

1 Throughout this chapter and in the rest of this book, I will use the standard acronym BiH for 'Bosnia and Herzegovina' in place of the long form of the name of the country adopted after the Dayton peace agreement and the acronym FRY for the 'Federal Republic of Yugoslavia' which existed up to 2004 when it became the State Union of Serbia and Montenegro.

2 The Vance–Owen plan proposed the cantonization of BiH, its vagueness over boundaries further stimulating the fighting for territorial control. The plan was initially designed by Finnish diplomat Martti Ahtisaari, who later drew up the plan for the final status of Kosovo in 2007.

3 David Chandler in a critical review called this system a 'parody of democracy' (Chandler 1999: 191).

4 Forty-two countries and twelve international NGOs took part in the conference.

5 When Yugoslavia collapsed, BiH along with the other republics inherited a portion of former Yugoslavia state debt, which amounted to $400 million (Kreimer *et al.* 2000). The Bank held meetings with officials from BiH in January 1995 in Warsaw, well before the cessation of hostilities, at which a plan for refinancing the debt was agreed.

6 The laws were not implemented until 1998 due to a political crisis in Republika Srpska, IMF (1998) Country Report, 98/96.

7 The first governor was a Frenchman, Serge Robert, who acted as Governor of the Bank from 1996 to 1997. He was succeeded by a New Zealander, Peter Nichol, who was Governor until the post was transferred to a Bosnian at the end of 2004.

8 1KM = €0.5113.

9 Sead Numanović, 'Bosnia: Ashdown raises expectations', *IWPR Balkan Crisis Report No. 342*, 12 June 2002.

10 Paddy Ashdown 'Bosnia: reform will bring justice and jobs', *IWPR Bosnia Crisis Report No. 341*, 7 June 2002.

11 The scandal was revealed in a report by the EU-funded Customs and Fiscal Assistance Office (CAFAO). The report charged that the head of the RS customs service department for fighting smuggling led the scam, which involved false invoicing for textile goods imported from Turkey, Bulgaria and Hungary, the procurement of bribes from the importers. The goods were sold on the free 'Arizona' market near the autonomous district of Brčko.

12 IWPR staff in London 'Bosnia: Ashdown reins in Bosnian Serbs', *IWPR Balkan Crisis Report No. 420*, 4 April 2003.
13 The problem was made more complex by the existence of large government domestic liabilities to citizens. These had built up in respect of claims for compensation for war damage, frozen foreign currency accounts, expenditure arrears and privatization coupons. The estimated extent of these liabilities amounted to over 200 per cent of GDP. Under a law adopted in 2004, these claims were to be compensated by the issue of KM 'Zero Coupon' bonds repayable in fifty years, combined with cash payouts. However, the Constitutional Court declared that this would be unjust and ruled against this system of compensation. In the case the frozen foreign currency accounts, it insisted that bonds should be issued for maximum period of fifteen years and should carry a fair market rate. The IMF criticized the decision on the grounds that it would place unsustainable pressure on the government budget and would make the budget deficit reduction targets unattainable.
14 UN Security Council Resolution 757 (1992), 30 May. According to a later IMF report 'The regional war took an enormous toll on FRY's economy owing to the loss of markets, the interruption of long-established production relations, and the imposition of crippling sanctions. The effects of these developments on the economy were aggravated by macroeconomic mismanagement', IMF Country Report No. 01/07, January 2001, p. 5.
15 UN Security Council Resolution 787 (1992), 16 November.
16 UN Security Council Resolution 820 (1993), 17 April.
17 The coalition consisted of the SPS, New Democracy (ND) and the Yugoslav United Left (JUL). Milošević ended his term as president of Serbia and became president of FRY in July 1997.
18 Even before the NATO air strikes began, there were already large numbers of displaced people within Kosovo. By the end of 1998, the International Federation of the Red Cross and Red Crescent societies reported that there were 90,000 Kosovar refugees outside the province, and 400,000 internally displaced persons within the province, although many had returned to their homes by March 1999.
19 Possibly as many as 10,000 people were killed in Kosovo during the war, see 'Crimes in Kosovo: taking turns in violence', AIM Podgorica, 21 August 1999.
20 UNHCR News Kosovo Crisis Update, 31 May 1999.
21 R. Boyes, 'An economy cut dead by conflict', *The Times*, 13 April 1999.
22 S. Erlanger, 'Who pays the bill for wrecked factories?' *Guardian*, 4 May 1999.
23 'The damage from defiance', Institute for War and Peace Reporting, 16 May 1999.
24 S. Shah, 'War "cost US$60bn for Yugoslavia"', *The Times* 23 August 1999.
25 It was not only the opposition that felt the increased tension, erstwhile allies of Milošević were also subjected to violence. An attempt was made on the life of Vuk Drašković, while Milošević's former mentor, Ivan Stambolić, disappeared while out jogging never to be seen again.
26 The new state union which was created soon afterwards was popularly referred to as 'Solania'.
27 Željko Cvijanović, 'Serbia: Djindjić versus Dinkić', *Balkan Crisis Report No. 398*, 16 January 2003.
28 The large and ornate federal government building in Belgrade became practically an empty space with a few high-level officials conducting business in surroundings that appeared to the visitor more like the 'Marie Celeste' than a functioning government of a modern state.
29 Most prominent among the detainees were members of the notorious Zemun gang, who were alleged to have organized the assassination. A shopping centre and residential complex in Belgrade owned by the gang's leader was demolished. The infamous Red Berets elite interior ministry unit, accused of complicity with the criminal gangs and with the organization of the assassination, was disbanded, and some of its leaders

arrested. Among those arrested were former State Security Minister Jovica Stanišić and his deputy Franko Simatović. Both were later extradited to the ICTY in the Hague. Another high-profile war crimes suspect, Veselin Šljivančanin, was arrested in June following a ten-hour siege of his apartment. Šljivančanin had been responsible for war crimes committed in the Croatian city of Vukovar in 1991. He was transferred to the Hague in July. His arrest removed a further threat from the USA to block a multi-million dollar aid package to Serbia. In April, the two main suspects in the murder were killed while resisting arrest, and a further forty-five people were charged with murder and conspiracy to commit murder.

30 This party was set up in April 1998.

31 One of the legacies of the UN sanctions against FRY was the persistence of smuggling into the post-sanctions era. Each year, some 17,000 tons of contraband cigarettes were being smuggled into FRY from Montenegro, threatening the viability of the four socially owned tobacco companies in Serbia. Nebojša Medejović, representative of the Montenegrin Agency for Restructuring the Economy, claimed that this smuggling 'couldn't have been realized without the support and protection from the authorities' most powerful men, especially the Federal Customs Administration', Business Yugoslavia, No. 8, 15 October 1997.

32 *Financial Times*, 22 May 1999.

33 The Kosovo economy became a haven for private enterprise but not of the type envisaged by the international community. According to one of the directors of the International Narcotics Enforcement Officers' Association, the Kosovo conflict turned the province into a centre of the international heroin trade due to the lack of border controls. In 1999, as much as two-fifths of the heroin reaching Western Europe passed through Kosovo, on its way from Asia and Turkey, through Albania, to the small ports in Southern Italy run by the Italian mafia or by road through Serbia direct to Hungary, the Czech Republic and Germany, report by Eve-Ann Prentice 'Kosovo is mafia's heroin gateway to the West', *The Times*, 24 July 1999.

34 In September 1999, I visited the University Library in Prishtina and witnessed the absence of books on the library shelves.

35 The Steering Group is co-chaired by the European Union and the World Bank. It includes the Special Coordinator of the Stability Pact, representatives of the International Monetary Fund, European Investment Bank, European Bank for Reconstruction and Development, the United Nations and finance ministers of the major donor countries.

36 'First Donors' Conference for Kosovo: conclusions', Brussels, July 28, 1999. Online, available at: www.seerecon.org/Calendar/Cal-28–7-99-Conclusions.htm (accessed 5 August 1999).

37 The Democratic Party of Kosovo (PDK) led by former KLA leader Hashim Thaqi won twenty-six seats, a smaller Albanian party, Alliance for the Future of Kosovo (AAK), won eight seats and the Serb coalition Povratak, the party of Kosovo's Serbs, gained twenty-two seats (including ten reserved seats).

38 Patrick Moore, 'Kosova and Serbia hold dialogue of the deaf', *RFE/RL Balkan Report 7(35)*, 17 October 2003.

39 Kosovo today is both an economic and a political failure. Western military intervention was supposed to create a multi-ethnic society. This has not happened, and there is quite frankly no prospect whatsoever of any such development in the future. Today the land of Kosovo and Metohija is less multi-ethnic than it has ever been in its history.

(O'Shea 2005: 61)

40 Human Rights Watch, 'Failure to protect: anti-minority violence in Kosovo'. Online, available at: http://hrw.org/reports/2004/kosovo0704/1.htm.

5 Privatization and foreign direct investment

1 In Albania, the Law on Foreign Investments (1993); in BiH, the Law on the Policy of Foreign Direct Investments (1998); in Croatia, the Investment Promotion Act (2000); in Macedonia, the Constitution and the Law on Trading Companies (2004); in Montenegro, the Law on Foreign Investments (2000); and in Serbia, the Law on Foreign Investments (2002).
2 The investment promotion agencies are Albinvest, the Foreign Investment Promotion Agency in BiH, the Trade and Investment Promotion Agency in Croatia, the Agency for Foreign Investments of the Republic of Macedonia, the Montenegrin Investment promotion Agency and the Serbia Investment and Export Promotion Agency.
3 These have included a five-year corporate tax exemption for foreign subsidiaries in BiH, and for three years in Macedonia, while tax exemptions are available in Free Zones and in less-developed regions in Croatia.
4 Companies based in the Skopje Free Economic Zone are exempt from VAT on intermediate goods produced there, from customs duties on products imported into the zone for production of export goods, on services within the zone that support exporters, on taxes on costs of connection to water, sewerage, heating, gas and power supply networks and from property tax and profits tax for a period of ten years. Investments in capital assets in the zone can be offset against tax after a period of ten years and one day from the commencement of business. Land within the free zone may be leased to foreign investors for a period of fifty years with the possibility to extend the lease for another twenty-five years.
5 This was called the 'Basic Law on Transformation of Socially Owned Assets'.
6 The fund has ... great powers and no direct accountability. In its portfolio it has shares from almost all enterprises in the economy, making it the largest asset owner ... it appoints managers and can initiate privatization when and how it sees fit.

(Bićanić 1993: 428)

7 The local company started up with eighteen employees backed by a collateral guarantee provided by the town council. Employment increased to 120 after the involvement of the foreign investor. Interview with Pakrac town council, 18 November 2003.
8 This was the Law on the Transformation of Enterprises with Social Capital.
9 Management buyouts accounted for DM1.3 billion of assets out of a total value of assets of privatized enterprises of DM3.5 billion.
10 Kerin Hope, 'Obstacles have been removed', *Financial Times*, 27 July 1995.
11 Kerin Hope, 'Still prosperous', *Financial Times*, 27 July 1995.
12 In autumn 2002, an economist at the Institute of Economics in Skopje summarized the effects of privatization by saying that management buy-outs have

enabled managers to transform their control rights into property rights, it has strengthened the power of high-level policy makers, and has led to collusion of the industrial and political elite. A handful of people have privatized state property with an estimated value of $6–$8 million.

13 Following the independence from the Ottoman Empire in 1912, most agricultural land in Albania was owned by just five families, each with about 60,000 hectares of farmland and forests. Subsequent land sales fragmented these family holdings, but by 1945 ownership was still very unequal with 3 per cent of the population owning 27 per cent of the land. The communist regime broke up the large landholdings under a land reform in 1945. The land was subsequently collectivized into agricultural cooperatives and nationalized in 1976. In the early 1990s, the pre-1945 landowners organized in the 'Property with Justice' movement mounted a vigorous political campaign for the restitution of their land. Under a 1995 law, they were compensated with seaside and tourist properties (Cungu and Swinnen 1999: 607).

14 The land reform was much more radical in Albania than in many communist countries in the Soviet bloc since in Albania land had been nationalized, whereas in other countries even land in cooperatives was formally under the private ownership of the cooperative members. In other countries, when the cooperatives were broken up, land was returned intact to the formal owners, rather than being distributed in an egalitarian manner to the rural population.

15 These areas were concentrated in the mountainous northeast of Albania, especially in the Kukes region.

16 Agency for Privatization in the Federation of BiH, 'Model of Privatization in the Federation of B&H'.

17 In practice, the desire for speed turned out to be based on an optimistic assessment of the administrative capacity of the bureaucracy. The initial hurdle to be overcome in the privatization process was the registration of citizens' claims for vouchers. Beginning in April, the Payments Bureau had to issue vouchers in the form of 'Unique Citizens' Accounts' or 'UCAs'. The issuing of vouchers was expected to last one month after which time individuals were able to appeal against mistakes in the valuation of their voucher accounts. Yet by early June, after the first sales of small enterprises had begun, the Payments Bureau had still failed to deliver over 800,000 UCAs, of the two million which had been printed. Moreover as many as 30 per cent of those which had been delivered turned out to have mistakes or were challenged. To deal with the problem, the Payment Bureau opened 300 special counters in its offices throughout the Federation.

18 A further distinctive element of the privatization process was that state-owned housing units were also included in the list of assets which could be bought with the privatization vouchers.

19 For example, the article 'Bosnian tycoons lying in wait for certificates', *Dnevni Avaz*, 11 April 1999.

20 Vinko Banović in interview with Večernji List, 29/30 May 1999, said:

> In the mass emission of certificates it is realistic to expect that those who have cash will buy certificates, i.e. shares from those who do not know what to do with them and yet need the money. Citizens in need will sell certificates to 'torbari' below their true value, but neither the CPA nor anybody else can prevent that from happening. Shares or certificates are regarded as private property

21 'Ethnic privatization: Croats hold 180 companies in HNK', *Oslobodjenje*, 6 June 1999. One analyst observed that 'Bosnia's economic transition has been heavily tainted by ethnic politics and corruption' and that 'the only locals with resources to buy state-owned enterprises were members of a rather unholy alliance among the ruling parties, the increasingly powerful mafia, and elements of the old socialist nomenklatura' (Donais 2002: 5).

22 'Certificates in ads: 20,000 marks in paper for 3,500 marks in cash', *Oslobodjenje*, 4 June 1999.

23 'Demobilized soldiers seek exemption form cash requirement in small scale privatization', *Dnevni Avaz*, 17 June 1999.

24 See 'Avaz reflects on certificate sales and items for small-scale privatization', *Dnevni Avaz*, 5 July 1999.

25 'Unsuccessful privatization start in Federation', *Dnevni Avaz*, 28 July 1999.

26 According to Sejfudin Zahirović, director of the Tuzla Canton Privatization Agency:

> The agency has registered for privatization items worth 230 million KM. Accordingly, it takes between 80 and 90 million KM to conduct the obligatory 35 per cent cash payment. There are not 90 million in cash in the state, let alone potential buyers. We do not have local demand.

> (Report on NTV Hyat, 6 June 1999)

27 'Trade Unions: "Westendorp responsible for ethnic privatization"', *Oslobodjenje*.
28 Avramović had spent his career working in the World Bank and for UNCTAD in Geneva, becoming a senior advisor to the UN Secretary General. He returned to Belgrade in 1989. In an interview with the daily newspaper *Vreme*, he said 'personally, I'm against the privatization of big companies, because it is always followed by a big robbery', Vreme News Digest Agency No. 174, 30 January 1995.
29 *Financial Times*, 16 December 1998.
30 Privatization Law, Official Gazette of Montenegro, 23/96.
31 Ibid., 6/99.
32 Interview with enterprise managers, Prizren, September 2003.
33 Tatjana Matić, 'Serbia angered by Kosovo privatization', Balkan Crisis Report no. 433, 30 May 2003.
34 Banking and Payments Authority of Kosovo, Annual Report 2005.

6 Entrepreneurship and SME policies

1 Statistički godišnjak Jugoslavije, 1989, Table 105-1.
2 John Allcock cited reports that in 1988, there were sixty dollar millionaires living in Zagreb (Allcock 1992: 405).
3 *Statistički godišnjak Jugoslavije 1997* [Statistical Yearbook of Yugoslavia 1997], Beograd: Savezni Zavod za Statistiku, 1997, p. 49. Of these, 127,340 were private enterprises without limited liability (sole proprietorships) and 57,916 were limited liability companies (društva sa ograničenom odgovornošću – d.o.o.).
4 *Statistički ljetopis 1995* [Statistical Yearbook 1995], Zagreb: Državni zavod za statistiku, p. 54. There were 31,050 private enterprises (privatna poduzeća) and 96,561 limited liability companies (društva s ograničenom odgovornošću – d.o.o.).
5 Of these 50,946 were private enterprises and 32,832 were limited liability companies (drushtva so ogranichena odgovornost – d.o.o.), see *Statistichki Godishnik na Republika Makedonija 1996* [Statistical Yearbook of the Republic of Macedonia], Skopje: Zavod za Statistika na Republika Makedonija, p. 70.
6 *Statistički godišnjak Jugoslavije 1997* [Statistical Yearbook of Yugoslavia 1997], Beograd: Savezni Zavod za Statistiku (1997: 49). Of these, 127,340 were private enterprises without limited liability (sole proprietorships) and 57,916 were limited liability companies (društva sa ograničenom odgovornošću – d.o.o.).
7 *Statistički ljetopis 2004* [Statistical Yearbook 2004], Zagreb: Državni zavod za statistiku, p. 71, excluding public administration and defence and compulsory social security.
8 Statistical Office of Serbia, *Socio-economic Trends*, 2003.
9 These organizations, which provided the central clearing function for business payments and receipts outside the commercial banking system, have all been privatized, having come under criticism by international advisors on the grounds that they were a relic of the past. However, the privatization has not always been successful owing to the weakness of the commercial banking systems, and the fact that many banks until recently remained in state ownership. In Croatia, the Payments Accounting Office was replaced by a private agency, FINA.
10 In Croatia, FRY and Macedonia, a small company was defined as one which employed fifty or less employees, medium-sized companies as those employing between fifty-one and 250 workers and large companies as those employing over 250 workers.
11 'Number and structure of business entities, March 2005', *First Release September 2005*, Zagreb: State Statistical Office.
12 In Montenegro in 1996, there were 15,640 registered small firms of which 5,606 were active, employing 13,596 workers, producing 17 per cent of total social product (Šišević and Vukčević 1997: 52–4).

13 'Report on small and medium-sized enterprises and entrepreneurship in 2004', Ministry of Economy, Republic Development Bureau, Belgrade, November 2005.

14 Taking small- and medium-sized enterprises together, the employment shares were 48.4 per cent in Slovenia, 50.6 per cent in Croatia, 41.4 per cent in Yugoslavia and 37.7 per cent in Macedonia. These data can be compared to the 66 per cent share of employment in SMEs in the European Union.

15 In the Croatian case, this amounted to DM5,000 according to the Company Law of 1993.

16 Croatian government response to the questionnaire of the European Commission, 2004, Chapter 16, p. 1. The Crafts Law that regulates the registration of craft firms and requires that the owner should have a professional qualification or master craftsman's certificate.

17 Statistical Office of Serbia, *Statistical Yearbook 2006*, Table 3.14.

18 Ibid., Table 5.13.

19 ''Bosnia: reform will bring justice and jobs' [speech by Paddy Ashdown] quoted in IWPR's *Balkan Crisis Report No. 341*, 7 June 2002.

20 A team of researchers from BiH, Macedonia and Slovenia and myself carried out the survey of 800 small businesses in the three countries based on stratified random samples drawn from company listings, using Slovenia as the benchmark case. Details of the organization and structure of the survey which was financed by European Commission's PHARE-ACE programme can be found in Bartlett and Bukvič (2002).

21 A recent report by the World Bank emphasizes the negative impact of employment protection legislation on job creation in the South East European economies, where it is identified as being very rigid in BiH, Croatia and Macedonia, intermediate in Serbia and Montenegro and 'flexible' in Albania (Rutkowski and Scarpetta 2005: 36–7).

22 The Croatian government began to develop an institutional support structure for SMEs in the 1990s, passing a Law on the Encouragement of Small Business Development in 2002. The Albanian government adopted a Medium Term Strategy for SME development in 2001 and an SME Law in 2002 and established an SME Development Agency in 2003. RS adopted a Law on the Development of Small and Medium-Sized Enterprises in the same year. National strategies for SMEs were adopted in Macedonia in 2002 and in Serbia in 2003. Only FBiH lacks a formal basis for support to the development of the SME sector.

23 This section is based on the findings of a research project on SME policies in Croatia funded by the British Council ALIS programme in 1997–8, carried out jointly with Professor Vojmir Franičević from the Economics Faculty, University of Zagreb.

24 A Law on Cooperatives was passed in 1995 (amended in 2002). The Company Law was amended in 1999; the Craftsmen Law was amended in 1996 and 2001.

25 Interview, Čakovec Centre for Entrepreneurship, October 1998.

26 In war-affected areas and on the islands, the subsidy was 75 per cent.

27 In Split, consultants' fees were only paid after approval by the HGA. Elsewhere, fees were paid immediately after approval by the bank.

28 Similar effects were noticed from the results of a survey carried out in Russia and Ukraine by a group of American economists who found that weak property rights discouraged firms from reinvesting their profits (Johnson *et al.*, 2002).

29 Interview, Osijek City Council, October 1998.

30 Interview, Osijek Centre for Entrepreneurship, October 1998.

31 Production resumed in 1992 and in 1994, the company was commercialized as a joint stock company. It was privatized in 1998.

32 Of the 3,000 enterprises in the county, 2,800 were small businesses.

33 Interview, Osijek county administration, October 1998.

34 Anthony Robinson, *Financial Times*, Survey, 19 February 2001, p. 14, quoted in Jeffries (2002: 247):

In communist times Macedonia was industrialized but jobs in both the socialized industries and the local administration were overwhelmingly given to Macedonians ... The Albanian population, largely excluded from the state sector, was also excluded from the privatization process. It continued to send its young men to work abroad or develop private farming and enterprise, including an informal family-based financial banking system. As a result, Albanians suffered less from the virtual collapse of the state enterprises.

35 The decision to close the NEPA was taken following a hostile evaluation report carried out by international consultants.
36 The Serbian Employment Bureau introduced a programme to encourage self-employment under which unused capacity in large socially owned firms could be rented by small businesses on a short term basis, on condition that they employed some of the redundant workers from the socially owned firm.
37 Interview, Montenegrin Development Fund, March 2003.
38 The subsidies were limited to €15,000 for up to five employees.
39 Interview, Montenegrin Employment Bureau, March 2003.
40 Interview, Podgorica, Montenegro, March 2003.
41 Interview, Berane, Montenegro, March 2003.

7 Growth, employment and trade

1 Furthermore, successful outcomes strengthen pro-reform coalitions and therefore stimulate further reform (Barlow and Radulescu 2005).
2 The position of BiH is not represented as data are unavailable for the war years between 1992 and 1995.
3 The composite index used here takes an average of the individual scores for the degree of reform in the following dimensions: large-scale privatization, small-scale privatization, enterprise restructuring, price liberalisation, trade and foreign exchange system, competition policy, banking reform and interest rate liberalisation, securities markets and non-bank financial institutions. The index is measured on a scale from 1 to 4.33, with a score of 4.33 representing the completion of the reform process, and that a country has reached 'standards and performance typical of advanced industrial economies', see EBRD Transition Report 2004, p. 199. I use the index for Serbia as a proxy for Serbia and Montenegro.
4 The regression results suggest a point estimate of 8 per cent in lagged GDP growth before employment growth would turn positive.
5 See Chapter 6 for a discussion of this survey.
6 Interview with Employers' Association, Banja Luka, RS, 15 September 2004.
7 On regional disparities in Serbia see Arandarenko (2006), in Montenegro (Bartlett 2006), and in Eastern Slavonia IMC (2004).
8 Labour Force Survey data, Statistical Office of the Republic of Serbia, 2007.
9 The coverage rate is only 8.4 per cent in Serbia and Montenegro, 10 per cent in Albania and Macedonia, 13 per cent in BiH and 17 per cent in Croatia.
10 FRY has also adopted a managed float since January 2001. See IMF Country Report No. 02/103, May 2002, p. 14.
11 The dollar had depreciated against the euro between 2000 and 2006, and so the data are adjusted to reflect this as most of the export earnings were in euros.
12 Limited concessional duty-free tariff quotas were offered to FRY before the fall of the regime for aluminium products, which were produced only in Montenegro, as a reward for the anti-Milošević stance of the Montenegrin government.
13 A study for the World Bank noted that '[t]he conflicts and sanctions imposed on Serbia and Montenegro, the Greek embargo on FYR Macedonia, the weak customs administration throughout the region, all contributed to a large underground economy,

much smuggling and diversion of trade from normal channels' (Michalopoulos 2003: 3).

14 In these cases, the FTAs had come into force at an earlier date; 2002, in the case of BiH–Croatia.

15 The FTA between the two countries had been introduced in 1997 and was revised to Stability Pact standards in May 2005 when a new agreement was initialled.

16 They ranged from companies in the food processing industry, to industrial processing, and transport. Nine were domestically owned private companies, two had sold a controlling interest to larger Greek companies (one of which was actually a state owned company in Greece) and one was a branch company of a Slovenian parent company.

8 Social policies and welfare reforms

1 The Open Method of Coordination sought to encourage the harmonization of policies through regular reports and meetings, to allow countries to learn from one another's achievements and draw policy lessons from best-practice examples within the EU. An important element of this process was the agreement on a set of common indicators to measure social conditions (the Laeken indicators), against which progress in meeting social policy targets can be measured.

2 Household Survey, Institute for Strategic Studies and Prognoses, Podgorica, 2002.

3 Croatian Statistical Office data.

4 The Law on Mandatory Fully Funded Pension Insurance was approved in April 2002.

5 This pension was introduced because the contribution records of many Kosovar workers had been lost during the 1999 conflict, apparently due to the destruction of the pension records office by NATO bombing.

6 Employees may opt to increase their contribution rate to 15 per cent.

7 According to David Snelbecker, an advisor to KPST, the Kosovo pension reform was designed to 'avoid international record of poor financial performance of politically controlled public funds' and to 'avoid creation of a typical European fiscally unsustainable PAYG system that reduces savings' (Snelbecker 2003).

8 However, this has not been very successful, and an agreement on the transfer of acquired pension rights has not been observed, with the consequence that in 2004 RS was paying the pensions of 20,000 people who acquired their pension rights in FBiH.

9 About 10 per cent of the working population suffers from a disability.

10 The authorities had lost control of the central database of social contributions as a result of an allegedly illegal privatization in 1999, and the pension fund had to purchase its own data back from the database owner.

11 This difficulty was explained to me by Merita Xhumari.

12 According to the European Agency for Reconstruction, out of a total housing stock of 250,000 housing units in Kosovo, 120,000 had been damaged or destroyed of which 41,000 were less seriously damaged, 32,000 were badly damaged and 47,000 were effectively destroyed, with often only the foundations remaining.

13 The World Bank has usefully initiated cadastral registration projects in both Croatia and Serbia.

14 Organization for Security and Cooperation in Europe, 'Return and Integration', Return Update. Online, available at: www.osce.org/missions/croatia/return/return_new.htm.

15 Data are for 30 June 2003, see 'Bosna i Hercegovina: Ministarstvo za ljudska prava i *izbeglice*, bilten 2003', Sarajevo, October 2003, p. 16.

16 Interview, Ministry of Health, Skopje, June 2004.

17 Information supplied by Mirjana Karahasanović, Sarajevo, June 2004.

18 Interview, Ministry of Health, Tirana, June 2004.

19 Interview Ministry of Health, Belgrade, May 2004.

20 Interview, Kosovo Ministry of Health, Pristina, September 2004.

21 The Act on Determining Representativeness of Higher-Rank Associations of Trade Unions in Tripartite Bodies on the National level, 1999.
22 Interview with representatives of RS Gender Centre and Croatian Office for Gender Equality, September 2004.
23 Interview with Ombudsperson for Gender Equality, Zagreb, July 2004. According to the Ombudsperson, despite the creation of a legal framework, the implementation of the law is problematic due to a lack of support from high-level politicians.
24 Interviews in Croatia, Macedonia and Albania, 2004.
25 Interview, Dragana Petrović, Ministry of Labour, Employment and Social Policy, June 2004.
26 Interview with Zineta Daci, vice-president of Kosova Chamber of Commerce, and head of Women's Business Network, Prishtina, September 2004.

9 International aid and regional cooperation

1 BBC News report, 'Blair pledges Balkan aid', Friday, 23 April 1999.
2 To take just one example, an independent evaluation of the EU assistance programme in Macedonia in 2002 found that the programme was inefficient, badly coordinated and hampered by bureaucracy. The report noted that road building projects had not always gone to the most efficient or cheapest companies. See S. Jovanovska and G. Icevska, 'Macedonia: EC aid under fire', IWPR Crisis Report 310, Part II, 21 January 2002.
3 IMF Factsheet, 'Poverty Reduction Strategy Papers (PRSP)', February 2005.
4 World Bank press release, 5 March 2005.
5 The shareholders of the Bank are the governments of the Member States, and its main strategic priorities are to support economic and social cohesion, innovation, trans-European transport networks and environmental protection and improvement. In 2005, support for SMEs was adopted as a fifth new strategic objective. Due to its favourable credit rating, the EIB is able to issue bonds through the capital market to finance low-cost long-term loans to its clients. It is able to finance up to 50 per cent of the cost of an investment project and often co-finances projects alongside EU assistance funds. By 2004, total lending volume reached over €43 billion. Although most of its lending takes place within the EU, it has also developed its activities to finance projects outside the EU.
6 Between 1977 and 1990, the EIB lent a total of €560 million to the former Yugoslavia, mainly to the individual republics. The last loan, to Serbia in 1990, was €100 million for the trans-Yugoslav highway.
7 'European Investment Bank in Serbia once again', Serbia Info News, 9 July 2001.
8 The shareholders include the EU, sixty-two sovereign governments including transition countries, and the EIB. The EBRD is able to raise funds on international capital markets at favourable interest rates and provide loans at lower interest rates than commercial banks. As a result of its shareholder base, it has a lower level of risk aversion than commercial banks and is therefore able to operate at the margin of commercial possibilities and plays an important role as a demonstrator of project viability.
9 The standard minimum involvement of the EBRD is €5 million per project, with an average value of around €18 million.
10 Croatia and Macedonia joined the Council of Europe Development Bank in 1997, Albania followed in 1999, BiH in 2003 and Serbia and Montenegro in 2004.
11 Council of Europe Development Bank, Report of the Governor, 2004.
12 The UK aid agency, DfID, is disengaging with the Balkan region as resources are diverted to Afghanistan and Iraq in pursuit of the latest geo-political imperative.
13 The Stability Pact was signed by all the Balkan states (with the exception of FRY), the Member States of the EU, Russia, USA, Canada and Japan, the European Commission and international organizations including OSCE, UNHCR, OECD, NATO,

WEU, the Council of Europe and international financial institutions including the IMF, World Bank, EBRD and the EIB.

14 'Common Position concerning the launching of the Stability Pact of the EU on South-East Europe, Annex to Council Conclusions', Brussels, 17 May 1999. The additional aims of the Stability Pact were to combat organized crime, prevent forced population displacement and ensure the safe return of refugees to their homes.

15 Moldova also joined at a later date.

16 From 2002, the Special Coordinator was Dr Erhard Busek, former Vice Federal Chancellor of Austria.

17 In all, representatives of forty-seven countries and thirty-six international institutions attended the conference.

18 'Regional Funding Conference Brussels, March 29–30 2000: chairmen's conclusions'. Online, available at: www.seerecon.org/Calendar/2000/Events/RC/conclusions. htm (accessed 17 April 2000).

19 This term was introduced by Paul Sabatier who developed the idea that policies are often not the result of rational deliberation but of conflict between competing advocacy coalitions representing discrete groups of institutions and organizations involved in the policy process (Sabatier 1988).

20 The EPPAs were carried out in 2003, 2004 and 2005 before being replaced by the Integrated Reform Index.

21 Stability Pact Working Table II Progress Report, May–November 2005.

22 The CEI manages a matchmaking system based upon the submission of networking forms by project proposers which are distributed to project funders for consideration for funding.

23 A Core Network of transport infrastructure covers 4,300 km of railways, 6,000 km of roads, major ports and airports and the Danube and the Sava Rivers.

24 'EBRD Activities in Croatia' London, European Bank for Reconstruction and Development, 28 August 1996.

25 The World Bank credit was issued with a ten-year grace period and a thirty-five-year maturity and was supplemented by a contribution of €25 million from the EU.

26 Bank of Albania Annual Report, Tirana, 2005.

27 In his personal account of the Dayton negotiations, Richard Holbrook wrote: 'The most difficult meetings were with Izetbegović. In the last of our three meetings that day, we tried to talk in personal terms to the Bosnian leader. We reminded him of all the benefits that peace would bring ...'. The list of benefits included 'the $5 billion World Bank package that awaited the country after a peace agreement' (Holbrooke 1999).

28 The first Emergency Recovery Project began in February 1996 and provided resources to fund critical imports for agriculture, power and transport, lines of credit for SMEs, support for key government institutions. An Emergency Social Fund to give cash grants to the poorest households for subsistence. Specific projects covered reconstruction of transport systems, agriculture, district heating, education, electric power, housing, hospitals, war victims' rehabilitation, military demobilization and reintegration, landmine clearance, public works, and employment, industry restart and local initiatives. A transition assistance credit was provided to cover fiscal and balance-of-payments deficits. The World Bank initiated a Priority Reconstruction Programme to contribute to the aid effort, and the EU contributed a separate Essential Aid Programme. The US contribution was provided through the official aid organization USAID.

29 Speech by the High Representative Carlos Westendorp to the fifth Donors' Pledging Conference for BiH, Brussels, 20 May 1999.

30 Ibid.

31 The inflow of international aid was so vast that by 2004 almost one-half of BiH's international debt was owed to the World Bank, and by 2005 the country's debt service obligations were almost equivalent to the amount of new lending inflows.

32 IMF (1998), Country Report 98/96, p. 8.
33 'Leaders in Bosnia are said to steal up to $1 billion', *New York Times*, 17 August 1999. The figure of $1 billion was later shown to have been exaggerated.
34 Interview, Banja Luka, September 2004.
35 'Evaluation of the Assistance to Balkan Countries under CARDS Regulation 2666/2000, Synthesis Report Volume 1, June 2004'. Online, available at: www.ear.org.
36 'Role of the World Bank in the Kosovo Crisis', New World Bank Backgrounders, July 1999.
37 The World Bank was able to provide small amounts of finance in the form of Special Assistance Grants.
38 'European Commission Launches First Programme for Reconstruction at Shattered Village of Cabra', EU Press Release. Online, available at: www.seerecon.org/PressRelease/press013-8-99.htm (accessed 19 September 1999).
39 Online, available at: www.um.dk/publikationer/Danida/English/Evaluations/Kosovo 2005/32.asp.
40 This comparison is made on the basis of visits to Prishtina in September 1987 during a research visit funded by the British Academy, and subsequent visits in September 1999 funded by the Soros Open Society Foundation, and in September 2003 funded by USAID.
41 Investment Compact for South East Europe, Annual Report of Activities, November 2006, p. 5 (data include Moldova among group of least advanced countries).
42 Senior Review Group report on the future of the Stability Pact, November 2005.
43 Special Coordinator Busek, 2006.
44 Annual Report, Stability Pact for South Eastern Europe, 2006.
45 In a meeting of the Stability Pact in Zagreb in May 2007, a Croatian politician, Hido Biščević, State Secretary at the Ministry of Foreign Affairs and European Integration, was appointed to be the first Secretary General of the RCC when it is established in early 2008. It was also decided that the RCC Secretariat would be based in Sarajevo.

10 European integration

1   A Trade Agreement was negotiated in 1970, and in 1973 which allowed Yugoslavia duty-free entry of many industrial goods to the EEC markets (the EU was called the European Economic Community – EEC – at the time), in 1983, the EEC signed a Cooperation Agreement with Yugoslavia and in 1990 Yugoslavia was included in the PHARE programme. By 1990, Yugoslavia was in a leading position among East European countries in its prospects for early EU membership, but the collapse of the state and the outbreak of war brought the relationship to an end. The last meeting of the Cooperation Council took place in December 1990, and the Cooperation Agreement was terminated on 15 November 1991.
2   Financial assistance provided by the EU has been mainly in the form of grants (in contrast to the concessional loans provided by the IFIs). PHARE projects were implemented by EU-based consultancy companies with limited local participation which gave rise to criticism that much of the financial assistance flowed back to the EU in the form of fees and charges. Whilst there was some point to the complaint, the main purpose of the arrangement was the transfer of knowledge and skills from the EU to the recipient countries, and on the whole these were willingly received.
3   See Annex III to Council Conclusions – Brussels 26 and 27 February 1996. Online, available at: http://europa.eu.int/comm/external_relations/see/docs/reg_approach_96.htm.
4   OBNOVA covered the years 1996–9 and was subsequently extended to 2000. Its main aims were the reconstruction of war-damaged infrastructure, the return and integration of refugees and displaced persons, the promotion of regional cooperation,

cross-border and 'good neighbour' projects, encouraging the consolidation of democracy, support for civil society and support for the SME sector.

5 The pre-accession strategy was adopted at the Essen European Council in December 1994. It placed PHARE 'at the heart of the political and economic relations between the European Community and the partner countries of Central Europe', PHARE Annual Report 1995, p. 2.

6 See Annex III to Council Conclusions – Luxembourg 29/30 April 1997. Online, available at: http://europa.eu.int/comm/external_relations/see/docs/conditionality_29_april.htm.

7 Ibid.

8 Croatia became eligible for PHARE funding in early 1995, but the programme was suspended on account of the military action involved in the offensive against the Krajina Serb mini-state in September of that year.

9 Commission Communication on the Stabilization and Association Process for Countries of South-Eastern Europe, COM (99) 235.

10 As the European Commission noted demurely in 1999: 'progress, particularly in respect of the objectives of the Regional Approach has been patchy . . .'. Commission Communication on the Stabilization and Association Process for Countries of South-Eastern Europe, COM (99) 235.

11 The Paris Club agreed to defer all debt payments for Albania and Macedonia for the year ahead.

12 Conclusions of the Presidency, Santa Maria de Feira European Council, 19–20 June 2000, para. D.67.

13 Regional cooperation was to take place in the fields of political dialogue, establishing a regional free trade area, ensuring close cooperation in the fields of justice and home affairs and combating organized crime, corruption, money laundering, illegal immigration and trafficking.

14 Many of the elements of the acquis communautaire, for example those governing environmental standards, while desirable in themselves, are geared towards the requirements of economies at a high level of development. They might be quite expensive to implement in poorer countries or even unsuitable to the prevailing conditions and customs.

15 These regional cooperation actions were to be enshrined in regional cooperation conventions which would form part of the SAA and which countries which signed an SAA with the EU would be expected to implement with one another.

16 Three sets of Stabilization and Association Reports were prepared by the Commission in 2002, 2003 and 2004. The Commission had previously monitored compliance with the Regional Approach criteria through factual reports on compliance between 1996 and 1999, see Commission Staff Working Paper SEC (99) 714 of 17 May 1999.

17 This was inspired by the pre-accession process for the ten accession states which had just signed the Athens Treaty on their EU membership in March 2003.

18 Commission of the European Communities COM (2003) 285 final, p. 3.

19 The Twinning idea had been widely used in the pre-accession process in the new Member States and had already begun to be used in Croatia and Albania.

20 Western Balkans Council Conclusions, 17 May 2004.

21 See EAR (2006: 13).

22 The full list of programmes was set out in an announcement of the General Affairs Council of 22 November 2004.

23 CARDS was the acronym for 'Community Assistance for Reconstruction, Development and Stabilization'.

24 Schimmelfennig and Sedelmeier (2004) refer to this as the 'external incentives' model of enlargement governance.

25 The Serb population had fallen from the 12 per cent share it had in 1990 owing to the mass exodus following the retaking of the Krajina in 1995.

26 Public Opinion in the European Union: First Results, Eurobarometer 66, December 2006 (National Report Summary for Croatia).
27 Doris Pack, chairwoman of the European Parliament's delegation for South East Europe, said that the application was premature and that Macedonia should rather focus on implementing the conditions of the recently signed Stabilization and Association Agreement.
28 RFE/RL, 8 October 2004, Volume 8, Number 37.
29 This reticence to establish a unified command did not extend to the armed forces. In December 2005, the Council of Ministers agreed on a new state-level defence law, and a single defence system for the country, bringing the armed forces under a unified command structure for the first time.
30 'Communication from the Commission to the Council and the European Parliament on the Instruments for External Assistance under the Future Financial Perspective 2007–2013', COM (2004) 626 final.

Bibliography

Acevska, B., Bartlett, W. and Stojanova, V. (2002) 'Barriers to SME development in the Republic of Macedonia', in W. Bartlett, M. Bateman and M. Vehovec (eds) *Small Enterprise Development in South-East Europe: policies for sustainable growth*, Dordrecht: Kluwer, 241–66.

Adamovich, L.S. (1995) 'Economic transformation in former Yugoslavia, with special regard to privatisation', in S.P. Ramet and L.S. Adamovich (eds) *Beyond Yugoslavia: politics, economics, and culture in a shattered community*, Boulder: Westview Press, 253–80.

Alderman, H. (2002) 'Do local officials know something we don't? Decentralization of targeted transfers in Albania', *Journal of Public Economics*, 83(3): 375–404.

Allcock, J.B. (1992) 'Economic development and institutional underdevelopment: tourism and the private sector in Yugoslavia', in J.B. Allcock, J.J. Horton and M. Milivojević (eds) *Yugoslavia in Transition: choices and constraints*, Oxford: Berg, 387–413.

Amable, B. (2003) *The Diversity of Modern Capitalism*, Oxford: Oxford University Press.

Andreas, P. (2004) 'The clandestine political economy of war and peace in Bosnia', *International Studies Quarterly*, 48: 29–51.

Anusić, Z., Rohatinski, Z. and Šonje, V. (1995) *A Road to Low Inflation: Croatia 1993/1994*, Zagreb: Government of the Republic of Croatia.

APP (2006) *Annual Report 2005 for the SME Sector*, Skopje: Agency for the Promotion of Entrepreneurship.

Arandarenko, M. (2003) 'The development of social policy in Serbia and Montenegro', *SCEPP AIA Report No. 6*, Beograd: Savetodavni centar za ekonomska i pravna pitanja.

Arandarenko, M. (2004) 'International advice and labour market institutions in South-East Europe', *Global Social Policy*, 4(1): 27–53.

Arandarenko, M. (2006) *Mapa tržišta rada Srbije*, Beograd: Centar za visoke ekonomske studije.

Aslund, A., Boone, P. and Johnson, S. (1996) 'How to stabilize: lessons from post-communist countries', *Brookings Papers on Economic Activity*, 1: 217–313.

Baletić, Z., Esterrajher, J., Jajčinović, M., Klemenčić, M., Milardović, A., Nikić, G. and Visnar, F. (1994) *Croatia between Aggression and Peace*, Zagreb: AGM.

Barakat, S. and Kapisazovic, Z. (2003) 'Being Lokalci: evaluating the impact of international aid agencies on local human resources: the case of post-war Sarajevo, Bosnia and Herzegovina', *European Journal of Development Research*, 15(1): 55–72.

Barlow, D. and Radulescu, R. (2005) 'The sequencing of reforms in transition economies', *Journal of Comparative Economics*, 33: 835–50.

Barr, N. (2005) 'From transition to accession', in N. Barr (ed.) *Labor Markets and Social Policy in Central and Eastern Europe: the accession and beyond*, Washington, DC: The World Bank, 1–30.

Bartlett, W. (1979) *Economic Development, Institutional Reform and Unemployment in Yugoslavia, 1945–1975*, unpublished PhD thesis, University of Liverpool.

Bartlett, W. (1987a) 'The problem of indebtedness in Yugoslavia: causes and consequences', *Rivista Internazionale di Scienze Economiche e Commerciale*, 34(11/12): 1179–95.

Bartlett, W. (1987b) 'Enterprise investment and public consumption in a self-managed economy', *Advances in the Economic Analysis of Participatory and Labor-Managed Firms*, 2: 165–82.

Bartlett, W. (1990) 'Labor market discrimination and ethnic tension in Yugoslavia: the case of Kosovo', in M.L. Wyzan (ed.) *The Political Economy of Ethnic Discrimination and Affirmative Action: a comparative perspective*, New York: Praeger, 197–216.

Bartlett, W. (1997a) 'European economic assistance to the post-socialist Balkan states', in S. Bianchini and M. Uvalić (eds) *The Balkans and the Challenge of Economic Integration: regional and European perspectives*, Ravenna: Longo Editore, 65–84.

Bartlett, W. (1997b) 'The transformation and demise of self-managed firms in Croatia, Macedonia, and Slovenia', in S. Sharma (ed.) *Restructuring Eastern Europe: the microeconomics of the transition process*, Cheltenham: Edward Elgar, 139–57.

Bartlett, W. (1999) 'Serbia and Montenegro', in P. Heenan and M. Lamontagne (eds) *The Central and Eastern Europe Handbook* (Regional Handbooks of Economic Development: prospects into the 21st century), London: Fitzroy Dearborn, 92–103.

Bartlett, W. (2000) ' "Simply the right thing to do": Labour goes to war', in M. Little and M. Wickham-Jones (eds) *New Labour's Foreign Policy: a new moral crusade?* Manchester: Manchester University Press, 131–46.

Bartlett, W. (2003a) 'Barriers to SME development in Bosnia and Herzegovina, Macedonia and Slovenia: a comparative analysis', in V. Franičević and H. Kimura (eds) *Globalization, Democratization and Development*, Zagreb: Masmedia, 363–76.

Bartlett, W. (2003b) *Croatia: between Europe and the Balkans*, London: Routledge.

Bartlett, W. (2006) 'International aid, policy transfer and local economic development in North Montenegro', in B. Dallago (ed.) *Transformation and European Integration: the local dimension*, Houndmills: Palgrave, 147–57.

Bartlett, W. (forthcoming) 'Economic restructuring, job creation and the changing demand for skills in the Western Balkan area', in A. Fetsi (ed.) *Labour Markets in the Western Balkan Countries: challenges for the future*, Turin: European Training Foundation.

Bartlett, W. and Bukvič, V. (2002) 'What are the main barriers to SME growth and development in South-East Europe?' in W. Bartlett, M. Bateman and M. Vehovec (eds) *Small Enterprise Development in South-East Europe: policies for sustainable growth*, Dordrecht: Kluwer, 17–38.

Bartlett, W. and Hoggett, P. (1996) 'Small firms in South East Europe: the importance of initial conditions', in H. Brezinski and M. Fritsch (eds) *The Economic Impact of New firms in Post-Socialist Countries: bottom-up transformation in Eastern Europe*, Cheltenham: Edward Elgar, 151–74.

Bartlett, W. and Samardžija, V. (2000) 'The reconstruction of South-East Europe, the Stability Pact and the role of the EU: an overview', *Moct-Most: Economic Policy in Transition Economies*, 11(2): 245–63.

Bateman, M. (2002) 'Small enterprise development in the Yugoslav successor states: institutions and institutional development in a post-war environment', *Moct-Most: Economic Policy in Transition Economies*, 11(2): 171–206.

Baumol, W. (1990) 'Entrepreneurship: productive, unproductive, and destructive', *Journal of Political Economy*, 9895: 893–921.

Bayliss, K. (2005) 'Post-conflict privatization: a review of developments in Serbia and Bosnia-Herzegovina', *mimeo*, London: Overseas Development Institute.

Bićanić, I. (1993) 'Privatization in Croatia', *East European Politics and Societies*, 7(3): 422–39.

Bićanić, I. (1996) 'The economic divergence of Yugoslavia's successor states', in I. Jeffries (ed.) *Problems of Economic and Political Transformation in the Balkans*, London: Pinter, 131–50.

Bieber, F. (2003) 'Montenegrin politics since the disintegration of Yugoslavia', in F. Bieber (ed.) *Montenegro in Transition: problems of identity and statehoood*, Baden-Baden: Nomos Verlagsgesellschaft, 11–42.

Blanchard, O. (1997) *The Economics of Post-Communist Transition*, Oxford: Clarendon Press.

Bogdani, M. and Loughlin, J. (2007) *Albania and the European Union: the tumultuous journey towards integration and association*, London: I.B. Taurus.

Boone, P. (1996) 'Politics and the effectiveness of foreign aid', *European Economic Review*, 40(2): 289–329.

Brunhart, R. and Gajić, N. (2005) 'Policing the economic transition in Serbia: assessment of the Serbian police service's capacities to fight organised crime', *mimeo*, Belgrade: OSCE Mission to Serbia.

Bukvič, V., Bartlett, W., Rus, A., Sehič, D. and Stojanova, V. (2001) 'Barriers to SME development in Slovenia, Bosnia and Herzegovina, and Macedonia', final report to PHARE/ACE Programme, Report No. P97-8089-R, Ljubljana: Gea College of Entrepreneurship.

Cani, S. (1997) 'Restructuring the banks in Albania', in S. Sharma (ed.) *Restructuring Eastern Europe: the microeconomics of the transition process*, Cheltenham: Edward Elgar, 158–66.

Cazes, S. and Nesparova, A. (2007) *Flexicurity: a relevant approach in Central and Eastern Europe*, Geneva: International Labour Office

CEDB (2004) *Housing in South East Europe: solving a puzzle of changes*, Paris: Council of Europe Development Bank.

Cerović, B. (2005) 'Effects of privatisation on enterprise performance and investment climate in Serbia', in B. Cerović (ed.) *Privatisation in Serbia: evidence and analysis*, Belgrade: Faculty of Economics, 19–48.

Chandler, D. (1999) *Bosnia: Faking democracy after Dayton*, London: Pluto Press.

Christie, E. and Holzner, M. (2004) 'Household tax compliance and the shadow economy in Central and Southeastern Europe', *Global Development Network*, Vienna: Vienna Institute for International Economic Studies.

Cigar, N. (2001) *Vojislav Kostunica and Serbia's Future*, London: Saqi Books.

Cohen, L.J. (2001) *Serpent in the Bosom: the rise and fall of Slobodan Milošević*, Boulder: Westview Press.

Collier, P. and Hoeffler, A. (2004) 'Aid, policy and growth in post-conflict societies', *European Economic Review*, 48(5): 1125–45.

CoM-BiH (2004) *BiH Medium Term Development Strategy – PRSP*, Sarajevo: Council of Ministers BiH.

Coricelli, F. and Rocha, R. (1991) 'Stabilization programs in Eastern Europe: a Comparative Analysis of the Polish and Yugoslav Programs of 1990', *WPS 732*, Washington, DC: The World Bank.

Crampton, R.J. (2002) *The Balkans Since the Second World War*, London: Longman.

Crnković-Pozaić, S. (2005) 'Flexibility and security in the labour market: Croatia's experience', *Flexicurity Paper 2004/1*, Budapest: International Labour Office.

Cungu, A. and Swinnen, J.F.M. (1999) 'Albania's radical agrarian reform', *Development and Cultural Change*, 47: 605–19.

Čičić, M. and Šunje, M. (2002) 'Micro-credit in transition economies: the case of Bosnia-Herzegovina', in W. Bartlett, M. Bateman and M. Vehovec (eds) *Small Enterprise Development in South-East Europe: policies for sustainable growth*, Dordrecht: Kluwer, 145–70.

Čučković, N. and Bartlett, W. (2007) 'Entrepreneurship and competitiveness: the Europeanization of small and medium-sized enterprise policy in Croatia', *Southeast European and Black Sea Studies*, 7(1): 37–56.

Dalgaard, C.J. and Hansen, H. (2001) 'On aid, growth and good policies', *Journal of Development Studies*, 37(6): 17–41.

de Melo, M., Denizer, C., Gelb, C. and Tenev, S. (2001) 'Circumstances and choice: the role of initial conditions and policies in transition economies', *The World Bank Economic Review*, 15(1): 1–31.

Deacon, B. and Stubbs, P. (1998) 'International actors and social policy development in Bosnia-Herzegovina: globalism and the "new feudalism"', *Journal of European Social Policy*, 8(2): 99–115.

Deacon, B., Hulse, M. and Stubbs, P. (1997) *Global Social Policy: international organizations and the future of welfare*, London: Sage Publications.

Deets, S. (2006) 'Public policy in the passive-aggressive state: health care reform in Bosnia-Hercegovina 1995–2001', *Europe-Asia Studies*, 58(1): 57–80.

Demekas, D.G., Horvath, B., Ribakova, E. and Wu, Y. (2005) 'Foreign direct investment in Southeastern Europe: how (and how much) can policies help?' *IMF Working Paper WP/05/110*.

de Soto, H. (1989) *The Other Path: the economic answer to terrorism*, New York: Basic Books.

Devine, V. and Mathiesen, H. (2005) 'Corruption in Bosnia and Herzegovina – 2005 – options for Swedish Development Cooperation 2006–2010', *CMI Reports*, Bergen: Chr Michelsen Institute.

Dimitrova, A. (2002) 'Enlargement, institution-building and the EU's administrative capacity requirement', *West European Politics*, 25(4): 171–90.

Dirlam, J.B. and Plummer, J.L. (1973) *An Introduction to the Yugoslav Economy*, Columbus: Charles E. Merrill.

Djankov, S. and Murrell, P. (2002) 'Enterprise restructuring in transition: a quantitative survey', *Journal of Economic Literature*, 40(3): 739–92.

Djurić, D. (2002) 'Social dialogue in Southeast European countries', *South East European Review*, 5(3): 19–52.

Dogandžić, S. (1987) 'Razvoj i strukturne promene u privredi SAP Kosovo posmatrane sa aspekte društvenog proizvoda', in M. Hadžibulić (ed.) *Problemi mogućnosti bržeg razvoja nedovoljno razvijenih područja Jugoslavije*, Prishtina: Savez Ekonomista SAP Kosova, 223–33.

Dolowitz, D.P. and Marsh, D. (2000) 'Learning from abroad: the role of policy transfer in contemporary policy-making', *Governance*, 13(1): 5–24.

Donais, T. (2002) 'The politics of privatisation in post-Dayton Bosnia', *Southeast European Politics*, 3(1): 3–19.

Donia, R.J. and Fine, V.A., Jr (1994) *Bosnia and Herzegovina: a tradition betrayed*, New York: Columbia University Press.

Dostal, J.M. (2004) 'Campaigning on expertise: how the OECD framed welfare and labour market policies – a why success could trigger failure', *Journal of European Public Policy*, 11(3): 440–60.

Dragutinović-Mitrović, R. (2006) 'The aims and effects of privatisation in Serbia: quantitative and qualitative analysis', in B. Cerović (ed.) *Privatisation in Serbia: evidence and analysis*, Belgrade: Faculty of Economics, 3–17.

Drulović, M. (1978) *Self-Management on Trial*, Nottingham: Spokesman Books.

Dubey, V. (1975) *Yugoslavia: development with decentralization*, Baltimore: The John Hopkins University Press.

Dyker, D.A. (1990) *Yugoslavia: socialism, development, and debt*, London: Routledge.

EAR (2003) *The European Union at Work: managing EU Assistance Programmes 2000–2003*, Thessaloniki: European Agency for Reconstruction.

EAR (2006) *Annual Report to the European Parliament and the Council: January to December 2005*, Thessaloniki: European Agency for Reconstruction.

Earle, J.S. and Sakova, Z. (2000) 'Business start-ups or disguised unemployment? Evidence on the character of self-employment from transition economies', *Labour Economics*, 7(5): 575–601.

Elster, J., Offe, C. and Preuss, U.K. (1998) *Institutional Design in Post-communist Societies: rebuilding the ship at sea*, Cambridge: Cambridge University Press.

EIB (2004) *Annual Report 2004, Volume I: activity report*, Luxembourg: European Investment Bank.

EBRD (2004) *Transition Report*, London: European Bank for Reconstruction and Development.

EBRD (2005a) *EBRD-EU Cooperation in the Western Balkans*, London: European Bank for Reconstruction and Development.

EBRD (2005b) *Transition Report: business in transition*, London: European Bank for Reconstruction and Development.

EC (2002) *CARDS Assistance Programme to the Western Balkans: Regional Strategy Paper*, Brussels: European Commission.

Esping-Andersen, G. (1990) *The Three Worlds of Welfare Capitalism*, Cambridge: Polity Press.

Estrin, S. (1983) *Self-Management: economic theory and Yugoslav practice*, Cambridge: Cambridge University Press.

ETF (2005a) 'Labour market review of former Yugoslav Republic of Macedonia', *Working Paper*, Turin: European Training Foundation.

ETF (2005b) 'Labour market review of Montenegro', *Working Paper*, Turin: European Training Foundation.

ETF (2006a) *Labour Market Review of Albania*, Turin: European Training Foundation.

ETF (2006b) *Labour Market Review of Bosnia and Herzegovina*, Turin: European Training Foundation.

European Commission (2004) 'The Western Balkans in transition', *European Economy Occasional Papers No. 5*, Brussels: European Commission Directorate General for Economic and Social Affairs.

European Commission (2005a) 'Progress towards meeting the economic criteria for accession: 2005 Country assessment', *Enlargement Papers No. 26*, Brussels: Directorate-General for Economic and Financial Affairs.

European Commission (2005b) *Working Together for Growth and Jobs: integrated guidelines for growth and jobs (2005–08)*, Luxembourg: European Communities.

Eurostat (2007) *Europe in Figures 2006–7*, Luxembourg: Eurostat.

Falcetti, E., Sanfey, P. and Taci, A. (2003) 'Bridging the gaps? Private sector development, capital flows and the investment climate in south-eastern Europe', *EBRD Working Paper No 80*, London: European Bank for Reconstruction and Development.

Falcetti, E., Lysenko, T. and Sanfey, P. (2006) 'Reforms and growth in transition: re-examining the evidence', *Journal of Comparative Economics*, 34: 421–45.

FEC (1990) *Programme of Economic Reform and Measures for Its Implementation in 1990*, Belgrade: Federal Executive Council Secretariat for Information.

Fischer, S. and Gelb, A. (1991) 'The process of socialist economic transformation', *Journal of Economic Perspectives*, 5: 91–105.

Flakierski, H. (1989) *The Economic System and Income Distribution in Yugoslavia*, Armonk, NY: M.E.Sharpe, Inc.

Fornero, E. and Ferraresi, P. (2007) 'Pension Reform and the Development of Pension Systems: an evaluation of World Bank assistance', *Background Paper Macedonia Country Study*, Washington DC: The World Bank.

Franičević, V. and Bartlett, W. (2002) 'Small business development policy in Croatia: design and implementation', in W. Bartlett, M. Bateman and M. Vehovec (eds) *Small Enterprise Development in South-East Europe: policies for sustainable growth*, Dordrecht: Kluwer, 267–94.

Gagnon, V.P., Jr (2004) *The Myth of Ethnic War: Serbia and Croatia in the 1990s*, Ithaca: Cornell University Press.

Geyer, R.R. (2000) *Exploring European Social Policy*, Cambridge: Polity Press.

Gibson, C.G., Andersson, K., Ostrom, E. and Shivakumar, S. (2005) *The Samaritan's Dilemma: the political economy of development aid*, Oxford: Oxford University Press.

Gjorgjev, D., Bacanović, A., Cicevalieva, S., Sulevski, Z. and Grosse-Tebe, S. (2006) 'The former Yugoslav Republic of Macedonia: Health system review', *Health Systems in Transition*, 8(2): 1–98.

Goati, V. (1997) 'The disintegration of Yugoslavia: the role of political elites', *Nationalities Papers*, 25(3): 455–68.

GoC (1999) *Ratna steta republike Hrvatske: zavrsno izvjesce*, Zagreb: Vlada Republike Hrvatske Komisija za Popis i Procenju Ratne Stete.

GoM (2002) *National Strategy for Poverty Reduction in the Republic of Macedonia*, Skopje: Ministry of Finance.

GoS (2004) *Poverty Reduction Strategy Paper for Serbia*, Belgrade: Government of Serbia.

Gow, J. (2003) *The Serbian Project and Its Adversaries: a strategy of war crimes*, London: C. Hurst & Co.

Gros, D. and Steinherr, A. (2004) *Economic Transition in Central and Eastern Europe: planting the seeds*, Cambridge: Cambridge University Press.

Haderi, S., Papapanagos, H., Sanfey, P. and Talka, M. (1999) 'Inflation and stabilisation in Albania', *Post-Communist Economies*, 11(1): 127–41.

Hall, G. (1995) *Surviving and Prospering in the Small Firm sector*, London: Routledge.

Hamilton, F.E.I. (1968) *Yugoslavia: patterns of economic activity*, London: G. Bell and Sons, Ltd.

Hanley, E. (2000) 'Self-employment in post-communist Eastern Europe: a refuge from poverty or a road to riches?' *Communist and Post-Communist Studies*, 33: 379–402.

Hashi, I. (2001) 'Financial and institutional barriers to SME growth in Albania: results of an enterprise survey', *MOCT-MOST*, 11: 221–38.

Hashi, I. and Xhillari, L. (1999) 'Privatisation and transition in Albania', *Post-Communist Economies*, 11(1): 99–125.

Hellman, J.S. (1998) 'Winners take all: the politics of partial reform in postcommunist transitions', *World Politics*, 50: 203–34.

Holbrooke, R. (1999) *To End a War*, New York: The Modern Library.

Hyde, A.G. (2004) 'Seizing the initiative: the importance of regional cooperation in Southeast Europe and the prominent role of the Southeast European Cooperation Process', *Southeast European and Black Sea Studies*, 4(1): 1–22.

ICG (2000) 'Macedonia's public secret: how corruption drags the country down', *International Crisis Group Report No. 133*, Brussels: ICG.

IFC (2006) *Micro, Small, and Medium Enterprises: a collection of published data*, Washington, DC: Small and Medium Enterprise Department, International Finance Corporation.

ILO (2005) *Social Security Spending in South Eastern Europe: a comparative review*, Geneva: International Labour Office.

IMC (2004) *Territorial Assessment Report*, Cardiff: IMC Consulting Ltd.

IMF (1998) *Bosnia and Herzegovina: selected issues*, Country Report 98/96, Washington, DC: International Monetary Fund.

IMF (2000) 'Bosnia and Herzegovina: fourth and fifth reviews under the stand-by arrangement and requests for extension and rephasing of the arrangement – staff report', *IMF Country Report No. 01/08*, Washington, DC: International Monetary Fund.

IMF (2001) 'Federal Republic of Yugoslavia: memorandum on economic and financial policies', *IMF Country Report No. 01/93*, Washington, DC: International Monetary Fund.

IMF (2004) 'Serbia and Montenegro: fourth review under the extended arrangement', *IMF Country Report No. 05/13*, Washington, DC: International Monetary Fund.

IMF (2005) 'Albania: ex-post assessment of longer-term program engagement', *IMF Country Report No. 05/88*, Washington, DC: International Monetary Fund.

INSTAT (2004) *Albania in Figures*, Tirana: Institute of Statistics.

Jarvis, C. (1998) 'The rise and fall of the pyramid schemes in Albania', *IMF Working Paper WP/98/101*, Washington, DC: International Monetary Fund.

Jeffries, I. (2002) *The Former Yugoslavia at the Turn of the Twenty-first Century: a guide to the economies in transition*, London: Routledge.

Jelavich, B. (1983) *History of the Balkans: twentieth century*, Cambridge: Cambridge University Press.

Johnson, S., McMillan, J. and Woodruff, C. (2002) 'Property rights and finance', *American Economic Review*, 92(5): 1335–56.

Judah, T. (2000) *Kosovo: war and revenge*, New Haven, CT: Yale University Press.

Kaminski, B. and de la Rocha, M. (2003) 'Policy-induced integration in the Balkans: policy options and their assessment', in *Trade Policies and Institutions in the Countries of South Eastern Europe in the EU Stabilization and Association Process: regional report*, Washington, DC: The World Bank.

Kekić, L. (2001) 'Aid the Balkans: the addicts and the pushers', *Journal of Southeast European and Black Sea Studies*, 1(1): 20–40.

Kim, B. and Pirtillä, J. (2006) 'Political constraints and economic reform: empirical evidence from the post-communist transition in the 1990s', *Journal of Comparative Economics*, 34: 446–66.

Kok, W. (2003) *Jobs, Jobs, Jobs: creating more employment in Europe*, Luxembourg: European Communities.

Kolodko, G.W. (2000) 'Transition to a market and entrepreneurship: the systemic factors and policy options', *Communist and Post-Communist Studies*, 33(2): 271–93.

Kornai, J. (1993) 'Transformational recession: a general phenomenon examined through the example of Hungary's development', *Economie Appliquée*, 46(2): 181–227.

Kovačević, M. (1998) 'Small and medium sized enterprise: legal and institutional framework', in J. Minić and A. Denda (eds) *How to Support SMEs in Yugoslavia*, Belgrade: Institute of Economic Sciences, 78–84.

Kraft, E. (1995) 'Stabilizing Inflation in Slovenia, Croatia and Macedonia: how independence has affected macroeconomic policy outcomes', *Europe-Asia Studies*, 47(3): 469–92.

Kraft, E. (2002) 'Bank lending to SMEs in Croatia: a few things we know', in W. Bartlett, M. Bateman and M. Vehovec (eds) *Small Enterprise Development in South-East Europe: policies for sustainable growth*, Dordrecht: Kluwer, 127–43.

Kramer, M. (1997) 'Social protection policies and safety nets in East-Central Europe: dilemmas of the postcommunist transformation', in E.B. Kapstein and M. Mandelbaum (eds) *Sustaining the Transition: the social safety net in postcommunist Europe*, New York: Council on Foreign Relations Press, 46–123.

Kreimer, A., Muscat, R., Elwan, A. and Arnold, M. (2000) *Bosnia and Herzegovina: post-conflict reconstruction*, Washington, DC: World Bank Operations Evaluation Department.

Krugman, P. (1993) *Geography and Trade*, Cambridge, MA: The MIT Press.

La Cava, G., Lytle, P. and Kolev, A. (2005) *Young People in South Eastern Europe: from risk to empowerment*, Washington, DC: The World Bank.

Lampe, J.R. (1966) *Yugoslavia as History: twice there was a country*, Cambridge: Cambridge University Press.

Layne, C. (2000) 'Collateral damage in Yugoslavia', in *NATO's Empty Victory: a post-mortem on the Balkan war*, Washington, DC: Cato Institute, 51–9.

Lazić, M. and Sekelj, L. (1997) 'Privatisation in Yugoslavia (Serbia and Montenegro)', *Europe-Asia Studies*, 49(6): 1057–70.

LeBor, A. (2002) *Milošević: a bibliography*, London: Bloomsbury.

Lemel, H. (1998) 'Rural land privatisation and distribution in Albania: evidence from the field', *Europe-Asia Studies*, 50(1): 121–40.

Linz, J.J. and Stepan, A. (1996) *Problems of Democratic Transition and Consolidation: Southern Europe, South America, and post-communist Europe*, Baltimore: The John Hopkins University Press.

Lopandić, D. (2001) *Regional Initiatives in South Eastern Europe*, Belgrade: European Movement in Serbia.

Lydall, H. (1984) *Yugoslav Socialism: theory and practice*, Oxford: Clarendon Press.

Lydall, H. (1989) *Yugoslavia in Crisis*, Oxford: Clarendon Press.

Lyon, J. (1996) 'Yugoslavia's hyperinflation, 1993–1994: a social history', *East European Politics and Society*, 10(2): 293–327.

Madžar, L. (1992) 'The economy of Yugoslavia: a brief outline of its genesis and characteristics', in J. Allcock, J.J. Horton and M. Milivojević (eds) *Yugoslavia in Transition: choices and constraints*, New York: Berg, 64–96.

Mahmutćehajić, R. (2000) *The Denial of Bosnia*, Pennsylvania: The Pennsylvania State University Press.

Malarek, V. (2004) *The Natashas: the new global sex trade*, London: Vision Paperbacks

Malcolm, N. (1994) *Bosnia: a short history*, London: Macmillan.

Malcolm, N. (1998) *Kosovo: a short history*, London: Macmillan.

Mansoor, A. and Quillin, B. (2006) *Migration and Remittances: Eastern Europe and the former Soviet Union*, Washington, DC: The World Bank.

Massari, M. (2005) 'Do all roads lead to Brussels? Analysis of the different trajectories of Croatia, Serbia-Montenegro and Bosnia-Herzegovina', *Cambridge Review of International Affairs*, 18(2): 259–73.

Matković, H. (1998) *Povijest Jugoslavije (1918–1991): Hrvatski pogled*, Zagreb: P.I.P. Pavičić.

Mencinger, J. (2003) 'Does foreign direct investment always enhance economic growth?' *Kyklos*, 56(4): 491–508.

Micevska, M. (2004) 'Labor market institutions and policies in Southeast Europe', *mimeo*, Bonn: Centre for Development Research, University of Bonn.

Michalopoulos, C. (2003) 'The Western Balkans in World Trade', in World Bank Report No. 24460, *Trade Policies and Institutions in the Countries of South Eastern Europe in the EU Stabilization and Association Process: Regional Report*, Washington, DC: The World Bank, 1–22.

Mihailović, K. (1982) *Ekonomska stvarnost Jugoslavije*, Belgrade: IRO Ekonomika.

Mircev, D. (1993) 'Ethnocentrism and strife among political elites: the end of Yugoslavia', *Governance*, 6(3): 372–85.

Moore, J.H. (1980) *Growth with Self-management: Yugoslav industrialization 1952–1975*, Stanford: Hoover Institution Press.

Muço, M., Sanfey, P. and Taci, A. (2004) 'Inflation, exchange rates and the role of monetary policy in Albania', *EBRD Working Paper No. 88*, London: European Bank for Reconstruction and Development.

Mueller, J. (2000) 'The banality of "ethnic war"', *International Security*, 25(1): 42–70.

Muent, H., Pissarides, F. and Sanfey, P. (2001) 'Taxes, competition and finance for Albanian enterprises: evidence from a field study', *MOCT-MOST*, 11: 239–51.

Mulaj, I. (2006) 'Redefining property rights with specific reference to social ownership in successor states of former Yugoslavia: did it matter for economic efficiency?' MPRA Paper No. 243. Online, available at: http://mpra.ub.uni-muenchen.de/243/.

Nordyke, R.J. and Peabody, J.W. (2002) 'Market reforms and public incentives: finding a balance in the Republic of Macedonia', *Social Science & Medicine*, 54: 939–53.

OECD (2003a) *Enterprise Policy Performance Assessment: FYR Macedonia*, Paris: Organization for Economic Cooperation and Development.

OECD (2003b) *South East Europe Region – Enterprise Policy Performance: a regional assessment*, Paris: Organization for Economic Cooperation and Development.

OECD (2004) *The Informal Economy in Albania: analysis and policy recommendations*, Paris: Organization for Economic Cooperation and Development.

OECD (2006) *Progress in Policy Reforms to Improve the Investment Climate in South East Europe*, Paris: Organization for Economic Cooperation and Development.

O'Shea, B. (2005) 'Kosovo: the triumph of ignorance', *Studies in Conflict & Terrorism*, 28: 61–5.

Ott, K. (2002) 'The underground economy in Croatia', *Occasional Paper No. 12*, Zagreb: Institute or Public Finance.

Pashko, G. (1991) 'The Albanian economy at the beginning of the 1990s', in Ö. Sjöberg and M.L. Wyzan (eds) *Economic Change in the Balkan States: Albania, Bulgaria, Romania and Yugoslavia*, London: Pinter Publishers, 128–46.

Pavković, A. (2000) *The Fragmentation of Yugoslavia: nationalism and war in the Balkans*, Basingstoke: Macmillan.

Petrášová, A. (2006) 'Social protection in the European Union', *Statistics in Focus: Population and Social Conditions*, 14.

Petričić, D. (2000) *Kriminal u hrvatskoj pretvorbi: tko, kako, zasto*, Zagreb: Abakus.

Petrović, M. (2001) 'Post-socialist housing policy transformation in Yugoslavia and Belgrade', *European Journal of Housing Policy*, 1(2): 211–31.

Petrović, N. (2007) 'Liberalization of electric power market in Southeast European countries – reforming process and policy doubts', update of paper presented at the *Coimbra Group Research Symposium: Building a Common Future – Conflict Management and Regional Cooperation in the Balkans, University of Bristol, November 2005*, Belgrade: Confida Consulting.

Petrović, P., Bogetić, Ž., and Vujošević, Z. (1999) 'The Yugoslav hyperinflation of 1992–1994: causes, dynamics, and money supply process', *Journal of Comparative Economics*, 27: 335–53.

Pissarides, F. (1999) 'Is lack of funds the main obstacle to business growth? EBRD's experience with small-and-medium sized businesses in Central and Eastern Europe', *Journal of Business Venturing*, 14: 519–39.

Popović, D. (1997) 'Yugoslavia's prospects for sustained growth', in J. Minic (ed.) *EU Enlargement: Yugoslavia and the Balkans*, Belgrade: European Movement in Serbia, Institute of Economic Sciences, Ekonomska politika, and Friedrich Ebert Stiftung, 161–8.

Popović, P. (1995) *Preduzetnistvo: granice rasta*, Beograd: Ekonomski Institut.

Pošarac, A. (1993) *Social Transfers in the Former Yugoslavia, 1978–1989*, Socialist Economies Reform Unit Research Paper Series, Paper Number 5, Washington, DC: The World Bank.

Pošarac, A. (1997) 'Yugoslav economic crisis and its social consequences', in J. Minić (ed.) *EU Enlargement: Yugoslavia and the Balkans*, Belgrade: European Movement in Serbia, 149–61.

Prifti, P.R. (1978) *Socialist Albania since 1944: domestic and foreign developments*, Cambridge, MA: MIT Press.

Pula, B. (2004) 'The emergence of the Kosovo "parallel state," 1988–1992', *Nationalities Papers*, 32(4): 797–826.

Račić, D., Babić, Z. and Podrug, N. (2004) 'Segmentation of the labour market and the employees rights in Croatia', *Revija Za Socijalnu Politiku*, 12(1): 45–65.

Raik, K. (2004) 'EU accession of central and eastern European countries: democracy and integration as conflicting logics', *East European Politics and Societies*, 18(4): 567–94.

Roland, G. (2000) *Transition and Economics: politics, markets, firms*, Cambridge, MA: MIT Press.

Ruli, G. (2003) 'Albania: the weakness of the state', in van Meurs (ed.) *Prospects and Risks Beyond EU Enlargement*, Opladen: Leske + Budrich, 151–62.

Rus, A. and Iglič, H. (2005) 'Trust, governance and performance: the role of institutional and interpersonal trust in SME development', *International Sociology*, 20(3): 371–91.

Rutkowski, J. (2003) 'Does strict employment protection discourage job creation? Evidence from Croatia', *World Bank Policy Research Working Paper 3104*, Washington, DC: The World Bank.

Rutkowski, J.J. and Scarpetta, S. (2005) *Enhancing Job Opportunities: Eastern Europe and the former Soviet Union*, Washington, DC: The World Bank.

Sabatier, P.A. (1988) 'An advocacy coalition framework of policy change and the role of policy-oriented learning therein', *Policy Sciences*, 21: 129–68.

Sanfey, P., Falcetti, E., Taci, A. and Tepić, S. (2004) *Spotlight on South-Eastern Europe: an overview of private sector activity and investment*, London: European Bank for Reconstruction and Development.

Schafer, A. (2006) 'A new form of governance? Comparing the open method of coordination to multilateral surveillance by the IMF and the OECD', *Journal of European Public Policy*, 13(1): 70–88.

Schiff, M. and Winters, L.A. (2003) *Regional Integration and Development*, Washington, DC: The World Bank.

Schimmelfennig, F. and Sedelmeier, U. (2004) 'Governance by conditionality: EU rule transfer to the candidate countries of Central and Eastern Europe', *Journal of European Public Policy*, 11(4): 661–79.

Šišević, B. and Vukčević, Z. (1997) 'Development of small and medium-sized enterprises in Montenegro – dynamics of growth, structural changes, incentive measures', in J. Minić and A. Denda (eds) *How to Support SMEs in Yugoslavia*, Belgrade: Institute of Economic Sciences, 35–56.

Sjöberg, Ö. (1991) 'The Albanian economy in the 1980s: coping with a centralised system', in Ö. Sjöberg and M.L. Wyzan (eds) *Economic Change in the Balkan States: Albania, Bulgaria, Romania and Yugoslavia*, London: Pinter Publishers, 115–27.

Škreb, M. (1995) 'Recent macroeconomic developments and financial sector changes in Croatia', *Moct-Most: Economic Policy in Transition Economies*, 5(3): 37–52.

Snelbecker, D. (2003) 'Governance of Public Pension Funds: The Kosovo Pension Savings Trust (KPST)', *2nd Public Pension Fund Management Conference*, May 5–7, Washington, DC: The World Bank.

SOK (2002) *Statistical Overview of Registered Businesses till December 31, 2002*, Prishtina: Statistical Office of Kosovo.

Šošić, V. (2005) 'Poverty and labor market policies in Croatia', *Financial Theory and Practice*, 29(1): 55–73.

Szajkowski, B. (2000) 'Macedonia: an unlikely road to democracy, in G. Pridham and T. Gallagher (eds) *Experimenting with Democracy: regime change in the Balkans*, London: Routledge, 249–72.

Tanner, M. (1997) *Croatia: a nation forged in war*, New Haven, CT: Yale University Press.

T&B Consult (2004) *Evaluation: humanitarian and rehabilitation assistance to Kosovo, 1999-2003*, Copenhagen: Danish Ministry of Foreign Affairs.

Teokarević, J. (1996) 'Neither war nor peace: Serbia and Montenegro in the first half of the 1990s', in D.A. Dyker and I. Vejvoda (eds) *Yugoslavia and After: a study in fragmentation, despair and rebirth*, London: Longman, 179–95.

Thomas, R. (1999) *Serbia under Milošević: politics in the 1990s*, London: Hurst & Company.

Tosić, I. (2005) 'City development in Central and Eastern Europe since 1990: the impacts of internal forces', in F.E.I. Hamilton, K. Dimitrovska Andrews and N. Pichler-Milanović (eds) *Transformation of Cities in Central and Eastern Europe: towards globalization*, Tokyo: United Nations University Press, 44–78.

Treichel, V. (2002) 'Stabilization policies and structural reforms in Albania since 1997 – achievements and remaining challenges', *IMF Policy Discussion Paper PDP/02/2*, Washington, DC: International Monetary Fund.

Tsenkova, S. (2005) *Trends and Progress in Housing Reforms in South Eastern Europe*, Paris: Council of Europe Development Bank.

Tyson, L.d'A., Petrin, T. and Rogers, H. (1994) 'Promoting entrepreneurship in Eastern Europe', *Small Business Economics*, 6: 165–84.

UNDP (2003) *Employment, Labour Market and Standard of Living in Montenegro*, Podgorica: UNDP Liaison Office.

UNECE (2002) *Country Profiles of the Housing Sector – Albania*, Geneva: United Nations Economic Commission for Europe.

UNICEF (2002) *Trafficking in Human Beings in Southeastern Europe*, Belgrade: UNICEF Area Office for the Balkans (in collaboration with UNHCHR and OSCE/ODIHR).

UNMIK (2002) *Progress Report on Kosovo*, Pristina: European Union Pillar IV.

Uvalić, M. (1992) *Investment and Property Rights in Yugoslavia: the long transition to a market economy*, Cambridge: Cambridge University Press.

Uvalić, M. (1997) 'Privatization in the Yugoslav successor states: converting self-management into property rights', in M. Uvalić and D. Vaughan-Whitehead (eds) *Privatization Surprises in Transition Economies: employee ownership in Central and Eastern Europe*, Cheltenham: Edward Elgar, 266–300.

Uvalić, M. (2000a) 'Regional cooperation in Southeast Europe', *South East Europe and Black Sea Studies*, 1(1): 55–75.

Uvalić, M. (2000b) 'Privatisation and corporate governance in FR Yugoslavia', paper presented at the *10th Conference of the International Association for the Economics of Participation*, 6–8 July, University of Trento.

Uvalić, M. and Vaughan-Whitehead, D. (1997) 'Introduction: creating employee capitalism in Central and Eastern Europe', in M. Uvalić and D. Vaughan-Whitehead (eds) *Privatization Surprises in Transition Economies: employee ownership in Central and Eastern Europe*, Cheltenham: Edward Elgar, 1–48.

Vachudova, M.A. (2003) 'Strategies for democratisation and European integration in the Balkans', in M. Cremona (ed.) *The Enlargement of the European Union*, Oxford: Oxford University Press, 141–60.

Vasić, M. (2005) *Atentat*, Belgrade: Politika.

Vaughan-Whitehead, D. (1999) *Albania in Crisis: the predictable fall of the shining star*, Cheltenham: Edward Elgar.

Vickers, M. (1998) *Between Serb and Albanian: a history of Kosovo*, London: Hurst & Company.

Vlahinić-Dizdarević, N., Buterin, V. and Zagar, A. (2006) 'The external debt sustainability in Southeast European countries: the analysis of debt indicators', *International Conference 'From Transition to Sustainable Development: the Path to European Integration'*, Sarajevo: School of Economics and Business.

Vujović, D. (2004) 'Why have we stopped reforms?' *G17 Review*, 4(46–7): 1–4.

WHO (2006) *Health and Economic Development in South-Eastern Europe*, Copenhagen: World Health Organization.

Woodward, S. (1995) *Socialist Unemployment: the political economy of Yugoslavia 1945–1990*, Princeton: Princeton University Press.

World Bank (2000) *The Road to Stability and Prosperity in South Eastern Europe: a Regional Strategy Paper*, Washington, DC: The World Bank.

World Bank (2001) *Former Yugoslav Republic of Macedonia: Transitional Support Strategy*, Washington, DC: The World Bank.

World Bank (2002) *FYR of Macedonia: public expenditure and institutional review*, Washington, DC: The World Bank.

World Bank (2003a) *A Strategy for Growth through European Integration*, Washington, DC: The World Bank.

World Bank (2003b) *Albania: poverty assessment*, Washington, DC: The World Bank.

World Bank (2003c) *Macedonia: country economic memorandum – tackling unemployment*, Washington, DC: The World Bank.

World Bank (2003d) *Bosnia and Herzegovina: poverty assessment*, Washington, DC: The World Bank.

World Bank (2004a) *Bosnia and Herzegovina: country assistance evaluation*, Washington, DC: The World Bank.

World Bank (2004b) *Kosovo: economic memorandum*, Washington, DC: The World Bank.

World Bank (2004c) 'Labor markets', *Republic of Serbia: an agenda for economic growth and employment*, Washington, DC: Poverty Reduction and Economic Management Unit.

World Bank (2004d) *Macedonia, Former Yugoslav Republic of Poverty Assessment for 2002–2003*, Washington, DC: The World Bank.

World Bank (2005a) *Kosovo – Poverty Assessment – Promoting Opportunity, Security, and Participation for All*, Washington, DC: The World Bank.

World Bank (2005b) *Republic of Montenegro: a policy agenda for growth and competitiveness*, Washington, DC: The World Bank.

World Bank (2005c) *Growth, Poverty and Inequality: Eastern Europe and the former Soviet Union*, Washington, DC: The World Bank.

World Bank (2005d) *Bosnia and Herzegovina: country economic memorandum*, Washington, DC: The World Bank.

World Bank (2006) *Doing Business in 2006: creating jobs*, Washington, DC: The World Bank.

Wyzan, M. (1992) 'First steps to economic independence in Macedonia', *Working Paper No. 59*, Stockholm: Institute of Soviet and East European Economics.

Xheneti, M. (2005a) *Barriers to SME Growth in Transition Economies: the case of Albania*, unpublished PhD thesis, School for Policy Studies, University of Bristol.

Xheneti, M. (2005b) 'Exploring the role of business support infrastructure in Albania: the need for a rethink?' *Environment and Planning C: Government and Policy*, 23: 815–32.

Xheneti, M. and Bartlett, W. (2006) 'SME development in Albania – an analysis of the determinants of business growth', in *Proceedings of the ICES 2006 Conference 'From Transition to Sustainable Development: the Path to European Integration'*, Sarajevo: School of Economics and Business, 255–60 [abstract, full paper on CD ROM].

Xhumari, M. (2003) *Procesi edhe Institucionet e Politikës Sociale*, Tiranë: Shtëpia Botuese e Librit Universitar Tiranë.

Xhumari, M. (2004) 'The functioning of the social sector administration in Albania: background report for the CARDS Strategic Study on Social Sector Administration in the Western Balkans', *mimeo*, Tirana.

Zalduendo, J. (2003) 'Enterprise restructuring and transition: evidence from the former Yugoslav Republic of Macedonia', *IMF Working paper WP/03/136*, Washington, DC: International Monetary Fund

Zarezankova-Potevska, M. (2000) *Perspektivite na maloto stopanstvo*, Skopje: Neol-Risto-DOOEL.

Index

CL

338.
949
6
BAR